A Guide to References and Resources in Child Abuse and Neglect

Second Edition

Editor
Jerry G. Jones, MD
Little Rock, AR

Coeditor
Carolyn J. Levitt, MD
St Paul, MN

Associate Editors

Ann S. Botash, MD
Syracuse, NY

Stephen Ludwig, MD
Philadelphia, PA

Mary M. Carrasco, MD
Pittsburgh, PA

Lynn Anne Platt, MD
Savannah, GA

V. Denise Everett, MD
Raleigh, NC

Gerald E. Porter, MD
Marshfield, WI

Roberta A. Hibbard, MD
Indianapolis, IN

Paul R. Prescott, MD
Mesquite, TX

Kent P. Hymel, MD
Washington, DC

David P. Schor, MD, MPH
Lincoln, NE

Paula K. Jaudes, MD
Chicago, IL

Suzanne P. Starling, MD
Nashville, TN

David L. Kerns, MD
San Jose, CA

James J. Williams, MD
Torrance, CA

Section on Child Abuse and Neglect
American Academy of Pediatrics
141 Northwest Point Blvd
PO Box 927
Elk Grove Village, IL 60009-0927

Department of Marketing and Publications
American Academy of Pediatrics
PO Box 747
Elk Grove Village, IL 60009-0747
1-800/433-9016
http://www.aap.org

Library of Congress Catalog No. 97-74709

ISBN No. 0-910761-93-0

MA0061

The recommendations in this publication do not indicate an exclusive course of treatment or serve as a standard of medical care. Variations, taking into account individual circumstances, may be appropriate.

Most of the references in this manual are followed by brief summaries, which are provided for the convenience of the reader. These annotations are not intended to serve as a standard of patient care. The original article should be reviewed before the information in the annotation is applied to a specific patient, to make certain that the context is applicable. Statements and opinions expressed in references are those of the authors and not necessarily those of the American Academy of Pediatrics.

Section on Child Abuse and Neglect

Introduction

The Section on Child Abuse and Neglect of the American Academy of Pediatrics is pleased to present the Second Edition of the *Guide to References and Resources in Child Abuse and Neglect*. The first edition of the *Guide* was extremely useful to the pediatric community and was well received. The second edition updates the references presented in the first guide and includes new material as well.

The Section is indebted to Jerry G. Jones, MD, and to the committee he directed. Dr Jones and his group have crafted a useful and comprehensive resource. While the target audience for the *Guide* is members of the Academy, the *Guide* will most likely be useful to other professionals who work with children as well.

The Section on Child Abuse and Neglect sponsors ongoing educational programs at the AAP Annual and Spring Session meetings, produces a scintillating quarterly newsletter, and is producing a new slide set on child sexual abuse that will serve as a companion piece to the recently published *Visual Diagnosis of Child Physical Abuse*. The Section welcomes new members from the Academy of Pediatrics who would be interested in learning more about the difficult problem of child abuse and neglect.

We appreciate the dedicated work of the AAP staff, including Tammy Piazza, Scott Allen, and the AAP Department of Marketing and Publications. Their superb, professional work makes projects such as the *Guide to References and Resources in Child Abuse and Neglect* possible.

Carole Jenny, MD
Chairperson, Section on Child Abuse and Neglect

Preface to the Second Edition

The health care of children who have been abused or neglected is a complex responsibility. It requires recognition, evaluation, reporting, crisis intervention, long-term treatment, and court testimony in a multidisciplinary, interagency approach. These components have been described in several excellent textbooks. However, members of the American Academy of Pediatrics recognized in 1991 that the rapid accumulation of information in clinical and research journals makes it difficult to readily synthesize and implement advances. A vision of a collection of up-to-date annotated references in child maltreatment developed and culminated in publication in 1994 of the first edition of *A Guide to References and Resources in Child Abuse and Neglect.* Edited by Carolyn J. Levitt, MD, as chairperson of the 1992 to 1993 Education Committee of the Section on Child Abuse and Neglect, this publication received an enthusiastic response.

A collection of annotations must be kept current to be useful. Almost as soon as the first edition was published, a second Education Committee was appointed to begin developing the next one. The goals of the *Guide* were to remain the same: to provide a reference manual and resource for continuing education for physicians and other health care professionals, a tool for teaching pre- and post-doctoral learners, and a resource for professionals when they encounter clinical issues. The second edition includes updated references, although annotations in the first edition have been retained when current. Several new sections of annotations have been added. Members of the Education Committee wrote most of the sections, but they utilized expertise and authorship outside the committee for several sections. All sections were reviewed by at least two committee members. The second part of the manual, which identifies sources of professional support, has also been updated.

The Foreword to the first edition, which is reprinted on the following page, provided a word of caution that should be repeated. Readers should not apply the annotations, clinical principles, or comments to specific cases without reviewing the original articles for content and completeness.

As chairperson of the 1994 to 1997 Education Committee, I wish to thank Carolyn Levitt, co-chairperson of the committee and coeditor of the *Guide,* the other members of the committee, and the additional contributors. Their selections of articles, carefully written annotations, review of other manuscripts, and adherence to a time line have been superb. The AAP staff, including Tammy Piazza, also deserve much praise.

To you, the reader, we hope this second edition will be helpful in your evaluation and management of abused and neglected children and their families, whatever your professional role.

Jerry G. Jones, MD
Chairperson, 1994 to 1997 Education Committee
American Academy of Pediatrics
Section on Child Abuse and Neglect

Preface to the First Edition

Three years ago, the members of the Section on Child Abuse and Neglect Education Committee set out together to develop a manual for those who would like to learn more about the medical diagnosis and treatment of child abuse and neglect. We wanted to create a handbook to support the efforts of pediatricians and others seeking to respond effectively to suspected or potential child abuse and neglect. We knew that we could not provide all the answers, but we hoped to chart a path through the child advocacy system and the current medical literature. Pediatricians, we felt, should be able to identify observations which should raise their index of suspicion, and know where to go for confirmation and consultation.

Each of our contributors selected a field of interest within the discipline, and provided a list of current articles and texts. Many included brief annotations for the convenience of the reader. The annotations highlight areas of interest; they are not complete summaries. The annotations are provided to expedite your research, but are no substitute for the original materials. Please do not apply the annotations or the general comments to specific situations without reviewing the original articles for context and completeness.

The second half of this manual identifies sources of support within the medical and child advocacy communities. We have listed medical and diagnostic programs, state chapter representatives of the Academy, local chapters of the National Committee to Prevent Child Abuse, and other resources. We hope that this manual will make it easy for the busy pediatrician to locate and access these resources.

In closing, as chairperson of the Education Committee, I would like to take this opportunity to thank the committee members for their hours of work and thoughtful evaluation. This manual is the result of our efforts, along with those of other colleagues who came forward to join us.

Contributing authors, who were the backbone of this project, are indicated throughout. I would like to single out Larry Ricci, MD, Roberta Hibbard, MD, Charlie Johnson, MD, James Noel, MD, Ed Gustavson, MD, and Bob Touloukian, MD, who contributed the first chapters and established our editorial structure.

I would also like to highlight the special efforts of those who worked so hard in recent months to meet the deadlines that were required to bring this project to fruition. In particular, I would like to thank Jerry Jones, MD, the director of the Children at Risk program at the Arkansas Children's Hospital, for his thorough review of the later drafts. He recognized and responded to the need for a final content editor, fine-tuning some sections, and adding essential material in the final weeks. Randy Alexander, MD, and Carol Berkowitz, MD, also extended moral support, and devoted many hours to provide critical review of problem sections.

When we recognized in the closing weeks that our work would be incomplete without updates on sexually transmitted diseases and poisoning, Sue White, MD, in New Orleans, and Jan Bays, MD, in Portland, responded. Kathy Christoffel, MD, in Chicago, provided a critical review of Jerry Jones' new section on homicide.

Special thanks, also, to my colleague, Kim Martinez, RN, CPNP, who provided the initial summaries of many of the articles in this manual for my editorial review; to Mariann Stephens, the managing editor; and to Laura Aird, the manager of the Section on Child Abuse and Neglect.

If you find our manual helpful for the work that you do with abused children, our efforts will be truly rewarded.

Carolyn Levitt, MD
Chairperson, 1992 to 1993 Education Committee
Section on Child Abuse and Neglect

Contributors

Randell C. Alexander, MD, PhD
Associate Professor of Pediatrics, University of Iowa, Iowa City, IA
Statistics of Child Abuse

Jan Bays, MD
C.A.R.E.S. Northwest, Emanuel Children's Hospital, Portland, OR
Compassion Fatigue

Ann S. Botash, MD*
Associate Professor of Pediatrics, SUNY Health Science Center at Syracuse; Director of CARE, University Health Care Center, Syracuse, NY
Developmental Disabilities and Child Abuse

Mary M. Carrasco, MD*
Associate Professor of Pediatrics, University of Pittsburgh School of Medicine; Director of Section of Community Health, Children's Hospital of Pittsburgh; Assistant Professor of Health Services Administration, University of Pittsburgh Graduate School of Public Health, Pittsburgh, PA
Prevention of Child Abuse

Janice K. Church, PhD
Assistant Professor of Pediatrics, University of Arkansas for Medical Sciences, Little Rock, AR
Psychological Impact of Child Maltreatment

Susan Elek, RN, PhD, CPNP
Assistant Professor, College of Nursing, University of Nebraska Medical Center, Lincoln, NE
Homicide and Child Fatality Review Teams

V. Denise Everett, MD*
Clinical Assistant Professor of Pediatrics, University of North Carolina at Chapel Hill, School of Medicine; Director, Child Sexual Abuse Team, Wake Medical Center, Raleigh, NC
Domestic Violence and Child Abuse

Lori Frasier, MD
Assistant Professor of Child Health, University of Missouri-Columbia, Columbia, MO
Interviewing Children Who May Have Been Abused

Roberta A. Hibbard, MD*
Associate Professor of Pediatrics, Indiana University; Director of Child Abuse Programs, Indiana University School of Medicine; Department of Pediatrics, Indianapolis, IN
Knowledge of Professionals
Munchausen Syndrome by Proxy

Dirk Huyer, MD
Assistant Professor, Department of Pediatrics, University of Toronto; Physician, Suspected Child Abuse and Neglect (SCAN) Program, Hospital for Sick Children, Toronto, Ontario, Canada
Thoracic Trauma

Kent P. Hymel, MD*
Chief, USAF Medical Consultant for Child Abuse, Washington, DC
Falls
Head Injuries
Retinal Hemorrhages
Shaken Impact/Shaken Baby Syndrome

Paula K. Jaudes, MD*
Professor of Clinical Pediatrics, University of Chicago; Director of the Child Abuse and Neglect Program, University of Chicago Children's Hospital and LaRabida Children's Hospital and Research Center, Chicago, IL
Failure to Thrive
Neglect

Charles Felzen Johnson, MD
Professor of Pediatrics, Ohio State University; Director, Child Abuse Program, Children's Hospital, Columbus, OH
Culture and Child Maltreatment

Jerry G. Jones, MD*
Professor of Pediatrics, University of Arkansas for Medical Sciences; Director, Programs for Children at Risk, Arkansas Children's Hospital, Little Rock, AR
Corporal Punishment
Ear and Orofacial Injuries
Homicide and Child Fatality Review Teams
Photographic Documentation of Child Abuse
Sexually Transmitted Diseases and Child Sexual Abuse
Sibling Studies
Textbooks, Journals, Audiovisuals, and Booklets

David L. Kerns, MD*
Chairman, Department of Pediatrics; Director,
    Center for Child Protection, Santa Clara Valley
    Medical Center; Clinical Professor of Pediatrics,
Stanford University School of Medicine,
    San Jose, CA
Sexual Abuse of Children
Sexually Transmitted Diseases and
    Child Sexual Abuse

Carolyn J. Levitt, MD *
Assistant Professor of Pediatrics, University of
    Minnesota; Director, Midwest Children's
    Resource Center of Childrens Health Care,
    Minneapolis and St Paul, MN
Drowning: Child Abuse and Bathtub Drownings
Falls
Fractures
Head Injuries
Retinal Hemorrhages
Sexual Abuse of Children
Shaken Impact/Shaken Baby Syndrome

Howard B. Levy, MD
Associate Professor of Pediatrics, Rush Medical
    College; Chairperson, Department of Pediatrics,
    Columbia Grant Hospital, Chicago, Illinois;
    Director, Pediatric Ecology Program,
    Chicago, IL; President, International Society for
    the Prevention of Child Abuse and Neglect
Reabuse (Revictimization)

Stephen Ludwig, MD*
Professor, Department of Pediatrics, University
    of Pennsylvania School of Medicine; Asso-
    ciate Physician-In-Chief for Education,
    The Children's Hospital of Philadelphia;
    Philadelphia, PA
Emotional Abuse

Kim Martinez, RN, CPNP, MPH
Midwest Children's Resource Center of
    Childrens Health Care, Minneapolis and
    St Paul, MN
Falls
Fractures
Head Injuries
Retinal Hemorrhages
Sexual Abuse of Children
Shaken Impact/Shaken Baby Syndrome

Michael W. Mellon, PhD
Assistant Professor of Pediatrics, University of
    Arkansas for Medical Sciences; Co-director of
    Elimination Disorders Clinic, AR
Children's Hospital, Little Rock, AR
Contested Divorce and Child Abuse

LTC James M. Noel, Jr, MD
Pediatric Gastroenterology, Madigan Army
    Medical Center, Tacoma, WA
Fractures

Jan E. Paradise, MD
Associate Professor of Pediatrics, Boston
    University School of Medicine; Boston
    Medical Center, Boston, MA
Corporal Punishment

Lynn Anne Platt, MD*
Assistant Director of Pediatric Education,
    Backus Children's Hospital at Memorial
    Medical Center, Inc, Savannah, Georgia;
    Professor of Pediatrics, Mercer University,
    Macon, Georgia; Professor of Pediatrics,
    Medical College of Georgia, Augusta, GA
Abdominal Blunt Trauma

Gerald E. Porter, MD *
Clinical Professor of Pediatrics and Family
    Medicine, University of Wisconsin;
    Department of Pediatrics, Marshfield Clinic,
    Marshfield, WI
Munchausen Syndrome by Proxy
Poisoning as Child Abuse
Substance Use Disorders and Child Abuse

Paul R. Prescott, MD *
Mesquite, TX
Fractures

Lawrence R. Ricci, MD
Director, Spurwink Child Abuse Program,
    Portland, ME
Corporal Punishment
Photographic Documentation of Child Abuse
Sibling Studies

David P. Schor, MD, MPH*
Associate Clinical Professor of Pediatrics,
  University of Nebraska Medical Center;
  Chair, Nebraska Child Death Review Team,
  Lincoln, NE; Medical Advisor, Nebraska
  Health and Human Services
Homicide and Child Fatality Review Teams
Prevention of Child Abuse

Madeleine U. Shalowitz, MD
Assistant Professor of Clinical Pediatrics,
  University of Chicago, Pritzker School of
  Medicine; Director, Failure to Thrive Program,
  LaRabida Children's Hospital and Research
  Center, Chicago, IL
Failure to Thrive

Rebecca R. S. Socolar, MD
Clinical Assistant Professor of
Pediatrics, University of North Carolina School
  of Medicine, Chapel Hill, NC
Corporal Punishment

Suzanne P. Starling, MD*
Assistant Professor of Pediatrics, Vanderbilt
  University; Director, Child Abuse and Neglect
  Program, Vanderbilt University Medical Center;
  Medical Director, Our Kids Program,
  Nashville, TN
Courts and Court Testimony

H. Patrick Stern, MD
Associate Professor of Pediatrics, University of
  Arkansas for Medical Sciences; Chief, Section
  of Behavioral Pediatrics, Little Rock, AR
Contested Divorce and Child Abuse

Susanne Tropez-Sims, MD, MPH
Professor and Chair; Department of Pediatrics,
  Meharry Medical College, Nashville, TN
Sexually Transmitted Diseases and
  Child Sexual Abuse

Den A. Trumbull, MD
Pediatric Healthcare, Montgomery, AL
Corporal Punishment

James J. Williams, MD*
Assistant Professor, Department of Pediatrics,
  UCLA School of Medicine; Medical Director,
  Child Abuse Crisis Center, Harbor-UCLA
  Medical Center, Torrance, CA
Cutaneous Manifestations of Child Abuse

Karen Boyd Worley, PhD
Assistant Professor of Pediatrics, University of
  Arkansas for Medical Sciences, Little Rock, AR
Psychological Impact of Child Maltreatment

* Member, Education Committee (1994 to 1997)
  of the AAP Section on Child Abuse and Neglect

Table of Contents

Part 1: Annotated Bibliography

Abdominal Blunt Trauma

See Also:
Fractures (AAP Statement *Diagnostic Imaging of Child Abuse)*

Clinical Principles

▼ Significant violent force is required to cause a life-threatening abdominal injury.

▼ The mortality rate in abusive abdominal injuries is 40% to 50%.

▼ Bruising of the abdominal wall is not typical in abusive trauma.

▼ Hollow viscus and liver (left lobe) injuries are typical in abusive trauma.

▼ Duodenal hematomas are often the result of inflicted injury.

▼ Pancreatitis is unusual in childhood. Abusive injury is part of the differential diagnosis.

Bibliography

General

Huyer D. Abdominal injuries in child abuse.
The APSAC Advisor. 1994;7:5-7, 24
Major blunt abdominal trauma due to child abuse is second only to head injuries as a cause of death in inflicted childhood trauma. The incidence of abusive blunt abdominal trauma is low. The associated mortality is high. O'Neill and Associates observed an 8% incidence of abusive injuries with a 40% to 50% mortality. (O'Neill J, Meacham W, Griffin P, Sawyers, J. Patterns of injury in the battered child syndrome. *J Trauma.* 1973; 13:332-339). In several large reviews of all presentations of blunt abdominal trauma, child abuse represents 1% to 11%.

Many factors contribute to the high mortality rate in cases of abuse:

1. *Delay in seeking care:* Caretakers are fearful of self-incrimination or, unaware of the serious nature of the injury, delay. Complications that can develop during the delay are peritonitis with septic shock and hemorrhagic shock, resulting from liver lacerations.

2. *Inaccurate or misleading histories result in delayed diagnosis:* The history is often the most significant component in the planning of evaluation and treatment. Victims are typically preverbal. A high index of suspicion must be maintained.

3. *Children have unique anatomical and physiologic features:*

   a. The ribs are flexible and cover only a small portion of the upper abdomen.

   b. The abdominal wall offers only limited protection due to the less well-developed muscles and small fat layer.

   c. The small body size results in organs that are in close proximity.

   d. Pediatric organs are proportionately larger in size. The blood volume is smaller. Therefore, injuries producing hemorrhage can result in significant physiologic changes.

Forces that produce blunt abdominal trauma are direct (such as a kick or punch) or indirect shearing (as in the rapid deceleration of a body when thrown across a room). The direct forces from abdominal blows crush organs against the immobile vertebral column or lower rib cage. Laceration and hemorrhage result. A direct blow compresses the contents of the hollow visceral organs leading to a sudden overdistention and rupture. In the indirect shearing injuries, the partially mobile organs continue in motion during body deceleration, resulting in shearing of the intestinal mesentery.

Literature on accidental abdominal injuries suggests that violent forces are required to cause a life-threatening abdominal injury. Accidental injuries are high velocity and frequently associated with other injuries. Ledbetter (1988) reported a 21% mortality rate in accidentally injured children. In that series, five of the seven deaths were in children with serious head injury. Two were isolated abdominal injury.

The child with an inflicted abdominal injury is usually young (age 2 years is typical), often male, infrequently has no other serious, acute injuries and may have old pattern injuries typical for child abuse. Abdominal wall bruising is atypical since the force is transmitted to the intra-abdominal structures. *In accidental injury, the spleen, kidney, and liver are the most frequent sites of injury. Hollow viscus injuries are common in abusive injury.* There is some overlap of injury sites. In abuse, the liver is the most common solid organ injured.

Intestinal injuries, especially injuries of the small intestine, are observed in abuse. The proximal small intestine in its fixed position seems very susceptible to compression injury. *In cases of abuse involving intestinal injuries with perforations, perforations are seen most frequently in the jejunum (60%), with 30% seen in the duodenum and 10% in the ileum.*

In children, the signs of intestinal perforation are subtle and vary in time of appearance. The most reliable indicator of perforation is found through repeated clinical examination, looking for the development of peritoneal irritation. It has been postulated that early sealing of the injury occurs since pneumoperitoneum is seen in only a minority of children with intestinal perforations. The most sensitive radiographic view is an upright chest. Left lateral decubitus and then the upright abdomen views follow in declining levels of sensitivity. Intraperitoneal fluid on computed tomography (CT) scan without evidence of other injury is suggestive of sealed hollow viscus perforation.

Intramural hematomas of the intestine are frequently the result of inflicted abdominal trauma. Without an explicit explanation of events, *duodenal hematomas are highly suspicious for child abuse.* The fixed position of the duodenum makes it highly susceptible to crushing injuries, which cause bleeding into the wall.

The onset of symptoms is delayed from 1 hour to 2.5 days. Masses and abdominal wall bruising are infrequent. The presentation is vomiting, often bilious, abdominal pain, and tenderness. Concomitant pancreatic injury may occur.

The upper gastrointestinal series (UGI) is the gold standard of diagnosis. Plain abdominal film results are typically normal but may show dilation of the stomach. Ultrasound and CT may demonstrate a mass, but the UGI should be done. On the UGI, a large, smooth, rounded, intramural mass is typically seen in the lateral wall of the duodenum encroaching on the lumen. When the contrast is passed, a "coiled spring" appearance can be

appreciated. Kleinman (1986) recommends that a UGI be obtained in children suspected of having abusive, blunt abdominal trauma regardless of symptomatic improvement, since characteristic radiographic patterns may persist.

The pancreas sits deep in a fixed position anterior to the vertebral column. Injury to it is uncommon, but deep crushing is possible due to the fixed position. Isolated injuries have been reported following falls onto small objects such as bicycle handles. One study (Chadwick, Mertem, and Reece, 1994) revealed that 1 of 27 children run over by cars had an elevated value for serum amylase.

Since pancreatitis is unusual in children, trauma should always be considered in the differential diagnosis. The presentation of pancreatitis is abdominal pain, vomiting, and fever. Onset of symptoms is gradual. An epigastric tenderness and a mass may be found. Laboratory evaluation will reveal elevated levels of serum and urinary amylase.

Six days to 16 weeks following blunt abdominal trauma, a pancreatic pseudocyst may arise. In the acute injury, ultrasound may reveal enlargement of the gland secondary to edema. Repetitive ultrasound evaluations allow for detection of pseudocyst formation (Kleinman, 1987).

The liver is the solid organ most frequently injured in abusive trauma (Cooper, 1992). Injuries are typically caused by a direct blow with a laceration resulting. Decelerating injuries can result in vascular disruption in the areas of ligamentous attachments. In accidental injury, the right lobe is more frequently injured, while in abusive injuries the left is frequently the site of injury (Coant et al, 1992).

Liver enzymes have been shown to be predictive of liver injury. Coant and associates (1992) showed that no children had demonstrable injury on CT with SGOT (AST) levels less than 200 IU coupled with SGPT (ALT) less than 100 IU. Alkaline phosphatase levels are usually not elevated in cases of blunt abdominal trauma. Computed tomography is the most sensitive noninvasive technique to assess hepatic injury (Kleinman, 1987).

Tepas JJ. **Blunt abdominal trauma in children.** *Curr Opin Pediatr.* 1993;5:317-324
Blunt abdominal trauma can present with inaccurate histories. The physical examination and close monitoring of evolving physical findings remain the basis for management and evaluation. The evolution of the nonoperative care of blunt abdominal trauma has made diagnostic imaging a central part of the evaluation, and CT has become the universally accepted modality. The three findings most relevant to CT evaluations are the presence of free fluid within the peritoneal cavity, the configuration of the solid viscera, and the distribution of bowel loops as an indicator of free air or fluid in an unusual or unexpected space.

Specific/Technical

Benhaim P, et al. **Post-traumatic chylous ascites in a child: recognition and management of an unusual condition.** *J Trauma.* 1995;39:1175-1177
A case of post-traumatic chylous ascites in an abused toddler is presented.

Coant PN, et al. **Markers for occult liver injury in cases of physical abuse in children.** *Pediatrics.* 1992;89:274-277
The use of liver transaminase values to evaluate for occult liver damage as part of the routine protocol for evaluating suspected child abuse victims is discussed. (Reviewed in first edition.)

Fossum RM, Deschencaux KA. **Blunt trauma of the abdomen in children.** *J Forensic Sci.* 1991;36:47-50
The author discusses the presentation of an injury to the small bowel with emphasis on diagnostic and investigative difficulties.

McAleer I, Kaplan GW. **Pediatric genitourinary trauma.** *Urol Clin North Am.* 1995;22:177-188
This is a review of pediatric genitourinary trauma with emphasis on mechanisms of injury, evaluation, and management.

Pisters PW, Heslin MJ, Riles TS. **Abdominal aortic pseudoaneurysm after blunt trauma.** *J Vasc Surg.* 1993;18:307-309
Case review and literature review of an unusual late complication of blunt abdominal trauma are provided.

Tso EL, Beaver BL, Haller JA. **Abdominal injuries in restrained pediatric passengers.** *J Pediatr Surg.* 1993;28:915-919
The mechanism of injury with seat belt systems is rapid deceleration and flexion over the belt, which makes the abdominal viscera and spine very vulnerable. This is a retrospective study of injuries sustained in motor vehicle accidents while passengers were restrained.

Acknowledgment

This section and its annotations were prepared by Lynn Anne Platt, MD, and Paul Robert Prescott, MD.

Clinical Principles

▼ Professionals who work primarily in the field of child abuse are vulnerable to variations of this condition, whether called compassion fatigue, burnout, chronic serial grief, or vicarious victimization. The symptoms can be identified.

▼ Modalities and resources for prevention and management are available.

Bibliography

Bays J. Compassion fatigue: a side effect of working with victims of child abuse. In: *Good grief: a group process modality for handling professional burnout.* Presented at the San Diego Conference on Responding to Child Maltreatment; January 31, 1997; San Diego, CA
After 10 years working with victims of child abuse, I found myself in a deep clinical depression. I lost interest in food, found no pleasure in gardening, dreaded going to work, and was irritable with family and friends. I thought about quitting the work that I had once loved. I realized that if I (considered one of the strongest people in our program, a person whose natural state is joy, curiosity, and anticipation) left the work without discovering what was wrong and how to treat it, I would be leaving my best friends and co-workers to face the same problems, but without my support and without a remedy. I began to read. I found that several names have been given to this group of symptoms. What follows is a summary of some of the ways of framing the problem and brief accounts of my personal experiences with these issues.

Burnout occurs when we set our goals too high and cannot change them when people try to give us feedback. When I first began this work, there were only a few physicians in the state who would evaluate abused children. Calls began pouring in. I answered these calls myself, made appointments, saw the families, typed my own reports on the computer, and did my own billing. One hellish week I saw 11 children in the outpatient clinic while functioning as the clinic attending! When I received subpoenas for three different counties for the same trial date, I finally realized I was dividing myself too thinly and began to set limits. I would only see children from the four counties whose courthouses were less than a 40 minutes' drive away. I had only so many appointments in a week. Although parents and agencies felt that every appointment was an emergency, I defined true emergencies, cases in which the child had acute injuries or needed evidence collection. Most cases benefited from a few days' wait for an appointment. I have found that when people plead extraordinary circumstances ("You're the only one who can…") and I make an exception to these rules, I almost always regret it.

Post-traumatic stress disorder includes a set of symptoms that are familiar to those who work "in the trenches" with abused children. After attending autopsies on children who have been raped and tortured, I find myself sitting and staring out the window, emotionally and mentally numb. This is a blessed protection against letting the feelings of horror come up, against my mind's attempts to imagine the child's last hours. The protective effects become disabling when this "going unconscious" lasts and renders me unable to respond to my own child's distress over a skinned knee or unable to remember the words to use in a lecture on child abuse the next day.

I am a visual person, and intrusive imagery has become a problem. Children describe abuse in vivid terms. Good interviewers put away adult ways of thinking and try to enter the minds of the children to understand the events from their perspective. An adult might say, "He raped me." A child says, with a look of revulsion, "He stuck his dick in my mouth and yucky white stuff came out and I threw up." After a week of interviewing children about sexual abuse, I have found that Friday night is not the best time to make love. Sometimes I ask just to be held and comforted, with kisses or a back rub. It can take a day of gardening or a few hours of meditation to clear my mind of images and to calm my inner child so I can enjoy healthy adult sexuality.

I am very fortunate. I have a husband who also works in the field. He is sympathetic and has learned just to listen (not try to offer solutions) when I am full to the brim with suffering after a bad Friday after a bad week, and I just need to be held, to pour out my distress, and sometimes to cry for a while. I have a colleague whose husband cannot understand why she does not want to watch *Terminator Three* on Friday evening. Another colleague's partner said, "Don't ever tell me about one of those cases again. I can't stand it." Isolation occurs, from loved ones and even strangers. When people at parties ask me what I do, I am evasive. They don't really want to know that I just saw a child whose father raped her and shot himself to death in her bed. If they push until I say that I work with abused children, they usually respond, "How awful. I could never do that work." They then begin to talk about the weather. Or worse, they want to tell me about a case in which a child was "unjustly" taken away. I may know the awful details of the case, but confidentiality laws render me dumb, suddenly grateful to escape into talk about the weather. *There are very few people we can really talk to about what we do. We become walled off, able to unload only with an "in group."*

Vicarious traumatization refers to the cumulative negative effect of exposure to traumatic stories or events. Our hospital chaplain made me aware of the literature on vicarious traumatization when she was working with nurses in our pediatric intensive care unit. She explained that human beings usually face one traumatic event at a time, like the death of a parent. We become acutely distressed, grieve, and then slowly regain a sense of normalcy. When traumatic events follow in rapid succession, we do not have time to regain our balance and sense of normalcy. It is akin to being in a war zone. We need to use extraordinary means to treat ourselves in order to stay healthy.

We have six basic psychological needs that are sensitive to disruption by actual or vicarious traumatization: safety, trust, esteem, intimacy, power or control, and frame of reference. Each person differs, depending on factors like genetic temperament and personal history, as to which need(s) is critical. These needs, as well as the results of prevention and/or treatment of their disruption, are described in the excellent book on traumatic stress by Pearlman and Saakvitne. The reference and an outline derived from the book are included in this section.

We experienced a sudden shattering of our sense of safety last year when the child of a co-worker in the field of child protection was shaken to death by a babysitter. The sitter was the mother's best friend and the spouse of another child welfare worker. The usual disbelief and divisiveness that compounds a case of abuse penetrated inside our ranks, through all our friends and co-workers. Underneath was the horrible realization that if a child could not be safe with your best friend in the home of a child welfare professional, then there was no guarantee of safety anywhere. Worse, it broke through our denial that, given the right circumstances, we ourselves might injure or even kill a child.

I believe the most profound effect of this work is on our spiritual well-being. When we remove children from abusive homes and they are subjected to worse cruelty in foster homes, what have we accomplished? Who is the enemy? It becomes hard to hold the larger framework, the higher purpose that gives our lives a sense of direction and meaning.

One day I realized that underlying all my stress and problems working in this field was a deep grief, a **chronic serial grief.** As I drove home at night, a silly sentimental song came on the radio and I found myself sobbing. Despite my gardening, meditation, square dancing, music classes, and a loving, understanding husband, I had a well of accumulated sadness that was full to the top and spilling over. I grieve that the world is not safe for children, that I cannot guarantee the safety of my own children, and that my own inner child suffers in the work to help other children. I grieve that human beings are so pitiful, so violent and suffer so much that they have to take their fear and anguish out by beating and shaking infants; that sex offenders are so lonely that the only way they can find intimacy is to trick or frighten little children into talking to them or touching them. I grieve that sometimes we hurt each other in our work and that we have become part of the problem.

We formed a "Good Grief" group at our child abuse program. We meet once a month to talk openly about our reactions to the work and to help each other find tools for coping and healing. Sometimes we invite people from outside the program, if we have worked together on a particularly traumatic case and their stress and grief are evident.

If we do not recognize the stress of our job and find mechanisms to deal with it, our sadness may spill out as anger. Worst is when the anger is directed toward our colleagues in the work. When I hear myself think or say "Those stupid...," I know I'm in trouble. When co-workers begin to scapegoat each other, our program is in trouble. When child welfare agencies begin fighting with each other, we are all in trouble. I see law enforcement as particularly isolated. They have the added stress of being the first on the scene of violence, plunged into the raw anger and chaos, splattered with the blood of the victims. They have the fewest institutional mechanisms to deal with the stress. I believe *job stress should be acknowledged by multidisciplinary child abuse teams and mechanisms developed to help each other continue in the work.*

Compassion fatigue, burn-out, chronic serial grief, and vicarious victimization are all names for the symptoms experienced by those working in the child abuse field. Health care and mental health workers may need to lead the way by detecting the symptoms, discussing the diagnosis, and helping others learn how to treat this illness.

Pearlman LA, Saakvitne KW. *Traumatic Stress: Countertransference and Vicarious Victimization in Psychotherapy with Incest Survivors.* **New York, NY: WW Norton & Co; 1995**
The authors discuss six psychological needs sensitive to disruption by actual or vicarious victimization. They are as follows:

1. **Safety:** Working with victims heightens the sense of personal vulnerability and the fragility of life. *Symptoms: preoccupation with safety, not letting anyone babysit, hypervigilance.*

2. **Trust:** Through exposure to the many cruel ways people deceive, betray, or violate the trust of others, therapists may become suspicious and cynical. "I used to believe that the majority of people were trustworthy. Now I believe the opposite." *Symptoms: self-criticism, not trusting one's own instincts, isolation.*

3. **Esteem:** Esteem is defined as the need to perceive others as benevolent and worthy of respect. Encountering so much human cruelty can shatter therapists' world views and lead to cynicism, pessimism, and anger at individuals or mankind in general. Or it can lead to musing about the fate of the human race. *Symptoms: degrading oneself or others (anyone not doing the work is useless), overidealization of others.*

4. **Intimacy:** A sense of alienation may emerge from exposure to horrific imagery that cannot be shared with others, either because others pull away in horror or disbelief, or because of confidentiality requirements. It is particularly painful if your spouse cannot bear to hear what you are doing in life or what is worrying you. A "club" develops, with a sense of distrust of those outside who can never understand your world. *Symptoms: emotional numbing, withdrawal from intimacy.*

5. **Power or control:** Two reactions are seen with repeated exposure to clients' powerlessness. The first is for therapists to try to increase their sense of power in the world, such as by taking self-defense classes or by becoming more dominant. The second is to experience despair about the uncontrollable forces of natural or human violence. *Symptoms: personal freedom restricted through fears and measures to relieve anxiety about safety, loss of control at work or with clients.*

6. **Frame of reference:** "Why did this happen?" A fundamental human need is to develop a meaningful frame of reference. We try to figure out the motive of the bad guy or what the victim did wrong. Or we lose our frame of reference and become pervasively uneasy.

Signs to pay attention to are:

- ▼ Intrusion of client's imagery into our imagination
- ▼ Loss of empathy for clients, self, and others
- ▼ Self-numbing through addictive behavior (including work)
- ▼ Withdrawal from intimacy — spouse, friends, community
- ▼ Fear of people walking behind
- ▼ Not looking in the mirror

Some solutions for prevention and management are as follows:

1. **Environmental**

   Balance a clinical caseload with teaching and research.

   Limit exposure: Balance victim and non-victim work.

   Set boundaries: Limit weekend and night work. Time really off.

   Find a way to work for social change.

2. **Interpersonal**

   Don't work alone.

   Get support from professional colleagues.

   Supervision and consultation (consultation on TV).

   Develop support groups where feelings can be discussed, separate from business.

3. **Personal**

   Find healthy ways to mentally leave the past behind, remain in the present moment, and not obsess about future problems and events.

   Understand that vicarious victimization is a normal response. Use it for growth.

   Use individual therapy to work on areas that are particular problems.

   Strive for a balance between personal and professional life.

   Make time for non–victim-related activities that renew a sense of hope and optimism. The most common are exercise, rest, gardening, music, dance, art work, pets, time with healthy children, travel, being outdoors, and doing nothing!

4. **Spiritual**

   Attend to empathy.

   Stay anchored in the present.

   Develop a sense of connection to something beyond oneself.

   Seek spiritual renewal.

A World Wide Web site called The Wounded Healer. The address is:

http://idealist.com/wounded_healer/

This site features points of departure (links) for psychotherapists and others who have survived child abuse and other trauma. The Wounded Healer has been rated in the top 5% of sites on the Internet.

Acknowledgment

This section and its annotations were prepared by Jan Bays, MD.

Contested Divorce and Child Abuse

Clinical Principles

▼ An increase in allegations of abuse, especially sexual abuse, in contested cases of divorce has been reported in the popular media and in some published case reports. However, few large-scale and systematic studies have been done. Thus far, the literature does not support an epidemic of false allegations of abuse, especially sexual abuse, in contested cases of divorce.

▼ The uncommon allegations of sexual abuse, in a study of custody-visitation disputes, subsequently were founded in half the cases.

▼ Multiple criteria have been proposed to assist the professional in determining the validity, or lack thereof, of abuse allegations raised in divorce cases.

▼ A careful comprehensive evaluation that includes the children, all relevant adults, and a multimodal and multidisciplinary team approach is recommended whenever abuse issues are raised in contested divorce cases.

Bibliography

Benedek EP, Schetky DH. Problems in validating allegations of sexual abuse. Part 2: clinical evaluation. *J Am Acad Child Adolesc Psychiatry.* 1987;26:916-921
The authors discuss the family dynamics of false accusations, with variables to consider in determining the level of credibility of an allegation. Relevant variables include a child's language, spontaneous drawings/play, affect/behavior, child's motives, memory, cognitive development, child giving a credible history, physical exam, and relationship with parents.

Ehrenberg MF, Elterman MF. Evaluating allegations of sexual abuse in the context of divorce, child custody and access disputes. In: Ney T, ed. *True and False Allegation of Child Sexual Abuse — Assessment and Case Management.* New York, NY: Brunner/Mazel Publishers; 1995:209-230
This in-depth review of historical, legal, and research issues and divorce-related family dynamics provides key factors needed to conduct a quality, comprehensive evaluation including recommendations for a multimodal and a multidisciplinary team approach. The key factors provide guidance to emphasize a research-based approach, competence in the evaluators, and stress factual information that will lead to probability estimates of credibility of the accusation.

Elterman MF, Ehrenberg MF. Sexual abuse allegations in child custody disputes. *Int Law Psychiatry.* 1991;14:269-286
This article proposes sexual abuse allegations be defined as probable and improbable. It discusses the dynamics and suggests 12 indicators associated with improbable allegations in custody and visitation disputes. These indicators were based on the known empirical studies of improbable allegations, the recommendation of experienced mental health professionals working in the area, and general findings from the child sexual abuse literature.

Faller K, Corwin DL, Olafson E. Literature review: research on false allegations of sexual abuse in divorce. *The APSAC Advisor.* 1993; 6:7-10
The authors note that articles suggesting there is an epidemic of false allegations of sexual abuse in divorce cases provide no data to support their statements. After reviewing the research, they conclude it is difficult to support the assertion.

Faller K, DeVoe E. Allegations of sexual abuse in divorce. *Child Sexual Abuse.* 1995;4:1-25
This article reviewed 215 cases in which allegations of sexual abuse were raised in families also involved in divorce. The relationship of the timing of the allegation of sexual abuse relative to the divorce, hierarchy of factors affecting the professionals' impressions, and the legal outcomes are summarized. Of the 215 cases, 73% were classified as likely, 7% as uncertain, and 20% as unlikely. In the 73% the authors classified as likely abusive, a court decision concurred in almost half.

McGraw JM, Smith HA. Child sexual abuse allegations amidst divorce and custody proceedings: refining the validation process. *Child Sexual Abuse.* 1992;1:49-62

The authors reviewed 18 cases of child sexual abuse allegations, in which only one was initially founded through traditional clinical methods. After applying the clinical process of validation used at the Kempe Center in Denver, eight cases were categorized as founded. The need for the use of a systematic process of evaluation of all cases of sexual abuse that arise in relation to divorce is emphasized.

Sorenson E, Goldman JW, Ard M, et al. Judicial decision-making in contested custody cases: the influence of reported child abuse, spouse abuse, and parental substance abuse. *Child Abuse Negl.* 1995;19:251-260

In a sample of 60 contested custody and/or visitation cases, maltreatment allegations were raised against the father/stepmother vs the mother/stepfather in the following percentages: child neglect, 15%/35%; sexual abuse, 17%/7%; emotional abuse, 28%/28%; physical abuse, 15%/8%; and previous child abuse, 5%/18%.

Theonnes N, Tjaden PG. The extent, nature, and validity of sexual abuse allegations in custody/visitation disputes. *Child Abuse Negl.* 1990;14:151-163

and

McIntosh JA, Prinz RJ. The incidence of alleged sexual abuse in 603 family court cases. *Law Hum Behav.* 1993;17:95-101

Theonnes et al and McIntosh et al, who reviewed 9,000 and 603 court cases, respectively, involving custody/visitation disputes, found only 2% involved allegations of sexual abuse. In a sample of 169 out of the 9,000 cases in which sexual abuse allegations were raised, 50% were founded, 33% were unfounded, and 17% were undetermined.

Acknowledgment

This section and its annotations were prepared by H. Patrick Stern, MD, and Michael W. Mellon, PhD.

Corporal Punishment

See Also:

AAP Section on Child Abuse and Neglect Statement *Corporal Punishment in the Home: Commentary* **and** *Corporal Punishment in Schools,* **which follow**

Clinical Principles

▼ The proportion of parents who report they spank or hit their children declined between 1988 and 1997. However, the number of parents between ages 18 and 24 years who reported use of spanking and hitting increased dramatically.

▼ Mothers' belief in spanking as a method of behavior management may be correlated with a belief in a negative approach to discipline, as well as with spanking their toddler-age children.

▼ An association between corporal punishment and aggressive behavior in children has been reported in numerous studies. However, the causal nature of this relationship is not clear. In addition, it is unclear whether corporal punishment alone or other parenting practices (eg, inconsistency, negative demeanor) associated with corporal punishment account for the increased aggressive behavior.

▼ Abusive parents tend to use different disciplinary practices than nonabusive parents. Most physical abuse seems to begin with parental frustration over child misbehavior. Abusive parents are more likely to use hostile, non-contingent, punitive, and severe physical discipline practices. They are less likely to use reasoning, but equally likely to use spanking.

▼ Mild nonabusive corporal punishment of young children, especially spanking, has rarely been distinguished from severe corporal punishment in empirical studies. The few studies that focused explicitly on nonabusive corporal punishment of young children found that spanking is associated with short-term compliance.

▼ The effects of disciplinary spanking, or any disciplinary practice, are determined by the total pattern of parental control and parental nurturance.

▼ The opinions of physicians regarding use of nonabusive corporal punishment in the home appear to be diverse. Physician surveys reveal majority support for the selective use of spanking by parents.

▼ Corporal punishment in schools has been banned in 27 states and many foreign countries.

Bibliography

Corporal Punishment in the Home

Anonymous. Consensus statements. *Pediatrics.* 1996;98:853 (Proceedings of a conference entitled The Short- and Long-Term Consequences of Corporal Punishment. Sponsored by the American Academy of Pediatrics and Albert Einstein College of Medicine/Montefiore Medical Center, February 9 and 10, 1996) Twenty-four recognized investigators were invited to present and discuss research findings and develop consensus statements reflecting the current state of knowledge about the short- and long-term consequences of corporal punishment. The participants reflected a range of opinions regarding spanking. Each consensus statement required agreement by 75% of the participants. Corporal punishment was defined as bodily punishment of any kind. Spanking was defined as physically noninjurious, intended to modify behavior, and administered with an open hand to the extremities or buttocks. The statements developed are as follows:

1. Recommendations concerning the discipline of children should be based on a reasoned interpretation of currently available data regarding the short- and long-term effectiveness and consequences of differing parts of a system of discipline.

2. Any disciplinary technique, including spanking, should be endorsed only if research demonstrates that the short- and long-term benefits outweigh the short- and long-term harm to the child or the caregiver (parent).

3. Spanking a child should not be the primary or only response to a misbehavior used by a caregiver.

4. Escalation from spanking to abusive levels of punishment may occur when caregivers have uncontrolled anger. Spanking should be avoided under these circumstances because of the risk of significant injury.

5. Spanking is not recommended in infants and children under 2 years of age because escalation, should it occur, carries a greatly increased risk of causing physical injury.

6. There are no data bearing on the effectiveness of spanking to control misbehavior short-term in the average family. Limited data on preschool children with behavior problems suggest that spanking may increase the effectiveness of less aversive disciplinary techniques. Data relative to the long-term consequences of spanking of preschool children are inconclusive.

7. Noncorporal methods of discipline of children have been shown to be effective in children of all ages, including reasoning, modeling, positive reinforcement of desired behaviors, and aversive consequences of misbehavior. Correct implementation of these procedures, especially timeout, is important to their effectiveness. Family education and support have also been shown to help prevent behavior problems and should be recommended.

8. Currently available data indicate that corporal punishment, as previously defined, when compared with other methods of punishment of older children and adolescents, is not effective and is associated with increased risk of dysfunction and aggression later in life.

9. Corporal punishment is one of many risk factors for poor outcomes in children. Characteristics of the child, parent, family, and community, including temperament, stress, and resources, may increase or decrease the risk.

10. Efforts aimed at reducing the use of corporal punishment through family, school, and community-wide programs should be culturally sensitive and coupled with efforts to teach the many alternative methods of discipline shown to be effective.

11. Findings relative to parental discipline are not applicable to the school setting. Data indicate that corporal punishment within the schools is not an effective technique for producing a sustained, desired behavioral change and is associated with the potential for harm, including physical injury, psychological trauma, and inhibition of school participation.

12. Concerning forms of corporal punishment more severe than spanking in infants, toddlers, and adolescents, the data suggest that the risk of psychological or physical harm outweighs any potential benefits.

13. Although sufficient data currently exist to allow for these consensus statements, and much is known about effective disciplinary strategies, additional research is still needed to clarify issues relative to optimal disciplinary approaches to children. Our conclusions should be viewed as subject to revision and clarification as data continue to accumulate.

Baumrind D. The development of instrumental competence through socialization. *Minnesota Symp Child Psychiatry.* 1973;7:3-46

Baumrind identified three general parenting styles and evaluated the effects these styles had on the children's development. A child's instrumental competence was defined by social responsibility, independence, achievement orientation, and vitality.

1. *Authoritarian parents* were more controlling, more restrictive, less inclined to explain, more punitive, detached, less warm, and expressed more anger with child disobedience. They used love withdrawal, fear, little encouragement, and often corporal punishment.

2. *Permissive parents* were markedly less controlling, minimally demanding, freely granting of the child's demands, uninvolved with the child, and warmer than authoritarian parents. They did not feel in control of their children's behavior. They were affirming, accepting, and benign toward the child's impulses and actions. They used love withdrawal, ridicule, guilt provocation, little power and reasoning, and rarely corporal punishment. Permissive parents admitted to "explosive attacks of rage in which they inflicted more pain or injury on the child than they had intended."

They became more "violent because they felt they could neither control the child's behavior nor tolerate its effect upon themselves."

3. *Authoritative parents* employed a combination of firm control and positive encouragement of a child's independence. They affirmed the child's qualities, yet set a standard for future conduct. They made reasonable demands of their children, promoted respect for authority, and were more consistent with discipline. Authoritative parents used less love withdrawal and fear/guilt provocation than #1, and they used corporal punishment more often than #2. They used reason, power, and reinforcement to achieve objectives. They favored corporal punishment over other negative sanctions.

The authoritative parents who balanced firm control with encouragement reared children who displayed more achievement orientation, friendliness toward peers, cooperativeness with adults, social dominance, nonconforming behavior, and purposiveness. Evidence from this study "did not indicate that negative reinforcement or corporal punishment per se were harmful or ineffective procedures, but rather the total patterns of parental control determined the effects on the child of these procedures."

Baumrind D. A blanket injunction against disciplinary use of spanking is not warranted by the data. *Pediatrics.* 1996;98:828-831

The author cites several psychological propositions for why a blanket injunction against spanking is not scientifically supportable. Periodically, negative consequences are needed to enforce reasoning with childhood disobedience. Power-assertion methods such as physical punishment, when used with reasoning, can encourage a child's internalization. The outcomes of physical punishment are critically influenced by the cultural context, the child's developmental level, and the manner in which it is used.

Daro D: *Public Opinion and Behaviors Regarding Child Abuse Prevention: A Ten Year Review of NCPCA's Public Opinion Poll Research.* Chicago, IL: National Committee to Prevent Child Abuse, 1997

In this 10-year review of the annual public opinion polls of the NCPCA, one-quarter fewer parents reported the use of corporal punishment in 1997 than in 1988. The one exception to this pattern of general decline was an increase in the reported use of spanking among the youngest respondents, parents ages 18 to 24 years. During the 10-year reporting period, the percentage of parents in this age category who reported the use of spanking and hitting increased from 45% in 1988 to 62% in 1997.

In each year of the 10-year period, only one third of the respondents believed hitting or spanking often or very often harms a child. A greater proportion of respondents from the eastern and western portions of the United States expressed concern over the negative impacts of corporal punishment than those living in the South.

Larzelere RE. A review of the outcomes of parental use of nonabusive or customary physical punishment. *Pediatrics.* 1996;98: 824-828

A review of scientific studies on nonabusive physical punishment (ie, spanking) published from 1961 through 1995 found only 35 articles meeting minimal methodologic criteria. A pervasive weakness among the studies was a failure to control for the severity or frequency of child problem behavior encountered by the parents. The strongest studies found beneficial short-term outcomes of spanking with children 2 to 6 years of age. Detrimental outcomes were more typical with physical punishment of adolescents. When and how parents use discipline tactics and the overall parent-child relationship may be more important than the methods used, the author suggests.

McCord J. Unintended consequences of punishment. *Pediatrics.* 1996;98:832-833

The theoretical reasons to expect negative outcomes of punishment, including corporal punishment, are noted by the author to be the following:

1. Punishments give pain and therefore teach children that at least under some conditions, it is all right to give pain to others.

2. Punishments reduce the ability of punishers to influence the behavior of children, such as by example or discussion.

3. Punishments enhance the value of that which is being punished, by making the forbidden more attractive.

4. The use of punishment introduces an option or alternative to the action that is desired, such as an option to accept punishment and commit the offense again.

5. The use of punishment teaches children to be egocentric, such as by avoidance of personal pain rather than consideration of others.

McCormick KF. Attitudes of primary care physicians toward corporal punishment. *JAMA.* 1992;267:3161-3165

Randomly selected family physicians and pediatricians in Ohio were surveyed regarding their attitudes toward corporal punishment, with 1,200 (61%) respondents. Use of corporal punishment was supported by 70% of the family physicians and 59% of the pediatricians.

Morris JL, Johnson CF, Clasen M. To report or not to report: physicians' attitudes toward discipline and child abuse. *Am J Dis Child.* 1985;139:194-197

Interviews were conducted with 58 family physicians and pediatricians practicing within 50 miles of Columbus, Ohio. In varying proportions, physicians who cared for children rated as inappropriate such physical punishments as a light spanking on the bottom using an open hand (10%), spanking on the bottom that leaves a red mark (45%), a light slap on the face using an open hand (59%), spanking with a belt (etc) lightly (72%), and spanking with a belt that leaves a red mark (88%).

Roberts MW, Powers SW. Adjusting chair timeout enforcement procedures for oppositional children. *Behav Ther.* 1990;21:257-271
and

Bean AW, Roberts MW. The effect of timeout release contingencies on changes in child noncompliance. *J Abnorm Child Psychol.* 1981;9:95-105
and

Day DE, Roberts MW. An analysis of the physical punishment component of a parent training program. *J Abnorm Child Psychol.* 1983;11:141-152

The goal of the authors was to determine which back-up procedure was most effective in controlling a child's escape from timeout. The spank procedure was tested against three other procedures: barrier, hold, and release procedures. In randomized clinical field trials, the spank and barrier procedures were found to be the most effective. With the spank procedure, the escaping child was given two spanks to the buttocks and returned to timeout. With the barrier procedure, the child was taken to a small 4' x 5' carpeted room and barricaded inside with a sheet of plywood for a brief period of time, then returned to timeout.

Although the spank and the barrier were equally effective, parents preferred the spank procedure in the home setting (64%). The barrier procedure, with its room requirement, is less practical for many homes.

Socolar RRS, Stein REK. Spanking infants and toddlers: maternal belief and practice. *Pediatrics.* 1995;95:105-111

In this study, mothers of children less than 4 years of age were recruited from an inner-city teaching hospital pediatric clinic and a private pediatrician's suburban office. They were interviewed utilizing a structured questionnaire designed to assess their beliefs about spanking and approach to discipline. The authors found that a belief in spanking correlated significantly with a belief in a negative approach and with the practice and severity of spanking. Nineteen percent of the mothers believed there are times when it is appropriate to spank a child less than 1 year old, and 74% believed this about children 1 to 3 years old.

The authors stated that the correlation between belief and practice of spanking suggests that belief rather than impulse largely explains spanking of children less than 4 years old.

Straus MA. Spanking and the making of a violent society. *Pediatrics.* 1995;98:837-842
The author concludes that none of the studies reviewed can show that spanking causes violence. However, he notes that all but a few studies, using a variety of methods, have shown an association of corporal punishment with violence.

Straus MA, Donnelly DA. *Beating the Devil Out of Them: Corporal Punishment in American Families.* New York, NY: Lexington Books; 1994
In this text, the author presents his evidence linking corporal punishment with poor adult outcomes such as alcohol abuse, marital violence, depression, and suicidal thinking.

Trickett PK, Kuczynski L. Children's misbehaviors and parental discipline strategies in abusive and nonabusive families. *Dev Psychol.* 1986;22:115-123
Twenty physically abusive families with children between the ages of 4 and 10 years and a matched control group of 20 families recorded their disciplinary practices for 5 consecutive days. Abused children showed more aggressive misbehaviors and were less compliant with parental discipline than control children. Abusive parents reported more anger, punishment, and severe corporal punishment and less reasoning than control parents. There was no difference in their usage of mild spanking and hand slapping.

Weiss B, Dodge KA, Bates JE, et al. Some consequences of early harsh discipline: child aggression and a maladaptive social information processing style. *Child Dev.* 1992;63:1321-1335
The authors selected two cohorts of kindergarten enrollees from three geographic regions of the United States. Assessing a total of 584 subjects and their parents, trained interviewers developed a physical punishment rating (harsh physical punishment or restrictive discipline) for each family. Harsh parental discipline early in life was found to be consistently related to late aggression in both cohorts. The punishment included acts that left bruises and scars, and harsher discipline was associated with greater aggression in a linear relationship (personal communication). However, the authors acknowledged that the parents who used harsh discipline may have been more emotionally or physically neglectful. Thus, they could not say with certainty that their findings are specific to harsh discipline.

Corporal Punishment in Schools

Hyman IA. *Pediatrics.* 1996;98:818-821
In this review article, the author observes that corporal punishment in schools has been banned in 27 states and most major cities. Most of the corporal punishment in the United States occurs in the South and Southwest. An estimated one-half million incidents per year occurred in the early 1990s, compared with an estimated 3 million incidents per year in the early 1980s. Corporal punishment occurs more frequently in the primary and intermediate grades and more often involves boys, minority and poor white children, and children with disabilities. Injuries most often are welts and hematomas on the legs and buttocks, although severe injuries and death have been reported.

Orentlicher D. Corporal punishment in the schools. *JAMA.* 1992;267:3205-3208
This article from the office of General Counsel of the American Medical Association notes that the abolishment of corporal punishment in schools has been advocated by the American Academy of Pediatrics, the American Psychiatric Association, the American Public Health Association, and other professional groups. Corporal punishment has been banned in schools in Great Britain, France, Germany, Spain, Greece, Italy, China, Russia, and many other countries.

The opposition to corporal punishment is based on the right of children to be free from physical assault, the lack of evidence showing a need for corporal punishment, the risk of serious harm to students, and the possibility that it will teach that physical force is an appropriate method of resolving conflicts. The continued use of corporal punishment in the US schools appears to reflect limited views of children's rights and the role of physical force in maintaining order in the schools.

The legal context, negative consequences, alternative techniques for responding to student misbehavior, and children's rights are discussed.

Acknowledgment

This section was prepared by Jerry G. Jones, MD; co-authors were Jan Paradise, MD, Rebecca Socolar, MD, and Den Trumbull, MD.

Corporal Punishment in the Home: Commentary

The following does not represent AAP policy but includes the views of the Section on Child Abuse and Neglect Executive Committee members regarding the use of corporal punishment in the home.

Corporal punishment is the purposeful infliction of bodily pain or discomfort as a penalty for unacceptable behavior. Corporal punishment includes any action that produces physical discomfort, such as spanking, shaking, pinching, ear pulling, jabbing, shoving, choking, forcing to assume positions that become painful over time, denying bathroom privileges, confining in an uncomfortable space, forcing to eat noxious substances, and withholding water or food.[1]

Proponents have offered religious beliefs and disciplinary philosophies as rationale for corporal punishment. Religious support comes from biblical proverbs such as "He who spares the rod hates his son, but he who loves him is diligent to discipline him" (Proverbs, 13:24). Certain discipline philosophies have held that corporal punishment builds character, is key to the development of a child's conscience, and generates respect for the adults administering the punishment.[1]

The American Psychological Association[2] and the American Public Health Association[3] have formulated positions against corporal punishment in the school. The American Academy of Pediatrics also opposes the use of corporal punishment in the school, believing that corporal punishment may adversely affect a student's image and school achievement and contribute to disruptive and violent student behavior.[1,4,5]

The main reason for not recommending corporal punishment is that it is not as effective as other means of managing behavior. At best it teaches children what not to do; it does not teach them what to do. In the absence of education about appropriate behavior, it has only a temporary effect and little educational value.[6,7] Corporal punishment may even make behavior worse.[1]

The negative effects of corporal punishment on the child include emotional and psychologic effects such as embarrassment, a feeling of worthlessness, mistrust, anger, resentment, and confusion. Spanking may contribute to delinquency and counterproductive behavior. Physical punishment, particularly when applied in anger, impairs a child's trust and confidence. It is humiliating and demeaning and conveys the idea that might makes right.[7,8]

No matter how controlled the person who inflicts the punishment, corporal punishment may result in serious injury. Major tissue damage, central nervous system hemorrhage, spinal injury, and sciatic nerve damage are documented complications.[7,8]

It is not enough for pediatricians to say to parents that they should not hit their children. Pediatricians must be prepared to provide parents with practical, effective alternatives to corporal punishment. Praise, discussion regarding values, and positive role models do more to develop character, respect, and values than does corporal punishment. Effective alternatives to corporal punishment include distraction, disapproval, timeouts, alternative activities, discussion of values, verbal reprimands, and natural and logical consequences. Behavioral modification research has shown that positive reinforcement is more effective and long-lived than adverse reinforcement.[1,6,9]

Pediatricians are in an ideal position, as advocates for children, to educate parents about the consequences and futility of corporal punishment and to offer practical and nonviolent alternatives.

Pediatricians should advocate for alternatives to corporal punishment and discourage the use of corporal punishment in the home. Pediatricians can make parents aware of these issues during well-child visits or with printed materials. Discussions should include the dangers and harmful effects of corporal punishment and alternative techniques of behavioral management.[1,6,10]

References

1. Poole SR, Ushkow MC, Nader PR, et al. The role of the pediatrician in abolishing corporal punishment in schools. *Pediatrics.* 1991;88:162-167

2. Policy Statement of the American Psychological Association. *Am Psychol.* 1975;30:632

3. Policy Resolution, Governing Council, American Public Health Association, November 7, 1979. *Am J Public Health.* 1980;70:308

4. Hyman IA, Wise JH, eds: *Corporal Punishment in American Education: Readings in History, Practice and Alternatives.* Philadelphia, PA: Temple University Press; 1979.

5. American Academy of Pediatrics, Committee on School Health: Corporal punishment in schools. *Pediatrics* 1991;88:173.

6. Christopherson ER. The pediatrician and parental discipline. *Pediatrics* 1980;66: 641-642.

7. Wessel MA. The pediatrician and corporal punishment. *Pediatrics.* 1980;66:639-641

8. Eichelberger SP, Beal DW, May RB. Hypovolemic shock in a child as a consequence of corporal punishment. *Pediatrics.* 1991;87:570-571

9. Schmitt BD. Discipline: rules and consequences. *Contemp Pediatr.* 1991;8:65-69

10. American Academy of Pediatrics, Committee on Psychosocial Aspects of Child and Family Health. The pediatrician's role in discipline. *Pediatrics.* 1983;72:373

AMERICAN ACADEMY OF PEDIATRICS

Committee on School Health

Corporal Punishment in Schools (RE9207)

It is estimated that corporal punishment is administered between 1 and 2 million times a year in schools in the United States.[1] Thirty states have statutes that allow school officials to use corporal punishment.

The American Academy of Pediatrics believes that corporal punishment may affect adversely a student's self-image and his or her school achievement, and that it may contribute to disruptive and violent student behavior.[2-4] Alternative methods of behavioral management have been shown to be more effective than corporal punishment.[2-4] It is also recognized that physical force or constraint by a school official may be required in selected situations to protect students or staff from physical injury or to disarm a student. In carefully selected circumstances, the use of physical force or constraint may also be justified to prevent property damage.

The American Academy of Pediatrics urges parents, educators, school administrators, school board members, legislators, and other adults to seek (1) the legal prohibition by all states of corporal punishment in schools and (2) the employment of alternative methods of managing student behavior.

COMMITTEE ON SCHOOL HEALTH, 1990 to 1991

Martin C. Ushkow, MD, Chairman
John R. Asbury, MD
Bradley J. Bradford, MD
Philip R. Nader, MD
Steven R. Poole, MD
Daniel C. Worthington, MD

Liaison Representatives
Penny Anderson, RN, MSN, CPNP, National Association of Pediatric Nurse Associates and Practitioners
Arthur B. Elster, MD, American Medical Association
Vivian Haines, RN, MA, SNP, National Association of School Nurses, Inc
Paul W. Jung, EdD, American Association of School Administrators
R. Dee Legako, MD, American Academy of Family Physicians
John Santelli, MD, American School Health Association
James H. Williams, MEd, National Education Association

REFERENCES

1. *1986–1987 Elementary and Secondary Schools Civil Rights Survey, National Summary of Projected Data.* Washington, DC: Office of Civil Rights, US Department of Education; 1987
2. Poole SR, Ushkow MC, Nader PR, et al. The role of the pediatrician in abolishing corporal punishment in schools. *Pediatrics.* 1991;88:162–167
3. Hyman IA, Wise JH, eds. *Corporal Punishment in American Education: Readings in History, Practice and Alternatives.* Philadelphia, PA: Temple University Press; 1979
4. Hyman IA, McDowell E, Raines B. In: Wise JH, ed. Proceedings: Conference on Corporal Punishment in the Schools: A National Debate. Washington, DC: National Institute of Education Contract N1E-P-77-0079; 1977

Courts and Court Testimony

See Also:
AAP Statements *Guidelines for Expert Witness Testimony* and *The Child as a Witness*, which follow

Clinical Principles

▼ Court testimony is an integral part of the evaluation of suspected child maltreatment. The responsibility of being a witness in a child abuse case is no less important than making an accurate medical diagnosis or prescribing a necessary medication.

▼ In order to interact effectively with the courts, physicians need to understand the legal system. Professionals dealing with child abuse should be well prepared for court.

▼ It is the lawyer's role to advocate; the physician's role is to educate. Expert witnesses should be objective and without bias.

▼ Physicians who diagnose and treat abused children may be asked to testify in several different types of court proceedings. These may include criminal prosecutions, proceedings to protect abused children, child custody and visitation litigation, and proceedings to terminate parental rights.

Bibliography

Journals

Chadwick DL. Preparation for court testimony in child abuse cases. *Pediatr Clin North Am.* 1990;37:955-970
This article outlines the preparation needed for a practitioner to be more effective during court testimony. Written by a pediatrician, it gives tips on reading the medical literature, reviewing the case, meeting with attorneys, and testimony in depositions and trials. The author stresses the important role physicians play in the substantiation of child abuse for the courts. He also discusses the ethics of medical testimony from a physician's perspective. Chadwick is the first physician to offer a medical definition of

"reasonable medical certainty" in the child abuse literature.

> Reasonable medical certainty': as certain as a physician should be in order to recommend and carry out treatment for a given medical condition. This definition requires that the nature of the condition, the probable untreated outcome and the risks of treatment also be described. Thus, 'reasonable medical certainty' for the diagnosis of leukemia and the recommendation of chemotherapy is quite different from that for the diagnosis of viral upper respiratory infection and the prescription of acetaminophen.

Chadwick DL, Krous HR. Irresponsible testimony by medical experts in cases involving the physical abuse and neglect of children. *Child Maltreatment.* 1997;2:313-321
The authors present three case reports of irresponsible testimony by medical experts testifying for the defense. They offer rebuttal for the defense testimony based on the relevant scientific literature. Additionally, the authors propose criteria to define irresponsible medical testimony and criteria to define medical expertise in the field of child abuse and neglect. They urge physicians and lawyers involved in child abuse cases to develop an expert testimony peer review process to expose and prevent irresponsible testimony.

Cross TP, Whitcomb D, De Vos E. Criminal justice outcomes of prosecution of child sexual abuse: a case flow analysis. *Child Abuse Negl.* 1995;19:1431-1442
The authors reviewed all cases of child sexual abuse referred for prosecution in four urban jurisdictions over the course of 1 year. They found that most cases were accepted for prosecution, with the vast majority resulting in guilty pleas. In their study, only 9% of child sexual abuse cases went to

trial, with the majority of the defendants convicted. Over 75% of those convicted were incarcerated. They concluded that the rate of prosecution and conviction for child sexual abuse was similar to overall national felony arrests, but sexual abuse cases were more likely to go to court and the sentences were more severe. The authors stress that more attention should be directed to the overall cases investigated and pleas bargained.

DeJong AR, Rose M. Legal proof of child sexual abuse in the absence of physical evidence. *Pediatrics.* 1991;88:506-511

The authors present a retrospective review of 1 year of court records in child sexual abuse cases. One hundred fifteen cases were reviewed, with 76% resulting in felony convictions. No significant difference was noted in the rate of felony convictions with or without physical evidence. Convictions were obtained in 67 (79%) of 85 cases without physical evidence and in 20 (67%) of 30 cases with physical evidence. The paper points out that successful prosecution depends on the quality of the verbal evidence in these cases and that physical evidence is not essential for prosecution.

Halverson KC, Elliott BA, Rubin MS, Chadwick DL. Legal considerations in cases of child abuse. *Prim Care.* 1993;20:407-416

This review article discusses practical aspects of forensic medicine such as reporting child abuse and interfacing with the courts. It discusses how to obtain and document a history that will stand up in court, as well as details of how to perform the physical examination and maintain the chain of evidence for forensic specimens. It concludes with preparation for and testimony in court.

Hanes M, Mcauliff T. Preparation for child abuse litigation: perspectives of the prosecutor and the pediatrician. *Pediatr Ann.* 1997; 26:288-295

The authors offer the unique perspectives of their professions in evaluating a child abuse case and preparing for legal intervention. Sections cover understanding the legal system, preparing for testimony, and testifying in various settings. The article also reviews appropriate interview techniques and proper documentation of forensic information. The authors stress the use of networking to coordinate services more effectively among community professionals involved in child abuse cases.

Myers JE. Role of physician in preserving verbal evidence of child abuse. *J Pediatr.* 1986;109:409-411

This article documents how physicians can obtain and preserve verbal evidence from children that can be effectively used in the courtroom. It discusses the use of hearsay evidence in court proceedings. It also emphasizes the use of nonleading questions in the interview of children. This is a useful paper for those who have first contact with a disclosing child, as well as those who may interview children regarding suspected abuse.

Myers JE, Bays J, Becker J, Berliner L, Corwin DL, Savwitz KJ. Expert testimony in child sexual abuse litigation. *Nebr Law Rev.* 1989;68:1-145

The authors provide a detailed legal review of child sexual abuse litigation, with sections on medical and behavioral science testimony by both physicians and mental health professionals. The article cautions that although expert testimony can be valuable in the courtroom, professionals should be highly qualified. It provides a medically related bibliography, as well as extensive legal case references.

Myers JE. Expert testimony regarding child sexual abuse. *Child Abuse Negl.* 1993; 17:175-185

This article discusses issues related to expert testimony in child sexual abuse cases from a lawyer's perspective. Although written specifically about sexual abuse, it is generally applicable to all forms of child abuse. It addresses the qualifications of an expert witness, where expert testimony is permitted, the "reasonable certainty" standard of expert testimony from a legal perspective, and the appropriateness of equating clinical decision making with legal degrees of proof. It concludes with a brief summary of the law concerning expert testimony.

Tjaden PG, Thoennes N. Predictors of legal intervention in child maltreatment cases. *Child Abuse Negl.* 1992;16:807-821
The authors examined the extent and nature of criminal and civil findings in 833 cases of substantiated child abuse from three diverse counties across the United States. They found legal intervention in child maltreatment to be uncommon; only 21% resulted in dependency hearings and 4% in criminal trials. Their findings are similar to the rates presented by The National Center on Child Abuse and Neglect in 1978. The data support the authors' position that despite the seeming trend toward increased prosecution, legal intervention in child abuse cases has not increased over the years.

Books

Myers JE. *Legal Issues in Child Abuse and Neglect.* Newbury Park, CA: Sage Publications; 1992
This book provides a well-written, easy-to-read overview of the legal implications involved in the evaluation of child abuse and neglect. It provides a description of the American legal system, as well as chapters on reporting laws, interviewing, expert testimony, cross-examination, and lawsuits against professionals working in the field of child abuse. This book is ideal for anyone starting out in the field with a need to know the basics of the legal system as it relates to child abuse.

Stern P. *Preparing and Presenting Expert Testimony in Child Abuse Litigation.* Thousand Oaks, CA: Sage Publications; 1997
Stern has written an excellent reference for both physicians and attorneys dealing with expert testimony in child abuse cases. It presents in-depth coverage of witness preparation, as well as direct and cross examination of witnesses. The book contains helpful tips for the prospective witness. It also explains the qualifications of expert witnesses and the steps necessary to ensure witness competence on the stand. This is a very helpful reference for professionals who anticipate regular courtroom testimony in the field of child abuse and neglect.

Acknowledgment
This section and its annotations were prepared by Suzanne P. Starling, MD. It was reviewed by Kent Hymel, MD, and David P. Schor, MD.

AMERICAN ACADEMY OF PEDIATRICS

Guidelines for Expert Witness Testimony in Medical Liability Cases(S93-3)

Committee on Medical Liability   (RE9431)

The American Academy of Pediatrics joins with other medical organizations in emphasizing the obligation of objectivity when its members respond to requests to serve as expert witnesses in the judicial system. Regardless of the source of the request, such testimony ought to embody the relevant facts and the expert's knowledge, experience, and best judgment regarding the case. At the same time, the Academy reiterates that it cannot condone participation of its members in legal actions in which their testimony will impugn some performances that clearly fall within the accepted standards of practice or, conversely, will endorse some obviously deficient practices.

The role of an expert witness in a medical liability case is to testify to the standards of care in a given case, and to explain how the defendant did or did not conform to those standards. An expert witness may be asked to testify as to whether a deviation from the standard of care caused the injury. Expert witnesses are also called upon to help an attorney determine if a case has merit, and in several states attorneys are required by law to consult an expert before a suit is filed. Because experts are relied upon to help courts and juries understand the "standards of practice" as applicable to a given case, care must be exercised that such "expert testimony" does not narrowly reflect the experts' views about applicable standards to the exclusion of other acceptable and perhaps more realistic choices. The standards of care for generalists may not necessarily be the standards of care for subspecialists. The Academy considers it unethical for any expert to provide testimony that does not adhere scrupulously to the goal of objectivity.

The Academy also recognizes its responsibility andthat of its Fellows for continued efforts to improve health care for children. However, some claims of medical malpractice may represent the response of our society to a technologically advanced form of health care that has, unfortunately, fostered some unrealistic expectations. As technology continues to become more complex, risks as well as benefits continue and sometimes increase, making the practice of medicine more and more complicated.

Under such circumstances, it becomes most important to distinguish between "medical maloccurrence" and "medical malpractice."[1] "Medical malpractice,"

according to *Black's Law Dictionary*,[1(p864)] is defined as follows:

In medical malpractice litigation, negligence is the predominant theory of liability. In order to recover from negligent malpractice, the plaintiff must establish the following elements: 1) the existence of the physician's duty to the plaintiff, usually based upon the existence of the physician-patient relationship; 2) the applicable standard of care and its violation; 3) a compensable injury; and 4) a causal connection between the violation of the standard of care and the harm complained of.

In contrast, medical maloccurrence is a less-than-ideal outcome of medical care which may or may not be related to the reasonableness of the quality of care provided. While a medical maloccurrence is always present in cases of malpractice, the converse is not true. Certain medical or surgical complications can be anticipated and represent unavoidable effects or complications of disease. Still other unavoidable complications arise unpredictably for the individual patient. Of course, others occur as a result of judgments and decisions carefully made by physicians and patients with informed consent but which turn out, in retrospect, to have been the least desirable of several options considered. Each of these situations represents maloccurrence rather than malpractice and is a reflection of the innate uncertainty inherent in medicine.

The potential for personal satisfaction, professional recognition, or financial reward appears to encourage "expert testimony" that overlooks the distinction between a simple maloccurrence and actual malpractice. The Academy considers it unethical for an expert to distort or misrepresent a maloccurrence in which the applicable standard of care was not violated as an example of medical malpractice—or the converse.

The Academy supports the concept of appropriate, prompt compensation to patients for injuries due to medical negligence. Under the present legal, insurance, and social tenets, such remuneration is sometimes made for medical maloccurrence in which no malpractice is present, on the assumption that the larger society should bear financial responsibility for such injuries.

The moral and legal duty of physicians to testify as called upon in a court of law in accordance with their expertise is recognized and supported. This duty implies adherence to the strictest ethics. Truthfulness is essential and misrepresentation or exaggeration of clinical facts or opinion to attempt to establish an absolute right or wrong may be harmful, both to the individual parties involved and to the profession as a whole. Furthermore, the acceptance of fees that are disproportionate to those customary for such professional endeavors is improper as the payment of such fees may be construed as attempting to influence testimony given by a witness.

The 1992 opinion of the American Medical Association on Medical Testimony states as follows:

As a citizen and as a professional with special training and experience, the physician has an ethical obligation to assist in the administration of justice. If a patient who has a legal claim requests a physician's assistance, the physician should furnish medical evidence, with the patient's consent, in order to secure the patient's legal rights.

The medical witness must not become an advocate or a partisan in the legal proceeding. The medical witness should be adequately prepared and should testify honestly and truthfully. The attorney for the party who calls the physician as a witness should be informed of all favorable and unfavorable information developed by the physician's evaluation of the case. It is unethical for a physician to accept compensation that is contingent upon the outcome of litigation.[2(p46)]

The Academy encourages the development of policies and standards for expert testimony. Such policies should embody safeguards to promote the accuracy and thoroughness of the testimony and efforts to encourage peer review of the testimony.

The following principles have been adopted as guidelines for the American Academy of Pediatrics and its members who assume the role of expert witness:

1. The physician should have current experience and ongoing knowledge about the areas of clinical medicine in which he or she is testifying and familiarity with practices during the time and place of the episode being considered as well as the circumstances surrounding the occurrence.
2. The physician's review of medical facts should be thorough, fair, objective, and impartial and should not exclude any relevant information in order to create a perspective favoring either the plaintiff or the defendant. *The ideal measure for objectivity and fairness is a willingness to prepare testimony that could be presented unchanged for use by either the plaintiff or defendant.*
3. The physician's testimony should reflect an evaluation of performance in light of generally accepted standards, neither condemning performance that clearly falls within generally accepted practice standards nor endorsing or condoning performance that clearly falls outside accepted practice standards.
4. The physician should make a clear distinction between medical malpractice and medical maloccurrence which is not the result of a violation of the applicant standard of care when analyzing any case. The practice of medicine remains a mixture of art and science; the scientific component is a dynamic and changing one based to a large extent on concepts of probability rather than absolute certainty.

5. The physician should make every effort to assess the relationship between the alleged substandard practice and the patient's outcome, because deviation from a practice standard is not always the cause of the less-than-ideal outcome at issue in the case.
6. The physician should be willing to submit transcripts of depositions and/or courtroom testimony for peer review.
7. The physician expert should cooperate with any reasonable efforts undertaken by the courts or by plaintiffs' or defendants' carriers and attorneys to provide a better understanding of the expert witness issue.
8. It is unethical for a physician to accept compensation that is contingent upon the outcome of the litigation.

COMMITTEE ON MEDICAL LIABILITY, 1993 TO 1994
Bradford P. Cohn, MD, Chairperson
Jan Ellen Berger, MD
Ian R. Holzman, MD
Jean Lockhart, MD
Mark Reuben, MD
William O. Robertson, MD
Steven Selbst, MD

CONSULTANT
Holly Myers, Esq

ACKNOWLEDGMENT

The Committee on Medical Liability gratefully acknowledges the contributions of the American College of Obstetricians and Gynecologists (Ethical Issues Related to Expert Testimony by Obstetricians and Gynecologists) and the Council of Medical Specialty Societies (Statement on Qualifications and Guidelines for the Physician Expert Witness) in the development of this policy statement.

REFERENCES

1. *Black's Law Dictionary.* 6th ed. St Paul, MN; West Publishing Co; 1990
2. *Current Opinions of the Council on Ethical and Judicial Affairs of the American Medical Association.* Chicago, IL: American Medical Association; 1992

BIBLIOGRAPHY

Ackerman AB. The physician expert witness: is peer review needed? *Generics.* 1985;(Dec):37–52
Brennan TR. Untangling causation issues in law and medicine: hazardous substance litigation. *Ann Intern Med.* 1987;107: 741–747
Brent RL. The irresponsible expert witness: a failure of biomedical graduate education and professional accountability. *Pediatrics.* 1982;70:754–762
Dyer C. Judge "not satisfied" that whooping cough vaccine causes permanent brain damage. *Br Med J.* 1988;296:1189–1190
Ethical Issues Related to Expert Testimony by Obstetricians and Gynecologists. American College of Obstetricians and Gynecologists; 1987
Fish R, Rosen P. Physicians should be expert witnesses. *J Emerg Med.* 1990;8:659–663
Higgins LC. MD (medical director) witnesses: who are these experts? *Med World News.* 1988;29:28–36
Lundberg GD. Expert witness for whom? *JAMA.* 1984;252:251
Miller D. Courtroom science and standards of proof. *Lancet.* 1987; 2:1283–1284
Robertson WO. *Expert Witness Controversies in Medical Malpractice: A Preventive Approach.* Seattle, WA: University of Washington Press; 1985:124–136
Robertson WO. Some 'experts' may not be all that expert. *WSMA Rep.* June 1988:4
Council of Medical Specialty Societies. *Statement on Qualifications and Guidelines for the Physician Expert Witness.* Council of Medical Specialty Societies; 1989

AMERICAN ACADEMY OF PEDIATRICS

The Child as a Witness   (RE9244)

Committee on Psychosocial Aspects of Child and Family Health

In the last two decades, there has been a dramatic increase in the recognition and reporting of child physical and sexual abuse. This, coupled with the current 50% divorce rate and the fact that many of these separations involve child custody decisions, has led to an increasing need for children to appear in court.

Custody decisions usually involve family or civil courts; however, allegations involving sexual abuse may require a child to appear as a witness in criminal court. Although the procedures and potential consequences of these legal processes are quite distinct, all situations in which children offer testimony can be quite stressful and merit the awareness and support of pediatricians.

Pediatricians can become involved with children who are to be witnesses at several levels, including: 1) supporting patients in the pediatric office; 2) participating in legal proceedings; and 3) advocating for legal reform.

SUPPORT IN THE PEDIATRIC OFFICE

The pediatrician is an important source of support for the child who is to be a witness, from the initial contact through preparation for court appearance, and after the court proceedings. A pediatrician should attempt to keep the legal process in the child's best interest and should help the child maintain a healthy adaptation to a stressful experience. The pediatrician should also address the psychological impact of the event responsible for the child's court appearance.

When parents plan to separate, pediatricians may help the family by discussing living arrangements and visitation during an office visit. If custody is disputed, which is the case in 10% of divorces, and a child is asked to appear in family court, the pediatrician can provide counseling to help prepare the child for the court appearance. If sexual abuse is suspected, the case will involve the criminal justice system, and a pediatrician is often the first person contacted. In such cases, the pediatrician needs the skills to sensitively and appropriately interview, examine, document, report, and provide ongoing counseling for the child. The pediatrician also needs to have knowledge of behavioral and physical indicators of abuse and of variations and current trends in sexually transmitted diseases.[1] In one study of sexually abused children, more than half of the children were involved in court cases, and 15% were asked to testify.[2]

Separate attention must be devoted to preparing a child for the stress that accompanies a legal hearing. Appearances in family court are often in the judge's chambers and are markedly different from criminal court experiences in which child witnesses may be examined for weeks by defense attorneys. Pediatricians can help prepare children for court appearances by explaining what will occur and that the child will always be accompanied by a supportive person, such as a parent. Pediatricians must be aware of children's concerns about recrimination. A pediatrician can help minimize a child's anxiety by explaining that the child will not be judged on his/her performance in the courtroom, that efforts will be made to ensure that the child will be safe from recrimination, and that the child should answer questions to the best of his/her ability.

Because of the stressful events leading up to and surrounding a court appearance, a follow-up visit with the pediatrician is indicated after a child appears as a witness. Children should be checked for behavioral manifestations of acute stress (sleep disorders, somatic complaints), adjustment, and functional status (school activities, resumption of usual activities, physical functioning, social functioning, mental health).

One study has shown that participating in legal proceedings may actually benefit a child psychologically.[2] The study showed that waiting for court proceedings was likely to prolong depression in sexually abused children, whereas testifying helped decrease children's anxieties.

PARTICIPATION IN LEGAL PROCEEDINGS

While the pediatrician's principal role is to support and help the child and family cope with the stresses of being involved in legal procedures, some pediatricians will choose to use their knowledge and spirit of advocacy to help with their patients' trial processes, or to serve as experts testifying on children's cognitive abilities. Pediatricians may also be asked to testify based on their knowledge of and relationship with the child.

Setting and Support

All children should have a supportive individual present during court proceedings to explain procedures, assist the child and parents, and provide support by advising the court of the child's needs. The courtroom and/or proceedings can also be adapted to

This statement has been approved by the Council on Child and Adolescent Health.

The recommendations in this publication do not indicate an exclusive course of treatment or serve as a standard of medical care. Variations, taking into account individual circumstances, may be appropriate.

make the legal process more comfortable for the child. Specific adaptations include exclusion of spectators, use of videotaped or closed circuit testimony, use of child-size furniture, and eye-level interviewing. However, a recent Supreme Court decision that affirmed the right of defendants in abuse cases to face their accusers has raised questions about accommodations provided by many state laws to protect children by using videotape.[3]

Interview

The purpose of interviewing a child in legal proceedings is to obtain accurate information. The setting, support persons, and interviewer's skills will influence the likelihood of success in accomplishing this task. A supportive environment is essential for two reasons: 1) so that the best interest of the child is served and the child is not subjected to undue stress, and 2) because the anxiety or emotional difficulties a witness feels due to the stress of a court appearance can hamper the process of obtaining valid and reliable information.

Individuals experienced in developmentally appropriate interactions should be involved. A variety of interviewing techniques may be appropriate, including use of behavioral observation techniques, play, story telling, and drawing, as well as verbal questioning. The use of a single, well trained interviewer capable of building rapport will enhance the process and minimize trauma to children. However, none of these techniques is completely accurate in determining whether a child may have been abused.[4,5]

Principles of interviewing that apply to children in the office apply to children in the courtroom. These include building rapport and asking clear, simple questions. For children testifying in abuse cases, a time for "warm-up" is especially important. Questioning should be general at first and should gradually become more specific.

Children may be confused by negatively worded statements. They may also be eager to please, anxious to provide the "right" answer, and may have a tendency to choose either the first or the last option when given a number from which to select. Therefore, it is essential that clearly worded questions that encourage children to provide answers that will be viewed non-judgmentally are used. Correct answers or scenarios should not be suggested as children may be influenced and are prone to suggestibility.

Determining Competence

The legal system is especially interested in three questions about a child's competence as a witness: 1) Can the child receive and relay information accurately? 2) Does the child know the difference between telling the truth and a lie? 3) Does the child understand the need to tell the truth in court?

For adults, lying is an intentional deception that involves either concealing or falsifying information directed at an unsuspecting individual.[6] Deception, as a developmental concept, has been studied extensively in young children, as has lying.[4,7-9] Ekman has classified the reasons children lie. They include "to avoid being punished; to get something you couldn't get otherwise; to protect friends from trouble; to protect yourself or another person from harm; to win the admiration or interest of others; to avoid creating an awkward social situation; to avoid embarrassment; to maintain privacy; and to demonstrate your power over an authority."[4]

When assessing the validity of information provided by children, many factors must be considered. Younger children may not remember with as much accuracy as older children, but the poignancy of an event may enhance memory.[7,8] A 3- or 4-year-old's ability to recall major events is excellent, although less important information is less well remembered. Three-year-olds have actually been effective witnesses.[10] A lack of accuracy may be due to the following:

1. poor recall of event or sequences in an event
2. misinterpretation or confusion around an event
3. suggestibility
4. delusion or other mental disorder
5. mental retardation
6. intentional deception initiated by the child or resulting from adult coercion.

Older children, who are capable of understanding the meaning of a lie, may be coerced into falsification by adults who label the action an act of secrecy. The child may conceptually consider a lie and a secret as two separate entities and, therefore, may not feel a lie is actually being told. Alternatively, children may be convinced that when a lie serves "a noble purpose" they are not really doing something wrong.

The amount of literature that addresses the accuracy of children as witnesses is growing.[4,9-16]

ADVOCATING LEGAL REFORM

Finally, pediatricians may wish to collaborate with other professionals to improve the legal procedures and policies for examining children.

Treating children sensitively throughout the pretrial period, along with the court's increased sensitivity to the special needs of children, will help make the legal examination easier for children. Specific actions that can be helpful include educating judges to be alert to lines of questioning that may confuse or intimidate a child. They must recognize signs of embarrassment or anxiety that may cloud or confuse a child's testimony and must take the initiative to help the child. For instance, a judge could call a recess to explore a child's discomfort.

It has been recommended that statutory reforms might be helpful. Possible reforms include: 1) abolishing competency requirements. Although state laws vary widely, traditionally, children have not been considered competent witnesses. Adoption of the more liberal Federal and Uniform Rules of Evidence, which allow children to testify and permit the trier of fact to determine the weight and credibility of the testimony, would facilitate justice in cases involving children. 2) Authorizing special hearsay exceptions for child sexual abuse victims. This would enable the child's statements to others, such as pediatricians and social workers, to be admitted as evidence.

Perhaps it is most important for pediatricians to understand the current rights of children in their states' legal systems so they can advise children and parents in their offices and determine what reforms may be needed in their states. Many states have made major legal strides in treating children sensitively as the following California codes illustrate: 1) "Every person, irrespective of age, is qualified to testify. . ."; 2) "The court should support, comfort, and protect child witnesses."; 3) "Up to two supporting persons in the courtroom are allowed for any child under 16."; 4) "The court is to take special care to protect the child from embarrassment and restrict the unnecessary repetition of questions."; 5) "The intent and purpose of the Legislature is to protect children from abuse. In any investigation of suspected child abuse, all persons participating in the investigation of the case shall consider the needs of the child victim and shall do whatever necessary to prevent psychological harm to the victim."; 6) "Contemporaneous closed circuit television testimony is allowed in criminal prosecution." This last accommodation may need to be reviewed based on the Supreme Court's recent decision to affirm the "right to confrontation" of the Sixth Amendment. Nevertheless, in a concurring opinion, Justice O'Conner suggested that the "compelling state interest of protecting a child witness" would allow for case-by-case decisions.[3]

In addition, it is possible for pediatricians to advocate for limiting the duration and frequency of child interviews, to recommend that professionals competent in child interviewing question witnesses, and to urge for expedient trials in abuse cases in order to hasten the child's healing process. Judges also have considerable discretion to exclude spectators from trials. Many other modifications in legal proceedings for children have been recommended (AACAP).[17]

Attempts to protect children from the stresses of a trial will continue to conflict with the rights of the accused to face an accuser and to have cross-examination of witnesses. We, therefore, anticipate that it will be necessary for pediatricians to engage in both ethical and legal debates in the process of working toward legal reform in the criminal court system. Nevertheless, all of the recommended accommodations can occur in civil, family, and juvenile courts.

SUMMARY

1. Children are often involved with the courts in cases of abuse and custody dispute and may be required to be witnesses.
2. Pediatricians have important roles in assisting children by providing psychosocial support for the precipitant life event and the event of subsequent appearance in court.

3. A pediatrician also may be able to contribute to a child's adaptation by advocating for accommodations in the legal process that are in the child's best interest.

COMMITTEE ON PSYCHOSOCIAL ASPECTS OF CHILD AND FAMILY HEALTH, 1991 TO 1992
Robert Pantell, MD, Chair
William B. Carey, MD
Stanford B. Friedman, MD
Michael S. Jellinek, MD
Lucy Osborn, MD
Ellen C. Perrin, MD
Martin T. Stein, MD
Mark L. Wolraich, MD

Liaison Representative
Mervyn Fox, MD,
    Canadian Paediatric Society

Consultants
John B. Reinhart, MD
George J. Cohen, MD
    National Consortium for Child
    Mental Health Services

REFERENCES

1. American Academy of Pediatrics, Committee on Child Abuse and Neglect. Guidelines for the evaluation of sexual abuse of children. *Pediatrics.* 1991;87:254–259
2. Runyan DK, Everson MD, Edelsohn GA, Hunter WM, Coulter ML. Impact of legal intervention on sexually abused children. *J Pediatr.* 1988;113:647–653
3. *Coy v Iowa,* 487 US 1012 (1988)
4. Ekman MAM. Kids' testimony in court: the sexual abuse crisis. In: Edman P, ed. *Why Kids Lie.* New York, NY: Scribners; 1989
5. Faust D, Ziskin J. The expert witness in psychology and psychiatry. *Science.* 1988;241:31–35
6. Edman, P. *Telling Lies: Clues to Deceit in the Marketplace, Politics, and Marriage.* New York, NY: WW Norton & Company; 1985
7. Johnson MK, Foley MA. Differentiating fact from fantasy: the reliability of children's memory. *J Soc Issues.* 1984;40:33–50
8. Loftus EF, Davies GM. Distortions in the memory of children. *J Soc Issues.* 1984;40:51–67
9. Nurcombe B. The child as witness: competency and credibility. *J Am Acad Child Psychiatry.* 1986;25:473–480
10. Jones DPH, Krugman RD. Can a three-year-old child be a witness to her sexual assault and attempted murder? *Child Abuse Negl.* 1986;10:253–258
11. Berliner L, Barbieri MK. The testimony of the child victim of sexual assault. *J Soc Issues.* 1984;40:125–137
12. Goodman GS. Child witness: an introduction. *J Soc Issues.* 1984;40:1–7
13. Goodwin J, Sahd D, Rada RT. Incest hoax: false accusations, false denials. *Bull Am Acad Psychiatry Law.* 1978;6:269–276
14. Green AH. True and false allegations of sexual abuse in child custody disputes. *J Am Acad Child Psychiatry.* 1986;25:449–456
15. Landwirth J. Children as witnesses in child sexual abuse trials. *Pediatrics.* 1987;80:585–589
16. Whitcomb D, Shapiro ER, Stellwagen LD. *When the Victim Is a Child: Issues for Judges and Prosecutors.* ABT Associates, Inc; 1985. Sr. Doc. No. J28.23:V66. Dept of Justice, 86-5135
17. American Academy of Child and Adolescent Psychiatry. Statement on Protecting Children Undergoing Abuse: Investigations & Testimony. February 9, 1986

Culture and Child Maltreatment

Clinical Principles

- Information about the incidence and manifestations of child abuse in other countries and cultures is not easily obtained or interpreted. The definitions of child abuse may vary intraculturally and interculturally.

- Research about cultural influences on child-rearing practices is limited but increasing in availability. Even if a government recognizes child abuse, data may not be made available.

- Because culture influences approaches to discipline, immigrants must be made aware of accepted US discipline and health care standards and definitions of child maltreatment. Immigrant children and adults should be screened for abuse histories and adherence to folk medicine.

- Studies in the United States review folk practices, such as *Cao Gio* and *Caida de Mollera,* and discipline approaches used by five general "cultural" classifications: white, African-American, Hispanic, Native American, and Asian. These reports may generalize and may not adequately subdivide families by risk factors. For immigrants, consideration must be given to length of time, or generations, in the United States. *Socioeconomic status, not race, is the major influence on the incidence of maltreatment.*

- Variables that influence the propensity to abuse — eg, adolescent pregnancy, drug use, single-parent families, closely spaced children, lack of a support system — all relate to poverty. Poverty may not be easily separated from culture and race variables in the United States.

Bibliography

Research Needs

Daro D. Enhancing child abuse prevention efforts: research priorities of the 1990s. National Committee to Prevent Child Abuse: Working Paper Number 844. July 1988
Prevention programs must consider the influence of race and culture, as well as socioeconomic and ethnic variables.

Ember CR, Ember M. Issues in cross-cultural studies of interpersonal violence. *Violence Vict.* 1993;8:217-233
This paper discusses the achievements and promise of cross-cultural (CC) studies of interpersonal violence (mainly focusing on homicide). Three aspects of child rearing are discussed in a review of CC results on interpersonal violence: frustrating socialization, conditions that may promote "protest masculinity" or machismo, and socialization for aggression. The result of these studies are reviewed, and suggestions are given for how CC studies of violence might be improved, both methodologically and theoretically.

Graham P, Dingwall R, Wolkind S. Research issues in child abuse. *Soc Sci Med.* 1985; 21:1217-1228
Research is needed on social, professional, economic, and cultural issues.

Korbin JE. Cross-cultural perspectives and research directions for the 21st century. *Child Abuse Negl.* 1991;15:67-77

Smith JA, Adler RG. Children hospitalized with child abuse and neglect: a case control study. *Child Abuse Negl.* 1991;15:437-445
Because child abuse is more prevalent in lower socioeconomic families, the association with many factors has been accepted as implying a causal relationship. Matching procedures, which attempted to eliminate confounding by social class and family structure, cast doubts on some previously held beliefs about the risk factors for child abuse. More studies are needed in this area.

"Cultures" in the United States

Featherman JM. *Jews and Sexual Child Abuse.* Thousand Oaks, CA: Sage Publications Inc; 1995

Fontes LA. *Sexual Abuse in Nine North American Cultures: Treatment and Prevention.* Thousand Oaks, CA: Sage Publications Inc; 1995

Hampton RL. *Child Abuse in the African American Community.* New Brunswick, NJ: Rutgers University Press; 1992

Hartz DT. Comparative conflict resolution patterns among parent-teen dyads of four ethnic groups in Hawaii. *Child Abuse Negl.* 1995;19:681-689
Parent-teen dyadic aggression levels for Americans of European, Japanese, Polynesian, and Filipino ancestry were compared. The adolescent children of Polynesian-American parents reported significantly higher parent aggression levels than did adolescents with parents of other ethnicity. Parent aggression was the best predictor of teen aggression directed toward parents. Aggression by one parent was highly correlated with aggression by the other parent. Aggression by either parent was more highly correlated with teen aggression toward the mother.

Heras P. Cultural considerations in the assessment and treatment of child sexual abuse. *J Child Sex Abuse.* 1992;1:119-124

Hong GK, Hong LK. Comparative perspectives on child abuse and neglect: Chinese versus Hispanics and whites. *Child Welfare.* 1991; 70:463-475

Rose SJ, Meezan W. Variations in perceptions of child neglect. *Child Welfare.* 1996;75:139-160
Members of minority groups perceive some types of child neglect as more serious than do their white counterparts. Workers see all types of child neglect as less serious than do the mothers.

Sanders-Phillips K, Moisan PA, Wadlington S, et al. Ethnic differences in psychological functioning among black and Latino sexually abused girls. *Child Abuse Negl.* 1995;19:691-706
Latino girls received significantly higher scores for depression than black girls. These differences in depression appeared to be related to ethnic differences in the circumstances of the abuse. Latino girls were abused at a younger age, more likely to be abused by a relative, and more likely to have had a sibling abused. Latinos were also more likely to report high levels of family conflict and somewhat lower levels of maternal support.

Saunders EJ, Nelson K, Landsman MJ. Racial inequality and child neglect: findings in a metropolitan area. *Child Welfare.* 1993;72:341-354
Despite contradictory evidence, child neglect is often believed to occur more frequently in the African-American than in the white population. African-American families in the neglect sample suffered more from economic inequality than those in the general population. Implications of the findings for social welfare policy and child welfare practice are discussed.

Taylor C, Fontes LA. *Seventh Day Adventists and Sexual Child Abuse.* Thousand Oaks, CA: Sage Publications Inc; 1995:303

Zayas LH, Solari F. Early childhood socialization in Hispanic families: context, culture, and practice implications. *Professional Psychology.* 1994;25:200-206
Parent and child behaviors are a result of different socialization processes that encompass specific cultural values.

Immigrants to United States of America

Abbott S. Holding on and pushing away: comparative perspectives on an eastern Kentucky child-rearing practice. *Ethos.* 1992;20:33-65
Although co-sleeping occurred across all social classes, as measured by occupation and education, co-sleeping was least likely to occur in families in which the father had achieved managerial status and/or in which the parents had attended a university. The pattern is shown to be similar to Japanese child rearing, which socialized infants toward a high level of familial interdependence. This interdependence is transferred to "corporate culture."

Fischler RS. Child abuse and neglect in American Indian communities. *Child Abuse Negl.* 1985;9:95-106
The interplay of government and Native American culture is discussed. Socioeconomic variables, divorce, alcoholism, and poverty are believed to influence the risk of child abuse.

Hummel RP, Greenhalgh DG, Barthel PP, et al. Outcome and socioeconomic aspects of suspected child abuse scald burns. *J Burn Care Rehabil.* 1993;14:121-126
Patient characteristics and initial nutritional parameters were similar except for race; a higher percentage of black children were in the abused group. A significantly longer length of hospital stay was found in the abused children. The number of operations and frequency of complications were increased in the abused group. Children suspected of being scalded intentionally were more likely to be part of a broken home, belong to a single parent, and have a younger mother than were children in the control group. The person suspected of performing the abuse was always a family member.

Korbin JE. *Child Maltreatment and the Study of Child Refugees.* Baltimore, MD: University Press; 1991

Lin CC, Fu VR. A comparison of child-rearing practices among Chinese, immigrant Chinese, and Caucasian-American parents. *Child Dev.* 1990;61:429-433
Parental control, encouragement of independence, expression of affection, and emphasis on achievement were measured. Chinese and immigrant Chinese parents rated higher on parental control, encouragement of independence, and emphasis on achievement than white American parents.

McKelvey RS, Webb JA. A pilot study of abuse among Vietnamese Amerasians. *Child Abuse Negl.* 1995;19:545-553
A group of Vietnamese Amerasians bound for the United States was studied. A history of physical and/or sexual abuse was reported by 22% of male and 18% of female Amerasians. Abused male Amerasians reported significantly higher levels of psychological distress than nonabused male Amerasians, while abused and nonabused female Amerasians did not differ in their levels of psychological distress.

Showers J, Bandman RL. Scarring for life: abuse with electric cords. *Child Abuse Negl.* 1986;10:25-31
Poverty and culture influence approaches to corporal punishment.

White S, Santilli G. A review of clinical practices and research data on anatomical dolls. *J Interpersonal Violence.* 1978;3:430-442
Cultural variables must be considered when using interview tools.

Other Countries

Corral-Verdugo V, Frias-Armenta M, Romero M, et al. Validity of a scale measuring beliefs regarding the "positive" effects of punishing children: a study of Mexican mothers. *Child Abuse Negl.* 1995;19:669-679
An indication of predictive validity was found in a high, significant structural correlation between the beliefs factor and a "corrective punishment" factor. Mothers reported as abusing their children produced higher scores on the "beliefs" scale compared with "control" mothers. The direct, significant effect of parents' beliefs on the punishment of children explains much about the child maltreatment problem in the society studied.

Davison JE. Parenting style and family environment of Caucasian-American versus Malaysian families. *Dissertation Abstracts Int.* 1990;51:1791

Fontes LA. Disclosures of sexual abuse by Puerto Rican children: oppression and cultural barriers. *J Child Sex Abuse.* 1993;2:21-35

Forjuoh SN. Pattern of intentional burns to children in Ghana. *Child Abuse Negl.* 1995;19:837-841
Of 650 childhood burns, 35 (5.4%) were purposefully inflicted. The perpetrators were mostly friends (43%) and siblings (37%) of the victims, and traditional healers (6%) who burned children by flame and contact with a hot object rather than through scalding, the most common cause of burns in this region.

Ho T, Kwok WM. Child sexual abuse in Hong Kong. *Child Abuse Negl.* 1991;15:597-600

Kojima H. Japanese child rearing advice in its cultural, social, and economic contexts. *Int J Behav Dev.* 1996;19:373-391
Japanese historical materials on child rearing are studied from a developmental point of view and their relation to cultural, social, and economic contexts in five historical epochs. A new term, the "ethnopsychological pool of ideas" (EPIs), is presented to denote a reservoir of knowledge, practices, sentiments, and values that maintains diverse components across historical periods.

Konanc E, Zeytinoglu S, Kozcu S. Analysis of child abuse and neglect court cases in three cities in Turkey. In *Critical Issues In Victimology: International Perspectives.* 1992;12:101-109

Krugman S, Mata L, Krugman R. Sexual abuse and corporal punishment during childhood: a pilot retrospective survey of university students in Costa Rica. *Pediatrics.* 1992;90:157-161
Students were asked to comment on their perceptions and experiences regarding various forms of punishment, and personal experiences of sexual abuse. Spanking was reported to be the most widely accepted and frequently employed form of corporal punishment.

Mehta MN, Prabhu SV, Mistry HN. Child labor in Bombay. *Child Abuse Negl.* 1985;9:107-111
Culture, economics, poverty, and neglect are discussed.

Mejiuni CO. Educating adults against socio-culturally induced abuse and neglect of children in Nigeria. *Child Abuse Negl.* 1991;15:139-145

Moghal NE, Nota IK, Hobbs CJ. A study of sexual abuse in an Asian community. *Arch Dis Child.* 1995;72:346-347
The existence and difference in the incidence, pattern of presentation, and management in cases of Asian sexual abuse are compared with those reported in the indigenous population.

Mutambirwa J. Health problems in rural communities, Zimbabwe. *Soc Sci Med.* 1989; 29:927-932
In many developing countries, particularly those with a strong oral tradition, cultural orientation greatly shapes individual perceptions regarding health, illness, and health care needs. Appropriate health assessment and determination of medical neglect require an understanding of the patient's culture.

Oneha MF, Magyary DL. Transcultural nursing considerations of child abuse/maltreatment in American Samoa and the Federated States of Micronesia. *J Transcult Nurs.* 1992;3:11-17
Defining features were derived from evaluation of child abuse and neglect laws in each specified population. The degree at which unreasonable harm becomes abuse is culturally dictated; hence, these territories of the Pacific Basin are seeking culturally specific terminology when defining child maltreatment.

dePaul J, Milner JS, Mugica P. Child maltreatment, childhood social support, and child abuse potential in a Basque sample. *Child Abuse Negl.* 1995;19:907-920

Payne MA. Use and abuse of corporal punishment: a Caribbean view. *Child Abuse Negl.* 1989;13:389-401
A written survey of 499 Barbadian adults aged 20 to 59 years determined that 70% generally approved of corporal punishment. Older and younger participants responded similarly. Culture may influence adherence to accepted American discipline standards in immigrants.

Pecnik N, Ajdukovic M. The child abuse potential inventory: cross-validation in Croatia. *Psychol Rep.* 1995;72:979-985

Porter B. "Abandoned" parents—loss of traditional family support systems: a challenge for health professionals. *Clin Pediatr (Phila).* 1990;29:401-404
Maternal incompetence in child rearing in three different cultural settings in southern Israel are illustrated in three case vignettes. Incompetence seemed to stem from abandonment of the parents by traditional family support systems and may have been reinforced by the inability or lack of readiness of the health system to supply the missing support mechanisms. Techniques for prevention include improving awareness of health case workers to this problem, teaching appropriate strategies for improving parental confidence and competence, and ensuring that maternal and infant care appropriately focus on issues of infant behavior and parental concerns.

Segal UA. Child abuse in India: an empirical report on perceptions. *Child Abuse Negl.* 1992;16:887-908

Skurray G, Ham R. Family poverty and child abuse in Sydney. *Aust Marriage Fam.* 1990;11:94-99

Tang NM. Some psychoanalytic implications of Chinese philosophy and child-rearing practices. *Psychoanal Study Child.* 1992;47:371-389

Child-rearing practices among Chinese include indulgence of the child as well as high expectations early on, instillment of the notion of duty to family and reciprocal responsibilities, the denial of affective experiences, and the lack of praise. While Americans value independence, autonomy, assertiveness, and open expression of feelings and opinions, the Chinese value interdependence on the family, restraint in emotions and personal views, and conformity to the rules of good behavior.

Wilson-Oyelaran EB. The ecological model and the study of child abuse in Nigeria. *Child Abuse Negl.* 1989; 13:379-387

A study of the relationship between race, culture, child neglect, and child exploitation, including child labor and begging, is presented.

Inter-Country Comparisons

Bornstein MH, Tal J, Tamis-LeMonda C. Parenting in cross-cultural perspective: the United States, France, and Japan: cultural approaches to parenting. In: Bornstein MH, ed. *Crosscurrents in Contemporary Psychology.* Hillsdale, NJ: Lawrence Erlbaum Associates Inc; 1991:69-90

A comparison of maternal behaviors in two Western and one Eastern culture provided data to help understand how patterns of parenting might be similar or vary cross-culturally.

Power TG, Kobayashi-Winata H, Kelley ML. Childrearing patterns in Japan and the United States: a cluster analytic study. *Int J Behav Dev.* 1992;15:185-205

United States middle-class mothers (USM) expected their children to follow more rules than did Japanese mothers (JM). The JM reported giving children more input into the socialization process. The USM reported responding more often to child misbehavior with material/social consequences. The JM were more likely than USM to report using physical punishment in situations where the child showed disrespect for adult authority.

Sigman M, Wachs TD. Structure, continuity, and nutritional correlates of caregiver behavior patterns in Kenya and Egypt. In: Bornstein MH, ed. *Cultural Approaches to Parenting: Crosscurrents in Contemporary Psychology.* Hillsdale, NJ: Lawrence Erlbaum Associates Inc; 1991:123-137

The authors were able to relate toddler nutritional status to measures of caregiver behavior patterns, utilizing two large samples in two cultures (Kenya and Egypt).

Solis-Camara P, Fox RA. Parenting among mothers with young children in Mexico and the United States. *Soc Psychol.* 1995;135:591-599

Mothers in Mexico and the United States, matched for education, marital status, and socioeconomic level, did not differ significantly in their developmental expectations or parenting practices. Both samples maintained higher expectations and reported more frequent use of discipline with older children than with younger children.

Reviews

Abney VD. Cultural competency in the field of child maltreatment. In: Briere J, Berliner L, Bulkley JA, et al, eds. *APSAC Handbook on Child Maltreatment.* Thousand Oaks, CA: Sage Publications Inc; 1996

Ahn HN. Cultural diversity and the definition of child abuse. In: Barth RP, Berrick JD, Gilbert N, eds. *Child Welfare Research Review.* New York, NY: Columbia University Press; 1994;1:28-55

Bell CC, Jenkins EJ. Effects of child abuse and race. *J Natl Med Assoc.* 1994;86:165-232

Bornstein MH. *Cultural Approaches to Parenting: Crosscurrents in Contemporary Psychology.* Hillsdale, NJ: Lawrence Erlbaum Associates Inc; 1991
A major issue in *Cultural Approaches to Parenting* is how children become members of the culture, given the behaviors, language, and physical surroundings they experience.

Bornstein MH. Cross-cultural perspectives on parenting. In: d'Ydewalle G, Eelen P. Bertelson P, eds. *International Perspectives on Psychological Science: The State of the Art.* New York, NY: Lawrence Erlbaum Associates, Inc; 1994;2:359-369
Explores the formative experiences parents provide young children that relate to the origins and development of contrasting cultural styles through an examination of families from different Western and Eastern cultures.

Brant R, Wyatt GE, Martin T. Case vignette: child abuse or acceptable cultural norms. *Ethics Behav.* 1995;5:283-293

Burgess RL. Social and ecological issues in violence toward children. In: Ammerman RT, Hersem M, eds. *Case Studies in Family Violence.* New York, NY: Plenum Press; 1991:15-38

D'Antonio IJ, Darwish AM, McLean M. Child maltreatment: international perspectives. *Maternal Child Nurs J.* 1993;21:39-52

Ellis GJ, Petersen LR. Socialization values and parental control techniques: a cross-cultural analysis of child-rearing. *Comp Fam Stud.* 1992;23:39-54
The relationship between socialization values, such as conformity and self-reliance and use of certain child-rearing techniques (eg, lecturing, corporal punishment) were evaluated in 122 societies. A high societal value placed on conformity was positively associated with corporal punishment, lecturing, and overall control. In cultures that stressed self-reliance and autonomy, such coercive techniques were less prevalent.

Glachan M. Child abuse: a social and cultural phenomenon. *Early Child Dev Care.* 1991;74: 95-102

Harkness S, Super C. Culture and parenting. In: Bornstein MH, ed. *Handbook of Parenting.* Mahwah, NJ: Lawrence Erlbaum Associates, Inc; 1995;2:211-234
Major issues and trends in the study of parenting, where culture is also an object of conscious attention, are presented by means of an integrated historical review of developments in both anthropological and psychological research.

Heath DT. Parents' socialization of children. In: Ingoldsby BB, Smith S, eds. *Families in Multicultural Perspective: Perspectives on Marriage and the Family.* New York, NY: Guilford Press; 1995:161-186
Cross-cultural research examples include parenting styles in China, Japan, and foreign-born and native-born Mexican-American subcultures in the United States, Japan, and Israel; parental class influences on Mizos of India, Thailand, and Malawi, urban blacks and whites in Great Britain, Xhosa of South Africa, Thailand and the United States; and benefits of close parent-youth relationships in adolescence in Hong Kong, Iran, Puerto Rico, Canada, Hispanics and whites in the United States, and Ojibway and Native Americans.

Mtezuka M. Issues of race and culture in child abuse. In: Fawcett B, Featherstone B, Hearn J, Toft C, eds. *Violence and Gender Relations: Theories and Interventions.* London, England: Sage Publications Inc; 1996:171-177

Rubin GB. Multicultural considerations in the application of child protection laws. Special issue: social distress and families in crisis: a multicultural perspective. *J Soc Dist Homeless.* 1992;1:249-271

Teaching Resources

Ratliff S, Ishizuka A. Southeast Asian Healing Practices, Birthmarks and Amulets (Poster). Children's Hospital, Columbia, OH
This poster features color photos with legends of Southeast Asian healing practices that leave marks on the skin that may be confused with abuse. These include coining, cupping, pinching, and moxibustion. Also demonstrated are Mongolian spots on an infant, as well as different kinds of traditional amulets and tattoos.

Posters and informational brochures may be purchased at a cost of $15.00 by writing the Education Department, Children's Hospital, 700 Children Dr, Columbus, OH 43205.

Acknowledgment

This section and its annotations were prepared by Charles Felzen Johnson, MD.

Cutaneous Manifestations of Child Abuse

See Also:
Ear and Orofacial Injuries

Clinical Principles

General

▼ Children who are beaten, bitten, or burned often have skin injuries.

▼ The skin is the most common body location for injury in physical abuse.

▼ The skin may be the first identifiable location for abuse, before visceral, skeletal, and central nervous system injuries become clinically apparent.

▼ Cutaneous injuries are often nonspecific in pattern.

▼ The skin is the most accessible location for non-health professionals to inspect for trauma.

▼ Photographic documentation and/or drawings of the injuries are necessary for the protection of the child and give immediate notice of evidence of abuse to the judiciary and child protective services system.

▼ Several new child abuse textbooks and photographic atlases demonstrate abusive pattern injuries of the skin. The Child Abuse and Neglect Committee and Section of the AAP has developed a slide set depicting abusive injuries that is also available in CD-ROM. These are described in the section *Textbooks, Journals, Audiovisuals, and Booklets.*

Bite Marks

▼ It is possible to narrow the search for, and even identify, the perpetrator of an abusive bite injury in some cases.

▼ Unique indentations, lacerations, or avulsions made by specific teeth may be seen on the skin and should be appropriately documented and preserved.

▼ Dental impressions can be made and then matched against the records of individuals who are suspected of causing the injury.

▼ Human bites appear as distinctive oval to horseshoe-shaped marks in which tooth impressions appear as bruises facing each other.

▼ They may appear anywhere on the body, but especially over soft tissues of the arms, chest, abdomen, buttocks, and thighs.

▼ Human bites, which measure at least 3.0 cm between canine impressions, indicate that the assailant was probably more than 8 years of age.

▼ The distance between the maxillary canine teeth in adults is usually 2.5 to 4.0 cm.

▼ Adult bites are virtually pathognomonic of inflicted abusive trauma.

▼ Evaluation of suspicious bite marks include:

1. Consultation with an experienced forensic dentist or evidence technician;

2. High-quality photography with a non-distorting lens, which is held perpendicular to the wound, and a rigid ruler, which is visible in the frame;

3. If fresh, the wound should be swabbed for possible recovery of the assailant's saliva for ABO secretory antigen typing and sloughed epithelial cells for DNA evidence;

4. Photographs may be repeated daily if the age of the wound is uncertain;

5. The victim's teeth should be examined and measured to exclude the possibility of a self-inflicted bite.

Bruises

▼ Bruise analysis by visual inspection is (still) rather limited in research basis.

▼ Studies do not permit the estimation of the age of a bruise with any precision based solely on its color.

Burns

▼ Burns account for 10% to 15% of child abuse cases.

▼ Awareness of the pattern of accidental vs abusive injuries is necessary to determine whether the burn is due to maltreatment.

▼ Burns inflicted by immersion have a "water-line" or sharp demarcation border between burned and not burned tissue. The border may completely encircle a limb, as in forced immersion, or it may appear in patches of burned skin, as in forced flow over a limb.

▼ The perineum and/or extremities are the most common locations of burns.

▼ The degree of a burn is dependent on the thickness of the skin, the temperature of the object, and the length of time of the contact.

▼ Burns in children younger than 2 years of age are frequently abusive in nature.

▼ Accidental burns tend to be asymmetrical in distribution.

Bibliography

Bite Marks

Jessee S. Physical manifestations of child abuse to the head, face, and mouth: a hospital survey. *J Dent Child.* 1995;62:245-249
This is a retrospective chart survey of 266 children seen at Texas Children's Hospital for suspected child abuse, 1993 to 1994. Injuries to the head, face, and neck made up 66% of all cases; face and mouth injuries were found in 31% of the cases; the head and neck were injured in 32% and 4% of the cases, respectively. Oral cavity injuries were seen in 2.6%, but this may be an underestimate.

Jessee SA. Recognition of bite marks in child abuse cases. *Pediatr Dent.* 1994;16:336-339

and

Kenney JP, Donoghue ER. Physician recognition and documentation of bite mark injuries in sexual assault and child abuse cases. *Chicago Medicine.* 1994;97:20-24

Sweet DJ. Bitemark evidence—human bitemarks: examination, recovery, and analysis. In: Bowers CM, Bell GL, eds. *Manual of Forensic Odontology.* Colorado Springs, CO; American Society of Forensic Odontology; 1995
The authors give a thorough description of the complexities of bite mark assessment and documentation.

Bruises

Feldman K. Patterned abusive bruises of the buttocks and the pinnae. *Pediatrics.* 1992;90: 633-636
Physical abuse often results in injuries in which the pattern of the object used may be discerned. The author speaks of both high and low velocity injuries. A high velocity injury, such as a slap or whipping, often results in an "unbruised negative image" or outline of the injuring object. The outline is composed of petechiae. A low velocity injury, such as tissue being squeezed or pinched, may result in a positive image or a bruise with a filled-in appearance without a petechial outline. In both cases, the shape of an object may be seen.

However, other patterned injuries may be explained by the contour of the body rather than by the shape of the object used in the attack. Examples of this include the body curves of the buttock and the external ear, where the bruises are prominent where the body surface is most curved.

The author concludes that neither the ears nor the buttocks are frequently injured in childhood accidents. Bruises of the buttocks or to the ears that conform to anatomic lines of stress are strong indicators of abuse.

Langlois NEI, Gresham GA. The aging of bruises: a review and study of the color changes with time. *Forensic Sci Int.* 1991;50:227-228
The clinical aging of bruises and comparison to the history offered is critical in many assessments for possible child abuse. The most frequently used technique compares the visible color of a bruise to established tables and charts (eg, Wilson EF. Estimation of age of cutaneous contusions in child abuse. *Pediatrics.* 1977;60:750-752). Wilson's study, often referred to by child abuse experts in court, presented and tabulated several disparate opinions on bruise evolution.

The research of Langlois and Gresham suggests that the development of bruise color is much more variable, however. For instance, the yellow color, cited as appearing rather late by Wilson, may sometimes appear much earlier than 8 days. Their study utilized 369 photographs of bruises of known ages of 89 subjects. The authors concluded the following from their data on color and age:

1. A bruise with any yellow must be older than 18 hours;

2. Red, blue, and purple or black may occur anytime from 1 hour of bruising to resolution;

3. Red has no bearing on the age of the bruise because red is present in bruises no matter what their ages; and

4. Bruises of identical age and cause on the same person may not appear as the same color and may not change at the same rate.

Schwartz AJ, Ricci LR. How accurately can bruises be aged in abused children? Literature review and synthesis. *Pediatrics.* **1996;97:254-257**

Schwartz and Ricci synthesize what is known about the aging of bruises. They found that various texts portray significant variation, not only as to when a color appears but also even in describing the colors. The authors reported, "There does seem to be broad agreement that bruises go through an evolution in color, that bruises initially appear red, violet, or black (perhaps blue as well), and that successive colors include brown, green, and yellow, although in no clearly predictable order or chronology." They cite Langlois and Gresham as the only published study on use of the visual aging technique and recommend repeat of the study.

The process of hemoglobin degradation as seen through the skin is responsible for the color of bruises and is affected by the depth and location of the bruises as well as ambient light and skin color. A superficial bruise may become apparent immediately while a deep bruise may take days, and some bruises have both superficial and deep components. Bruising appears sooner in poorly supported tissues such as genital and periorbital areas.

Studies do not permit the estimation of the age of a bruise with any precision based solely on its color. Practitioners should avoid too narrow an interpretation of their findings.

Stephenson T, Bialas Y. Estimation of the age of bruising. *Arch Dis Child.* **1996;74:53-55**

In this study, a single "blind" observer attempted to estimate the age of children's bruises solely on their photographic appearance. The bruises of 23 children, 8 months to 13 years of age, who had known accidental and timed injuries, were photographed by the authors. Thirty-six bruises and 50 photographs were reviewed (some children were photographed more than once, at a 3- to 9-day interval from their initial presentations). The bruises were ascribed to three categories: fresh (48 hours old or less), intermediate (between 48 hours old and 7 days old), and old (more than 7 days old). The actual ages of the bruises were 1.5 hours to 14 days old.

The authors found that age estimates of bruises from photographs are "much less precise than forensic textbooks imply." The observer estimated correctly in 24 of 44 cases, incorrectly in 20. Accuracy was unrelated to the age of the child, presence of a fracture, or site of the bruise. No photograph of an injury older than 48 hours was estimated to be fresh. The color red in a photograph indicated that the injury was less than a week old; a green or yellow color suggested that the injury was at least 24 to 48 hours old. Several different colors were present at the same time in one bruise; and, in one child, "the bruise on her leg had turned green/yellow while that on her arm remained blue, although both injuries had occurred during the same accident."

This is an important study, despite the shortcoming of only one reviewer. Further work on the appearance of bruises needs to be done. Perhaps experienced medical examiners implicitly realize that examinations in the clinical setting use other sensory data that are not as readily documented photographically, such as abrasions, swelling, and information obtained by palpation.

Wardinsky TD, Vizarrondo FE. The mistaken diagnosis of child abuse: a three year USAF Medical Center analysis and literature review. *Mil Med.* 1995;160:15-20

The mistaken diagnosis of abuse may occur if medical and/or cultural folk conditions that may mimic maltreatment are not considered. It is important to have a differential diagnosis for apparent bruises just as one would for an acute abdomen.

How often is the diagnosis of mistaken child abuse made? Over a 3-year period, 504 children were referred for suspected abuse to a child abuse medical evaluation team; 52% of cases were unsubstantiated, and 7% were initially diagnosed as abuse but found to have conditions that were misdiagnosed as abuse. However, in a study by Wheeler and Hobbs (Wheeler DM, Hobbs CJ. Mistakes in diagnosing nonaccidental injury: 10 years' experience. *BMJ.* 1988;296:1233-1236), only 3% of referred children were found to have conditions that mimicked abuse.

Burns

Moritz AR, Henriques FC. Studies of thermal injury: pathology and pathogenesis of cutaneous burns experimental study. *Am J Pathol.* 1947;23:915-941

The authors report the only experimental work on the time and temperature relationship to degree of the burn. However, it is 50 years old and based on piglet skin.

Yeoh C, Nixon JW, Dickson W, et al. Patterns of scald injuries. *Arch Dis Child.* 1994;71:156-158

In this retrospective analysis of 68 patients, 10 months to 13.5 years of age (mean, 40.4 months), 38 children fell into hot water, 8 were scalded by hot running tap water, 5 put their hands into hot water, and in 10 cases the hot water was turned on by a sibling. Four children were forcibly immersed; all had associated bruises, fractures, or evidence of neglect.

Acknowledgment
This section and its annotations were prepared by James J. Williams, MD. Selected annotations from the first edition were prepared by Carolyn Levitt, MD, and Kim Martinez, RN, CPNP.

Developmental Disabilities and Child Abuse

Clinical Aspects:

▼ Children with disabilities are believed to be maltreated at a higher rate than children in the general population. The indicators of abuse for children with disabilities are the same as those for the general population. Behavioral indicators of abuse may not be recognized or may be attributed to the disability.

▼ Disability refers to a physical or mental impairment that results in functional limitations in one or more of life's major activities of an individual older than the age of 5 years. Consistent with the Americans with Disabilities Act, a person has a disability if the person has such an impairment manifested before the age of 22 years, has a history of such an impairment, or is regarded as having such an impairment. Developmental disability applies to children from birth to 5 years old who have significant developmental delay or congenital or acquired conditions that may result in a disability if services are not provided.

▼ Increased risk of abuse may be due to enhanced vulnerability as a result of increased demands for care, chronic stress of child care providers, parental attachment problems, parental isolation, unrealistic expectations of child performance, aggressive behaviors in the child, concurrent risk factors that may be associated with abuse as well as disabilities such as alcohol or drug abuse in families, communication limitations resulting in a decreased ability to relay information about the abuse, inability to communicate needs (resulting in neglect), and dependency on an often large number of caretakers.

▼ Children with less severe disabilities may be at greater risk for abuse. Communicatively disabled children may be at higher risk for sexual abuse. Severely disabled children may be at higher risk of malnutrition and failure to thrive.

▼ Consequences of abuse may be more pronounced in children with disabilities because of their vulnerable physical and psychological state.

▼ Children of developmentally disabled parents may be at increased risk of child maltreatment and neglect.

Other Comments:

▼ Limitations of most studies include subject selection biases, disparities in the definitions of disabilities, differing operational definitions of maltreatment, heterogeneous populations of disabled individuals, lack of training in the assessment of disabilities by child protective service workers, difficulty in determining the causal relationship between the abuse and the disability, questionable validation of procedures for determining disabilities, exclusion of extrafamilial abuse from central registries, and probable underreporting of abuse in disabled populations.

▼ It is estimated that between 9% and 40% of children served by child protective services have a developmental disability. Rates of abuse and maltreatment in disabled populations have been reported to be between 3% and 61%. Current estimates suggest that children with disabilities are sexually abused at a much greater rate than the general population.

▼ The incidence of disabilities presumably caused by maltreatment has been reported to be 147 per 1,000 maltreated children. This incidence is based on reports of child protective agencies and may not necessarily reflect accurate diagnoses of disabilities. The incidence of pre-existing developmental disabilities has been reported to be as high as 70% in some populations.

▼ In order to develop better prevention methods, further study of risk factors for child maltreatment in developmentally disabled children is needed.

Bibliography

Prevalence and Risk Factors

Ammerman RT, Hersen M, Van Hasselt VB, Lubetsky MJ, Sieck WR. **Maltreatment in psychiatrically hospitalized children and adolescents with developmental disabilities: prevalence and correlates.** *J Am Acad Child Adolesc Psychiatry.* 1994;33(4):567-76

In this descriptive study, the authors prospectively examined factors associated with risk of child maltreatment and assessed maternal and child functioning in 138 hospitalized children and adolescents (aged 3 to 18 years) with both developmental disabilities and psychiatric disorders. Seventy-nine percent of the population was male and 83% was white. Most were from lower socioeconomic status backgrounds. Diagnoses included mental retardation, pervasive developmental disorders, disruptive behavioral disorders, and affective disorders.

Characteristics of mothers and children that might influence the severity of mother's disciplinary practices were examined utilizing a semi-structured interview, Child Abuse and Neglect Interview Schedule (CANIS), which was constructed by the authors for this study. According to their rating scales, arranged based on responses of the CANIS as disciplinary practices, care and attention scale and sexual abuse confidence scale, 61% of the children studied had experienced some form of maltreatment by a care provider during their lifetime. Mothers' use of more severe disciplinary techniques were associated with children who were young, oppositional, and higher functioning and with mothers who reported low levels of social support and increased anger reactivity.

The authors conclude that, in the psychiatric setting, children with these factors were at elevated risk for maltreatment and that maltreatment in psychiatrically hospitalized children and adolescents with disabilities is very prevalent.

Jaudes P, Diamond J. **The handicapped child and child abuse.** *Child Abuse Negl.* 1985;9:341-347

This descriptive study of 37 children with developmental disabilities and child abuse (from a cohort of 162 children diagnosed with cerebral palsy) reviews the problems of children whose development is affected by the compounded influences of maltreatment and the presence of a handicapping condition. Four problems are identified as crucial to the study of abuse and neglect with respect to the child with developmental disabilities: (1) abuse that causes disabilities, (2) abuse that occurs to the child with disabilities, (3) compromises in care that can occur when the child with disabilities becomes involved with the medical and legal systems, and (4) arrangements for foster care or other out-of-home placement for the child with disabilities.

Abused children were identified by parent interviews, reviews of medical records, court records, and protective service reports. In 14 of the 37 abused children, the abuse was believed to have caused the cerebral palsy. The abuse in these children involved severe head injuries before the age of 1 year resulting in brain injury. In 23, the abuse followed the diagnosis of cerebral palsy and in 3 children, the abuse both preceded and followed the diagnosis. Most of these children (15 of the 23) suffered from starvation/malnutrition, medical neglect, or abandonment. The remaining 8 were physically abused, burned, or sexually abused. The median age of maltreatment in this group was 4 years.

The authors point out that repeated battery in the homes of these children was a significant problem, occurring for five of the children. Nineteen of the children were placed in foster care, where six went to multiple placements. The authors discuss the need for pediatricians to identify abuse, advocate for the disabled abused child, and intervene in a way that affects the long-term outlook for developmentally disabled children.

Neglect

Amundson J, Sherbondy A, Van Dyke DC, Alexander R. **Early identification and treatment necessary to prevent malnutrition in children and adolescents with severe disabilities.** *J Am Diet Assoc.* 1994;94:880-883

These authors review and discuss two case presentations of severe malnutrition and growth retardation that complicated the course of medical treatment. Both adolescents, with severe mental retardation, cerebral palsy, seizure disorders, scoliosis, and growth retardation, were admitted to hospitals and evaluated for feeding disorders. Growth charts and hospital courses are detailed. In the first case, the child suffered from superior mesenteric artery syndrome that may have been precipitated by severe malnutrition with weight loss and lumbar lordosis.

In their discussion, the authors indicate that malnutrition in disabled children may be associated with poor oral intake, gastroesophageal reflux with aspiration, and chronic constipation. Those with central nervous system dysfunction often have abnormal weight-for-height ratios. There are few established parameters for defining expectations of growth and those with disabilities may differ from standard norms. Malnutrition is sometimes accepted as part of the disability. Children with disabilities may be at higher risk for serious nutrition problems and early identification and treatment of protein-energy malnutrition is crucial to avoid complications. Abnormal growth with or without the presence of wasting or edema should trigger a comprehensive evaluation.

Sexual Abuse

Elvik SL, Berkowitz CD, Nicholas E, Lipman JL, Inkelis SH. Sexual abuse in the developmentally disabled: dilemmas of diagnosis. *Child Abuse Negl.* **1990;14:497-502**
The authors describe their experience of evaluating 35 developmentally disabled females from a residential treatment facility for physical signs of sexual abuse. The task was undertaken after one of the residents became pregnant resulting in the suspicion of sexual abuse perpetrated at the facility. Patients ranged in age from 13 to 55 years, 69% were categorized as profoundly retarded, and no patients were able to provide a history. Two had prior histories of rape and two had prior histories of infection with *Chlamydia trachomatis.*

None of the patients had acute physical findings associated with recent penetrating trauma. The two with prior trachomatis infections had normal examinations. Two patients had prior histories of rape and had normal examination findings. Thirteen had abnormal genital findings that were consistent with healed penetration.

In these cases, no perpetrator was identified and the dilemma of determining the significance and implications of the abnormal genital findings was discussed. The authors recommend that practitioners who are longitudinally following a disabled patient perform a complete examination at every visit. When abuse is suspected, a team approach is recommended.

Sobsey D, Doe T. Patterns of sexual abuse and assault. *Sex Disabil.* **1991;9(3):243-259**
Over a 2-year period, disability advocacy groups and sexual assault treatment centers were asked to request that people with disabilities and their advocates fill out reports describing sexual offenses. 162 reports were studied. The victims represented a broad range of disabilities and ranged in age from 18 months to 57 years. Slightly less than half of this selected sample were children and adolescents, and 82% were female. The offenses were described and nearly 50% disclosed greater than 10 occasions of abusive incidents. Most reported little physical harm, but 18.5% reported severe injuries requiring treatment, and emotional, behavioral, and social consequences were common.

Most perpetrators were male (91%), and 44% had a relationship with the victim that was apparently specifically related to the victim's disability. No attempts were made to secure any treatment or support in 11% of cases, and many others (46%) experienced difficulty finding required treatment services. In cases in which services were located, 50% failed to meet the victim's special needs. The authors discuss a multifactorial, ecological model of abuse and recommend possible prevention strategies.

Communicative Disorders

Botash AS, Babuts D, Mitchell N, O'Hara M, Lynch L, Manuel J. Evaluation of children who have disclosed sexual abuse via facilitated communication. *Arch Pediatr Adolesc Med.* **1994;148:1282-1287**
This is a descriptive study of 13 children, referred to a tertiary care outpatient child sexual abuse program in Central New York after facilitated communication disclosures of sexual abuse. The children, aged 5 to 15 years, had various developmental diagnoses including autistic behavior, mental retardation, cerebral palsy, seizure disorders, and Down syndrome. Two of the cases are

described in detail; the others summarized. Four children had corroborating evidence of sexual abuse (one perpetrator confession, one verbal disclosure, and two with physical examination findings considered suspicious for sexual abuse); an additional five had other supportive evidence. The authors summarized the literature and issues concerning sexual abuse disclosures utilizing facilitated communication and conclude that the results do not support nor refute validation of this communication technique. Since many of these children had other indicators for sexual abuse, the authors recommend that all allegations of abuse in this population be evaluated, including a complete medical examination.

Sullivan PM, Brookhauser PE, Scanlan JM, Knutson JF, Schulte LE. Patterns of physical and sexual abuse of communicatively handicapped children. *Ann Otol Rhinol Laryngol.* **1991;100:188-194**
This report describes data collected as part of a longitudinal study of therapeutic efficacy among a group of abused children with documented and verified handicapping conditions. In 482 children consecutively referred to and evaluated at Boys Town National Research Hospital, impairment ranged from hearing problems to mental retardation, visual impairment, and others. Patients were mostly white (84%) and ranged in age from infancy to 21 years at the time of the first incident of maltreatment. Comparisons were made between children who were educated in mainstream schooling or were part of a residential program.

Results indicated that the most prevalent type of maltreatment for both boys and girls was sexual abuse (48%). Mainstreamed boys were somewhat more likely to be physically abused (35%) than sexually abused (30%), but boys in residential facilities were much more likely to be sexually abused (58.8%). Sexual abuse was the single most frequently reported type of maltreatment among each of the described handicap-specific subgroups. Stranger perpetrators accounted for no more than 3% of sexual abuse. Nearly 83% endured multiple episodes of abuse. When considering all types of abuse collectively, the most frequent site at which abuse was perpetrated was the child's home. The home was also the most common site for physical abuse (73.3%) and for combined abuse and neglect

(50.9%). However, the most common site for cases of isolated sexual abuse (39%) was the school (including residential schools).

The authors conclude that sexual and/or physical abuse as well as emotional abuse and/or neglect are significant risks for children with communication disorders and related disabilities. The implication is that the relatively increased risk of males for sexual abuse compared with the general population is due to two factors: (1) education and child care practices and (2) communication barriers.

Parents With Disabilities

Tymchuk AJ, Andron L. Mothers with mental retardation who do or do not abuse or neglect their children. *Child Abuse Negl. 1990;* **14:313-323**
This study describes results of a questionnaire in which 33 mothers and/or her caretaker(s) reported maternal demographics, family and paternal variables, and abuse and neglect histories in consecutive admissions to Project Parenting at the Department of Psychiatry at the University of California, Los Angeles, between September 1982 and July 1987. Seventeen mothers had a history of abuse/neglect to their children, and 16 had no such history. Only 2 of the 17 had abused their children, 15 had neglected them. The history of abuse/neglect to the mothers themselves did not predict abuse in their children. Two thirds of the mothers who abused/neglected their children were married (lived independently), while only one third of parents who did not abuse/neglect their children were married. More abusive/neglectful families had more than one child. Lower functioning mothers appeared less likely to abuse/neglect their children. The report also examined reasons for removal of children from parental care.

The author concludes that, if adequate child care is defined as not being abusive or neglectful and/or coming to the attention of child care agencies, some mothers with mental retardation provide adequate child care. Risk factors for abuse might include stresses of independent living, more than one child, and lack of approval by their families for their pregnancy/child. The results also suggest that abuse or neglect by a mother with mental retardation is not necessarily the primary reason for having a child removed. Rather, in addition to having abused/neglected her child, she must be unwilling to attend and participate in a parenting program, must have an additional problem (eg, seizures), and must not have anyone who can provide her with support. Further study to examine the predictors of abuse in this population are recommended.

Review Articles and Chapters

Alexander RC, Sherbondy AL. Child abuse and developmental disabilities. In: Wolraich ML, ed. *Disorders of Development and Learning: A Practical Guide to Assessment and Management.* St Louis, MO: Mosby Yearbook Inc; 1996

Dowdney L, Skuse D. Parenting provided by adults with mental retardation. *J Child Psychol Psychiatry.* 1993;34(1):24-47

Feldman MA. Parenting education for parents with intellectual disabilities: a review of outcome studies. *Res Dev Disab.* 1994;15:299-332

Garbarino J. Maltreatment of young children with disabilities. *Inf Young Children.* 1989; 2:49-57

Horton CB, Kochurka KA. The assessment of children with disabilities who report sexual abuse: a special look at those most vulnerable. In: Ney T, ed. *True and False Allegations of Child Sexual Abuse: Assessment and Case Management.* Mazil, NY: Brunner; 1995

Tymchuk AJ. Parents with mental retardation: a national strategy. *J Disabil Policy Studies.* 1990;1:43-55

Westcott H. The abuse of disabled children: a review of the literature. *Child Care Health Dev.* 1991;17:243-258

White R, Benedict MI, Wulff L, Kelley M. Physical disabilities as risk factors for child maltreatment: a selected review. *Am J Orthopsychiatry.* 1987;57:93-101

Other Resources

The ABCD (Abuse and Children Who Are Disabled) Training and Resource Pack c/o NSPCC National Child Protection Training Group, Leicester, United Kingdom

Baladerian NJ. Interviewing skills to use with abuse victims who have developmental disabilities. 1991. Available from Disability, Abuse & Personal Rights Project, Spectrum Institute, PO Box "T," Culver City, CA 90230

Council for Exceptional Children (CEC), 1920 Association Dr, Reston, VA 20191; 703/620-3660

Developmental Disabilities Assistance and Bill of Rights Act, 42 USCA, Section 6000 et seq, West Supp, 1993

Grayson J, ed. Child abuse & developmental disabilities. *Virginia Child Protection Newsletter.* 1992;37(703):568-614

National Association of Protection and Advocacy Systems (NAPAS), 900 2nd St NE, Ste 211, Washington, DC 20002; 202/408-9514/9521 (TDD)

National Association for the Protection From Sexual Abuse of Adults and Children With Learning Disabilities. *Annotated Bibliography.* Nottingham: NAPSAC; 1994

National Center for Youth with Disabilities, National Resource Library, University of Minnesota, Box 721, 420 Delaware St SE, Minneapolis, MN 55455-0392; 612/626-2825

National Information Center for Children and Youth With Disabilities (NICHCY), PO Box 1492, Washington, DC 20013-1492; 1-202/884-8200 (voice/TT)Y, 1-800/695-0285 (voice/TT)Y, nichy@aed.org

National Resource Center on Child Abuse and Neglect. *Maltreatment of Children with Disabilities: Information Sheet.* Englewood, CO: NCCAN - American Humane Association, 1995

National Resource Center on Child Abuse and Neglect. *A Report on the Maltreatment of Children With Disabilities.* Washington, DC: US Department of Health & Human Services; 1993

Bureau of Child Research, University of Kansas 3111 Haworth Hall, Lawrence, KS 66045; 913/864-7600. Contact for copies: The National Clearinghouse on Child Abuse & Neglect Information, PO Box 1182, Washington, DC 20013-1182; 1-800/FYI-3366

Office on the Americans With Disabilities Act, Civil Rights Division, US Dept of Justice, PO Box 6618, Washington, DC 20035-6118, 202/514-0301/0381 (TDD/TT) http://www.usdoj.gov/crt/ada/adahom1.htm

The PACER (Parent Advocacy Coalition for Educational Rights) Center Inc, Training, Resources, and Information (catalog), 4826 Chicago Ave S, Minneapolis, MN 55417-1098; 612/827-2966 or in MN; 1-800/53-PACER

Sobsey D, Wells D, Lucardie R, Mansell S, eds. *Violence and Disability: An Annotated Bibliography*. Baltimore, MD: Paul H. Brookes Pub Co; 1995

Sobsey D, Gray S, Wells D, Pyper D, Reimer-Heck B. *Disability, Sexuality & Abuse: An Annotated Bibliography*. Baltimore, MD: Paul H. Brookes Pub Co; 1991

Syracuse University Center on Human Policy, 805 South Crouse, Syracuse, NY 13244-2280; 1-800/894-0826; thechp@sued.syr.edu, http://soeweb.syr.edu/thechp/

Westcott L. *Abuse of Children and Adults With Disabilities*. London, England: National Society for Prevention of Cruelty to Children. 1993

Westat Inc for the National Center on Child Abuse and Neglect (NCCAN). *A Report of Children With Disabilities*. Washington, DC: US Government Printing Office; 1993

National Study of Maltreatment of Handicapped Children and Child Maltreatment in Substance Abusing Families. Rockville, MD: Westat Inc; 1992

Acknowledgment

Annotations were prepared by Ann S. Botash, MD and further reviewed by Paula K. Jaudes, MD.

Domestic Violence and Child Abuse

Clinical Principles

▼ Children of battered women should be considered at risk for child abuse.

▼ Possible mechanisms in which spousal abuse can lead to child abuse:
1. the child attempts to intervene and the spouse redirects the anger toward the child
2. the child is accidently struck by a blow that was directed at the spouse
3. battered women tend to overdiscipline their children in an effort to control the child's behavior, fearing that the partner may impose worse abuse upon the child

▼ Children who witness domestic violence often continue the cycle of abuse as they become adults.

▼ Child abuse is strongly associated with such factors as a history of lack of social support, history of childhood violence in the mother or her partner, and a partner suspected of child abuse or of harsh discipline.

Bibliography

Campbell JC. Child abuse and wife abuse: the connection. *Maryland Med J.* 1994;43:349-350
This article serves as a reminder that children of battered women should be considered at risk for child abuse and that in all cases of reported child abuse, the possibility of wife abuse should be contemplated. In addition, the children of women abused during pregnancy should be considered at risk for child abuse.

The author's literature review revealed that battered women were six times more likely than non-battered women to be reported for child abuse. A national random survey demonstrated a substantive correlation between wife abuse and child abuse. The author points out that health care professionals need to be aware of this correlation, and efforts should be made to ensure the safety of the children and the battered mother.

Kornblit AL. Domestic violence — an emerging health issue. *Soc Sci Med.* 1994;39:1181-1188
This paper explains some of the aspects included in the concept of family violence and summarizes the principal theoretical models proposed to explain it. The author also describes the principal syndromes included within the scope of the concept: battered woman, courtship violence, child abuse, child sexual abuse, child witnessing violence, sibling violence, and elder violence.

Upon review of the various models and syndromes associated with family violence, this paper reports that it is possible that prevention should center on the improvement of communication skills within the family so as to empower individuals to seek better resources to develop coping mechanisms.

Krugman RD. From battered children to family violence: what lessons should we learn? *Acad Med.* 1995;70:964-967
According to Dr Krugman, three lessons have been learned from our efforts dealing with child abuse:

1. The public has a much greater capacity for increasing its awareness of a problem than it does for implementing intervention and prevention programs.

2. It has never been stated clearly what this country's child protection policy (federal vs state) should be, which has led to confusion.

3. There have been failures resulting from inadequate research data. Reliable longitudinal incidence and outcome data would be extremely useful.

Dr Krugman states that our efforts to deal with family violence will require research, clinical work, and education.

McKay MM. The link between domestic violence and child abuse: assessment and treatment considerations. *Child Welfare League of America.* 1994:29-39
This excellent article reviews the research that suggests spouse abuse and child abuse are clearly linked within families. The need for both the

domestic violence agencies and the child welfare system to recognize the link between spouse and child abuse is emphasized. It is recommended that domestic violence service providers (1) help battered women recognize the link between domestic violence and child abuse during the assessment and planning phases of the treatment plan; (2) help the mother interact with the child welfare system; and (3) form a close working relationship with child protective services to ensure that both the battered women and their children are protected, rather than simply removing the children from the home. Child protective services workers should recognize indicators that (1) a woman is a victim of domestic violence; (2) children have witnessed domestic violence; and (3) a man may be a batterer. Furthermore, these providers should carefully consider the dynamics of domestic violence when assessing whether children or the batterer should be removed from the home. They should also be familiar with community resources for battered women in their effort to protect children.

More research is needed to understand fully the links between domestic violence and child abuse. A combined, coordinated effort is needed between both domestic violence and child protective service providers in order to eliminate violence within families.

O'Keefe M. Predictors of child abuse in maritally violent families. *J Interpersonal Violence.* 1995;10:3-25

This study supported data that children who are both witnesses of marital violence and victims of child physical abuse exhibit greater externalizing behavior problems (eg, aggression, acting out, delinquency, etc) than children who only witness spousal violence. Furthermore, it was found, as in previous studies, that spousal abuse is often accompanied by child abuse. It is likely that an interactive effect can be found between low marital satisfaction and child abuse (ie, stress from the marital relationship negatively affects the parent-child relationship, resulting in child abuse and the mother's increased dissatisfaction with the spousal relationship).

Ross S. Risk of physical abuse to children of spouse abusing parents. *Child Abuse Negl.* 1996;20:589-598

This study reinforces the positive correlation between marital violence and child physical abuse in the general population. There is a statistically significant relationship between husband-to-wife violence and physical child abuse by the father. Each additional act of violence toward the wife increases the odds of the husband physically abusing the child by an average of 12%.

Furthermore, violence by the wife toward the husband is a statistically significant predictor of the mother's physical abuse of her child. Each additional act of violence toward the husband increased the odds of the wife physically abusing the child by an average of 4%.

The study supports the presumption of custody to the mother if the child is to remain with one of the parents, especially when there is a high level of marital violence. However, given the relatively high predicted probability of child abuse by aggressive wives as well as aggressive husbands, perhaps the best custody decisions might be those coupled with counseling for the custodial parent.

Thormachlen DJ, Bass-Felf ER. Children: the secondary victims of domestic violence. *Maryland Med J.* 1994;43:355-359

This article stresses the importance of recognizing and responding to children who witness domestic violence. Counseling should be recommended to help child witnesses of domestic violence to (1) understand they should not feel responsible for the domestic violence; (2) identify and express their feelings in a healthy way; and (3) use coping mechanisms to deal with feelings of anger. Physicians should approach abused parents by making them aware that the abusive situation is detrimental to the physical and emotional well-being of the children and they should take measures to seek a safe environment. Furthermore, physicians should be supportive and nonjudgmental in the manner in which they approach victims of domestic violence.

Wilson LM, Reid AJ, Midmer DK, Biringer A, Carroll JC, Stewart DE. Antenatal psychosocial risk factors associated with adverse postpartum family outcomes. *Can Med Assoc J.* 1986;154:785-799

The purpose of this review was to determine the strength of the association between antenatal psychosocial risk factors and adverse postpartum outcomes in the family, such as assault of women by their partners, child abuse, postpartum depression, marital dysfunction, and physical illness. Child abuse and abuse of the mother by her partner were most strongly correlated with a history of lack of social support, recent life stressors, psychiatric disturbance in the mother, and an unwanted pregnancy. Child abuse was also strongly associated with a history of childhood violence in the mother or her partner, previous child abuse by the mother's partner, a poor relationship between the mother and her parents, low self-esteem in the mother, and lack of attendance at prenatal classes. Health care providers should begin routinely screening for psychosocial risk factors not only during the prenatal period, but also as a standard part of antenatal care.

Acknowledgment
This section and its annotations were prepared by V. Denise Everett, MD.

Drowning: Child Abuse and Bathtub Drownings

Clinical Principles

▼ Epilepsy or febrile seizures can lead to accidental drowning in the bathtub and must be carefully sorted out from intentional drowning. These children tend to be older and are consequently trusted to be alone in the bathtub.

▼ Children who drown accidentally are in the younger age group (8 to 15 months) and are left alone briefly or in the care of a sibling.

▼ Children who drown nonaccidentally in the bathtub tend to be older than 15 months, may have a past history of abuse or siblings who were abused, have a history inconsistent with the findings, have signs of inflicted trauma, and often are brought in late for emergency room services.

▼ However, often there are no markers for abuse. First responders, emergency room personnel, and physicians must recognize that two thirds of the cases should raise suspicion and one third of the drowning cases are likely due to child abuse.

▼ Hypothermia in critically ill children should alert emergency personnel to intentional cold water immersion.

▼ There needs to be cooperation between law enforcement, medical examiners, and emergency physicians to sort out accidental from intentional drowning.

Bibliography

General

Gillenwater M, Quan L, Feldman KW. Inflicted submersion in childhood. *Arch Pediatr Adolesc Med.* **1996;150:298-303**
This study compares 16 (8%) intentionally drowned or nearly drowned children with 186 unintentional drownings. The intentional group had physical findings of abuse, primarily bruises and inconsistencies between the history and physical findings, between subsequent interviews, and with the child's stage of development. Nine (26%) of 34 bathtub submersions were inflicted and the bathtub was the site in intentional submersion in 9 (56%) of 16 cases. Child victims of inflicted submersion were likely to be younger (median, 2.1 years) and were more likely to die from the submersion. The two groups did not differ in demographic or social attributes. The authors conclude that inflicted submersion is most likely to be associated with children showing other indications of abuse and with bathtub submersion.

Kemp MA, Mott AM, Sibert JR. Accidents and child abuse in bathtub submersions. *Arch Dis Child.* **1994;70:435-438**
The authors describe details of 44 children who drowned or nearly drowned in the bathtub in 1988 or 1989. Twenty-eight of the cases were determined to be accidental, most typically a 9-month-old infant being left unsupervised in a bath. Ten cases, made up of six drownings and four near-drownings, were thought to be intentional because of their inconsistent history, a previous history of abuse, and delay in seeking medical care. Four of the bathtub drownings were related to epilepsy.

Features that differentiate between accidental, nonaccidental, and homicidal submersion injuries to children are as follows:

Accidental submersion
- Typically a baby momentarily left alone or with a sibling in the bath
- Majority of children 8 to 15 months of age
- Child the youngest in the family
- No features suggesting child abuse

Epilepsy-related submersion
- Child with history of epilepsy
- Bathing alone
- A child older than 24 months

Nonaccidental submersions
- Atypical submersion description, with inconsistent details
- Late referral to hospital
- Associated history of child abuse
- Child outside 8- to 24-month age span
- Child left with unsuitable caregiver

Homicidal drowning
- Maternal history of mental illness
- Child outside the 8- to 24-month age range
- Previous history of child abuse or social needs

Lavelle JM, Shaw KN, Seidl T, Ludwig S. Ten-year review of pediatric bathtub near-drowning: evaluation for child abuse and neglect. *Ann Emer Med.* **1995;25:344-348**

These authors found 21 patients with bathtub near-drowning who were treated at their institution over a 10-year period. Sixty-seven percent had suspicion of child abuse or neglect raised by history and/or physical findings. Some had histories that were incompatible with the injury, other physical injuries, previous child abuse reports, psychiatric history of the caretaker, and/or psychosocial concerns in the child's environment. Forty-two percent of the children died. They reported 29% had either physical evidence or admitted intent of child abuse for bathtub near-drowning, which was considerably higher than prior reports ranging from 10% to 19%. Sixty-three percent had incompatible histories or multiple stories of the event; 38% had physical findings of abuse or severe neglect; and 25% had prior child abuse reports. One 6-year-old bathing alone nearly drowned due to a febrile seizure. These authors encourage emergency physicians to recognize bathtub near-drowning as likely to involve abuse or neglect and social services assessment is needed.

Schmidt P, Madea B. Death in the bathtub involving children. *Forensic Sci Int.* **1995;72:147-155**

This article from Cologne, Germany, is a retrospective review of 215 deaths occurring in the bathtub from 1980 through 1993. Twelve of the fatalities involved children from 9 months to 13 years. Seven of these were thought to be due to accidents: five of which were drowning and two scalding burns; two were attributed to natural death including epilepsy and heart failure due to an underlying condition; one was a homicide involving stabbing; two cases were thought to be undetermined, possibly attributable to a seizure; and one had other signs of maltreatment including a subdural hematoma. Three toddlers were left alone unattended in the bathtub and two were in the care of their siblings. It is difficult to compare this article with the other articles included here because the authors seem to accept the parents' history as the cause of the scalding burns and other injuries including subdural

hematoma and counted those cases as undetermined. Many of the accidental drownings might have been intentional and just misinterpreted.

Additional Studies

Griest KJ, Zumwalt RE. Child abuse by drowning. *Pediatrics.* **1989;83:41-46**

The authors first review the literature primarily by Nixon and Pearn (1977) describing features that distinguish accidental from nonaccidental drowning and then describe their experience with six homicides by drowning. Nixon and Pearn suggested that most nonaccidental drowning occurred in the bathtub at an unusual time of day with the drowned child alone in the bathtub. The family fit the "sociopathologic profile" of abusing parents and there was often a domestic crisis precipitating the drowning. They found that the child who was drowned in the bathtub was usually between 15 and 30 months of age, compared with 9 to 15 months, the age of the accidental drowning victims. In this review, in three of the six cases there was a prior history of abusive behavior by parents and four out of six caretakers delayed summoning help for their children. The wet clothing provided valuable clues in two of the six cases. Three of the six cases had postmortem pulmonary features of the post-immersion syndrome and five of six had cerebral edema indicating that time passed between the immersion and the death. One of their cases involved a toilet drowning of a newborn and they provide strategy for this specialized investigation. They summarize that all investigations of drowning require cooperation between the investigative agencies and the pathologist, a complete autopsy, a social history, and special studies at the site of the drowning.

Gustavson E, Levitt C. Physical abuse with severe hypothermia. *Arch Pediatr Adolesc Med.* **1996;150:111-112**

Four cases of severe nonaccidental hypothermia are reported, three of which involve prolonged cold water bathtub immersion. In one very instructive case, the caretaker admitted to holding the 19-month-old's body (not face) under the cold water in the bathtub for 1 hour as he struggled to get up. When he became unconscious, she dressed him in a diaper and blanket and waited for another hour before paramedics were summoned. His rectal temperature was 28.3° C on admission to the emergency room. He required intubation and ventilation but made a full recovery. The authors remind us that it is important to consider intentional injury (child abuse) when critically ill children present with hypothermia.

Rauchschwalbe R, Brennen R, Smith G. The role of bathtub seats and rings in infant drowning deaths. *Pediatrics electronic pages.* **1997;100:4. Available at http://www.pediatrics.org.**
Thirty-two infant drowning deaths (ages 5-15 mos) involving bathtub seats or rings were reported to the Consumer Product Safety Commission over 13 months. Lapse in adult supervision of up to 6 minutes accounted for these deaths and the adults reported being more likely to leave the infant alone when the ring or seat was being used.

Acknowledgment

This section and its annotations were prepared by Carolyn Levitt, MD, and reviewed by David Schor, MD.

Ear and Orofacial Injuries

See Also:
Cutaneous Injuries
AAP Statement *Oral and Dental Aspects of Child Abuse and Neglect,* **which follows**

Clinical Principles

▼ Trauma to the head and associated areas occurs in about 50% of abused children.

▼ Common *physical abuse* injuries include bruises, bite marks, lacerations, and burns, as well as fractures of the facial bones and teeth.

▼ A torn frenulum of the upper lip and intra-oral bruising are highly suspicious signs of physical abuse.

▼ Distinctive ear bruises, ipsilateral cerebral edema with obliteration of the basal cisterns, and retinal hemorrhages constitute the "tin ear syndrome."

▼ Signs of *sexual abuse* include lesions of sexually transmitted diseases.

▼ Erythema and petechiae at the conjunction of the hard and soft palates or the floor of the mouth suggest fellatio.

▼ Dental *neglect* may be suspected when extensive caries and oral infections persist despite the elimination of financial and transportation barriers to dental care.

Bibliography

Grace A, Grace S. **Child abuse within the ear, nose and throat.** *Otolaryngology.* 1987;16:108-111
A survey of 50 hospitals and child abuse units in England was carried out to determine the types of injuries inflicted to the ear, nose, and throat in verified cases of abuse. The authors concluded that most blows to the ear result in bruising of the pinna, hemotympanum, or perforation of the tympanic membrane. Nonaccidental injury to the nasal cavity is rare. Intra-oral bruising should invoke strong suspicions of abuse and mandate a search for other manifestations of nonaccidental injury. A torn frenulum of the upper lip can be considered pathognomonic of abuse. Lacerations within the ear, nose, or throat do not tend to occur accidentally, and they should also arouse suspicion.

Hanigan WC, Peterson RA, Njus G. **Tin ear syndrome: rotational acceleration in pediatric head injuries.** *Pediatrics.* 1987;80:618-622
The authors describe a clinical triad of signs in three children between 2 and 3 years of age. The children had similar unilateral bruises of their ears consisting of fresh purpuric hemorrhages in the antitragus, helix, triangular fossa, and interior folds of the ear. They also had diffuse retinal hemorrhages and radiographic evidence of ipsilateral cerebral edema with obliteration of the basal cisterns, consistent with uncal herniation. All three children died within 72 hours following admission. Necropsy revealed thin subdural hematomas without coup or contrecoup contusions. Past history and environmental circumstances in each child implicated abuse.

The authors hypothesize that the children sustained blunt injuries to their ears resulting in significant rotational acceleration of the head, stretching and tearing of the cortical veins with production of ipsilateral subdural hematoma, loss of vascular tone with severe cerebral hyperemia, uncontrollable intracranial hypertension, and tentorial herniation. They described a mathematical model to support their hypothesis.

Jessee SA. **Orofacial manifestations of child abuse and neglect.** *Am Fam Physician.* 1995;52:1829-1834
The author notes in this review article that common signs of physical abuse include fractures of the teeth, maxilla, mandible, and other facial bones; facial burns; lacerations of the lips and lingual frenum; and bite marks on the face and neck. Other injuries may include retinal hemorrhages, ptosis, and periorbital bruising of the eyes; nasal contusions and fractures; and damage to the tympanic membrane associated with bruising of the auricle and postauricular area. Sexual abuse should be suspected if erythematous, ulcerative, and vesiculopustular, pseudomembranous and condylomatous lesions due to syphilis, gonorrhea, or condylomata acuminata are present on the lips,

tongue, palate, face, or pharynx. Erythema and petechiae at the conjunction of the hard and soft palate or on the floor of the mouth may be signs of forced fellatio. Dental neglect should be suspected if rampant caries, oral infections, bleeding, and trauma persist despite the elimination of financial and transportation barriers to obtaining dental care.

Willging JP, Bower CM, Cotton RT. Physical abuse in children: a review and an otolaryngology perspective. *Arch Otolaryngol Head Neck Surg.* **1992;118:584-590**

In this retrospective study, 49% of 1,390 physically abused children had evidence of injury to the head and neck region, while 1% of 2,950 sexually abused children had such injuries. Most of the injuries were caused by blows with the hands (40%), an object (22%), or falls (19%);

89% of the injuries were to the face and scalp. Ecchymoses and abrasions accounted for 62% and 15% of the injuries, respectively. Lacerations, fractures, hematomas or hemorrhages, burns, blunt trauma, and shake injuries were less common. Most lacerations were on the lips and face. Most fractures were of the skull. Almost one fourth of the children had upper extremity injuries, and lower extremity injuries were also common. Eleven (1.6%) of the children died; nine of these children had severe head injuries.

Acknowledgment

This section and its annotations were prepared by Jerry G. Jones, MD.

AMERICAN ACADEMY OF PEDIATRICS

Committee on Early Childhood, Adoption, and Dependent Care

Oral and Dental Aspects of Child Abuse and Neglect (RE6068)

In all 50 states, physicians are required to report suspected cases of child abuse and neglect to social service or law enforcement agencies. Dentists are similarly required to report such suspected cases in most states and are allowed to report in all states; however, a minority of dentists are aware of these legal requirements.[1-4] Physicians and dentists could aid in educating each other and in collaborating to increase the detection, treatment, and prevention of these disorders. Physicians typically receive limited training in dental injury and disease and thus may not detect dental abuse or neglect as readily as they do child abuse and neglect involving other areas of the body.

PHYSICAL ABUSE

Because craniofacial injuries occur in half of child abuse cases,[3,5,6] evaluation of these injuries is essential. Some authorities believe the oral cavity may be a central focus for physical abuse because of its significance in communication and nutrition.[2] The injuries are most commonly inflicted as blunt trauma with an instrument, eating utensil, hand, or finger or by scalding liquids or caustic substances. The abuse may result in ecchymoses, lacerations, traumatized or avulsed teeth, facial fractures, burns, or other injuries. Discolored teeth may result from repeated trauma.[7,8] Gags applied to the mouth may leave bruises, lichenification, or scarring at the corners of the mouth.[9] Multiple injuries, injuries in different stages of healing, injuries inappropriate for the child's stage of development, and/or a discrepant history should arouse suspicion of abuse.

SEXUAL ABUSE

The oral cavity is a frequent site of sexual abuse in children. The presence of oral and perioral gonorrhea or syphilis in prepubertal children is pathognomonic of sexual abuse.[10] Pharyngeal gonorrhea is frequently asymptomatic. Therefore, when a diagnosis of gonorrhea is made, lesions should be sought in the oral cavity and appropriate cultures should be obtained even if no lesions are detected.[11-15]

When gonorrhea is diagnosed in a child, case finding efforts should include adults with whom the child had any contact during the preceding week, concentrating on asymptomatic men and women with a history of genital symptoms.[16] When obtaining oral or pharyngeal cultures for *Neisseria gonorrhoeae*, the physician must specifically ask for culture material that will grow and differentiate this organism from *Neisseria meningitidis*, which normally inhabit the mouth and throat. Gonococci will not grow in routine throat cultures.[17] In the rare case of syphilis in the sexually abused child, oral lesions should also be sought and darkfield examinations performed. Oral or perioral condylomata acuminata, although probably most frequently caused by sexual contact, may be the result of contact with verruca vulgaris or self-innoculation.[18] Unexplained erythema or petechiae of the palate, particularly at the junction of the hard palate and soft palate, may be evidence of fellatio.[19,20]

BITE MARKS

Bite marks are lesions that may indicate abuse. Dentists may be of special help to physicians in detecting and evaluating bite marks related to physical and sexual abuse. Bite marks should be suspected when ecchymoses, abrasions, or lacerations are found in an elliptical or ovoid pattern. Bite marks inflicted during sexual abuse may have a central area of ecchymoses or "suck mark." The normal distance between the maxillary canine teeth in adult humans is 2.5 to 4.0 cm, and the canine marks in a bite will be the most prominent or deep parts of the bite. Bites produced by dogs and other carnivorous animals tear flesh, whereas human bites compress flesh, causing only contusions.[9] If the intercanine distance is less than 3 cm, the bite may have been caused by a child. If the intercanine distance is larger, the bite was probably produced by an adult. The size, contour, and color(s) of the bite mark should be evaluated by a forensic odontologist (dentist) or forensic pathologist, if possible. If this specialist is not available, the bite mark's characteristics should be observed and documented by the attending physician. Repeated written observations and photographs will document the involution and further delineate age of the bite. Because each individual has a characteristic bite pattern, a forensic odontologist or forensic pathologist may be able to match molds (casts) of a suspected abuser's teeth with molds of the bite itself, if there is sufficient tissue damage to produce a meaningful mold.[8,21,22]

Blood group substances are secreted in saliva and may be deposited in bites. Even if dried, this saliva may be collected on a sterile cotton swab, moistened with isotonic saline, and replaced in a sealed vial. A control sample should be obtained from an uninvolved area of the child's skin. These samples should be sent to a forensic laboratory for prompt analysis. Although this technique is useful, results are not infallible.[21]

DENTAL NEGLECT

Failure to obtain proper dental care may result from (1) family isolation, (2) lack of finances (more of a problem for dental care than for medical care), (3) parental ignorance, or (4) lack of perceived value of oral health.[21]

As with child neglect in general, dental neglect has some definitional problems. Definitions of dental neglect in children include, "negligence or maltreatment that harms their oral health," and, somewhat more specifically, "failure by a parent or guardian to seek treatment for visual, untreated caries, oral infections and/or oral pain, or failure of the parent or guardian to follow through with treatment once informed that the above condition "exists."[23]

The problem physicians and dentists both face is, "when is it neglect?" An untreated small cavity in a deciduous tooth that will be shed in a few weeks is not neglect. Rampant caries with multiple alveolar abscesses is neglect. Between these extremes, it is difficult to determine the boundary.

Indicators of dental neglect include (1) untreated rampant caries, easily detected by a layperson; (2) untreated pain, infection, bleeding, or trauma affecting the orofacial region; and (3) history of a lack of follow-through for care in children with identified dental pathology.

In the presence of these indicators, the physician or dentist should be certain that the caretakers understand the explanation of the pathology and its implications and, when financial barriers to the needed care exist, attempt to assist these families in finding monetary aid or public facilities for needed services. If, in spite of these efforts, the parents continue to refuse therapy, such cases should be reported to appropriate social service departments.

CONCLUSION

In evaluation of physical or sexual abuse or neglect, physicians will benefit from consultation with dentists, especially those having experience or expertise with children—particularly abused children. Physician members of multidisciplinary child abuse and neglect teams should identify such dentists in their communities to serve as consultants for these teams. In addition, physicians with experience or expertise in child abuse and neglect should make themselves available to dentists and to dental organizations as consultants and educators. Such efforts will strengthen our ability to detect child abuse and neglect and enhance our ability to care for children.

COMMITTEE ON EARLY CHILDHOOD, ADOPTION, AND DEPENDENT CARE, 1985–1986
George G. Sterne, MD, Chairman
David L. Chadwick, MD
Richard D. Krugman, MD
Jean Pakter, MD
Gerald E. Porter, MD
Edward L. Schor, MD
Virginia Wagner, MD

Liaison Representatives
Elaine Schwartz, Children's Bureau, OHD, DHHS
Judy Abrahams, Child Welfare League of America
Bernice Weissbourd, National Association for the Education of Young Children

Section Representatives
Kay R. Lewis, MD (Child Development)
Carol Roberts Gerson, MD (Otolaryngology)

Consultant
Arthur J. Nowak, DMD (American Academy of Pediatric Dentistry)

REFERENCES

1. Davis GR, Domoto PK, Levy RL: The dentist's role in child abuse and neglect: Issues, identification, and management. *J Dent Child* 1979;46:185–192
2. Schwartz S, Woolridge E, Stege D: The role of the dentist in child abuse. *Quintessence Int* 1976;7(10):79–81
3. Becker DB, Needleman HL, Kotelchuck M: Child abuse and dentistry: Orofacial trauma and its recognition by dentists. *J Am Dent Assoc* 1978;97:24–28

4. Sognnaes RF, Blain SM: Child abuse and neglect: I. Diagnostic criteria of special interest to dentists, abstracted. *J Dent Res* 1979;58:367
5. Cameron JM, Johnson HRM, Camps FE: The battered child syndrome. *Med Sci Law* 1966;6:2–21
6. Tate RJ: Facial injuries associated with the battered child syndrome. *Br J Oral Surg* 1971;9:41–45
7. Kittle PE, Richardson DS, Parker JW: Two child abuse/child neglect examinations for the dentist. *J Dent Child* 1981;48:175–180
8. Blain SM, Winegarden T, Barber TK, et al: Child abuse and neglect: II. Dentistry's role, abstracted. *J Dent Res* 1979;58:367
9. McNeese MC, Hebeler JR: The abused child: A clinical approach to identification and management. *Clin Symp* 1977;29:1–36
10. Folland DS, Burke RE, Hinman AR, et al: Gonorrhea in preadolescent children: An inquiry into source of infection and mode of transmission. *Pediatrics* 1977;60:153–156
11. Chue PWY: Gonorrhea—Its natural history, oral manifestations, diagnosis, treatment, and prevention. *J Am Dent Assoc* 1975;90:1297–1301
12. Givan KF, Keyl A: The isolation of Neisseria species from unusual sites. *Can Med Assoc J* 1974;111:1077–1079
13. Jamsky RJ: Gonococcal tonsillitis: Report of a case. *Oral Surg* 1977;44:197–200
14. Nelson JD, Mohs E, Dajani AS, et al: Gonorrhea in preschool and school-aged children: Report of the prepubertal gonorrhea cooperative study group. *JAMA* 1976;236:1359–1364
15. Silber TJ: Pharyngeal gonorrhea in children. *Pediatrics* 1978;61:674
16. Potterat JJ, Markewich GS, Rothenberg R: Prepubertal infections with *Neisseria gonorrhoeae*: Clinical and epidemiologic significance. *Sex Transm Dis* 1978;5:1–2
17. Silber T, Controni G, Korin DE: Pharyngeal gonorrhea in children and adolescents. *Clin Proc* 1977;33:79–81
18. Seidel J, Zonana J, Totten E: Condylomata acuminata as a sign of sexual abuse in children. *J Pediatr* 1979;95:553–554
19. Giansanti JS, Cramer JR, Weathers DR: Palatal erythema: Another etiologic factor. *Oral Surg* 1975;40:379–381
20. Schlesinger SL, Borbotsina J, O'Neill L: Petechial hemorrhages of the soft palate secondary to fellatio. *Oral Surg* 1975;40:376–378
21. Sanger RG, Bross DC (eds): *Clinical Management of Child Abuse and Neglect: A Guide for the Dental Professional.* Chicago, Quintessence Publishing Co, Inc, 1984
22. Sims BG, Grant JH, Cameron JM: Bite-marks in the "battered baby syndrome." *Med Sci Law* 1973;13:207–210
23. *Policies of the American Academy of Pediatric Dentistry.* Chicago, American Academy of Pediatric Dentistry, 1983, pp 51–52

Emotional Abuse

See Also:
Domestic Violence and Child Abuse
Psychological Impact of Child Maltreatment

Clinical Principles

▼ Emotional abuse continues to be difficult to define both clinically and operationally for research purposes.

▼ The difficulty in defining emotional abuse leads to a small number of reports in this category of abuse (< 10%) despite its pervasive impact.

▼ Emotional abuse and psychological abuse are terms that are often used interchangeably. However, there may be differences between these, and we may need more precision in our terminology.

▼ The terms "emotional abuse" or "psychological abuse" include many subsets that impact on the child's physical health, mental health, and development. Impact may be short-term and situational, or long-term and fixed.

▼ Little is known or understood about individual resiliency and the factors that make one child more or less vulnerable to emotional abuse. Two children living in the same environment may have very different vulnerabilities for reasons social scientists have yet to describe.

▼ It has been well documented that violence in the household at the parental level has significant negative impact on the child. Interparental violence may have a negative effect as serious as if the child were directly physically abused.

Bibliography

Definitions

APSAC Practice Guidelines. *Psychosocial Evaluation of Suspected Psychological Maltreatment in Children and Adolescents.* **American Professional Society on the Abuse of Children. 1995**
The APSAC guidelines offer a good definition of psychological abuse:

> Psychological maltreatment means a repeated pattern of caregiver behavior or extreme incident(s) that convey to children that they are worthless, flawed, unloved, unwanted, endangered, or only of value in meeting another's needs. The term 'psychological,' instead of 'emotional,' is used because it better incorporates the cognitive, affective, and interpersonal conditions that are the primary concomitant of this form of child maltreatment. Professionals should be aware of legal definitions of psychological maltreatment that are applicable in their community. Psychological maltreatment includes acts of commission (eg, verbal attacks by a caregiver) as well as acts of omission (eg, emotional unavailability of a caregiver). Definitions specific to a particular state will generally be found in one or more of its civil or criminal statutes.

The guidelines point out that the impact of psychological maltreatment may lead to short-term and long-term effects. They caution that the physician or health care provider be aware of basic legal principles governing confidentiality and privilege.

In assessing a child and family, these guidelines suggest considering (a) global assessment, (b) child's developmental level, and (c) a variety of forms and levels of severity of psychological maltreatment. Definitions are given for "spurning," "rejecting," "terrorizing," "exploiting/corrupting," "denying emotional responsiveness," "isolating," and, "mental health, medical, and educational neglect." The guidelines also provide the definition for "severe emotional disturbances" as defined by the federal law, Individuals With Disabilities Education Act. Within the Act the term is defined by a condition exhibiting one or more of the following characteristics:

"(A) An inability to learn that cannot be explained by intellectual, sensory, or health factors;

(B) An inability to build or maintain satisfactory interpersonal relationships with peers and teachers;

(C) Inappropriate types of behavior or feelings under normal circumstances;

(D) A general pervasive mood of unhappiness or depression; or

(E) A tendency to develop physical symptoms or fears associated with personal or school problems."

In general, these guidelines form a good starting point for the understanding of emotional/psychological abuse, its definitions, and its assessment.

O'Hagan KP. Emotional and psychological abuse: problems of definition. *Child Abuse Negl.* 1995;19:449-461

Defining 'emotional abuse' and 'psychological abuse' is a task made difficult by uncertainty as to whether or not such terms are synonymous and/or interchangeable. There is an increasing tendency in child protection literature to regard them as synonymous, or at least, to make little distinction between them.

The purpose of this paper is to explore the origins of this tendency and to provide an alternative view, namely, that the terms are not synonymous, and there should be different definitions for each. Existing commonly used definitions are reviewed. The definitions that this paper provides stem from important concepts in emotional and psychological development.

This article calls for more precision in the use of terminology. It is representative of the fact that we are still struggling with basic definitions. It is no wonder that there is difficulty in moving beyond the basic level of understanding.

This author would suggest "emotional abuse" be applied to the abuse that impairs emotional life and impedes emotional development. Psychological abuse impairs mental life that includes emotional and other mental functions such as intelligence, memory, recognition, perception, attention, imagination, and normal development.

Thompson AE, Kaplan CA. Childhood emotional abuse. *Br J Psychiatry.* 1996;168:143-148

This article takes on the challenge of making some practical sense of the term emotional abuse. As practitioners, we have all seen emotionally abused children. As reporters of child abuse, we have rarely used this emotional abuse provision of our reporting law. As researchers, it is daunting to develop scientific operational definitions. This paper examines a number of existing definitions, both clinical and legal, and dissects out the important elements of each. Further, the authors look at the mechanistic approach to emotional abuse and a delineation of the consequences of abuse.

Measurement Tools

Brassard MR, Hart SN, Hardy DB. The psychological maltreatment rating scales. *Child Abuse Negl.* 1993;7:715-729

Psychological maltreatment is gaining recognition as one of the core concepts in child welfare; however, its utility has been limited by definitional problems and the absence of operationalized and validated instruments. These Psychological Maltreatment Rating Scales (PMRS) were developed for assessing psychological maltreatment in mother-child interaction, and were used to rate the videotaped interaction of 49 high-risk mother-child dyads and make predictions of child protective service involvement with the dyads. These predictions are compared with predictions based upon mothers' personal resources and social support. Results show that the PMRS is a moderately reliable and valid measure of psychologically maltreating and prosocial parental behavior that can discriminate between maltreating and comparison parents, and is a more effective predictor than maternal measures. Three factors of parenting emerged from an exploratory factor analysis: emotional abuse and two factors of positive parenting. Psychological abuse was the presence of hostile behavior, and psychological neglect the absence of positive parenting.

This study reports on the use of a scale-PMRS (Psychological Maltreatment Rating Scale) and its ability to identify maltreating parents. In the hands of this group of investigators, it appears that for a small group of children, 5 to 9 years old, the scale is both sensitive and specific. Nonetheless, the authors suggest that this kind of tool be used only in conjunction with collateral reports, not as a primary screening tool.

Sanders B, Becker-Lausen E. The measurement of psychological maltreatment: early data on the child abuse and trauma scale. *Child Abuse Negl.* 1995;9:315-323

This paper describes a self-report measure, the Child Abuse and Trauma Scale, which yields a quantitative index of the frequency and extent of various types of negative experiences in childhood and adolescence. Data on this measure are presented for two large samples of college students and for a small clinical sample of subjects with a diagnosis of multiple personality disorder. The strong internal consistency and test-retest reliability of the scale in the college population is documented, and its validity is attested to by demonstrating that it correlates significantly with outcomes such as dissociation, depression, difficulties in interpersonal relationships, and victimization, all of which have previously been associated with childhood trauma or abuse. The extremely high scores of the multiple personality subjects confer additional validity to the measure. The authors suggest that the construct of psychological maltreatment underlies the destructive elements of numerous forms of abuse and neglect, and that the scale they have developed may provide a useful index of this construct.

This report documents another set of efforts to identify emotional/psychological abuse. This paper describes the Child Abuse and Trauma (CAT) Scale. This is a self-administered survey given to young adults. The authors describe it as "one approach to the retrospective assessment of negative childhood experiences." There are three distinct scales: (1) negative home environment/neglect, (2) sexual abuse, and (3) punishment. The CAT Scale appears to be a worthwhile reasonable tool but does not offer any use in the clinical setting.

Mechanisms and Outcomes

Claussen AH, Crittenden PM. Physical and psychological maltreatment: relations among types of maltreatment. *Child Abuse Negl.* 1991;15:5-18

Maltreatment has serious consequences for the development of children, although the reason is not fully understood. The authors' hypotheses were that psychological maltreatment would be present in almost all cases of physical maltreatment and that it would be more related to detrimental outcomes for children than would severity of injury.

In this study of 175 maltreated children and 176 normative children, both hypotheses were supported. The study also provided evidence that psychological maltreatment can occur alone, parental psychologically maltreating behavior and negative child outcomes are highly correlated, and family income is related to psychological maltreatment in young children.

This case-controlled research investigates the central deleterious element in child maltreatment: *Is it the physical injury or is it the accompanying psychological message that is transmitted?* Results show that severity of physical injury was uncorrelated with other forms of maltreatment. Physical maltreatment rarely occurred in the absence of psychological maltreatment. Psychological maltreatment did occur in the absence of physical injury. This article supports the idea that we need to evaluate children more carefully and go beyond the skeletal survey and magnetic resonance studies. Some abused children may need rehabilitation services despite minor physical impairment.

Klosinski G. Psychological maltreatment in the context of separation and divorce. *Child Abuse Negl.* 1993;17:557-563

Children of separating or divorcing parents seldom escape suffering psychological stress, particularly when the parents are in open conflict. How much should such children be allowed to suffer? The author discusses the problem of defining the terms "emotional child abuse" and "psychological maltreatment" as they are used in the literature. Reviewing the common behavioral patterns that children in this situation resort to and the roles that they tend to take upon themselves, he attempts to distinguish between those instances of stress that can be regarded as acceptable and those that must be considered harmful. With respect to children in this situation, the following behavior patterns are discussed: (a) the inclination of the child to sacrifice itself for the sake of the parents, in particular for the 'weaker' one; (b) the tendency of the children to reach agreements among themselves about how they should be divided up; (c) the phenomenon of parentization in which the child assumes the role of the substitute partner for one or the other parent; and (d) the child's discovery of both its power and its helplessness with respect to the situation and the feelings of guilt awakened by this discovery.

This paper presents good background information on the definitions of emotional and psychological abuse and uses parental divorce as a model. It explores ways that children can be harmed by the divorce process and points out that *all divorces are stressors, but not all reach the level of emotional abuse.* The author offers his opinion on when emotional abuse may be identified.

Rogosch FA, Cicchetti D, Aber JL. The role of child maltreatment in early deviations in cognitive and affective processing abilities and later peer relationship problems. *Dev Psychopathology.* 1995;7:591-609

Despite considerable research demonstrating the adverse consequences of child maltreatment, including a heightened risk for adaptational failures and psychopathology, longitudinal evaluations of processes contributing to negative outcomes have been limited. Problems in peer relations constitute a critical developmental risk for future maladaptation among maltreated children, transferring relationship disturbance from the family to new interpersonal contexts. The linkages of a history of child maltreatment to early deviations in cognitive/affective processes which in turn lead to subsequent difficulties in peer relations were examined. Specifically, in a sample of 46 maltreated and 43 nonmaltreated low-income children, laboratory assessments of affect, understanding, and cognitive control functioning were conducted, followed by later peer and teacher assessments of peer relations in the school setting. *Maltreated children were shown to evidence early deviations in their understanding of negative affect as well as immaturity in their cognitive controls. Maltreated children also were shown to have lower social effectiveness and higher levels of undercontrolled and aggressive behavior in the school setting. Physically abused children were found to be more rejected by their peers.* Cognitive control functioning partially mediated the effect of maltreatment on later social effectiveness. Negative affect understanding mediated both the relation of maltreatment on later dysregulated behavior in the peer setting and the effect of physical abuse on later rejection by peers. The results were discussed in terms of their support for organizational/transactional theory and the implications they have for prevention and intervention.

This paper, although not specific to emotional abuse, begins to give some insight into the psychological mechanisms that lead to the long-term impact of abuse on personality and interpersonal interactions. The impact of abuse on peer relationships is explored.

Acknowledgment

This section and its annotations were prepared by Stephen Ludwig, MD.

Failure to Thrive

See Also:
Neglect

Failure to thrive (FTT) accounts for 1% of all pediatric hospitalizations. Historically, FTT has been divided into "organic" (disease related) and "nonorganic" (NOFTT) (secondary to family dysfunction), but these categories are not mutually exclusive. The term "FTT" may legally imply neglect and should be used thoughtfully. The discussion here will focus on FTT as pediatric undernutrition with possible adverse effects. The causes of undernutrition in the United States differ from those in developing countries, raising questions about how this cross-cultural phenomenon should be described and approached.

Clinical Principles

▼ Failure to thrive is used as a general description of a child who fails to maintain growth at an expected rate above the 3rd percentile for weight. The patterns of acute and chronic malnutrition result from the intake of insufficient calories for growth, come from the World Health Organization, and are defined as follows:

~ weight/length <10th percentile ("wasting")

and/or

~ weight and height each <3rd percentile ("stunting")

In addition, a dynamic view describes pediatric undernutrition as weight crossing two major percentile lines in less than 6 months, even though the weight is >3rd percentile.

▼ Failure to thrive may result from chronic disease or a challenging caregiver-child interaction or both. The differential diagnosis is expansive and must come from the history and physical exam. In the absence of a suspicion of a chronic disease, the yield of an extensive laboratory workup is essentially zero. The hallmark of a complete FTT evaluation is a multidisciplinary assessment of the child, the family, and the environment.

▼ Infants may evidence recurrent behavior patterns such as intense watchfulness, inappropriate stranger anxiety, diminished vocalizations, and unusual postures or motor movements. Developmental milestones may be delayed.

▼ Toddlers may show food refusal, a variety of behaviors that, in conjunction with professional pressure on parents to increase intake, cause conflicts over eating, including force-feeding.

▼ Intervention includes calories for maintenance and catch-up growth, improved structure and content of mealtime, improved social interaction around mealtime, and therapy for associated developmental delays. A 1- to 2-week hospitalization may be required for assessment and initial weight gain.

▼ Failure to thrive may result in developmental delays and increased morbidity secondary to illnesses. Long-term follow-up suggests an increased incidence of language and reading problems, difficulties with peer relationships, and attention problems.

Other Comments

▼ Cumulative risk factors cause escalating stress: parental inexperience or lack of knowledge, poor family resources, few social supports, negative emotional environment, and parent-child interaction issues that may stem from chronic illness, infant feeding problems, or temperament.

▼ Caregiver stressors may include health problems, separations, loss, unwanted child/pregnancy, pregnancy and birth complications, and parental affective disorders (eg, depression) or other psychiatric disorders including substance abuse.

Bibliography

Bithoney WG, McJunkin J, Michalek J, Snyder J, Egan H, Epstein D. The effect of a multidisciplinary team approach on weight gain in non-organic failure-to-thrive children. *J Dev Behav Pediatr.* 1991;12:254-258
The study shows that an intensive multidisciplinary team approach to outpatient NOFTT (N=53) can result in markedly superior weight gain compared with standard pediatric primary care (N=107) in the same institution. The improved weight gain (with no significant differences in hospital rates, though the index group was significantly more malnourished and was more difficult to manage) implies a potential cost-efficacy benefit. Three factors may have contributed: age-appropriate, high-calorie diets individualized by a nutritionist; behavioral protocols; and intensive social services with referrals for family.

Drotar D. Behavioral diagnosis in nonorganic failure-to-thrive: a critique and suggested approach to psychological assessment. *J Dev Behav Pediatr.* 1989;10:48-55
The author critically reviews studies of behavioral diagnoses in children with NOFTT. He suggests an alternative way to organize data from behavioral assessment that emphasizes the heterogeneity of NOFTT and the consequences of environmental and biologic risk factors on psychological development and outcomes.

Mathisen B, Skuse D, Wolke D, Reilly S. Oral-motor dysfunction and failure to thrive among inner-city infants. *Dev Med Child Neurol.* 1989;31:293-302
Among socioeconomically deprived inner-city infants, NOFTT may be associated with abnormal oral-motor function and socially adverse situations such as disorganized mealtimes. The authors rated oral-motor behavior objectively and tested matched pairs of children while they were being fed at home. The subject infants had immature and abnormal oral-motor development that made them less able to be fed successfully. Temperamentally, they were more "difficult" than the comparison infants, and they were less adept at signaling their needs during mealtimes. The subject infants were fed in age-inappropriate positions, with more distractions and less suitable utensils.

Moore JB. Project thrive: a supportive treatment approach to the parents of children with nonorganic failure to thrive. *Child Welfare.* 1982;61:389-399
An effective, cost-efficient intervention method with families of 28 FTT infants is described. The case managers were all social work student interns with a limited number of cases, to whom they devoted total attention. All families did well; none of the babies were rehospitalized during the 16 months. The author suggests "students often have a kind of ingenious belief in their client's ability to change...very enabling, a quality that many more experienced, harried workers may have lost."

Ramsey M, Gisel EG, Boutry M. Non-organic failure to thrive: growth failure secondary to feeding-skills disorder. *Dev Med Child Neurol.* 1993;35:285-297
The authors suggest NOFTT is a growth failure secondary to a feeding-skills disorder (FSD), neurophysiological in origin. Four clinical signs (two or more present at or near birth) contribute to an FSD diagnosis: abnormal duration of feeding time; poor/no appetite; food texture intolerance; and deviant feeding behaviors. In this study, a high percentage of the 60 infants with both organic and nonorganic FTT exhibited all four signs. The reported onset of FSD in both groups preceded or coincided with deceleration in weight gain, and in all cases preceded onset of FTT. The authors suggest overt feeding behavior and interactions at any age may be consequential to longstanding feeding difficulties and not mother-infant psychological dysfunction.

Skuse DH, Gill D, Reilly S, Wolke D, Lynch MA. Failure to thrive and the risk of child abuse: a prospective population survey. *J Med Screening.* 1995;2:145-149
Using a whole population 1986 birth cohort, the authors sought to identify the relative importance of FTT during infancy as a risk factor for later abuse or neglect. Of the 2,609 children, 47 were identified as having NOFTT by 12 months. The relative risk attributable to NOFTT exceeded other measured risk factors such as birth weight, but previous research has overstated its importance. Nonorganic FTT independently contributed to subsequent poor parenting, necessitating intervention.

Smith MM, Lefshitz F. Excess fruit juice consumption as a contributing factor in nonorganic failure to thrive. *Pediatrics.* **1994;93:438-443**

Eight children, from 14 to 27 months of age, were referred for FTT. In each case, deterioration of weight and linear growth progression coincided with excessive juice consumption, consumed for various reasons including children's preferences. After nutritional intervention, weight gain increased significantly in the first month and persisted for follow-up of 5 to 18 months. This large intake of fruit juices may displace more calorie- and nutrient-dense foods.

Acknowledgment

This section and its annotations were prepared by Paula K. Jaudes, MD, and Madeleine U. Shalowitz, MD. It was reviewed by Kent P. Hymel, MD.

Falls

See Also:
Fractures
Head Injuries
Retinal Hemorrhages
Shaken Impact/Shaken Baby Syndrome
Summary of Published Studies Regarding Pediatric Falls, which follows

Clinical Principles

▼ Child abuse should be suspected when life-threatening or fatal injuries result from uncorroborated short falls.

▼ Except for epidural hemorrhage, indoor accidental cranial impacts rarely cause severe or fatal intracranial injury in infants.

▼ Reports that serious injuries are the result of falls from bed, sofa, or crib should be viewed with skepticism. Serious head injury and CNS damage are extremely rare when infants and young children fall out of bed.

▼ Stairway falls of children do not result in life-threatening injury.

▼ The vast majority of accidental, infant walker-related injuries result from stairway falls and usually do not involve injuries to the trunk or extremities.

Bibliography

Barlow B, Niemirska M, Gandhi RP, Leblanc W. Ten years of experience with falls from a height in children. *J Pediatr Surg.* 1983;18:509-511

Chadwick DL, Chin S, Salerno C, Landsverk J, Kitchen L. Deaths from falls in children: how far is fatal? *J Trauma.* 1991;31:1353-1355
History and physical findings were compared for 317 children admitted for injuries allegedly sustained through falls. No deaths occurred in 65 children who fell 5 to 9 feet, although fatal falls occurred in 7 of 100 children whose families made uncorroborated reports of falls that were less than 4 feet. One death occurred among 118 children who had fallen 10 to 45 feet.

All but one of the deaths were caused by head injury: subdural hematoma, cerebral contusion with cerebral edema, or both. The inconsistency of these findings leads authors to conclude that child abuse should be suspected when parents give a history of short falls to explain fatal injuries. (CL/KM)

Chiaviello CT, Christoph RA, Bond GR. Stairway-related injuries in children. *Pediatrics.* 1994;94:679-681
These authors prospectively studied all children less than 5 years of age who presented to their emergency department over a 2-year period with a stairway-related injury. Demographic, epidemiologic, and injury severity information was analyzed. Children with suspected intentional trauma and walker-related injuries were excluded.

The median age of the 69 study patients was 2 years. Head and neck injuries occurred in 90% of study patients, extremity injuries in 6%, and truncal injuries in 4%. The majority of injuries were minor. None of the study patients sustained injuries involving more than one body region. However, the authors reported that 15 patients (22%) suffered "significant" injuries, including concussion in 11 (16%), skull fracture in 5 (7%), cerebral contusion in 2 (3%), subdural hematoma in 1 (1%), and a C-2 fracture in 1 (1%). The authors concluded that stairway-related injuries may be more common than previously reported.

In verbal discussions with authors regarding this study, we have learned that "significant injuries" were not associated with significant morbidity or mortality. Concussion was defined broadly in this study as "loss of consciousness and/or alteration in mental status (such as confusion, somnolence, or amnesia)." The single child with subdural hemorrhage in this study also sustained a skull fracture and underlying cerebral contusion (1 of 2 study patients with cerebral contusion). This child was being carried down the stairs in the arms of the mother when these injuries were sustained. Both study patients with cerebral contusion "did great" (according to author C.C.) after brief hospitalization for observation without deleterious complications. Another child whose stairway-related injuries were sustained while in the arms of the parent sustained a skull fracture. The authors hypothesized that more severe injuries are likely when infants fall with an adult while being carried on the stairs. (KH,GP)

Chiaviello CT, Christoph RA, Bond GR. Infant walker-related injuries: a prospective study of severity and incidence. *Pediatrics.* **1994;93:974-976**
Epidemiologic and demographic information was prospectively analyzed in 65 patients with walker-related injuries evaluated in the emergency department at the University of Virginia between 1989 and 1992. Infants with suspected inflicted trauma were excluded. Ninety-five percent of study patients were younger than 1 year of age. Mechanisms for walker-related injuries included stairway falls (71%), falls from a porch (3%), and burns (5%). Injuries predominantly involved the head and neck region (97%), with only a few injuries to the extremities (6%) and trunk (3%). Significant injuries to 19 of 65 study patients included skull fracture (15%), concussion (12%), intracranial hemorrhage (8%), full-thickness burns (3%), and cervical spine fracture (1 patient). The single study patient who died sustained cervical spine fracture, skull fracture, and subdural hematoma.

The authors concluded that the pattern of walker-related injuries can help clinicians to differentiate this accidental outcome from inflicted trauma. More specifically, the vast majority of accidental walker-related injuries result from stairway falls and do not involve injuries to the trunk or extremities. (KH)

Helfer RE, Slovis TL, Black M. Injuries resulting when small children fall out of bed. *Pediatrics.* **1977;60:533-535**
Parents of children 5 years or younger who fell 3 feet or less were asked to complete a questionnaire regarding the incident. Data were compared with those from pediatric hospital incident reports on falls from cribs, beds, or examination tables.

Parent questionnaires reported no observable injuries in 80% of instances. The remainder reported bumps or nonserious bruises in 17% and fractures in 3%. (The fractures included three clavicles, two skulls, and one humerus.) The hospital incident reports showed that 57 of 85 had no apparent injury; 17 had small cuts, scratches, or bloody noses; and 20 sustained bumps or bruises. One child in the hospital group suffered a fractured skull without significant sequelae.

The authors conclude that physicians should be very suspicious when serious injuries are said to have been caused by a fall from bed, sofa, or crib. Serious head injury and central nervous system damage are extremely rare when children aged 5 years or less fall out of bed. (CL/KM)

Joffe M, Ludwig S. Stairway injuries to children. *Pediatrics.* **1988;82:457-461**
This study considered 363 nonabused children aged 0 to 11 years who presented to an urban hospital after stairway falls. No patients had life-threatening injuries, and none required intensive care. Most of the injuries were superficial: 55% abrasions/contusions and 26% lacerations. Bone injuries, including fractures and dental damage, occurred in 7%. Head injury (concussion) occurred in 1%. No detectable injury was found in 11%.

Only 2.7% of the children injured more than one body part. Injuries to the head and neck were the most common (73%); these were much more likely among children younger than 4 years. Injuries to the extremities occurred in 28%; most were distal. Only 2% had truncal injuries. There were no pulmonary contusions or abdominal visceral injuries. (CL/KM)

Kravitz H, Criessen C, Gomberg R, Korach A. Accidental falls from elevated surfaces in infants from birth to 1 year of age. *Pediatrics.* **1969;44:869-876**

Lehman D, Schonfeld N. Falls from heights: a problem not just in the northeast. *Pediatrics.* **1993;92:121-124**

Lyons T, Oates RK. Falling out of bed: a relatively benign occurrence. *Pediatrics.* 1993;92: 125-127

This study described injuries resulting from falls from either cribs (N=124) or beds (N=83) in 207 children younger than 6 years old.

In this study there were only 31 injuries among the 207 falls in hospitals corroborated by incident reports. All but two injuries were "trivial." One 10-month-old who fell from a crib had a simple linear skull fracture, and one 22-month-old climbing over the rail had a fractured clavicle. (CL)

The authors review and comment on the literature regarding witnessed/corroborated and witnessed/uncorroborated falls. In another study (Selbst et al, referenced below), six who fell from the top bunk required hospitalization for either concussion (4), skull fracture and subdural hematoma (1), or laceration. (CL)

Mayr J, Gaisl M, Purtscher K, et al. Baby walkers—an underestimated hazard for our children? *Eur J Pediatr.* 1994;153:531

Musemeche C, Barthel M, Cosentino C, Reynolds M. Pediatric falls from heights. *J Trauma.* 1991;31:1347-1349

Nimityongskul P, Anderson L. The likelihood of injuries when children fall out of bed. *J Pediatr Orthop.* 1987;7:184-186

A study of 76 children aged 0 to 16 years who fell 1 to 3 feet in the hospital determined that serious injury is extremely rare when children fall from bed. Approximately half of the study patients (39/76) were younger than 3 years of age. Only one questionable occipital skull fracture occurred in the group; it required no treatment. The other injuries were minor and included no extremity or spinal injury. (CL/KM)

Rivara FP, Alexander B, Johnston B, Soderberg R. Population-based study of falls in children and adolescents resulting in hospitalization or death. *Pediatrics.* 1993;92:61-63

Selbst SM, Baker MD, Sharnes M. Bunk bed injuries. *Am J Dis Child.* 1990;144:721-723

Smith MD, Burrington JD, Woolf AD. Injuries in children sustained in free falls: an analysis of 66 cases. *J Trauma.* 1975;15:987

Williams R. Injuries in infants and small children resulting from witnessed and corroborated free falls. *J Trauma.* 1991;31:1350-1352

Data regarding injuries suffered by 106 children whose falls were witnessed and corroborated were compared with data on injuries sustained in 292 uncorroborated falls. Severe injuries were common in the uncorroborated group and included two deaths from falls of less than 5 feet.

Among the witnessed and corroborated free falls, there was one death, resulting from a 70-foot fall. But witnessed falls were not generally associated with serious trauma and, in fact, 43 children who fell more than 10 feet sustained only minor bruises, abrasions, and simple fractures. Witnessed falls included 15 uninjured patients, 7 of whom had fallen more than 10 feet. Authors concluded that serious injury from uncorroborated short falls is highly suspect. (CL/KM)

Acknowledgment

This section and its annotations were prepared by Kent Hymel, MD. The table included on the next page was prepared for the second edition by Carolyn Levitt, MD. Selected annotations from the first edition were written by Carolyn Levitt, MD, and Kim Martinez, RN, CPNP, MPH. The manuscript was reviewed by Gerald Porter, MD, and Suzanne Starling, MD.

SUMMARY OF PUBLISHED STUDIES REGARDING PEDIATRIC FALLS: 1969 to 1994

Reference	Number	Age, y	Height/Mechanism	Injuries/Deaths*
Short Falls				
Helfer, Slovis, Black (1977)	176	<6	Home: bed, sofa, etc	2 skull fxs and 1 humeral fx <6 mos; 3 clavicle fxs >6 mos
Helfer, Slovis, Black (1977)	85	<6	Hospital: bed, crib	1 skull fx (uncomplicated)
Nimityongskul & Anderson (1987)	76	<16	Hospital: bed, crib	1 skull fx (linear)
Kravitz, Criessen, Gomberg, Korach (1969)	336	<2	Home: changing table	1 skull fx; 1 subdural hematoma
Williams (1991)	44	<3	<10 feet	3 skull fxs (depressed)
Lyons & Oates (1993)	207	<7	Hospital: bed, crib	1 skull fx (linear); 1 clavicle fx
Selbst, Baker, Sharnes (1990)	68	<6	Bunkbeds	6 hospitalized; 7 fxs; 1 skull fx with subdural hematoma
Levitt, McCormick (unpublished)	336	<2	<8 feet	9 subdural hematomas; 7 with retinal hemorrhage (7 are SBS)
Chadwick, Chin, Salerno, Landsverk, Kitchen (1991)	165	<18	<10 feet	7 deaths; 7 subdural hematomas; 7 with cerebral edema, 5 with retinal hemorrhage; 5 subarachnoid hemorrhage (7 are SBS)
TOTAL	**1493**			
Stairway Falls				
Joffe, Ludwick (1988)	363	<19	24 in walker; 10 carried by adults	No intracranial hemorrhage or cerebral contusions; 22 fxs: 6 skullfxs (<3 y) and 16 extremity fxs (15 >4 y)
Chiavello, Christoph, Bond (1994)	69	<5	Excluded walkers; 3 carried by adults	5 skull fxs; 1 small subdural hematoma; 1 cervical spine fx; 2 cerebral contusions
Levitt, McCormick (unpublished)	156	<2	75 walkers	2 with subdural hematomas & retinal hemorrhage (1 flame)
TOTAL	**588**			
Falls > 1 Story				
Williams (1991)	62	<3	≥10 feet	1 death (70 feet)
Barlow, Niemirska, Gandhi, Leblanc (1983)	61	<16	≥1 story	14 deaths (>3 stories)
Smith, Burrington, Woolf (1975)	42	<15	≥1 story	2 deaths (4 stories)
Chadwick, Chin, Salerno, Landsverk, Kitchen (1991)	118	<18	≥10 feet	1 death (10-45 feet)
Musemeche, Barthel, Cosentino, Reynolds (1991)	70	<15	≥10 feet	No deaths
Lehman, Schonfeld (1993)	134	<16	Windows, balconies, rooftops	1 death
TOTAL	**487**			**19 deaths (18 >3 stories)**

* Fx indicates fracture; SBS, shaken baby syndrome.

Fractures

See Also:
Falls
Head Injuries
Shaken Impact-Shaken Baby Syndrome
Thoracic Trauma
AAP Statement *Diagnostic Imaging of Child Abuse,* **which follows**

Clinical Principles

▼ The body mass of a child younger than 12 months will not ordinarily generate sufficient force to fracture a normal bone in a simple fall from a bed, crib, or couch. Radiologic skeletal survey is recommended whenever the history is suspicious or not corroborated.

▼ One must suspect abuse when a nonambulatory child presents with fracture. In ambulatory children, aged 15 to 36 months, a high percentage of these fractures are also the result of child maltreatment.

▼ Transverse or oblique long bone fractures are more common with abusive injury than are spiral fractures.

▼ Tibial spiral fractures should be considered due to accidents unless they occur in non-ambulatory young infants.

▼ Radiologic skeletal survey is also recommended for all children younger than 2 years with fractures whose history is inconsistent or who have any signs of unexplained injury or when there has been undue delays in seeking treatment.

▼ Bone scans can sometimes be helpful in identifying subtle findings of soft tissue and intra-abdominal injuries.

Other Comments

▼ Children do not ordinarily suffer rib fractures as a result of cardiopulmonary resuscitation.

▼ The potential overlap between sexual and physical abuse should not be overlooked when evaluating a child who has suffered physical trauma.

▼ The hallmark finding in fractures caused by nonaccidental trauma is the lack of a plausible explanation.

▼ Fractures involving the metaphysis of long bones, posterior aspect of ribs, scapula, spinous processes of vertebrae or sternum are highly suggestive of abuse in infants, even without a history.

▼ Multiple fractures, fractures of different ages, epiphyseal separation, vertebral body fractures, and subluxation are moderately suggestive of child abuse and need to be carefully considered in light of the history.

▼ Fractures of the clavicle, shafts of the long bones, and linear skull fractures are very commonly seen due to accidents. However, they must be carefully reviewed whenever they occur in infants.

Bibliography

General

Howard JL, Barron BJ, Smith GG. Bone scintigraphy in the evaluation of extraskeletal injuries from child abuse. *Radiographics.* 1990;10:67-81
This presentation of the subtle findings revealed on bone scintigraphy points out that clinicians need to be alert to soft tissue and intra-abdominal findings that may appear on bone scans. (JMN)

Kleinman PK, ed. *Diagnostic Imaging of Child Abuse.* Baltimore, MD: Williams & Wilkins Co; 1987
This detailed evaluation of fractures in children covers the need for quality films when child maltreatment is suspected, the technique required, and the types of films to be obtained in a skeletal survey. The structural characteristics of the child's skeleton and mechanics required for children to obtain fractures are reviewed. Tables list fractures highly suggestive of abuse, as well as those less likely to be abuse related. The place of bone scan

in evaluation of the mistreated child is discussed, and suggestions are made for its most efficient use. Other tables act as quick references to date radiographic findings and enable a differential diagnosis for skeletal lesions. *This is an excellent text.* (JMN)

Kleinman PK, Belanger PL, Karellas A, Spevak MR. Normal metaphyseal radiologic variants not to be confused with findings of infant abuse. *Am J Roentgenol.* 1991; 6:781-783

This review reports a variety of metaphyseal variants that should not be confused with child abuse. (PRP)

Kleinman PK, Marks SC Jr. A regional approach to classic metaphyseal lesions in abused infants: the distal tibia. *Am J Roentgenol.* 1996;166:1207-1212

and

Kleinman PK, Marks SC Jr. A regional approach to the classic metaphyseal lesion in abused infants: the proximal tibia. *Am J Roentgenol.* 1996;166:421-426

Sixteen classic metaphyseal lesions of the distal and 17 of the proximal tibia were studied. In both studies, lesions found radiographically were always along the medial aspect of the metaphysis. Lateral involvement was only noted with more extensive injury. All were more easily recognized with healing. The typical medial injury separated a tall, triangular fragment radiographically. Histologically, hypertrophic chondrocyte extension from the growth plate into the region of the fracture was a consistent finding. (PRP)

Kleinman PK, Marks SC Jr. Relationship of the subperiosteal bone collar to metaphyseal lesions in abused infants. *J Bone Joint Surg Am.* 1995;77:1471-1476

This study explains the radiographic appearance of Caffey's "corner" and "bucket-handle" fractures in abused infants. (PRP)

Kleinman PK, Marks SC Jr, Nimkin K, Rayder SM, Kessler SC. Rib fractures in 31 abused infants: postmortem radiologic-histopathologic study. *Radiology.* 1996;200:807-810

Eighty-four fractures (51%) involved the ribs. Of these, only 30 (36%) were noted on routine skeletal survey, leading to the conclusion that high-detail skeletal radiography in live and deceased infants is justified. (PRP)

Kleinman PK, Marks SC Jr, Richmond JM, Blackbourne BD. Inflicted skeletal injury: a postmortem radiologic-histopathologic study in 31 infants. *Am J Roentgenol.* 1995; 165:647-650

Thirty-one infants with an average age of 3 months, all of whom died from child abuse, were examined with high-detail skeletal surveys, specimen radiography, and histopathologic analysis. A total of 165 fractures were discovered (excluding skull fractures in 13 cases); a total of 116 (70%) were healing, 36 (22%) were acute, and 13 (8%) were of indeterminate age. At least one healing fracture was found in 29 (93.5%) of the infants. Specimen radiography increased the yield of fractures noted on skeletal survey from 58% to 92%. Eighty-four (51%) were rib fractures, 72 (44%) long bone, 6 (4%) hand and foot, 2 (1%) clavicular, and 1 (< 1%) spinal. Metaphyseal fractures accounted for 64 (89%) of the 72 long bone fractures while the shaft was involved in 8 (11%).

The authors conclude that aggressive radiologic efforts exceeding the routine skeletal survey are justified in living and deceased infants. (PRP)

Leventhal J, Thomas S, Rosenfield N, Markowitz R. Fractures in young children: distinguishing child abuse from unintentional injuries. *Am J Dis Child.* 1993;147:87-92

Pediatric radiologists and child abuse consultants reviewed 253 fractures in 215 patients, aged 0 to 3 years (mean age, 15.7 months), to sort out diagnostic features of fractures due to abuse. Abuse occurred more frequently in boys and in children younger than 12 months of age (39%). Fractures of the rib or humerus were considered more frequently due to abuse, while fractures of the hand, foot, or clavicle were more likely due to unintentional injury. Rib fractures were most strongly associated with abuse. Skull fractures due to abuse were most commonly parietal, as were the unintentional fractures.

Long bone fractures were usually unintentional, except in children younger than 12 months of age (82%). Location is the most important distinguishing factor in humeral fractures. Midshaft or metaphyseal fractures were classified as abuse. Femur fractures as a result of abuse are most common in children, aged 12 months or less.

Falls were frequently alleged to be the cause of injury in abuse cases. Child abuse is a common cause of fractures in young children; skeletal surveys are helpful in diagnosis. (CL/KM)

Specific Fractures and Controversies

Ablin DS, Greenspan A, Reinhart MA. Pelvic injuries in child abuse. *Pediatr Radiol.* **1992; 22:454-457**
Reported pelvic injuries in child abuse are unusual. Two patients had pelvic fractures. One had heterotrophic ossification of the soft tissues of the pelvis and thigh corresponding to extensive bruising in the pubic, genital, buttock, and thigh areas. (PRP)

Anderson WA. The significance of fractures in children. *Ann Emerg Med.* **1982;11:174-177**
This study of 117 patients with fractures included 24 whose fractures were caused by abuse. The 24 included 15 who were younger than a year old, and 4 more younger than 2 years. Among the 117 patients, 5 had more than one fracture, and 41 had associated injuries. The most common cause of fracture was auto-pedestrian accident (n=37), followed by abusive incidents (n=24). Among the 24 abused children, 16 sustained no other injuries, while the remaining 8 patients accounted for 24 additional fractures. The 24 fractures due to abuse were 4 metaphyseal, 4 spiral, 7 transverse, 6 oblique, 2 torus, and 1 neck. The authors also noted the following: no patient with a closed-single femur fracture showed evidence of shock; boys generally predominate in childhood injuries; and single closed fractures are associated with a 1-g drop in hemoglobin and 3.35% drop in hematocrit levels. Tachycardia is a common presenting symptom, while hypotension is seen less often. (CL/KM)

Blakemore LC, Loder RT, Hensinger RN. Role of intentional abuse in children 1 to 5 years old with isolated shaft fractures. *J Pediatr Orthop.* **1996;16:585-588**
In this retrospective study of 42 children (average age, 3 ½ years) with isolated fractures, only one fracture was documented to be nonaccidental, while one other child had a prior history of intentional injury. In 14 (33%) the history was considered suspicious for child abuse, but only 5 of the 42 children had skeletal surveys. Little is documented regarding the medical investigation and questioning, leaving one to wonder about the abuse training of the examiners. The criterion for substantiation of abuse was somewhat unique, requiring confirmation at a legal hearing. The authors' belief that their findings suggest children, aged 1 to 5 years, can sustain femoral shaft fractures from relatively low-energy trauma such as a fall while running appears tenuous. However, their recommendation to clinicians appears appropriate:

> Although our data suggest that the probability of intentional injury as the cause of isolated shaft fracture in children 1 to 5 years of age appears to be low, the clinician should still have a high degree of vigilance and have the circumstances investigated when the history of physical findings are disturbing.

Inappropriate clinical application of this study could result in a failure to protect abused children. (PRP).

dos Santos LM, Stewart G, Meert K, Rosenberg NM. Soft tissue swelling with fractures: abuse versus nonintentional. *Pediatr Emerg Care.* **1995;11:215-216**
Thirty-seven children younger than 11 years of age presenting with long bone fractures were prospectively examined to define the amount of post-fracture swelling and to analyze the difference, if any, between accidental and nonaccidental cases. There was no difference in the reported age of the injury (15.5 Å 24.5 hours in the abuse group vs 14 Å 17.7 hours for the nonabused). After adjusting for injury age, the abuse group was found to have less post-injury swelling than the nonabused group. The authors speculate that the history and/or the timing of the injury may not be reliable in suspected abuse cases. (PRP)

Hobbs CJ. Skull fracture and the diagnosis of abuse. *Arch Dis Child.* **1984;59:246-252**
This discussion of skull fractures provides clues to findings that suggest abuse, and situations that affect the likelihood that the observed injury resulted from a fall. A detailed discussion of

fracture width and coexisting findings that further support nonaccidental trauma as an etiology for injury is presented. Fracture characteristics most common in abused children include multiple or complex configuration; depressed, wide, and growing fracture, involvement of more than one cranial bone; nonparietal fracture; and associated intracranial injury (including subdural hematoma). (JMN/CL)

Kleinman PK, Marks SC. Vertebral body fractures in child abuse: radiologic-histopathologic correlates. *Invest Radiol.* **1992;27:715-722**
Vertebral injuries are rarely reported in child abuse cases. Ten vertebral body fractures were identified in four abused infants and children 7 to 36 months of age, three of whom died from head injuries and one, from abandonment. Three pure vertebral body compression fractures, two superior end-plate fractures without compression deformity, and five anterosuperior end-plate fractures with associated compression deformity are described radiologically and histologically. Vertebral compression was generally mild (<25%). (PRP)

Kleinman PK, Marks SC, Nimkin K, Rayder SM, Kessler SC. Rib fractures in 31 abused infants: post mortem radiologic-histologic study. *Radiology.* **1996;200:807-810**
(See *Thoracic Trauma*)

Kleinman PK, Marks SC, Spevak MR, Richmond JM. Fractures of the rib head in abused infants. *Radiology.* **1992;185:119-123**
Seven abused infants who died with posterior rib fractures were studied. Fifty posterior rib fractures were identified, with 29 involving the rib head. Frontal x-rays clearly revealed injury in 4 (14%) of 29 cases only when periosteal reaction was present. The CT performed in two infants revealed 5 (26%) of 19 of the fractures.

Morphologic features support most fractures being caused by indirect force, a finding consistent with anteroposterior compression during assaults. (PRP)

Mellick LB, Reesor K. Spiral tibial fractures of children: a commonly accidental spiral long bone fracture. *Am J Emerg Med.* **1990;8:234-237**
Both medical and social services professionals have emphasized spiral fractures of the long bones as highly suspicious for child abuse. However, the majority of spiral tibial fractures are due to accidents. The authors review 10 cases (patients aged 9 to 44 months) seen over a 4-month period, and three cases (patients aged 2 to 19 months) from their child abuse reports over the last 5 years. All spiral tibial fractures were due to accidents, except for the 9-month-old and the 2-month-old infants. The authors warn that if the history of injury is compatible with the fracture, the "nature of the fracture" (spiral) is not sufficient reason to assume a nonaccidental etiology. (JMN/CL)

Pergolizzi R Jr, Oestreich AE. Child abuse fracture through physiologic periosteal reaction. *Pediatr Radiol.* **1995;25:566-567**
This article serves as a reminder that acute fractures can occur through the normal diaphyseal periosteal reaction seen in infants. Careful midshaft analysis is required in such cases, with repeat high-detail spot films obtained in selected cases. (PRP)

Strait RT, Siegel RM, Shapiro RA. Humeral fractures without obvious etiologies in children less than 3 years of age: when is it abuse? *Pediatrics.* **1995;96:667-671**
In a retrospective review of 124 children younger than 3 years of age with humeral fractures, abuse was diagnosed in 9 (36%) of 25 children younger than 15 months of age. Supracondylar fractures were considered abusive in 2 (20%) of 10, as were 7 (58%) of 12 spiral/ oblique fractures. In contrast, abuse was considered the cause in only 1 (1%) of 99 of those over 15 months. Of the other cases, 91 (73%) of 124 were considered nonaccidental, and 23 (18.5%) of 124 were indeterminate.

Although this study presents a lower incidence of abuse in children with humeral fractures than in the study of Thomas et al, which follows, one must remember the retrospective nature of the study and the 18.5% "indeterminate" rate. (PRP)

Strouse PJ, Owings CL. **Fractures of the first rib in child abuse.** *Radiology.* 1995; 197:763-765

Rib fractures from nonaccidental trauma were identified in 12 (34%) of 35 children. One neonate with congenital osteogenesis imperfecta had a first-rib fracture. Three others, all abused, had first-rib fracture (one bilaterally). Two additional children were identified from years prior to the study. Of this total of five abused children, first-rib fractures were isolated in four (80%). (PRP)

Thomas SA, Rosenfield NS, Leventhal JM, Markowitz RI. **Long-bone fractures in young children: distinguishing accidental injuries from child abuse.** *Pediatrics.* 1991;88:471-476

This study of 215 children younger than age 3 identified 39 children with either humeral or femoral fractures, 20 of whom were victims of abuse. Among the humeral fractures, 11 of 14 resulted from abuse, and 7 of those 11 children were younger than 1 year of age. All abusive fractures were midshaft, or distal or proximal metaphyseal. They included transverse, oblique, and greenstick. All nonsupracondylar humeral fractures were the result of abuse. These should be treated with suspicion in all children younger than 3 years of age.

Femoral fractures occurred more commonly. Nine of the 25 femoral fractures were due to abuse, 14 were accidental, and the etiology of the remaining 2 fractures could not be determined. Four of the nine abused children had other fractures; six of the nine were younger than 12 months of age. The femoral fractures were metaphyseal, and oblique and horizontal midshaft, with no specific pattern to distinguish them from accidental fractures.

This article points out that both femoral and nonsupracondylar humeral fractures are strongly associated with abuse. The authors consider the force needed to fracture a femur, and the mechanisms of femoral fracture seen in toddlers. They emphasize that the age of the child (young/non-ambulatory) is helpful in distinguishing abuse from accident but that the specific pattern of fracture is not. (CL/KM)

Wellington P, Bennet GC. **Fractures of the femur in childhood.** *Injury.* 1987;18:103-104

This review from Glasgow, Scotland, of 150 femoral fractures incurred between 1979 and 1983 found abuse was suspected or proven in 22% of those younger than age 5 years and 39% of those younger than age 1 year. Abuse was not suspected in the 23 children with high-energy injuries (eg, traffic accidents, falls from upper stories). Witnesses were often available to corroborate accounts of low-energy falls (eg, falls during play, low-speed traffic accidents). When the injuries were not witnessed, history was assessed for "reasonableness," and undue delay in seeking treatment was noted, along with the caretaker's explanation. The authors recommend a radiological skeletal survey for all children younger than 12 months with femoral fractures and all children younger than age 5 years whose histories are inconsistent or who have any signs of unexplained injury or delays in seeking treatment. This research suggests that the body mass of a child younger than 1 year of age will not ordinarily generate sufficient force to fracture a normal bone in a simple low-energy fall, such as that from a couch, crib, or bed. (CL/KM)

Clinical Conditions That Predispose Children to Fractures

Amir DS, Katz K, Grunebaum M, Yosipovich A, Wielunsky E, Reisner SH. **Fractures in premature infants.** *J Pediatr Orthop.* 1988;8:41-44

Decreased bone density is one cause of fractures. This article discusses reasons and risk factors that might predispose a premature infant to easy fractures. Evaluation of the infant's laboratory tests, radiographs, hospital course, and (perhaps) bone mineral content should provide clues and help to eliminate the potential diagnosis of brittle bones secondary to a metabolic condition. (JMN)

Chapman S. Hall CM. **Non-accidental injury or brittle bones.** *Pediatr Radiol.* 1997;27:106-110

and

Ablin DS, Sane SM. **Non-accidental injury: confusion with temporary brittle bone disease and mild osteogenesis imperfecta.** *Pediatr Radiol.* 1997;27:111-113

Copper deficiency, "temporary brittle bone disease," and mild (Type IV) osteogenesis imperfecta have been raised as possible etiologies for otherwise unexplained fractures, particularly in infancy. These two articles together provide an excellent summary and rebuttal.

"Temporary brittle bone disease" due to a temporary collagen defect, possibly due to copper deficiency, has been largely promoted by one author. The diagnoses were largely retrospective. No scientific support has been published, and this entity has not been corroborated by other authors. Furthermore, one author's statements in court have cast doubt on the accuracy of his conclusions.

Copper deficiency complicated by fractures has been reported twenty times in the world literature, and fractures have not been reported as a late sequelae of proven cases.

The same author has proposed that OI subtype IV-A has a higher prevalence than generally accepted. Criticisms of the published review, especially the availability of x-rays in only 17 of 78 patients, are discussed. The estimated incidence of OI type IV is 1:1,000,000 to 1:3,000,000 live births. Guidelines for collagen analysis are included.

Chapman and Hall go on to report that the British courts have sought to define what is acceptable opinion vs untried hypothesis. Untested and unacceptable views should not be put forward—advice American courts should take note of in this age of "pseudo-science" in the courtroom.

Cook SK, Harding AF, Morgan FL, et al. Association of bone mineral density and pediatric fractures. *J Pediatr Orthop.* 1987; 7:424-427

The authors compare recorded measurements of bone mineral density in a group of children with fractures and a group of children without fractures. They found that, in the absence of metabolic disease, decreased bone mineral density was unlikely to play a significant role in acute traumatic pediatric fracture. (JMN)

Dent JA, Paterson CR. Fractures in early childhood: osteogenesis imperfecta or child abuse? *J Pediatr Orthop.* 1991;11:184-186

In children younger than 5 years, 39 with osteogenesis imperfecta (OI) sustained 194 fractures, while 69 normal children had 84 fractures. Spiral and transverse fractures were the most common in the OI group, with metaphyseal fractures accounting for 15%. A specific fracture pattern does not rule out OI. (PRP)

Gahagan S, Rimsza ME. Child abuse or osteogenesis imperfecta: how can we tell? *Pediatrics.* 1991;88:987-991

Three cases of OI initially diagnosed as child abuse are reported. None of the children had osteopenia, and only one had characteristic blue sclera and a family history of OI. In one child, multiple fractures occurred with several different caretakers. The authors point out that a history incompatible with an injury (ie, a fall from a couch), the "hallmark" of abuse, can readily occur in OI. Osteogenesis imperfecta (OI) Types III and IV may not have blue sclera and Type I may not have typical radiographic findings.

The authors recommend biochemical studies if there are no other signs of abuse, the mode of injury appears minor, or there were fractures in different environments. (PRP)

Kleinman PK. Differentiation of child abuse and osteogenesis imperfecta: medical and legal implications. *Am J Radiol.* 1990;154:1047-1048

Paul Kleinman advises that the presence of blue sclera can sort out Types I and II of osteogenesis imperfecta from child abuse. Type III, which has normal sclera, has very severe bone fragility and osteopenia leading to multiple fractures and severe deformity of the long bones and spine, which is progressive. Type IV OI, which is less severe, can be confused with child abuse but is extremely rare and estimated to occur only once in 1 to 3 million births. Family history, wormian bones, dentinogenesis imperfecta, bony deformity, and demineralization are generally present in Type IV. (CL)

Lim HK, Smith WL, Sato Y, Choi J. Congenital syphilis mimicking child abuse. *Pediatr Radiol.* 1995;25:560-561

Steiner RD, Pepin M, Byers PH. Studies of collagen synthesis in the differentiation of child abuse from osteogenesis imperfecta. *J Pediatr.* 1996;128:542-547

Successful collagen studies are reported on 55 samples from suspected abuse cases sent to the authors for analysis. In 48 complete medical histories, none had an unequivocal family history of OI. A "family history" of fractures was noted in 16; 6 (12.5%) of 48 had biochemical evidence of OI. In 5 there were clinical signs of OI on physical examination sufficient to make the diagnosis strongly suspected.

The authors conclude that biochemical analysis should be obtained only when there is uncertainty after radiologic and clinical evaluation. When pathognomonic signs of child abuse are present (retinal hemorrhages, intracranial injury, lacerations, burns, signs of sexual abuse), collagen analysis should not be performed. Furthermore, normal collagen studies do not prove child abuse since normal results do not exclude OI, equivocal results are possible, and children with OI may still be the victim of child abuse. (PRP)

Clues to Assess the Plausibility of Alleged Etiology

Betz P, Liebhardt E. Rib fractures in children—resuscitation or child abuse? *Int J Legal Med.* 1994;106:215-218
Autopsy reports of 233 children between 5 days and 7 years were reviewed. The authors found that 190 (82%) died from natural and 43 (18%) from traumatic causes of death. Cardiopulmonary resuscitation was performed in 94 of the natural causes group. Bilateral rib fractures in the mid-clavicular line were present in 2 (2%). Fractures mainly of the posterior ribs occurred in 15 (35%) of 43 in the traumatic death group. These findings support previous conclusions that ventral fractures can occur in resuscitation efforts. Dorsal fractures remain a strong indication of nonaccidental trauma.

Resuscitation injuries were also caused almost exclusively by physicians, making claims of rib fractures due to panicked untrained resuscitation unlikely. (PRP)

Feldman KW, Brewer DK. Child abuse, cardiopulmonary resuscitation, and rib fractures. *Pediatrics.* 1984;73:339-342
Patients who experience cardiac arrest from injuries obtained through nonaccidental trauma often receive vigorous CPR. It has been argued that rib fractures might have been imparted by resuscitators. These authors point out that children do not ordinarily suffer fractures as a result of CPR, even when administered by someone with limited training. They suggest x-ray clues to distinguish between a rib fracture from abuse and one possibly caused by resuscitative efforts. It is noted that none of the patients resuscitated in this study had fractures attributable to CPR. (JMN)

Other Aspects of Interest

Hobbs CJ, Wynne JM. The sexually abused battered child. *Arch Dis Child.* 1990;65:423-427
This article is provided as a reminder. Evaluation for sexual abuse is often not a priority when confronted by massive trauma. These authors report 130 children with evidence of nonaccidental trauma, neglect, and sexual abuse. They direct attention toward the total involvement of the child in maltreatment, and stress that the trauma of the battered child is often pervasive. Statistics are provided concerning the overlap between sexual and physical abuse. (JMN)

Worlock P, Stower M, Barbor P. Patterns of fractures in accidental and non-accidental injury in children: a comparative study. *BMJ.* 1986;293:100-102
British researchers compared 826 nonabused children younger than age 12 years with 35 abused children younger than age 5 years, all of whom presented with fractures. The authors found that 85% of the nonabused children with fractures were older than 5 years, while 80% of the abused children with fractures were younger than 18 months. The most common inflicted injuries were multiple fractures, soft tissue head and neck injuries, rib fractures without major chest trauma, spiral or oblique fractures of long bones, subperiosteal new bone formation, and spiral fractures of the humeral shaft. (CL/KM)

Acknowledgment

This section and its annotations were prepared by Paul R. Prescott, MD. Selected annotations from the first edition were written by LTC James M. Noel, Jr, MD, Carolyn Levitt, MD, and Kim Martinez, RN, CPNP, MPH. The section was reviewed by Mary Margaret Carrasco, MD, and Lynn Anne Platt, MD.

AMERICAN ACADEMY OF PEDIATRICS

Section on Radiology

Diagnostic Imaging of Child Abuse (RE9204)

The concept of child abuse as a medical entity has its origins in the radiologic studies of the pediatric radiologist Dr John Caffey, as well as many other specialists in the field of diagnostic imaging. When all cases of child abuse and neglect are studied, the incidence of physical alterations documentable by diagnostic imaging is relatively small. However, imaging studies are often critical in the infant and young child with evidence of physical injury, and they also may be the first indication of abuse in a child who is seen initially with an apparent natural illness. As most conventional imaging studies performed in this setting are noninvasive and entail minimal radiation risks, recommendations regarding imaging should focus on examinations, which provide the highest diagnostic yield at acceptable costs.

SKELETAL IMAGING

Although skeletal injuries rarely pose a threat to the life of the abused child, they are the strongest radiologic indicators of abuse. In fact, in the young infant, certain radiologic abnormalities are sufficiently characteristic to allow a firm diagnosis of inflicted injury in the absence of clinical information. This fact mandates that imaging surveys performed to identify skeletal injury be carried out with the same level of technical excellence utilized in examinations routinely performed to evaluate accidental injuries. The "body gram" or abbreviated skeletal surveys have no place in the imaging of these subtle, but highly specific bony abnormalities.

In general, the radiographic skeletal survey is the method of choice for skeletal imaging in cases of suspected abuse. Modern pediatric imaging systems commonly use special film, cassettes, and intensifying screens to minimize exposure. Certain modifications of such low-dose systems are required to provide the necessary contrast and spatial resolution to image the subtle metaphyseal, rib, and other

unusual injuries which frequently elude detection with systems designed for chest and abdominal imaging. Many departments utilize a so-called "extremity" system that provides high detail images at modest increases in exposure. This improvement in image quality is obtained primarily by use of a high-detail film and a slower intensifying screen. Maximal detail results with a single emulsion film and a single intensifying screen. Use of cassettes with specially designed front plates utilizing material which allows more lower energy photons to strike the intensifying screen will provide significant improvement in contrast resolution at a lower radiation exposure. Systems of this type are readily available as a result of the technical developments in the field of mammographic imaging, an area where dose considerations are crucial. Knowledgeable radiologists, physicists, and radiologic technologists should choose systems which will perform well clinically, as well as conform to the practical requirements of individual departments.

Once the appropriate imaging system is chosen, a precise protocol for skeletal imaging must be developed to ensure consistent quality. In routine skeletal imaging, an accepted principle is that films must be coned or restricted to the specific area of interest. It is a common practice to encompass larger regions of the skeleton when skeletal surveys are performed. This results in areas of under- and overexposure, as well as loss of resolution due to geometric distortion and other technical factors. The skeletal survey, therefore, must use anteroposterior views of the arms, forearms, hands, femurs, lower legs, and feet, all on separate exposures. Lateral views of the axial skeleton are obtained, along with the routine frontal views in infancy, because of the occurrence of fractures involving the spine and sternum. Anteroposterior and lateral views of the skull are mandatory even when cranial computed tomography (CT) has been obtained, as fractures occurring in the axial plane may be missed with CT. Studies must be monitored by a radiologist for technical adequacy, as well as be assessed for additional lateral or oblique projections.

The skeletal survey is mandatory in all cases of suspected physical abuse in children less than 2 years of age. A screening skeletal survey beyond 5 years of age has little value. Patients in the 2-year to 5-year age group must be handled individually, based on the specific clinical indicators of abuse. At any age, when clinical findings point to a specific site of injury, the customary protocol for imaging that region should be used. Application of these guidelines to selected cases of neglect and sexual abuse is appropriate when associated physical maltreatment is suspected.

Radionuclide bone scans, when they are performed by experienced pediatric radiologists in large centers, may offer an alternative to radiography. Clearly, skeletal scintigraphy provides increased sensitivity for rib fractures, subtle shaft fractures, and areas of early periosteal elevation. However, data are limited regarding the sensitivity of scintigraphy for the metaphyseal fractures, particularly when they are bilateral, as well as for subtle injuries of the spine, features which carry a high specificity in young infants. Thus, although skeletal scintigraphy plays an important supplementary role to the radiologic skeletal survey, use of this modality as a primary tool should be exercised with extreme caution. Follow-up imaging studies in 1 to 2 weeks may be useful in selected cases, when initial studies are normal or equivocal, or when a repeat study may provide further evidence to allow more precise determination of the age of individual fractures.

INTRACRANIAL INJURY

All infants and children with suspected intracranial injury must undergo cranial CT and/or magnetic resonance imaging (MRI). Although ultrasonography may reveal intracranial abnormalities, it is inadequate to exclude or to evaluate fully intracranial injury. In cases of suspected acute central nervous system pathology, studies are designed to identify treatable conditions. Computed tomography is generally sufficient in this context. However, preliminary studies indicate that MRI is substantially more sensitive than CT in identifying and characterizing most intracranial sequelae of abusive assaults. Subdural hematomas, particularly over the convexities, cortical contusions, cerebral edema, and white matter injuries are well depicted with MRI. Only subarachnoid hemorrhage appears to be detected better with CT. Furthermore, MRI provides better characterization of the age of areas of hemorrhage than does CT. For this reason, MRI should be performed early in all cases of suspected intracranial injury when clinical findings are not explained adequately by CT. A strong argument can be made for a follow-up in all cases of suspected intracranial injury to better characterize the extent of parenchymal injury and to predict clinical outcome. In cases exhibiting chronic central nervous system alterations, and in infants with evidence of the shaken infant syndrome but no clinical evidence of central nervous system injury, MRI should be performed. As MRI becomes more available to the critically ill child, greater application of this elegant imaging modality can be expected.

THORACOABDOMINAL TRAUMA

Major blunt and penetrating thoracoabdominal injury is uncommon in the young infant; thus, imaging strategies are the most critical in the toddler and older child. In the massively traumatized patient, protocols similar to those used for accidental injury apply. Initial roentgenograms in the emergency department include a chest roentgenogram to evaluate for flail chest, pneumothorax, pleural effusion, and pulmonary parenchymal injury. Abdominal roentgenograms are insensitive indicators of solid visceral injury, but they will show gross pelvic fractures. It is prudent to obtain a lateral cervical spine roentgenogram before further diagnostic studies are performed. Once the patient is stabilized, CT is indicated. Computed tomography is the most effective and sensitive imaging technique to identify injuries of the lungs, pleura, and solid abdominal organs. Hollow visceral injury may be detected by the presence of small amounts of intraperitoneal air, as well as intramural and mesenteric blood. In particular, pancreatic injury and duodenal hematomas, two characteristic findings in abused children, are assessed well with CT. In children less than 1 year of age, ultrasonography may be a reasonable preliminary study to perform if abdominal injury is suspected.

In the child exhibiting lesser signs of injury, or a constellation of nonspecific abdominal signs and symptoms that cannot be explained by the history or a unifying diagnosis, ultrasonography is an acceptable initial procedure. Occult duodenal hematomas, pancreatic injury, and renal injuries are studied reasonably with ultrasonography. The diagnosis of duodenal hematoma, particularly if chronic, may be difficult with ultrasonography or CT. On occasion, an upper gastrointestinal tract series may be required to delineate the injury. Radionuclide scintigraphy plays a relatively small role in visceral injury, but it is of value in cases of renal contusion and myoglobinuria.

To obtain the most thorough diagnostic imaging assessment, caretakers accompanying children to the Radiology Department must receive advance preparation. Achievement of adequate studies in young children requires restraint and, in cases of skeletal surveys, numerous exposures. Excessive apprehension, hostility, and resistance usually will result in inadequate examinations. Therefore, caretakers should be handled by personnel in a professional and nonjudgmental manner. Questions regarding indications for the study as well as results should be directed to the referring physician. Imaging examinations must be viewed in the clinical context, and the implications of the examinations are best addressed by physicians and other health care workers familiar with the family and skilled in these sensitive interactions.

SECTION ON RADIOLOGY EXECUTIVE
COMMITTEE, 1990–1991
Jack O. Haller, MD, Chair
Paul K. Kleinman, MD, Editor
David F. Merten, MD, Editor
Harris L. Cohen, MD
Mervyn D. Cohen, MD
Patricia W. Hayden, MD
Marc Keller, MD
Richard Towbin, MD
Shashikant M. Sane, MD

REFERENCES

1. Ball WS Jr. Nonaccidental craniocerebral trauma (child abuse): MR imaging. *Radiology.* 1989;173:609–610
2. Caffey J. Multiple fractures in the long bones of infants suffering from chronic subdural hematoma. *AJR.* 1946;56:163–173
3. Kempe CH, Silverman FN, Steele BF, Droegemueller W, Silver HK. The battered-child syndrome. *JAMA.* 1962;181:17–24. Landmark Article
4. Kleinman PK. *Diagnostic Imaging of Child Abuse.* Baltimore: Williams & Wilkins; 1987
5. Kleinman PK, Blackbourne BD, Marks, SC, Karellas A, Belanger PL. Radiologic contributions to the investigation and prosecution of cases of fatal infant abuse. *N Engl J Med.* 1989;320:507–511
6. Kleinman PK, Marks SC, Blackbourne BD. The metaphyseal lesion in the abused child: A radiological-histopathologic study. *AJR.* 1986;146:895–905
7. Merten DF, Radkowski MA, Leonidas JC. The abused child: a radiological reappraisal. *Radiology.* 1983;146:377–381
8. Merten DF, Radkowski MA, Leonidas JC. Craniocerebral trauma in the child abuse syndrome: radiological observations. *Pediatr Radiol.* 1984;14:272–277
9. Sato Y, Yuh WTC, Smith WL, Alexander RC, Kao SCS, Ellerbroek CJ. Head injury in child abuse: evaluation with MR imaging. *Radiology.* 1989;173:653–657
10. Silverman FN. Unrecognized trauma in infants, the battered child syndrome, and the syndrome of Abroise Tardieu: Rigler lecture. *Radiology.* 1973;104:337–353
11. Sinal SH, Ball MR. Head trauma due to child abuse: serial computerized tomography in diagnosis and management. *South Med J.* 1987;80:1505–1512
12. Sivit CJ, Taylor GA, Eichelberger MR. Visceral injury in battered children: a changing perspective. *Radiology.* 1989;173:659–661
13. Sty JR, Starshak RJ. The role of bone scintigraphy in the evaluation of the suspected abused child. *Radiology.* 1983;146:369
14. Trefler M. Radiation exposure reduction using carbon fiber. *Radiology.* 1982;142:751–754

Head Injuries

See Also:
Falls
Fractures
Retinal Hemorrhages
Shaken Impact/Shaken Baby Syndrome

Child abuse must be considered the most likely diagnosis whenever there is:

▼ Infant intracranial injury, including subdural hematoma, in the absence of significant corroborated accidental trauma

▼ Multiple or complex skull fractures

▼ Involvement of more than one cranial bone

▼ Nonparietal, nonlinear skull fracture

▼ Depressed, wide, and "growing" cranial fractures in very small children

Other Comments

▼ Child abuse is the most common cause of serious head injury in children younger than 1 year of age.

▼ Perpetrators of pediatric abusive head trauma are more often males.

▼ Except for epidural hemorrhage, indoor accidental cranial impacts (eg, simple falls) rarely cause severe or fatal intracranial injury in infants.

▼ Epidural hemorrhage is not a specific indicator of inflicted pediatric cranial trauma.

▼ *Primary* brain injuries are those brain injuries that occur at the moment of injury. *Secondary* brain injuries result primarily from complicating hypoxia-ischemia, manifesting as cerebral edema.

▼ Primary and/or secondary brain injuries in shaken impact syndrome can be classified further as focal and/or diffuse.

▼ Primary diffuse brain injuries are associated with immediate loss of consciousness and/or apnea. Therefore, specific evidence of primary diffuse brain injury may provide an indication of the timing of cranial injury. Examples of primary diffuse brain injury include concussion and diffuse axonal injury associated with prolonged traumatic coma.

▼ Computed tomography (CT) appears to be the method of choice for initial evaluation of acute head injury when abuse is suspected.

▼ Magnetic resonance imaging (MRI) offers advantages in diagnosis of subacute and chronic head injuries, focal parenchymal lesions, and whenever clinical symptoms do not fit the CT findings.

Bibliography

General

Billmire ME, Myers PA. Serious head injury in young infants: accidents or abuse? *Pediatrics.* **1985;75:340-342**
This study reports on 84 children younger than 1 year old admitted to the University of Cincinnati Children's Hospital over a 2-year period with the diagnosis of head injury or abnormal findings on CT scan. Age range was 3 weeks to 11 months (mean age, 4.6 months). Accidental injuries were identified in 54 of 84 (mean age, 5 months). Injuries from abuse were identified in 30 of 84 (mean age, 4 months).

Accidental etiology was diagnosed when events were witnessed and there were no discrepancies between mechanism described and physical findings. Most resulted from falls or car accidents. In most accidental cases (40/54), a simple skull fracture was the sole injury.

Criteria for diagnosis of abuse included caretaker confession (10/30); multiple injuries (12/30); inadequate explanation for injuries (6/30); and serious discrepancy between history and physical findings (2/30). Characteristic injuries attributed to abuse were complex, depressed, or diastatic fractures and retinal hemorrhages. Associated characteristics included metaphyseal fractures and failure to thrive. Intracranial bleeding was due to abuse in 11 of 12 cases; 3 of the 3 with other intracranial injury were abused. All 4 with both skull fracture and intracranial bleeding were abused.

Accidental trauma rarely causes severe intracranial injury in infants. When uncomplicated skull fractures were excluded, 64% of all head injuries and 95% of serious or life-threatening head injuries were attributed to child abuse. The remaining 5% of cases in this study refers to a single patient with intracranial injury who had been unrestrained in a motor vehicle collision. Authors conclude that intracranial injury in infants (in the absence of significant accidental trauma such as a car accident) constitutes grounds for an official child abuse investigation. Physicians are encouraged to avoid delays in reporting while ruling out less likely, but more "acceptable," diagnoses. Child abuse is the most common cause of serious head injury in children younger than 1 year of age. (CL/KM/KH)

Duhaime AC, Alario AJ, Lewander WJ, et al. Head injury in very young children: mechanisms, injury types, and ophthalmologic findings in 100 hospitalized patients younger than 2 years of age. *Pediatrics.* **1992;90:179-185**
This is a prospective study of 100 children younger than 24 months admitted consecutively to three different hospitals with the diagnosis of head injury. The mechanism of injury, injury type, and associated injuries were documented. Criteria were set up for judging fall heights; a biomechanical profile and an algorithm were utilized in determining whether the head injury was presumptive inflicted vs suspicious for inflicted injury. All the children underwent a fundoscopic examination, and a detailed physical examination by a pediatrician, neurosurgeon, and, frequently, a trauma surgeon.

The mean age of the children studied was 9 months, with a range of 11 days to 24 months. There were 73 reported falls, 9 motor vehicle accidents, 14 patients with no history, 2 patients with admitted assaults, and 2 with impact by moving objects. Twenty-four patients were classified as having inflicted injuries. The reported histories in this group of 24 were a fall less than 4 feet in 8 patients, admitted assault in 2 patients, and no histories in 14 patients. Thirteen of these patients had subdural hemorrhages; 5 of the 13 also had skull fractures. Nine of the 24 had acute long bone fractures or healing fractures.

Retinal hemorrhages were found in 10 patients; 9 of the 10 were inflicted injuries (P<.0005). Seven of the 9 patients with inflicted injury, retinal hemorrhages, and subdural hemorrhages had seizures as part of their acute presentation. There were 4 deaths in the overall study, 3 of these as the result of inflicted injury.

The authors conclude that the results of this study confirm the notion that simple falls from low heights rarely, if ever, result in significant primary brain injury. It also confirms the observation that greater biomechanical forces produce more significant injuries. However, there were three epidural hematomas due to short falls. Subdural hematomas were found only in 3 of 76 and diffuse subarachnoid hemorrhage in 2 accidental injuries, all due to motor vehicle accidents, and in 16 of the 24 children abused in this study.

Retinal hemorrhages were overrepresented in nonaccidental cases (9 out of 24, P<.000002). The only retinal hemorrhage that was seen in the accidental group was the result of a motor vehicle accident. An additional three retinal hemorrhages were found, due to accidents, after the study was completed. They consisted of a motor vehicle accident, a 3-story fall that was fatal, and a fall down the stairs in a walker. It is important to note that 24% of all the admissions for head injury in this series were the result of inflicted trauma. (CL/KM)

Duhaime AC, Eppley M, Margulies S, Heher KL, Bartlett SP. Crush injuries to the head of children. *Neurosurgery.* **1995;37:401-406**

Hiss J, Kahana T. The medicolegal implications of bilateral cranial fractures in infants. *J Trauma.* **1995;38:32-34**

Hobbs CJ. Skull fracture and the diagnosis of child abuse. *Arch Dis Child.* **1984;59:246-252**
This account relates a study of 89 children with skull fractures seen at St James Hospital in Leeds, England. All were younger than 2 years of age. In total, 29 of 89 were diagnosed as abused; 19 of 20 deaths were among the abused children. The parietal was the most commonly fractured bone in both abused and accidental cases. Fracture characteristics most common in abused children include multiple or complex configuration; depressed, wide, and growing fracture; involvement of more than one cranial bone; nonparietal

fracture; and associated intracranial injury (including subdural hematoma). Accidental fracture characteristics include single, narrow, linear fractures, most commonly of the parietal bone with no associated intracranial injury.

In three children (one abused, one with abuse suspected, one involved in an accident), there were bilateral and symmetrical fractures in both parietal bones. Bilateral linear fractures are not easily assessed; they cannot be considered certain evidence of abuse but should be evaluated very carefully. A multiple or complex fracture configuration points strongly in favor of abuse. "Growing" fractures are almost unknown in the first few years of life. The exact mechanism is not completely understood. In this study, fractures more than 5 mm wide were considered to be growing. Dural tear and underlying cerebral injury are antecedents of growing fractures.

The authors strongly recommend measurement of maximum fracture width as an indicator of abuse; all accidents produced fractures less than 3 mm in width. The two most important corroborative facts in diagnosis of abuse were multiple injuries and inadequate explanation for the injuries. This study also confirms the important connection between subdural hematoma and abuse. The absence of a single case of subdural hematoma due to accident is remarkable. (CL/KM)

Hymel KP, Abshire TC, Luckey DW, Jenny C. Coagulopathy in pediatric abusive head trauma. *Pediatrics.* **1997;99:371-375**
The objectives of this study were to assess the frequency of coagulation defects in pediatric abusive head trauma and to analyze their relationship to parenchymal brain damage. Of 265 records retrospectively reviewed, 147 met study inclusion criteria: (1) radiologic evidence of head trauma, (2) multidisciplinary validation that head trauma had been inflicted, and (3) coagulation screening performed within 2 days of clinical presentation. Using nonparametric analysis, initial coagulation test results were compared between study patients *without* parenchymal brain damage and those *with* parenchymal brain damage.

Mild prothrombin time (PT) prolongations (median, 13.1) occurred in 54% of study patients *with* parenchymal brain damage and only 20%

of study patients *without* parenchymal brain damage. Among pediatric abusive head trauma patients with parenchymal brain damage *who died,* 94% displayed PT prolongations (median, 16.3) and 63% manifested evidence of activated coagulation.

The authors concluded that PT prolongation and activated coagulation are common complications of pediatric abusive head trauma. In the presence of parenchymal brain damage, it is highly unlikely that these coagulation abnormalities reflect a preexisting hemorrhagic diathesis. These conclusions have diagnostic, prognostic, and legal significance. (KH)

Levitt CJ, Smith WL, Alexander RC. Abusive head trauma: In Reece RM, ed. *Child Abuse: Medical Diagnosis and Management.* **Malvern, PA: Lea & Febiger; 1994:1-22**
This excellent overview on abusive head trauma is the first chapter within an exceptional text on child abuse medical issues. Three highly experienced child abuse clinicians present a thorough review of etiology, mechanisms, incidence, predisposing factors, diagnosis, differential diagnosis, management considerations, timing of injuries, outcome, and prognosis. Three case histories illustrate important diagnostic principles. (KH)

Ommaya AK. Head injury mechanisms and the concept of preventive management: a review and critical synthesis. In: Bandak FA, Eppinger RH, Ommaya AK (eds). *Traumatic Brain Injury Bioscience and Mechanics.* **Larchmont, NY: Mary Ann Liebert Inc; 1996:19-38**
This manuscript is the seminal paper of an extraordinary current text on traumatic head injury research. Ommaya provides a synthesis and conceptual integration of head injury research across four disciplines: epidemiological, biomechanical, basic neuroscientific, and clinicopathologic/therapeutic. Recognizing the need for interdisciplinary communication, Ommaya reviews head injury research activity scanning four decades, providing the "big picture" perspective. In depth and in breadth, Ommaya allows us to "catch up" with global head injury research endeavors of other disciplines. A detailed bibliography is provided for further in-depth reading. (KH)

Shugerman RP, Paez A, Grossman DC, Feldman K, Grady MS. Epidural hemorrhage: is it abuse? *Pediatrics.* 1996;97:664-668

The authors sought to determine whether children presenting with epidural hemorrhage (EDH) are as likely to have been abused as are children presenting with subdural hemorrhage (SDH). Cases of children younger than age 3 years presenting with EDH or SDH at two medical centers in Seattle, WA (n=94), were retrospectively reviewed for accidental vs inflicted injury, demographics, and associated injuries.

Results revealed that only 6% of children with EDH had been abused, compared with 47% of children with SDH. Employing a biomechanical description, the authors explained why their study revealed (1) EDH was frequently associated with simple and complex skull fractures and (2) SDH was frequently associated with long bone or rib fractures, patterned bruising, retinal hemorrhage, and/or parenchymal brain injury. The authors concluded, "EDH should not, in isolation, raise the same level of concern regarding abuse that is raised by the identification of a SDH." (KH)

Starling S, Holden JR, Jenny C. Abusive head trauma: the relationship of perpetrators to their victims. *Pediatrics.* 1995;95(2):259-262

One hundred fifty-one cases of pediatric abusive head trauma over a 12-year period were examined retrospectively for information regarding the perpetrator. Perpetrators included father (37%), mother's boyfriend (20.5%), female baby-sitter (17.3%), and mother (12.6%). Overall, 60% of the abusive head trauma was committed by males. The authors pointed out that female baby-sitters had not been previously recognized to be a significant perpetrator risk group. (KH)

William KY, Bank DE, Senac M, Chadwick DL. Restricting the time of injury in fatal inflicted head injuries. *Child Abuse Negl.* 1997;21:929-940

The study objective was to determine the clinical progression of fatal head injuries in children. Ninety-five cases of accidental fatal closed head injury involving children 16 years old or younger comprised the final study sample (mean age 8.5 years; range 99 days to 16.2 years). Fatal injury mechanisms in all but 2 of these 95 study cases involved a motor vehicle. For each case, the authors collected data on injury circumstances and mechanisms, detailed clinical information (including Glasgow Coma Scale score at the scene of injury), CT neuroimaging results, and autopsy findings. Despite the small sample size, retrospective design, and "older" patient sample (compared to fatal abusive head trauma cases), the conclusions of this study are highly relevant for child abuse clinicians.

The vast majority of children who die from fatal accidental blunt cranial trauma demonstrate immediate and significant changes (89.9% had Glasgow Coma Scale score <8 and 67.1% had fixed and/or dilated pupils at the scene of injury). The authors concluded: (1) fatal head injury that does not involve an epidural hemorrhage must have occurred after the last known time the child exhibited age-appropriate normal behavior, and (2) a delay in presentation to a medical facility after a fatal closed head injury suggests the need to investigate inflicted trauma rather than an indication that the child was asymptomatic for a period of time after the fatal head injury event. (KH)

Neuroimaging

Aoki N. Extracerebral fluid collections in infancy: role of magnetic resonance imaging in differentiation between subdural effusion and subarachnoid space enlargement. *J Neurosurg.* 1994;81:20-23

Berryhill P, Lilly MA, Levin HS, et al. Frontal lobe changes after severe diffuse closed head injury in children: a volumetric study of magnetic resonance imaging. *Neurosurgery.* 1995;37:392-399

Feldman KW, Brewer DK, Shaw DW. Evolution of the cranial computed tomography scan in child abuse. *Child Abuse Negl.* 1995;19:307-313

Hymel KP, Rumack CM, Hay TC, Strain JD, Jenny C. Comparison of intracranial computed tomographic (CT) findings in pediatric abusive and accidental head trauma. *Pediatr Radiol.* 1997;27:743-747

Study objectives were: (1) to compare the frequencies of six specific intracranial CT abnormalities in accidental and nonaccidental pediatric head trauma, and (2) to assess interobserver agreement regarding these CT findings. Three pediatric radiologists blindly and independently reviewed cranial CT scans of patients 4 years of age or younger who had sustained closed head trauma. Study cases included 39 patients with nonaccidental closed head trauma and 39 with inflicted cranial injuries.

The study revealed that interobserver agreement between pediatric radiologists was greater than 80% for all lesions evaluated, with the exception of frontal-parietal shearing tears (68%). Interhemispheric falx hemorrhage, subdural hemorrhage, large (nonacute) extra-axial fluid, and basal ganglia edema were discovered significantly more frequently in the nonaccidental trauma patient group. ($P<.05$). Though not statistically significant, all three cases of posterior fossa hemorrhage occurred in the inflicted head trauma group. (KH)

Sato Y, Yuh WTC, Smith WL, Alexander RC, Kao S, Ellerbroek CJ. Head injury in child abuse: evaluation with MR imaging. *Pediatr Radiol.* **1989;173:653-657**
This study of 30 physically abused infants and children identified 10% with significant head trauma. Both computed tomography (CT) and magnetic resonance (MR) imaging exams were administered for 19 of these 30 children. The age range was 3 weeks to 4 years; 79% were younger than 1 year of age.

The MR imaging was found to be a superior diagnostic method for subdural hematomas (15 cases); cortical contusions (6 cases); shearing injuries (5 cases); and for subacute or chronic head injuries. In acute subarachnoid hemorrhage, CT was more helpful. The authors note that when CT is used to assess chronic subdural hematomas associated with ventricular dilatation, it is difficult to distinguish the chronic subdural hematoma from cerebral atrophy. The authors recommend CT for initial evaluation of acute head injury in suspected abuse victims and MR imaging for subacute or chronic head injury or when the clinical symptoms are disproportionate to the CT findings. (CL/KM)

Sinal SH, Ball MR. Head trauma due to child abuse: serial computerized tomography in diagnosis and management. *South Med J.* **1987;80:1505-1512**
The authors reviewed clinical features and CT scans for 24 children who had acute head trauma as a result of child abuse. All but one child was younger than 1 year old. Whiplash shaken infant syndrome was diagnosed in 17. Serial CT, done in 50% of the cases, was found to be useful for medical, legal, and social aspects and in predicting neurologic outcome. Three children died, and 12 more suffered serious neurologic sequelae. The other five children demonstrated lesser degrees of deficit: three were neurologically normal on follow-up visits, and one was lost to follow-up. Two siblings of these children died of child abuse, which indicates the necessity of continuing intervention to prevent further abuse. (LRR)

Acknowledgments

This section and its annotations were prepared by Kent Hymel, MD. Selected annotations from the first edition were written by Carolyn Levitt, MD, Lawrence R. Ricci, MD, and Kim Martinez, RN, CPNP, MPH.

Homicide and Child Fatality Review Teams

See Also:
Abdominal Blunt Trauma
Head Injuries
Munchausen Syndrome by Proxy
Poisoning as Child Abuse
Two AAP Statements, *Investigation and Review of Unexpected Infant and Child Deaths*
   and *Distinguishing Sudden Infant Death Syndrome From Child Abuse Fatalities*

Clinical Principles

▼ The most vulnerable children are those younger than 2 years, born into poverty, with young or single parents. Blunt trauma is the most common mechanism of injury in abuse-related homicides.

▼ Only one out of seven child abuse fatalities may be recorded as such on death certificates.

▼ Child fatality review teams are now present in nearly every state. There are significant differences, however, in the missions, methods, jurisdictions, and products of these teams.

Bibliography

General

Christoffel KK. Child abuse fatalities. In: Ludwig S, Kornberg AE, eds. *Child Abuse: A Medical Reference.* **New York, NY: Churchill Livingston; 1992**
Homicide is among the 10 leading causes of death for children in all age groups under age 20 years. Approximately one fourth of these deaths affect children younger than 5 years old.

The possibility of abuse or neglect should be considered when a child from a group in which abuse is more prevalent dies or nearly dies. For children who are younger than 2 years of age, in urban areas, from poor families, with an unrelated man in the house, information must be collected to rule out abuse as a cause of death. In all cases, this is done most convincingly by establishing a nontraumatic cause of death.

Similarly, it is often difficult to ascertain whether a child who presents with a history of repeated apnea episodes has a medical disorder or is being repeatedly smothered. Appropriate testing before death, and review of medical records after death, should identify fatal causes of medical apnea. Environmental hazard apneas occur when a child is left in a situation that causes asphyxiation, such as an unsafe crib. In Munchausen syndrome by proxy apneas, disturbed parents smother their infants to obtain medical attention for themselves. The author notes that reports of recurrent sudden infant death syndrome (SIDS) in siblings of apnea patients must be viewed with great suspicion.

Other causes of apnea include child abuse asphyxiation, when an angry parent attempts to quiet a crying child. When there is other evidence of abuse, such as broken bones, child abuse asphyxiation is managed like any other kind of abuse. If there is no such evidence, extensive medical testing may be required to rule out medical causes. Elimination of apnea episodes in the hospital and in foster care, the access of the caretaker to the child having been restricted, would implicate some factor at home.

Information useful for determining whether death is due to child abuse or neglect is as follows:

1. Autopsy
2. Social work interview
3. Review of medical records
4. Skeletal survey
5. Police information on death
6. Previous child protection information on the family
7. Death scene investigation
8. Paramedic run sheets
9. Perinatal history

Multidisciplinary assessment, necessary to collect sufficient information, is almost always better than assessment by a single discipline. (JJ)

Durfee MJ, Gellert GA, Tilton–Durfee D. Origins and clinical relevance of child death review teams. *JAMA.* 1992;267:3172-3175

The incidence of fatal child abuse is difficult to estimate. Available statistics reflect varied levels of competence in detection, evaluation, and recording of child deaths, as well as variation in definitions used by different agencies. Estimates range from "over 1,000" to about 2,000 children annually.

Most suspicious child deaths occur among very young children. Studies of fatal child abuse indicate that 50% of the victims are younger than 1 year of age. The perpetrator is commonly a caretaker, and the death may be a result of neglect. These factors require a special approach to child death investigations and interagency communications.

Multi-agency child death review teams can improve the identification of suspicious deaths, lend greater clarity and coherence to case management, and help define intra-agency and inter-agency problems. They also increase the capability for criminal, civil, and social intervention, including intervention to protect siblings at risk.

The teams commonly include representatives from the coroner/medical examiner's office, law enforcement agencies, prosecuting attorneys, child protective services, pediatricians with child abuse expertise, and other health professionals. Teams may function at the state and/or local jurisdictional level. Many teams have expanded the focus on child maltreatment to address all coroners' cases, including suicide, accidental deaths, and natural deaths. The trend is toward establishing both local and state teams and, ultimately, building a national network. (JJ)

Monteleone JA. Review process. In: Monteleone JA, Brodeur AE, eds. *Child Maltreatment: A Clinical Guide and Reference.* St Louis, MO: GW Medical Publishing Inc; 1994:310-385

This chapter presents detailed summaries of several reports and studies of fatal child abuse, with particular emphasis on studies in Missouri leading to that state's Child Fatality Review Project. (Some of the Missouri efforts to document underreporting of child abuse maltreatment are also covered in Ewigman et al, *Pediatrics.*

1993;91:330-337.) The Missouri program established multidisciplinary and multijurisdictional investigations designed not only to improve the accuracy in reporting causes but also to provide comprehensive suggestions on methods of preventing child deaths and severe injuries. Strategies have included development of a comprehensive data collection system, multidisciplinary training, and production of protocols and checklists for on-scene use. Results have included a near-doubling of deaths attributed to abuse and neglect, more appropriate autopsies, and improved public and professional awareness of factors contributing to child deaths.

A selection of "basic investigation protocols" included with the chapter will be useful to most state and local teams. Materials include:

– serious crime/event scene checklist
– scene investigation checklists: infants, children 1 to 14 years of age
– roles and responsibilities for joint investigations
– basic interviewing techniques
– basic scene photography, sketching, and note taking
– case summary checklists

Risk Factors

McClain PW, Sacks JJ, Froehlke RG, Ewigman BG. Estimates of fatal child abuse and neglect, United States, 1979 through 1988. *Pediatrics.* 1993;91:338-343

This provocative report used information from Missouri studies of deaths of children younger than 5 years and from the FBI Uniform Crime Reporting system to generate synthetic estimates of abuse-related child deaths. The authors note that without a history of physical battering or a finding of criminal neglect or abandonment, death of an infant who was intentionally stabbed by a parent would not be coded as abuse-related, nor would there be a notation of the perpetrator. In the more general circumstances where the certifier is unsure, unaware, or concerned about recriminations, child abuse deaths will tend to be categorized as due to other causes or to undetermined ones.

The authors used the Missouri and national data to estimate the proportion of homicide, undetermined, unintended, natural, and sudden infant deaths that were instead due to child abuse. Overall, this study suggests only about 1 in 7 child abuse deaths are recorded as such on death certificates. By the authors' methodology, child abuse and neglect death rates did not increase over the decade. Children younger than 5 years make up 90% of child abuse fatalities; about 40% of the fatalities occur among infants.

Schlosser P, Pierpont J, Poertner J. Active surveillance of child abuse fatalities. *Child Abuse Negl.* 1992;16:3-10

Birth and death certificates were correlated with information in the Kansas Child Abuse and Neglect Registry on 104 abuse-related fatalities. Significant findings included (1) a very young age of parents at first pregnancy; (2) a high rate of single parenthood; (3) significantly lower educational achievement among victims' mothers; (4) late and inadequate prenatal care; (5) complications during pregnancy; and (6) low birth weight among victims. Children younger than age 2 years made up 85% of the victims; more than 65% were younger than 1 year old.

This study of child abuse fatalities also demonstrates the value of active surveillance efforts, which go beyond the passive receipt of reports. An assessment of the characteristics of child abuse victims and perpetrators provides information that can be used to guide prevention-oriented policies and programs and monitor their success. (JJ)

Diagnosis

Hicks RA, Gaughan DC. Understanding fatal child abuse. *Child Abuse Negl.* 1995; 19:855-863.

This paper emphasizes the role of subdural hemorrhage due to blunt trauma or shaking with impact in the deaths of a dozen physically abused children who ranged in age from neonates to not quite 3 years old. It reinforces and adds to a series of cited studies generally describing fatally abused children as young, poor, and unknown to child protective services, with the method of injury typically being blunt trauma inflicted by a parent in the home.

The authors identified 14 fatalities as due to abuse (12) or neglect (2), representing about 4%

of child deaths at Children's Medical Center in Dayton, OH, from 1988 through 1992. Nine additional fatalities were excluded, although the very brief histories and clinical/autopsy findings place some of these in what Richard Krugman, in an accompanying editorial, called a "gray" area: "not enough information to be certain that abuse occurred, but too much not to worry." Only 2 of the 14 had prior involvement with child protective services, although sibling abuse was noted in additional cases, and only 2 had histories of prior injury. However, 3 of 12 physically abused victims had findings supporting past shaking injury.

All physical abuse fatalities showed soft tissue head injury, and acute subdural hemorrhage was the most common brain injury (9/12). The authors refer to the debate as to whether violent shaking by itself (without impact) can produce injuries of shaken infant syndrome, noting that in all of their (fatal) cases there was at least autopsy evidence of soft tissue head injury, presumably from impact.

Meadow R. Suffocation, recurrent apnea, and sudden infant death. *J Pediatr.* 1990; 117:351-357

The author reviewed records of 27 young children who were suffocated by their mothers. Nine of the children had died; of the 18 living children, 1 had severe brain damage. Repetitive suffocation usually began between ages 1 and 3 months and continued until it was discovered or the child died 6 to 12 months later. The 27 children had 15 living older siblings and 18 others who had died suddenly and unexpectedly in early life. Among the 18 siblings who had died, 13 had recurrent apnea, cyanosis, or seizures, and the cause of death in most was recorded as sudden infant death syndrome (SIDS).

In most of the children, suffocation was suspected because no satisfactory cause was found for the apnea. In some cases, it was the ill-explained deaths of previous siblings that provoked suspicion. Suffocation, even when it results in death, may leave no incriminating findings on physical examination or autopsy. The diagnosis sometimes can be made with covert video recording.

The features of suffocation were compared with the usual features of SIDS. Suffocation was associated with previous apnea in 90% of cases but in less than 10% of SIDS cases. A previous unexplained disorder was associated with 44% of suffocation cases but with less than 5% of SIDS cases. Less than 15% of SIDS victims, but 55% of suffocation victims, were more than 6 months old. Finally, 48% of suffocated babies had siblings who had died, compared with 2% of the SIDS babies.

Distinguishing suffocation from SIDS can be difficult. The author believes that recurrent apnea in a previously healthy child without viral infection or cardiac, respiratory, metabolic, or neurologic abnormality is rare.

Finally, the author contrasts suffocation with a typical presentation of Munchausen syndrome by proxy. In suffocation, some deaths resulted from a single act, and direct harm to the child occurred. Also in suffocation some mothers admitted that although they knew at the time it was not necessary to suffocate the child in order to attract a physician's attention, they felt hatred for their child. (JJ)

Reece RM. Fatal child abuse and sudden infant death syndrome: a critical diagnostic decision. *Pediatrics.* 1993;91:423-429

In 1989 the National Institute of Child Health and Human Development promulgated the following definition of SIDS: "The sudden death of an infant under one year of age which remains unexplained after the performance of a complete postmortem investigation, including an autopsy, an examination of the scene of death and review of the case history."

Thus distinguishing SIDS from fatal child abuse involves an examining physician, radiologist, pathologist, child protective services worker, and others. *Criteria to distinguish SIDS from fatal child abuse and other medical conditions are provided in the Table on the next page.*

The author's recommendations for evaluation of these complex cases include the following steps:

- Accurate history-taking by emergency responders and medical personnel at the time of death
- Examination of the dead infant at a hospital emergency department
- Protocol postmortem examinations within 24 hours of death, including toxicology and metabolic screening where appropriate
- Prompt death scene investigation by knowledgeable individuals, including careful interviews of the household members

- Collection of previous medical records from all sources of medical care and interviews of key medical providers
- Detailed collection of medical history from caretakers
- Locally based infant death review teams to review the collected data (JJ)

Southall DP, Plunkett MCB, Banks MW, Falkov AF, Samuels MP. Covert video recordings of life-threatening child abuse: lessons for child protection. *Pediatrics;* 1997;100:735-760

The authors report results of in-hospital covert video surveillance (CVS) of 39 children (median age 9 months, range 2 to 44 months) with apparent life-threatening events (ALTE). Representing about 15% of children with ALTE seen at national center hospitals in the United Kingdom, those undergoing CVS were generally selected through multi-agency planning meetings. Duration of CVS averaged 29 hours, with the middle half range being about 5 to 60 hours.

In 33 cases surveillance identified abuse, often attempted suffocation while asleep. Many of the proffered explanations might have been plausible were it not for the video. Some parents repeatedly pinched or otherwise injured their children prior to a suffocation attempt. The authors reviewed the mechanisms of ALTE in apparently healthy infants and children and identified several associations with child abuse as the cause, including bleeding from the nose or mouth, having a sibling who died suddenly and unexpectedly, abuse of a sibling, and petechial hemorrhage of the face. Premature birth was less common, and ALTE occurred somewhat later on average in this population when compared with infants suffering ALTE from a respiratory mechanism. Personality disorder among the parents was relatively more common, although the authors did not obtain adequate information in many cases. The authors noted that attention-seeking behavior seemed to be important to many of the parents. They suggest that dramatic presentations, episodes occurring during times of parental stress, the absence of independent observers at the onset, and ceasing of episodes following parental separation may also be associated with similar cases elsewhere.

The authors recommend new strategies for assessing infants with ALTE, including a "low-threshold" for obtaining skeletal survey, retinal exam, and brain imaging studies; evaluation of siblings and their medical histories; and reviews

TABLE. Criteria for Distinguishing SIDS from Fatal Child Abuse and Other Medical Conditions

	Consistent With SIDS	Less Consistent With SIDS	Highly Suggestive or Diagnostic of Child Abuse
History surrounding death	Apparently healthy infant fed, put to bed. Found lifeless. Silent death. EMS resuscitation unsuccessful.	Infant found apneic. EMS transports to hospital. Infant lives hours to days. Substance abuse, family illness.	History atypical for SIDS. Discrepant history. Unclear history. Prolonged interval between bedtime and death.
Age at death	Peak 2–4 mo. 90% <7 mo. Range 1–12 mo.	8–12 mo.	>12 mo.
PE and laboratory studies at time of death	Serosanguinous watery, frothy, or mucoid nasal discharge. PM lividity in dependent areas. Possible marks on pressure points of body. No skin trauma. Well-cared-for baby.	Organomegaly of viscera. Stigmata of disease process (PE, laboratory, x-ray).	Cutaneous injuries. Traumatic lesions of body parts (conjunctiva, fundi, scalp, intraoral, ears, neck, trunk, anogenital extremities, malnutrition, neglect. Fractures.
History of pregnancy, delivery, and infancy	Prenatal care—minimal to maximal. Frequent history of cigarette use during pregnancy. Some future SIDS victims are premature or LBW. Subtle defects in state, feeding, cry, neurological status (hypotonia, lethargy, irritability). Less postneonatal height and weight gain. Twins, triplets. Spitting, GE reflux. Thrush, pneumonia, illnesses requiring hospitalization, tachypnea, tachycardia, cyanosis. Usually: No signs of antecedent difficulty.	Prenatal care—minimal to maximal. History of recurrent illnesses and/or multiple hospitalizations. "Sickly" or "weak" baby. Specific diagnosis of organ system disease.	Unwanted pregnancy. Little or no prenatal care. Late arrival for delivery. Birth outside of hospital. Few or no well baby care. No immunizations. Use of cigarettes, drugs/alcohol during and after pregnancy. Baby described as hard to care for or to "discipline." Deviant feeding practices.
Death scene investigation	Crib, bed in good repair. No dangerous bedclothes, toys, plastic sheets, pacifier strings, pellet pillows. No cords, bands for possible entanglement. Accurate description of position with attention to possible head/neck entrapment. Normal room temperature. No toxins, insecticides. Good ventilation, furnace equipment.	Defective crib/bed. Use of inappropriate sheets, pillows, sleeping clothes. Presence of dangerous toys, plastic sheets, pacifier cords, pellet pillows. Cosleeping. Poor ventilation, heat control. Presence of toxins, insecticides. Unsanitary conditions.	Chaotic unsanitary crowded living conditions. Evidence of drugs/alcohol. Signs of terminal struggle in crib, bed, bedclothes or other equipment. Discovery of blood-stained bedclothes. Evidence of hostility by caretakers. Discord between caretakers. Display of violence between caretakers. Admission of harm. Accusations.
Previous infant deaths in family	First unexplained and unexpected infant death.	One previous unexpected or unexplained infant death.	More than one previous unexplained or unexpected infant death.
Autopsy findings	No adequate cause of death at PM. Normal: skeletal survey, toxicology, chemistry studies (blood sugar may be high, normal, or low), microscopic examination, metabolic screen. Presence of: large numbers of intrathoracic petechiae; dysmorphic, dysplastic, or anomalous lesions; gliosis of brainstem; sphincter dilation. Occasionally subtle changes in liver, including fatty change and extramedullary hematopoiesis.	Subtle changes in liver, adrenal, myocardium. Few or no intrathoracic petechiae.	Traumatic cause of death (IC or visceral bleeding). External bruises, abrasions, or burns. No intrathoracic petechiae. Malnutrition. Fractures. Subgaleal hematoma. Abnormal body chemistry values (Na, Cl, K, BUN, sugar; liver, pancreatic enzymes; CPK). Abnormal toxicology.
Previous CPS or LE involvement	None.	One.	Two or more. One or more family member arrested for violent behavior.

* Abbreviations: SIDS, sudden infant death syndrome; EMS, emergency medical services; PM, postmortem; PE, physical examination; LBW, low birth weight; GE, gastroesophageal; WBC, well baby care; IC, intracranial; BUN, blood urea nitrogen; CPK, creatine phosphokinase; CPS, children's protective services; LE, law enforcement.

†Reece RM. Fatal Child Abuse and Sudden Infant Death Syndrome: A Critical Diagnostic Decision. *Pediatrics.* 1993;91:423-430

of child abuse registries. In cases with bleeding from the nose or mouth or histories of sudden death of siblings in childhood, they call for "a full and forensic analysis." They note that in 30% of the positive CVS cases, the referring pediatrician offered no hint that ALTE might have been due to abuse. They believe that CVS provided critical information necessary to protect children in a majority of the cases. They recommended CVS as standard practice. Finally, they discuss strategies for identifying and protecting children from abuse at the hands of deceptive and sadistic parents. In an accompanying editorial (*Pediatrics* 1997;100:890-891), Krugman notes that CVS may not be required of all pediatricians, but he exhorts us all to "overcome our professional and societal denial" of abuse and neglect by supporting relevant research (eg, a "nurturing defect" in mice associated with a single gene) and working harder in diagnosis. (DS)

Investigation

Kaplan SB, Granik LA. *Child Fatality Investigative Procedures Manual*. Chicago, IL: American Bar Association Center on Children and the Law and the American Academy of Pediatrics; 1991
The unexpected death of a child should trigger investigations by the medical examiner, law enforcment, and child protective services. Specific guidelines and procedures for each of these agencies are needed to ensure complete investigations, good records, and interagency cooperation. Examples of such documents are provided under the categories of medical examiner, law enforcement, child protective services, and interagency activities. This publication, number 549-0230, may be ordered from Order Fulfillment, American Bar Association, 750 North Lake Shore Drive, Chicago, IL 60611. (JJ)

Parrish R. Battered child syndrome: investigating physical abuse and homicide.
In: *Portable Guides to Investigating Child Abuse*. Washington, DC: Office of Juvenile Justice and Delinquency Prevention, US Department of Justice; 1991
This 16-page guide, written by the chief of the children's justice division of the Utah Attorney General's Office, is designed to help law enforce-

ment investigators and others collect evidence to be used in prosecuting physical child abuse. It emphasizes obtaining photographs and expert medical evaluations and discusses strategies for interviewing key witnesses.

Sections of the booklet are devoted to guidelines for child death investigations, features of shaken baby syndrome, and Munchausen syndrome by proxy as well as SIDS. References and a list of additional resources complete the guide.

Multi-Agency Death Review Teams

Anderson TL, Wells SJ. *Data Collection for Child Fatalities: Existing Efforts and Proposed Guidelines*. Chicago, IL: American Bar Association Center on Children and the Law and the American Academy of Pediatrics; 1991
The authors address the need for more accurate identification of the circumstances contributing to child deaths and the need for more precise and uniform data collection systems nationally. The use of child death review teams to better identify cause of death and collect data is discussed.

Two data sets are recommended. The first is designed to allow epidemiologists to identify trends in the incidence and causes of child deaths. It represents the minimum data that should be collected by child death review teams and generally represents a retrospective review. The second data set focuses also on suggested elements believed to promote and improve case management efforts in child maltreatment fatalities. It is generally completed as the investigation proceeds, or shortly thereafter. See preceding reference of Kaplan for ordering information; this is publication number 549-0228. (JJ)

Gellert GA, Maxwell RM, Durfee MJ, Wagner GA. Fatalities assessed by the Orange County child death review team, 1989 to 1991. *Child Abuse Negl.* 1995;19:875-883
This paper describes the review process, demographics of reviewed deaths, and comparisons between reviewed (unattended or questionable causes) and unreviewed deaths of children younger than 13 years old. The team reviewed 44% of the 1,463 child deaths occurring in the 2-year interval: 35% of infant deaths and 73% of older children's deaths. Most children who die are younger than

1 year of age, and most infants who die are younger than 1 month of age, largely due to the impacts of birth defects, prematurity, and SIDS. In addition, most suspicious child deaths occur in infants and toddlers. As a result of these factors, over 70% of reviewed deaths were in children younger than 2 years old.

Child abuse deaths (defined in this study as homicide by caretaker) accounted for 10 of 32 intentionally caused deaths. All abuse deaths, and 72% of other homicides, occurred in children younger than 5 years. The authors describe some of the barriers to accurate understanding of factors contributing to death from abuse or neglect, including difficulty accessing records and issues of confidentiality, and they cite some of the efforts undertaken in Orange County to address them.

Granik LA, Durfee M, Wells SJ. *Child Death Review Teams: A Manual for Design and Implementation.* **Chicago, IL: American Bar Association Center on Children and the Law and the American Academy of Pediatrics; 1991**
This manual offers a blueprint for jurisdictions or agencies contemplating the development of a review team. The authors provide an analysis of different goals and structures of the teams. A step-by-step approach to forming and operating child death review teams is outlined. The appendices include a questionnaire to be used in community self-assessment, a preliminary step to team development. It also provides copies of written materials used by various jurisdictions to establish and operate a team and two examples of reports resulting from team activity. See preceding reference of Kaplan for ordering information; this is publication number 549-0229. (JJ)

Kaplan SR. *Child Fatality Review Teams: Training for the Future.* **Chicago, IL: American Bar Association Center on Children and the Law; 1997**
This publication provides a model training curriculum for Child Fatality Review Teams. It includes modules for team establishment and development; investigation by law enforcement officers, medical examiners and coroners, child protective services workers, and prosecutors; and legal issues. See preceding reference of Kaplan for ordering information. (JJ)

Acknowledgment

This section and its annotations were prepared by David Schor, MD, MPH, assisted by Susan Elek, RN, PhD, CPNP. Selected annotations from the first edition were written by Jerry G. Jones, MD.

AMERICAN ACADEMY OF PEDIATRICS

Investigation and Review of Unexpected Infant and Child Deaths

(RE9336)

Committee on Child Abuse and Neglect and Committee on Community Health Services

A significant proportion of infant and child deaths are preventable. Of the 55 861 deaths of children aged 14 and younger in the United States in 1989, more than three fourths occurred in children under the age of 2 years.[1] Approximately one third of the latter were unexpected, including those due to sudden infant death syndrome (SIDS) or trauma, or deaths that were otherwise unexplained. Child abuse deaths occur in greatest numbers among infants, followed by those in toddlers and preschool children.[2] Children younger than 6 years of age are most vulnerable to abuse because of their small size, incomplete verbal skills, and often limited contact with adults other than their primary caretakers.[3]

With few exceptions, throughout the United States there is no uniform system for the investigation of infant and child deaths. Many jurisdictions lack appropriately trained pathologists, interagency collaboration that would facilitate sharing of information about the family, and a surveillance system to evaluate data regarding infant deaths. As a result, progress in the understanding of SIDS is inhibited, cases of child abuse and neglect may be missed, familial genetic diseases go undiagnosed, public health threats may be unrecognized, and inadequate medical care may be undetected. Lack of adequate infant and child death investigation is an impediment to preventing illness, injury, and death of other children at risk.

Adequate death investigation requires the participation of numerous individuals including medical examiner/coroner, public health officials, the patient's physician, the pathologist, and personnel from agencies involved with child welfare and social services and law enforcement. Collaboration between agencies enhances the ability to determine accurately the cause and circumstances of death. Information about the death of one child may lead to preventive strategies to protect the life of another.

ADEQUATE DEATH INVESTIGATION

An adequate death investigation includes a complete autopsy, investigation of the circumstances of death, review of the child's medical and family history, and review of information from relevant agencies and health care providers. A complete autopsy consists of an external and internal examination of the body, microscopic examination, and toxicologic,

microbiologic, and other appropriate studies. When possible, the autopsy should be performed by a forensic and/or pediatric pathologist, using a standard infant and child death autopsy protocol.[4] Investigation of the circumstances of death should include a scene investigation and interview with caretakers and responders by trained death investigators who are sensitive to issues of family grief. By current national standards, the diagnosis of SIDS cannot be made without a complete autopsy with appropriate ancillary studies and scene investigation.[5]

Interagency cooperation and review of all relevant records are necessary parts of a death investigation. Relevant records include, but are not limited to, all medical records including those from birth on, social services reports including those from Children's Protective Services, emergency and paramedic records, and law enforcement reports.

INFANT AND CHILD DEATH REVIEW

Thorough retrospective review of child deaths is one approach to ensure quality in death investigation. A centralized data base could aid in the proper functioning of infant and child death review and would allow for the identification of preventable deaths. Several models have been established and are operational at both state and local levels.[6] The American Academy of Pediatrics (AAP) also has developed a model bill on child death investigation. Infant and child death review requires the participation of many agencies. An appropriately constituted child death review team should evaluate the death investigation process, reexamine difficult or controversial cases, and monitor death statistics and certificates. Benefits of such death review include (1) quality assurance of death investigation at local levels, (2) identification of barriers to death investigation, (3) enhanced interagency cooperation, (4) improved allocation of limited resources, (5) enhanced awareness and education on the management and prevention of infant and child death, (6) better epidemiologic data on the causes of death, and (7) improved accuracy of death certificates.

RECOMMENDATIONS

Recommendations regarding child death investigation are as follows:

1. Pediatricians should advocate proper death certification for children, recognizing that such certification is not possible in sudden, unexpected deaths in the absence of comprehensive death investigation including autopsy.

This statement has been approved by the Council on Child and Adolescent Health and the Council on Pediatric Practice.
The recommendations in this policy statement do not indicate an exclusive course of treatment or serve as a standard of medical care. Variations, taking into account individual circumstances, may be appropriate.

2. Pediatricians and AAP chapters should support state legislation that requires autopsies of all deaths of children younger than 6 years that result from trauma; that are unexpected, including SIDS; and that are suspicious, obscure, or otherwise unexplained. It should never be assumed that the death of a child with a chronic impairment occurred as a result of that impairment.

3. Pediatricians and AAP chapters should support state legislation and other efforts that establish comprehensive child death investigation and review systems at the local and state levels.

4. Pediatricians should be involved in the training of death scene investigators so that appropriate knowledge of issues such as SIDS, child abuse, child development, and pediatric disease is used in the determination of cause of death.

5. Pediatricians should accept the responsibility to be involved with the death review process.

6. The AAP supports public policy initiatives directed at preventing childhood deaths, based on information acquired both locally and at the state level from adequate death investigations, accurate death certifications, and systematic death reviews.

COMMITTEE ON CHILD ABUSE AND NEGLECT, 1993 TO 1994
Richard D. Krugman, MD, Chair
Judith Ann Bays, MD
David L. Chadwick, MD
Mireille B. Kanda, MD
Carolyn J. Levitt, MD
Margaret T. McHugh, MD, MPH

Liaison Representatives
Marilyn B. Benoit, MD, American Academy of Child and Adolescent Psychiatry
Kenneth E. Powell, MD, MPH, Centers for Disease Control
Marshall D. Rosman, PhD, American Medical Association

Section Liaison
Robert H. Kirschner, MD, Section on Pathology

COMMITTEE ON COMMUNITY HEALTH SERVICES, 1993 TO 1994

Renee Jenkins, MD, Chair
Stanley I. Fisch, MD
Rudolph E. Jackson, MD
Alan Kohrt, MD
Arthur Lisbin, MD
Carolyn J. McKay, MD
Philip F. Merk, MD
R. Larry Meuli, MD
Donna O'Hare, MD
Michael Weitzman, MD
Harry L. Wilson, MD

Liaison Representatives
Janet S. Schultz, RN, National Assoc of Pediatric Nurses & Practitioners
Anne E. Dyson, MD, AAP Partnership for Children
Jennie McLaurin, MD, Migrant Clinicians Network
Paul Melinkovich, MD, Project Advisory Committee on Community-Based Programs
Yvonne Russell, MD
Bruce E. Schratz, MD, American Academy of Family Physicians
James F. Steiner, DDS, American Academy of Pediatric Dentistry

REFERENCES

1. Centers for Disease Control/National Center for Health Statistics. Advance report of final mortality statistics, 1989. *Monthly Vital Statistics Report.* January 7, 1992;40(S):2
2. Ewigman B, Kivlahan C, Land G. The Missouri child fatality study: underreporting of maltreatment fatalities among children younger than 5 years of age, 1983 through 1986. *Pediatrics.* 1993;91:330–337
3. McClain PW, Sacks JJ, Froehlke RG, Ewigman BG. Estimates of fatal child abuse and neglect, United States, 1979 through 1988. *Pediatrics.* 1993;91:338–343
4. Task Force for the Study of Non-Accidental Injuries and Child Deaths convened by the Illinois Dept of Children and Family Services and the Office of the Medical Examiner-Cook County. *Protocol for Child Death Autopsies.* Chicago, IL: Illinois Dept of Children and Family Services; 1987
5. Willinger M, James LS, Catz C. Defining the sudden infant death syndrome (SIDS): deliberations of an expert panel convened by the National Institute of Child Health and Human Development. *Pediatr Pathol.* 1991;11:677–684
6. Durfee MJ, Gellert GA, Tilton-Durfee D. Origins and clinical relevance of child death review teams. *JAMA.* 1992;267:3172–3175

AMERICAN ACADEMY OF PEDIATRICS

Distinguishing Sudden Infant Death Syndrome From Child Abuse Fatalities

Committee on Child Abuse and Neglect   (RE9421)

Public and professional awareness of sudden infant death syndrome (SIDS) has increased in the 28 years since the establishment of the National Sudden Infant Death Foundation, now called the National SIDS Alliance.[1] Similarly, awareness of child abuse has increased in the 30 years since the publication of the first article on the battered child.[2] In the majority of cases, when an infant younger than 1 year dies suddenly and unexpectedly, the cause is SIDS. Sudden infant death syndrome is far more common than infanticide. In a few difficult cases, legitimate investigations for possible child abuse have resulted in an insensitive approach to grieving parents or caretakers. This statement provides professionals with information and guidelines to avoid distressing or stigmatizing families of SIDS victims while allowing accumulation of appropriate evidence in the uncommon case of death by infanticide.

INCIDENCE AND EPIDEMIOLOGY

Sudden infant death syndrome, also called crib or cot death, is "the sudden death of an infant under 1 year of age which remains unexplained after a thorough case investigation, including performance of a complete autopsy, examination of the death scene, and a review of the clinical history."[3] Sudden infant death is the most common cause of death between 1 and 12 months of age. Eighty percent of cases occur before age 5 months, with a peak incidence between 2 and 4 months of age. Sudden infant death syndrome occurs in 1.5 to 2 per 1000 live births, resulting in 6000 to 7000 infant deaths each year in the United States.[4] While rates of infant mortality from other causes have declined over the past decade in the United States, the incidence of SIDS has not changed appreciably.

Death due to SIDS is much more common than death due to recognized child abuse. It is uncommon for death due to child abuse to be confused with SIDS. Although precise data are lacking, authors of a recent article estimate that less than 5% of apparent SIDS deaths are actually due to abuse.[5] In one recent study 170 infants dying suddenly and unexpectedly were given full postmortem evaluations including autopsy, full-body radiographs, and viral and bacterial cultures. Of the 170 deaths, 101 (59.4%) were

classified as SIDS and 61 (35.9%) were attributed to natural causes other than SIDS. Six infants (3.5%) died as a result of abuse or neglect, and two other infants (1.2%) died under questionable circumstances.[6] To comfort a family whose infant has died unexpectedly, in the absence of evidence of injury, an immediate diagnosis of "probable SIDS" can be given. This diagnosis conveys to the family that they could not have prevented their infant's death, and is correct about 95% to 98% of the time.

ETIOLOGY

Despite nearly 3 decades of intensive study, the etiology of SIDS is unknown. There is no diagnostic test for SIDS. Recent research has focused on such diverse causes as sleep apnea, arousal mechanisms, sleep-state organization, cardiac arrhythmias, thermoregulation abnormalities, occult viral infection, infant medications, sleeping position, allergy, metabolic disease, chronic hypoxia, and autonomic instability.[4,7-10] In the past, many causes of SIDS have been postulated and have either remained unconfirmed or have been disproved.

Risk factors associated with a higher incidence of SIDS include the following[4,8]:

- low socioeconomic status;
- an unmarried mother;
- maternal age younger than 20 years at first pregnancy or younger than 25 years during subsequent pregnancies;
- maternal smoking during pregnancy;
- illicit drug use during pregnancy;
- inadequate prenatal care;
- an interval of less than 12 months since the preceding pregnancy;
- prematurity;
- low birth weight;
- low APGAR scores;
- prone sleeping position.[9]

Unfortunately, many factors associated with a higher risk of sudden infant death are also associated with an increased risk of child abuse and other causes of infant mortality.

CLINICAL PRESENTATION

The typical presentation in SIDS is the sudden unexpected death of a seemingly healthy infant. SIDS deaths are more common during winter months. The infant may have been suffering from a mild upper respiratory or gastrointestinal infection, and fed before taking a nap or sleeping at night. After some hours unobserved, the infant is found dead. Death is silent and occurs during apparent sleep. A review of the medical history, scene investigation, radiographs, and autopsy are unrevealing.

PATHOLOGY

Pathologists establish the diagnosis of SIDS by exclusion when they are unable to identify other specific causes for a child's death.[11] The pathologic feature considered characteristic, but not pathognomonic, of SIDS is intrathoracic petechiae.[8]

The autopsy finding of intrathoracic petechiae (on the thymus, heart, lungs, parietal pleura, pericardium, and diaphragmatic pleura) is suggestive, but not diagnostic, of SIDS. Research on animals indicates that intrathoracic petechiae can be caused by induced airway obstruction or by oxygen deficit in inspired air without obstruction. Petechiae are more common after repeated tracheal occlusion and vigorous efforts to breathe. In humans, petechiae are seen following suffocation and more commonly in suffocated neonates than suffocated adults. Intrathoracic petechiae are found in known cases of infant suffocation, carbon monoxide asphyxia, and drowning, but seem to be more common in SIDS.[12]

THE IMPORTANCE OF AUTOPSY, SCENE INVESTIGATION, AND CASE REVIEW

Without a complete autopsy, a careful scene investigation, and a review of the medical history a diagnosis of SIDS cannot be made. Without these measures, progress in the understanding of SIDS is inhibited, cases of child abuse and neglect may be missed, familial genetic diseases may go unrecognized, public health threats may be overlooked, inadequate medical care may go undetected, and product safety issues will not be identified. Through thorough investigation of apparent SIDS deaths, the potential hazards of products including defective infant furniture, water beds, and bean bag mattresses have been identified and remedied.[13,14]

A death should be ruled as due to SIDS when:

- a complete autopsy is done, including cranium and cranial contents, and autopsy findings are compatible with SIDS;
- there is no gross or microscopic evidence of head trauma, intracranial injury, cerebral edema, cervical cord injury, retinal hemorrhage, or mechanical asphyxia;
- there is no evidence of trauma on skeletal survey;[15]
- other causes of death are adequately ruled out, including meningitis, sepsis, aspiration, pneumonia, myocarditis, abdominal trauma, dehydration, fluid and electrolyte imbalance, significant congenital lesions, inborn metabolic disorders, carbon monoxide asphyxia, drowning, or burns; and
- there is no evidence of current alcohol, drug, or toxic exposure.

A group of experts assembled by the National Institutes of Health has stated that infant deaths without postmortem examination should not be diagnosed as SIDS. Cases that are autopsied and carefully investigated but which remain unresolved may be designated as undetermined, unexplained, or the like."[3]

There is a small subset of infants who die unexpectedly, whose deaths are attributed to SIDS, but who may have been smothered or poisoned. Autopsy cannot distinguish death by SIDS from death by suffocation.[8,11] A study of infants suffocated by their parents indicates that certain features should raise the possibility of suffocation. These include previous episodes of apnea in the presence of the same person, previous unexplained medical disorders such as seizures, age at death older than 6 months, and previous unexpected or unexplained deaths of one or more siblings or the previous death of infants under the care of the same, unrelated person.[16]

If appropriate toxicological tests are not done, the few deaths due to accidental or deliberate poisoning will be missed.[6,11] Two recent studies indicate that occult cocaine exposure is widespread and potentially lethal. One reviewer found that 17 (40%) of 43 infants who died before 2 days of age without an obvious cause of death at autopsy had toxicologic evidence of cocaine exposure.[17] A second review of 600 infant deaths revealed evidence of cocaine exposure in 16 infants (2.7%) younger than 8 months who died suddenly and unexpectedly.[18] The relationship between cocaine exposure and infant death found in these studies is not clear.

MANAGEMENT

The appropriate professional response to any child death is compassionate, empathic, supportive, and nonaccusatory. At the same time it is vital to discover the cause of death if possible. Unless there is a history of significant antecedent illness or there are obvious injuries, the parents can be told that death appears to be due to SIDS, but that only with a thorough scene investigation, postmortem examination, and review of records can other causes be excluded. It can be explained to the parents that these procedures will enable them and their physician to understand why their infant died and how other children in the family, including children born later, might be affected.

The family is entitled to an opportunity to see and hold the infant once death has been pronounced. A protocol may help in planning how and when to address the many issues that require attention, including baptism, grief counseling, funeral arrangements and religious support, cessation of breastfeeding, reactions of surviving siblings,[19,20] and the risk of SIDS in subsequent siblings. All parents should be provided with information about SIDS[21] and the telephone number of the local SIDS support group.

The majority of sudden infant deaths occur at home. Parents are shocked, bewildered, distressed, and often feel responsible. Parents innocent of blame in their child's death feel guilty nonetheless, imagining ways in which they might have contributed to or prevented the tragedy.[11,19] When it is appropriate, parents should be reassured that neither they nor a physician could have prevented their infant's death. Inadvertent comments as well as necessary questioning by medical personnel and investigators are likely to cause additional stress.

It is important for those in contact with parents during this time to be supportive while at the same time conducting a thorough investigation. Personnel in first response teams should be trained to make observations at the scene such as the position of the infant, marks on the body, body temperature and rigor, type of bed or crib and any defects, amount and position of clothing and bedclothes, room temperature, type of ventilation and heating, and reaction of the caretakers. Paramedics and emergency room personnel should be trained to distinguish normal findings such as postmortem anal dilation and lividity from trauma due to abuse.[11,22,23]

A family's anxiety can be further increased if there is a delay in notification of the autopsy results. In most cases parents can be informed promptly of the results of the gross autopsy without waiting for the microscopic examination results.

In many states multidisciplinary teams have been established to review child fatalities.[24] Sharing data among agencies helps ensure that deaths due to child abuse are not missed and that surviving and subsequent siblings are protected. Some child fatality teams routinely review deaths due to apparent SIDS. These teams should include physicians or other professionals with expertise in SIDS.

The American Academy of Pediatrics endorses the following management scheme for evaluating sudden and unexpected infant deaths:

- universal performance of autopsies on infants dying suddenly and unexpectedly;[25]
- a standardized protocol for child deaths;[19,26]
- prompt notification to the family of the autopsy results;
- use of the term SIDS when appropriate;
- training of first response teams;
- counseling for parents of SIDS victims; and
- follow-up through the pediatrician's office or the public health department.

If all professionals involved in handling infant deaths are well trained and cooperate in a multidisciplinary approach, most deaths due to child abuse can be distinguished from sudden infant deaths and grieving families treated with compassion. If we are able to alter the risk factors common to child abuse and SIDS, we may be able to decrease the incidence of both.

COMMITTEE ON CHILD ABUSE AND NEGLECT, 1993–1994
Richard D. Krugman, MD, Chair
Judith Ann Bays, MD
David L. Chadwick, MD
Mireille B. Kanda, MD
Carolyn J. Levitt, MD
Margaret T. McHugh, MD, MPH

LIAISON REPRESENTATIVES
Marilyn B. Benoit, MD, American Academy of Child and Adolescent Psychiatry
Kenneth E. Powell, MD, MPH, Centers for Disease Control
Marshall D. Rosman, PhD, American Medical Association

SECTION LIAISON
Robert H. Kirschner, MD, Section on Pathology

REFERENCES

1. Bergman AB. Twenty-fifth anniversary of the National Sudden Infant Death Syndrome Foundation. *Pediatrics.* 1988;82:272–274
2. Kempe CH, Silverman FN, Steele BF, et al. The battered child syndrome. *JAMA.* 1962;181:17–24
3. Willinger M, James LS, Catz C. Defining the sudden infant death syndrome (SIDS): deliberations of an expert panel convened by the National Institute of Child Health and Human Development. *Pediatr Pathol.* 1991;11:677–684
4. Goyco PG, Beckerman RC. Sudden infant death syndrome. *Curr Probl Pediatr.* 1990;20:297–346
5. McClain PW, Sacks JJ, Froehlke RG, Ewigman BG. Estimates of fatal child abuse and neglect, United States, 1979 through 1988. *Pediatrics.* 1993;91:338–343
6. Perrot LJ, Nawojczyk S. Nonnatural death masquerading as SIDS (sudden infant death syndrome). *Am J Forensic Med Pathol.* 1988;9:105–111
7. Southall DP. Role of apnea in the sudden infant death syndrome: a personal view. *Pediatrics.* 1988;81:73–84
8. Valdes-Dapena M. A pathologist's perspective on possible mechanisms in SIDS. *Ann NY Acad Sci.* 1988;533:31–36
9. AAP Task Force on Infant Positioning SIDS. Positioning and SIDS. *Pediatrics.* 1992;89:1120–1126
10. Hardoin RA, Henslee JA, Christenson CP, Christenson PJ, White M. Colic medication and apparent life-threatening events. *Clin Pediatr.* 1991;30:281–285
11. DiMaio DJ, DiMaio VJM. *Forensic Pathology.* New York, NY: Elsevier; 1989:289–321
12. Beckwith JB. Intrathoracic petechial hemorrhages: a clue to the mechanism of death in sudden infant death syndrome? *Ann NY Acad Sci.* 1988;533:37–47
13. Kemp JS, Thach BT. Sudden death in infants sleeping on polystyrene-filled cushions. *N Engl J Med.* 1991;324:1858–1864
14. Ramanathan R, Chandra S, Gilbert-Barness E, Franciosi R. Sudden infant death syndrome and water beds. *N Engl J Med.* 1988;318:1700
15. Kleinman PK, Blackbourne BD, Marks SC, Karellas A, Belanger PL. Radiologic contributions to the investigation and prosecution of cases of fatal infant abuse. *N Engl J Med.* 1989;320:507–511
16. Meadow R. Suffocation, recurrent apnea, sudden infant death. *J Pediatr.* 1990;117:351–357
17. Rogers C, Hall J, Muto J. Findings in newborns of cocaine-abusing mothers. *J Forensic Sci.* 1991;36:1074–1078
18. Mirchandani HG, Mirchandani IH, Hellman F, English-Rider R, Rosen S, Laposata EA. Passive inhalation of free-base cocaine ('crack') smoke by infants. *Arch Pathol Lab Med.* 1991;115:494–498
19. Limerick S. Family and health-professional interactions. *Ann NY Acad Sci.* 1988;533:145–154
20. Committee on Psychosocial Aspects of Child Family Health. The pediatrician and childhood bereavement. *Pediatrics.* 1992;89:516–518
21. SIDS Alliance, 10500 Little Patuxent Parkway, Suite 420, Columbia, MD 21044, 1-800-221-7437
22. Bass M, Kravath RE, Glass L. Death-scene investigation in sudden infant death. *N Engl J Med.* 1986;315:100–105
23. Kirschner RH, Stein RJ. The mistaken diagnosis of child abuse: a form of medical abuse? *Am J Dis Child.* 1985;139:873–875
24. Granik LA, Durfee M, Wells SJ. *Child Death Review Teams: A Manual for Design and Implementation.* Chicago, IL: American Bar Association; 1991
25. Investigation review of unexpected infant child deaths. *Pediatrics.* 1993;92:734–735
26. Kaplan SR, Granik LA, eds. *Child Fatality Investigative Procedures Manual.* Chicago, IL: American Bar Association; 1991

Interviewing Children Who May Have Been Abused

Clinical Principles

▼ The history provided by the child may be the only evidence of sexual abuse, and the physician must be equipped to obtain that history, as well as preserve that evidence without "tainting" or leading the child.

▼ The physician's role in reporting what a child says has a legal stature and is an exception to the hearsay rule in most states.

▼ A child's history provided to a physician may indicate an immediate need for protection and custody.

Bibliography

Davies D, Cole J, Albertella G, et al. A model for conducting forensic interviews with child victims of abuse. *Child Maltreatment.* 1996; 1:189-199
A forensic interview protocol is described here, with emphasis on *forensic.* The protocol describes the phases of the interview and use of anatomically detailed dolls, open-ended vs direct questioning, and strategies to cope with avoidant children. Physicians can find guidance and strategies for conducting medical interviews that will hold up to forensic scrutiny. (LF)

Everson M, Boat B. Putting the anatomic doll controversy in perspective: an examination of the major uses and criticisms of the dolls in child sexual abuse evaluations. *Child Abuse Negl.* 1994;18:113-129
Doctors Boat and Everson carefully outline the history of and controversies surrounding the use of anatomically detailed dolls. Although not commonly used in the medical office, such tools may be helpful to the physician who performs sexual abuse evaluations. The authors describe seven functional uses of the dolls: Comforter, Icebreaker, Anatomic Model, Demonstration Aid, Memory Stimulus, Diagnostic Screen, and Diagnostic Test. These functional uses are described in light of some of the criticisms. In a medical setting, using dolls for Comforter, Icebreaker, and Anatomic Model may be very helpful with young children; however, this article outlines potential pitfalls and criticisms that may arise even in such limited use. It is important for a medical provider to be aware of such issues if dolls are used for historical purposes. (LF)

Frasier L. The pediatrician's role in child abuse interviewing. *Pediatr Ann.* 1997; 26:306-311
This is a recent update reminding physicians that they have a unique role eliciting an unbiased medical history including drop in grades, sexually precocious behavior, vaginal irritation, and a teenager's sexual activity, drug, or alcohol usage. The importance of interviewing the child alone, building rapport, watching for emotional cues and evasiveness, reassurance, and closure is highlighted. The author points out there is no gold standard, but guidelines have been established for interviewing. Physicians are often reticent to interview for fear of contaminating the child's history or becoming too involved in a time-consuming and adversarial process. It is important to pose questions in an open-minded manner, so that the answers are not in the questions, and to elicit details children have learned through the sexual encounter. There are special challenges of interviewing adolescents and developmentally disabled children. Accurate documentation may be pivotal to the protection of the child. Physicians are reminded that the sexually abused child's medical history is usually recognized by the courts as reliable. The author summarizes that the purpose of the physician's interview is the health, well-being, and protection of the child and should be considered a supplement to, but not replacing, a skilled forensic interview. (CL)

Levitt C. The medical examination in child sexual abuse: a balance between history and exam. *J Child Sexual Abuse.* 1992;1:113-121
Dr Levitt concisely integrates the physical evaluation with the history-taking process in the evaluation of child sexual abuse. In addition to a discussion of physical findings and the use of the colposcope, she emphasizes the importance of a precise and well-documented medical history. The process, described as "two-pronged," integrates the history and physical examination as is done in all other medical diagnostic

encounters; this standard process should not be abandoned in the evaluation of sexually abused children. (LF)

Myers JEB. The role of the physician in preserving verbal evidence of child abuse. *J Pediatrics.* **1986;109:409-411**

This article by a well-known lawyer emphasizes the role of the physician in eliciting and then preserving vital verbal evidence. The author carefully describes why hearsay evidence is important and why it is considered more reliable when elicited by a professional such as a physician, particularly when it is obtained in the course of taking a medical history for diagnosis and treatment. He reminds us it is the judge's responsibility to determine whether a child's statement is hearsay, and what factors are considered in this determination. How that history is documented is very important, and the author provides suggestions for documentation. He also tells how to elicit a history while avoiding leading or suggestive questions. This article was one of the first that addressed the physician's role in obtaining verbal evidence. It continues to be pertinent, timely, and an excellent guide for physicians. (LF)

Acknowledgment

This section and its annotations were prepared by Lori Frasier, MD, with the assistance of Carolyn Levitt, MD.

Knowledge of Professionals

Clinical Aspects

▼ Studies continue to document the need for multidisciplinary education and training in child abuse and neglect.

▼ Studies continue to demonstrate inadequacies in knowledge of the indicators of abuse/neglect and of procedures for reporting suspected cases, the latter among professionals mandated to report. Continuing education does increase this knowledge and may increase reporting of suspected cases.

Other Comments

▼ There is surprisingly little new information on professional knowledge in child abuse and neglect.

▼ Evaluations of resident training programs in child abuse are needed.

▼ Studies on the most effective and efficient methods of improving professional knowledge are urgently needed.

Bibliography

Ashworth CS, Fargason CA, Fountain K. Impact of patient history on residents' evaluation of child sexual abuse. *Child Abuse Negl.* 1995;19:943-951
Pediatric residents who viewed 15 slides of children's genitalia had difficulty identifying abnormal physical findings when the history did not include abuse. Responses were most correct when the history and physical exam were both normal. These results challenge the assumption (at least among residents) that physical examination interpretation is not influenced by expectation bias. The poor performance in incongruent cases (49% correct when history was normal but results of exam were abnormal) raises concern because these are often the cases in which sociolegal professionals expect doctors to have some special ability.

This study is a good example demonstrating the need for more education. A similar assessment of practicing pediatric, family practice, and emergency room physicians would be interesting.

Palusci VJ, McHugh MT. Interdisciplinary training in the evaluation of child sexual abuse. *Child Abuse Negl.* 1995;19:1031-1038
This report evaluates the effectiveness of a training program (didactic presentations, case discussions, videotapes, and direct participation in patient evaluation) on the knowledge and assessment of child sexual abuse by medical students, pediatric residents, fellows, and attending physicians. While all participant groups showed an increase in knowledge, the increase was most notable among the resident physicians.

Reiniger A, Robison E, McHugh M. Mandated training of professionals: a means for improving reporting suspected child abuse. *Child Abuse Negl.* 1995;19:63-69
Substantial numbers of professionals participating in mandated child abuse training in New York state were not aware of the indicators of child abuse. They were somewhat more knowledgeable about abuse than the legal obligations and procedures for reporting. Differences among professionals were found. If child abuse legislation is to be effective, professionals must be able to identify and report it.

Socolar RR. Physician knowledge of child sexual abuse. *Child Abuse Negl.* 1996; 20:783-790
This study of 113 physicians participating in a statewide program on the evaluation of child abuse demonstrated knowledge deficiencies in the areas of chlamydia infections, Tanner staging, and documentation of history and physical findings. More knowledge was demonstrated by physicians participating in continuing education courses in child abuse and by those with specialization in pediatrics.

Tilden VP, Schmidt TA, Limandri BJ, et al. Factors that influence clinicians' assessment and management of family violence. *Am J Public Health.* 1994;84:628-633
This survey of professionals from six disciplines in dentistry, medicine, psychology, and social work revealed that one third of the respondents had no formal training in child abuse, spouse abuse, or elder abuse. Those with training were

more likely to identify suspected abuse. A significant number of respondents did not view themselves as responsible for dealing with family violence problems. The authors encourage the expansion of curricula on family violence and the reexamination by legislators of current statutes regarding reporting.

Von Burg MM, Hibbard RA. Child abuse education: do not overlook dental professionals. *ASDC J Dent Child.* **1995;62:57-63**
This report describes an educational program for dental professionals with assessment of pre- and post-course knowledge. Seventy percent had no previous training, 65% had suspected abuse among their patients, but only 19% had ever reported abuse. Dental professionals attending this program were considered generally knowledgeable about some topic areas but lacking in others. They demonstrated improvement in knowledge, and many professionals reported that they further disseminated the program information to their colleagues.

Acknowledgment

This section and its annotations were prepared by Roberta A. Hibbard, MD, and reviewed by Gerald E. Porter, MD.

Legislation

See Also:
AAP Model Bills *Child Abuse Victim Protection Act,* **and** *Child Death Investigation Act*
AAP Statements *Public Disclosure of Private Information About Victims of Abuse,* **and**
Religious Objections to Medical Care, **which follow**

The following model bills and policy statements of the American Academy of Pediatrics relate to child abuse:

▼ Child Abuse Victim Protection Act

▼ Child Death Investigation Act

▼ Public Disclosure of Private Information about Victims of Abuse

▼ Religious Objections to Medical Care

These model bills and policy statements are on the pages which follow.

Bibliography

Kaplan SR. *Child Fatality Legislation in the United States.* Chicago, IL: American Bar Association Center on Children and the Law; 1997
This review of current legislation focuses on child death review teams, multidisciplinary child abuse teams, mandated agency responses to child death, and recent state initiatives. It includes summaries of current child fatality–related legislation and sample state legislation establishing local and state child death review teams. This publication, number 549-0231, may be ordered from Order Fulfillment, American Bar Association, 750 North Lake Shore Drive, Chicago, IL 60611.

AMERICAN ACADEMY OF PEDIATRICS

Child Abuse Victim Protection Act

**A BILL TO PREVENT PUBLIC DISCLO-
SURE OF THE IDENTITY OF CHILD ABUSE
VICTIMS.**

**BE IT ENACTED BY THE LEGISLATURE
OF THE STATE OF _____:**

Section 1. Title. This act shall be known and may be cited as the "CHILD ABUSE VICTIM PROTECTION ACT."

Section 2. Purpose. The purpose of this statute is to provide courts with discretion to prevent the public disclosure of information that identifies victims of child abuse or neglect in order to protect the victims from community stigmatization, promote rehabilitation efforts, and reduce the trauma associated with or caused by such public disclosure.

Section 3. Application. This statute shall apply in all criminal and civil proceedings involving actual or alleged child abuse or neglect, including, without limitation, child custody and visitation proceedings.

Section 4. Definitions.

(a) "proceeding to which this statute applies" means any proceeding described in Section 3.

(b) "child victim" refers to a person who was a victim or alleged victim of child abuse or neglect.

(c) "child abuse or neglect" means the physical or mental injury, sexual abuse or exploitation, negligent treatment, or maltreatment of a person under the age of eighteen, by a person (including any employee of a residential facility or any staff person providing out-of-home care) who is responsible for the child's welfare, under circumstances which indicate that the child's health or welfare is harmed or threatened thereby.

(d) "family member" refers to a person related by blood or law to a child victim;

(e) "parent" refers to any of the following: biological parent, adoptive parent, guardian, de facto parent, foster parent, or any other adult charged with the custody, care and control of a child victim;

(f) "public" refers to all persons except the following persons involved in a proceeding to which this statute applies:

(1) judge presiding over a trial;

(2) members of a jury;

(3) a defendant and the attorney and an investigator for the defendant;

(4) the prosecuting attorney and an investigating officer for the state;

(5) the parents of the child victim;

(6) a guardian ad litem or attorney for the child victim;

(7) an adult for whom the child victim has developed a significant emotional attachment, and who can provide emotional support for the child victim while he or she testifies;

(8) court personnel, including those essential for taking the testimony.

Section 5. Protective Measures.

(a) In a proceeding to which this statute applies, the court may, upon its own motion, the motion of one of the parties or a request by or on behalf of a child victim, take any of the following measures to prevent the public disclosure of information that identifies the victim of child abuse or neglect:

(1) exclude the public from the proceeding during the testimony of the child victim;

(2) exclude the public from the entire proceeding;

(3) order that the name, address, or identifying information of the child victim not be placed in the indictment or any other public record. Instead, a Jane Doe or John Doe designation shall appear in all public records. Sealed records containing the child's name and necessary biographical information shall be maintained. For purposes of this subsection, identifying information includes the name, address, and other information about a parent or family member that could lead to the identification of such child victim unless the parent or other family member is the named defendant, in which case subsection (4) hereof shall govern the disclosure of identifying information with respect to that parent or other family member;

(4) if a parent or other family member is a defendant in the action, order:

(i) that the entire record be sealed from the public; or

(ii) that a pseudonym be used for the defendant in the record;

(5) urge the news media and other persons not to print or publish, broadcast, televise, or disseminate through any other medium of public dissemination or cause to be printed or published, broadcasted, televised or disseminated in any newspaper, magazine periodical, or other publication the name, address, or other identifying information (including the name, address or other information about the parents or family members that would lead to identification) concerning any victim of child abuse or neglect; or

(6) to the extent otherwise permissible, limit or prohibit broadcasting, televising, recording or photographing in the courtroom an area immediately adjacent thereto during the proceedings or recesses between sessions.

(b) The court may only take one or more of the measures enumerated in subsection (a) upon an express finding that the measure is necessary in order to reduce the trauma for the child victim, promote rehabilitation efforts or protect the child victim from community stigmatization. Factors to be considered by the court in making such a determination shall include the likelihood of identification of the child victim to the public if the protective measure is not taken, whether protecting the family from publicity would encourage the resolution of family problems, the nature of the crime, the victim's age or level of maturity, and the desires of the child victim.

Section 6. Other Laws. Nothing in this statute shall be interpreted to be inconsistent with or apply to the requirements of any law governing:

(a) the reporting of instances of child abuse or neglect,

or

(b) the maintenance of information in a central registry of a victim of child abuse or neglect, or the release of such information to authorized personnel as specified by statute.

February 1989
Reaffirmed June 1995

AMERICAN ACADEMY OF PEDIATRICS

Child Death Investigation Act

A BILL TO REQUIRE DEATH INVESTIGATIONS IN THE CASE OF UNEXPECTED DEATHS OF CHILDREN UNDER SIX YEARS OF AGE

BE IT ENACTED BY THE LEGISLATURE OF THE STATE OF _____:

Section 1. Short Title. This act shall be known and may be cited as the "CHILD DEATH INVESTIGATION ACT."

Section 2. Legislative Findings and Purpose.

(a) The legislature hereby finds and declares that:

(1) Protection of the health and welfare of the children of this state is a goal of its people and the unexpected death of infants and young children is an important public health concern that requires legislative action.

(2) The threat of unexpected death is particularly acute in the case of children below the age of six (6) years, who are especially helpless, and whose welfare is generally not monitored outside of the home.

(3) The parents, guardians, or other persons legally responsible for the care of a young child who dies unexpectedly have a right to know the cause of death as determined by an autopsy.

(4) Collecting accurate data on the cause and manner of unexpected deaths will better enable the state to protect some infants and young children from preventable deaths, and thus will help reduce the incidence of such deaths.

(5) Identifying persons responsible for abuse or neglect resulting in unexpected death will better enable the state to protect other children who may be under the care of the same persons, and thus will help reduce the incidence of such deaths.

(6) Multidisciplinary reviews of child deaths can assist the state in the development of a greater understanding of the incidence and causes of child deaths and the methods for preventing such deaths and in identifying gaps in services to children and families.

(b) The purpose of this Act is to aid in the reduction of the incidence of injury and death to infants and young children by accurately identifying the cause and manner of death of children under six (6) years of age, by requiring that a death investigation be performed in the case of all unexpected deaths of children under six (6) years of age; and by establishing a State Child Death Review Panel to collect data from such investigations and report to the legislature regarding the causes of such deaths.

Section 3. Definitions. As used in this Act, the following terms have the following meanings:

(a) "Autopsy" means a post-mortem external and internal physical examination conducted in accordance with accepted medical practice and the laws of this State using a standardized child death investigation protocol performed by a forensic pathologist or, if a forensic pathologist is unavailable, a pathologist qualified to conduct such an examination under such laws.

(b) "Death investigation" means the process of determining the cause and manner of death by scene and circumstance evaluation, complete autopsy, and history and record review.

(c) "Unexpected death" means a death which is unanticipated, is the result of trauma, or the circumstances of which are suspicious, obscure or otherwise unexplained. A clinical diagnosis of death due to Sudden Infant Death Syndrome (SIDS) shall be deemed an unexpected death.

(d) "Medical Examiner" means the physician or other individual elected or appointed pursuant to state or local law to investigate certain deaths of human beings.

Section 4. State Child Death Review Panel.

(a) There is hereby established the State Child Death Review Panel within the [Department of Health].

(b) The State Panel shall:

(1) establish or approve a standardized child death investigation protocol which shall require at a minimum that all child death investigations be completed within ninety (90) days of the report of the death. The protocol shall include procedures for law enforcement agencies, district attorneys' offices, medical examiners, and departments of social services to follow in response to a child death;

(2) collect, review, and analyze child death certificates, child death summary data, including patient records or other pertinent confidential information (not withstanding the confidential nature of any such records or information), and

such other information as the State Panel deems appropriate, to use in preparation of reports to the legislature concerning the causes and manner of child deaths;

(3) recommend interventions to the legislature that will prevent unexpected deaths of infants and young children based on an analysis of the cause and manner of such deaths; and

(4) recommend changes within the agencies represented on the State Panel which may prevent child deaths; and

(5) maintain the confidentiality of any patient records or other confidential information reviewed under this section.

(c) The State Panel shall be composed of at least twelve (12) persons. Members of the State Panel shall include:

(1) the State's chief medical examiner or a representative of the medical examiner system or his designee,

(2) the head of the State department of public health or his designee,

(3) the head of the State child protective services agency or his designee,

(4) the chief of the state law enforcement agency or his designee,

(5) the chief of the State's vital statistics bureau or his designee,

(6) the State's attorney general or his designee,

(7) a pediatrician with expertise in SIDS appointed by the Governor, for a term of three (3) years,

(8) a health professional with experience in diagnosing and treating child abuse and neglect appointed by the Governor for a term of three (3) years,

(9) a pediatrician appointed by the Governor for a term of three (3) years from a list submitted by the state chapter of the American Academy of Pediatrics,

(10) a pathologist with expertise in diagnosing and evaluating infant and child death appointed by the Governor for a term of three (3) years,

(11) a representative from the Governor's office, and

(12) a citizen of the State appointed by the Governor for a term of three (3) years.

(d) The State Panel may establish local or regional panels to which it may delegate some or all of its responsibilities under subsections (b)1, (b)2, and (b)4 of this section.

(e) There shall be no monetary liability on the part of, and no cause of action for damages shall arise against, any member of the State Panel, or of any local or regional panel appointed under section 4(d), for any act or proceeding undertaken or performed within the scope of the functions of the State Panel if the member acts without malice.

Section 5. Requirements for Death Investigation.

(a) In the case of every unexpected death of a child under six (6) years of age, a death investigation shall be performed by the medical examiner or by another qualified physician appointed and supervised by the medical examiner, in accordance with the child death investigation protocol established by the State Panel, or another child death investigation protocol approved by the State Panel. The results of the death investigation shall be reported to appropriate authorities, including the police and child protective services if appropriate, within three (3) days of the conclusion of the death investigation.

(b) Child death certificates shall be provided to the State Panel within one month of the conclusion of the death investigation.

(c) The cause of death as determined by the autopsy shall be reported to parents, guardians or other persons legally responsible for care of the child within ten (10) days of the conclusion of the death investigation.

Section 6. Report to Legislature.
The State Panel shall report to the legislature annually concerning the causes and manner of unexpected deaths of infants and young children. The report shall include analysis of factual information obtained through review of death certificates.

Section 7. Effective date.
This Act shall become effective sixty (60) days after being enacted into law.

February 1993

AMERICAN ACADEMY OF PEDIATRICS

Committee on Child Abuse and Neglect

Public Disclosure of Private Information About Victims of Abuse (RE9201)

Media publication of information about child abuse victims and their families may be detrimental to the victims. This is particularly true in cases of sexual abuse, but it may be just as serious in some cases of physical abuse or neglect. Many states lack laws that restrict publicity concerning the identity of child abuse victims and their families. As a result, serious harm to children can occur, not only at the time of the trial or hearing, but when subsequent stories appear years later.

The American Academy of Pediatrics recommends that all states adopt laws to prevent public disclosure of information that identifies victims of child abuse. The laws should grant courts the discretion to take one or more of the following measures during hearings of alleged civil or criminal child abuse/neglect: (1) exclude the public and media from a proceeding during the testimony of the child victim; (2) exclude the public (but not the media) from an entire proceeding; and (3) use pseudonyms in court records for the child victim and his or her family members.

Criteria by which the need for such protective measures should be judged include (1) the likelihood of identification of the child victim to the public if the protective measure is not taken; (2) the nature of the conduct that is the basis for the proceeding; (3) the child victim's age and level of maturity; (4)

the desires of the child victim; and (5) in cases in which a family member is the defendant, the need to protect the family from publicity to encourage the resolution of family problems.

In addition to recommending that all states adopt such laws, the American Academy of Pediatrics also recommends that the media exercise great caution in publishing any information that includes the names of children who are victims of sexual or physical abuse or neglect.

This policy is not intended to shield the subject material or content of the trial from the public. Rather, its aim is to reduce the trauma for the child victim, promote rehabilitation efforts, protect the child victim from stigmatization, and protect the identity and privacy of child victims.

COMMITTEE ON CHILD ABUSE AND
  NEGLECT, 1990–1991
Richard D. Krugman, MD, Chairman
Judith Ann Bays, MD
David L. Chadwick, MD
Carolyn J. Levitt, MD
Margaret T. McHugh, MD, MPH
J. M. Whitworth, MD

Liaison Representatives
Thomas Halversen, MD, American
  Academy of Child and Adolescent
  Psychiatry
Marshall D. Rosman, PhD, American
  Medical Association

Section Liaison
Robert H. Kirschner, MD, Section on
  Pathology

PEDIATRICS (ISSN 0031 4005). Copyright © 1991 by the American Academy of Pediatrics.
Reaffirmed 5/94

Religious Objections to Medical Care

ABSTRACT. Parents sometimes deny their children the benefits of medical care because of religious beliefs. In some jurisdictions, exemptions to child abuse and neglect laws restrict government action to protect children or seek legal redress when the alleged abuse or neglect has occurred in the name of religion. The American Academy of Pediatrics (AAP) believes that all children deserve effective medical treatment that is likely to prevent substantial harm or suffering or death. In addition, the AAP advocates that all legal interventions apply equally whenever children are endangered or harmed, without exemptions based on parental religious beliefs. To these ends, the AAP calls for the repeal of religious exemption laws and supports additional efforts to educate the public about the medical needs of children.

ABBREVIATION. AAP, American Academy of Pediatrics.

THE PROBLEM

The American Academy of Pediatrics (AAP) recognizes that religion plays a major role in the lives of many children and adults in the United States and is aware that some in the United States believe prayer and other spiritual practices can substitute for medical treatment of ill or injured children. Through legislative activity at the federal and state levels, some religious groups have sought, and in many cases attained, government recognition in the form of approved payment for this "nonmedical therapy" and exemption from child abuse and neglect laws when children do not receive needed medical care. The AAP opposes such payments and exemptions as harmful to children and advocates that children, regardless of parental religious beliefs, deserve effective medical treatment when such treatment is likely to prevent substantial harm or suffering or death.

The US Constitution requires that government not interfere with religious practices or endorse particular religions. However, these constitutional principles do not stand alone and may, at times, conflict with the independent government interest in protecting children.[1] Government obligation arises from that interest when parental religious practices subject minor children to possible loss of life or to substantial risk of harm.[2,3] Constitutional guarantees of freedom of religion do not permit children to be harmed through religious practices, nor do they allow religion to be a valid legal defense when an individual harms or neglects a child.[4]

Acute Illness or Injury

The AAP asserts that every child should have the opportunity to grow and develop free from preventable illness or injury.[5] Children also have the right to appropriate medical evaluation when it is likely that a serious illness, injury, or other medical condition endangers their lives or threatens substantial harm or suffering. Under such circumstances, parents and other guardians have a responsibility to seek medical treatment, regardless of their religious beliefs and preferences. Unfortunately, certain groups have obtained exemptions from legal sanctions and state child abuse and neglect reporting laws based on the child's "treatment" by spiritual means, such as prayer.[6] The overall effect has been to limit the government's ability to protect children from abuse or neglect.

The AAP is concerned about religious doctrines that urge parents to avoid seeking medical help when their children are seriously ill. Each year, some parents' religious views lead them to eschew appropriate medical care for their children, resulting in substantial harm or suffering or death due to treatable conditions such as meningitis, bowel obstruction, diabetes mellitus, or pneumonia (*Boston Globe.* August 12, 1993:1; *Pittsburgh Post-Gazette.* March 16, 1991:B1).[4,7] The AAP considers failure to seek medical care in such cases to be child neglect, regardless of the motivation. The basic moral principle of justice requires that children be protected uniformly by laws and regulations at the local, state, and federal levels. Parents and others who deny a child necessary medical care on religious grounds should not be exempt from civil or criminal action that otherwise would be appropriate. State legislatures and regulatory agencies should remove religious exemption clauses from statutes and regulations to ensure that all parents understand that they should seek appropriate medical care for their children.

Preventive Care

Some religious tenets hold that members should not seek or receive medical care for any condition, including pregnancy. These beliefs can result in increased perinatal and maternal mortality.[8] Some religious groups deny children the benefits of routine preventive care. For example, some parents, acting in accord with state laws, refuse to have their children immunized because of religious beliefs. The AAP does not support the stringent application of medical neglect laws when children do not receive recommended immunizations. Although the risk to unimmunized individuals is relatively low, serious adverse reactions to vaccination are rare and the AAP strongly endorses universal immunization. Recent outbreaks of vaccine-preventable infectious diseases, with consequent serious complications and deaths, have been linked to groups that refused immunization for religious reasons.[9–12]

The AAP therefore supports the use of appropriate public health measures, such as mandatory mass vaccinations in epidemic situations, when necessary to protect communities and their unimmunized members. In addition, the AAP is concerned that children unimmunized for any reason may expose young children, not yet old enough to be protected, to infections such as pertussis or invasive *Haemophilus influenzae* disease. The risk is especially high in child care facilities. In such situations, all parents of children in the facility should be informed of the hazards.

Mature Minors

The weight given to parental religious beliefs in decisions affecting their children's well-being declines with the child's increasing age and development. That is, as minors mature, their interest in and capacity for participating in health care decisions affecting themselves increases, as does their ability to make decisions regarding their parents' religious views. The law and AAP policy recognize the doctrine of the "mature minor."[13] This concept acknowledges that many children, usually beginning in adolescence, can contribute to or make medical decisions, including those about life-sustaining treatment. Thus, in selected cases, disputes may be avoided when a minor has the capacity to make an independent decision in light of religious values and recommended medical therapy.

Need for Care and Respect

The AAP wishes to underscore its recognition of the important role of religion in the personal, spiritual, and social lives of many individuals and cautions physicians and other health care professionals to avoid unnecessary polarization when conflict over religious practices arises. Pediatricians should seek to make collaborative decisions with families whenever possible and should take great care when considering seeking authority to override parental preferences. Nevertheless, physicians who believe that parental religious convictions interfere with appropriate medical care that is likely to prevent substantial harm or suffering or death should request court authorization to override parental authority or, under circumstances involving an imminent threat to a child's life, intervene over parental objections. When caring for children whose prognoses are grave even with treatment, physicians should use restraint in pursuing a court order to initiate or continue treatment when parents object to it. In such situations, physicians should work with the parents and children to ensure provision of appropriate palliative care. Threatening or seeking state intervention should be the last resort, undertaken only when treatment is likely to prevent substantial harm or suffering or death. Even under these circumstances, physicians should respect parental religious beliefs and the role of parents in rearing their children. Of course, a physician may withdraw from these cases, after securing acceptable alternative medical care, when continuing in the doctor-patient-family relationship would violate the physician's own moral precepts.

The AAP emphasizes that all children who need medical care that is likely to prevent substantial harm or suffering or death should receive that treatment. The AAP opposes religious doctrines that advocate opposition to medical attention for sick children. Adherence to such views precludes appropriate assessment and intervention to protect the children. The AAP believes that laws should not encourage or tolerate parental action that prevents implementing appropriate medical treatment, nor should laws exempt parents from criminal or civil liability in the name of religion.

RECOMMENDATIONS

The AAP calls for all those entrusted with the care of children to:

1. show sensitivity to and flexibility toward the religious beliefs and practices of families;
2. support legislation that ensures that all parents who deny their children medical care likely to prevent death or substantial harm or suffering are held legally accountable;
3. support the repeal of religious exemption laws; and
4. work with other child advocacy organizations and agencies and religious institutions to develop coordinated and concerted public and professional action to educate state officials, health care professionals, and the public about parents' legal obligations to obtain necessary medical care for their children.

COMMITTEE ON BIOETHICS, 1995 TO 1996
Joel E. Frader, MD, Chairperson
Lucy S. Crain, MD
Kathryn L. Moseley, MD
Robert M. Nelson, MD
Ian H. Porter, MD
Felipe E. Vizcarrondo, MD

LIAISON REPRESENTATIVES
Watson Bowes, MD
    American College of Obstetricians &
    Gynecologists
Alessandra Kazura, MD
    American Academy of Child &
    Adolescent Psychiatry
Ernest F. Krug III, MD
    American Board of Pediatrics

SECTION LIAISON
Donna A. Caniano, MD
    Section on Surgery

LEGAL CONSULTANT
Nancy M. P. King, JD

REFERENCES

1. *Planned Parenthood of Central Missouri v Danforth*, 428 US 52, 74(1976)
2. *Prince v Commonwealth of Massachusetts*, 321 US 158, 170(1944)
3. *Jehovah's Witnesses v King County Hospital Unit No. 1*, 278 F Supp 488

(WD Wash 1967), affirmea per curiam 390 US 598(1968)

4. *Walker v Superior Court*, 763 P2d 852, 860 (Calif 1988), *cert denied*, 491 US 905(1989)

5. *UN Convention on the Rights of the Child*. New York, NY: United Nations; 1989

6. Skolnick A. Religious exemptions to child neglect laws still being passed despite convictions of parents. *JAMA*. 1990;264:1226, 1229, 1233

7. *State of Minnesota v McKown*, 475 NW2d 63 (Minn 1991), *cert denied*, 112 S Ct 882(1992)

8. Kaunitz AM, Spence C, Danielson TS, Rochat RW, Grimes DA. Perinatal and maternal mortality in a religious group avoiding obstetric care. *Am J Obstet Gynecol*. 1984;150:826–831

9. Rodgers DV, Gindler JS, Atkinson WL, Markowitz LE. High attack rates and case fatality during a measles outbreak in groups with religious exemption to vaccination. *Pediatr Infect Dis J*. 1993;12:288–292

10. Etkind P, Lett SM, Macdonald PD, Silva E, Peppe J. Pertussis outbreaks in groups claiming religious exemptions to vaccinations. *AJDC*. 1992; 146:173–176

11. Novotny T, Jennings CE, Doran M, et al. Measles outbreaks in religious groups exempt from immunization laws. *Public Health Rep*. 1988;103: 49–54

12. Centers for Disease Control. Outbreak of measles among Christian Science students—Missouri and Illinois, 1994. *MMWR*. 1994;43:463–465

13. Committee on Bioethics, American Academy of Pediatrics. Informed consent, parental permission, and assent in pediatric practice. *Pediatrics*. 1995;95:314–317

Munchausen Syndrome by Proxy

See Also:
Poisoning as Child Abuse

Clinical Principles

▼ Munchausen Syndrome by Proxy (MSBP) is a malignant disorder of parenting in which false stories and/or fabricated evidence result in repetitive and needless medical evaluations, testing, and hospitalizations. The fabricated illnesses may be simulated or actually produced.

▼ The diagnosis should be considered when the child's medical history is unusual, extensive, cannot be confirmed, or does not make sense in terms of the expected clinical course. Signs and symptoms often "occur" only in the presence of the perpetrator.

▼ Some children may have real medical conditions as well, but exaggeration and fabrication in these cases result in undue testing, procedures, and hospitalizations.

▼ The emphasis in evaluation and protection of these children should be placed on assessing the harm (physical, psychological) to the child, not on making a specific diagnosis of MSBP. This is important, because the social/legal systems understand harm, but not always MSBP.

▼ Evaluation and management should include resolution of the medical dilemmas and cessation of unnecessary evaluation and treatment; thorough education of child protection and law enforcement personnel, as well as county attorneys, regarding the dilemmas and risks posed by investigation of MSBP; detailed review of medical records of the patient (and often family members); psychiatric/psychological evaluation of the alleged perpetrator; and ongoing monitoring of the child's health by individuals knowledgeable about the nature of the child's problems and family. Separation of the perpetrator and child for evaluation and protection may be prudent.

Other Comments

▼ The diagnosis of a falsified or factitious illness is primarily a medical diagnosis based on evaluation of the medical information for the child, rather than psychological evaluation of the alleged perpetrator.

▼ Do not rely on a specific profile of alleged perpetrators to identify possible victims. Some common motivations and characteristics of perpetrators (95% mothers) may help identify this condition, but they vary and are not always present.

▼ Controversy abounds in terms of the scope of what should be included in the diagnosis of MSBP—from a broad spectrum of factitious disorders with varying motivations to a very narrow range of factitious illnesses with the sick role by proxy as a specific motivation. (Also see references.) Many professionals have begun referring to the problem as factitious disorder by proxy to avoid the controversy of the specificity of the label, but agreement has not yet been reached on how to handle the dilemma.

▼ Most authors suggest a clear description of the nature of the harm to the child is more helpful than the label. A specific diagnosis or identified motivation in the alleged perpetrator, when identified, may be helpful in determining a plan of action.

Bibliography

Research and Review

Rosenberg DA. Web of deceit: a literature review of Munchausen Syndrome by Proxy. *Child Abuse Negl.* 1987;11:547-563
This is the most extensive review of this subject to date, detailing 117 cases reported until 1987 with 98 references.

Munchausen Syndrome by Proxy is a syndrome cluster consisting of the following:

1. Illness in a child that is simulated and/or produced by a parent;
2. Presentation of a child for medical assessment and care that is usually persistent and often results in multiple medical procedures;
3. Denial by the parent perpetrator as to the etiology of the child's illness; and
4. Acute signs and symptoms of the child that improve or disappear when the child is separated from the parent perpetrator.

The paper describes the many means abusers (almost always mothers) use to simulate and induce illnesses in their children and enlist medical professionals as "co-abusers." The prototypical mother spends much time at the hospital, may appear very knowledgeable about medical terminology (frequently having some medical or nursing training), and may appear to be the "ideal parent" although she does not display emotions appropriate to the seriousness of the situation.

Any age child may be affected, but the majority are infants or toddlers. Multiple organ systems may be involved, but the more frequent presentations were bleeding, seizures, central nervous system (CNS) depression, apnea, diarrhea, vomiting, fever, and rash. The symptomatology continues in the hospital 70% of the time. All affected children suffered acute and many also long-term morbidity. The overall mortality was 9%. Ten siblings of index cases died under unusual circumstances.

The psychopathology in the perpetrators is poorly defined and, when they are examined by psychiatrists and psychologists, frequently no definitive diagnoses are established. Effective therapy is difficult, especially since these mothers continue to deny the abuse.

The diagnosis of MSBP is frequently delayed for months or even years because of the failure of the physician to consider it instead of searching for very rare diagnoses. The clinician's denial of its possibility also plays a role. Once diagnosis is considered, further investigation is best accomplished by a multidisciplinary team. (GP) (Be sure to read Meadow's comments on this article, which follow).

Bools C, Neale B, Meadow R. Munchausen syndrome by proxy: a study of psychopathology. *Child Abuse Negl.* 1994;18:773-788
This study describes the follow-up of 56 families of approximately 100 known to the authors. Sufficient information was available on 47 mothers to report lifetime psychiatric histories. Somatizing disorders (72%), alcohol/drug misuse (21%), and self-harm (55%) were common problems. Of a subset of 19 mothers who were interviewed, 17 had personality disorders, predominantly histrionic and borderline types.

Bryk M, Siegel PT. My mother caused my illness: the story of a survivor of Munchausen by proxy syndrome. *Pediatrics.* 1997;100:1-7
This article chronicles the actual experiences of an MSBP victim through 8 years of medical abuse at the hands of her mother. It provides the victim's account of what happened to her, describes what her family was like, details the long-term consequences on emotional and physical development, identifies the factors that influence recovery, and details the impact of family relationships.

Gray J, Bentovim A. Illness induction syndrome: paper I - a series of 41 children from 37 families identified at the Great Ormand Street Hospital for Children NHS Trust. *Child Abuse Negl.* 1996;20:655-673
The authors describe a case review study of 41 children who had induced illnesses. Four patterns emerged: failure to thrive through withholding of food, allegation of allergy and food withholding, fabrication of medical symptoms, and active interference by poisoning or disrupting medical treatment. No specific characteristics of the child or family differentiated the types. The process of illness induction was conceptualized as starting with the parent's perception of the child being ill and subsequently using this as a way to solve major personal family or marital difficulties. The authors are trying to be more specific in describing and categorizing the details of the abuse and demonstrate that such categorization can be done.

Meadow SR. Munchausen syndrome by proxy (letter). *Child Abuse Negl.* 1990;14:289-290

Dr Meadow points out that the data from Dr Rosenberg's review of the literature, unbeknownst to her (or any other reader), included multiple reports on some patients, thus invalidating morbidity and mortality rates. He also notes that confrontation of a parent at the time the articles were written was fairly mild and did not usually include legal proceedings. He recommends using the information in the article (Rosenberg DA. Web of deceit: a literature review of Munchausen syndrome by proxy. *Child Abuse Negl.* 1987; 11:547-563) for qualitative aspects of the syndrome, but not quantitative aspects.

McClure RJ, Davis PM, Meadow SR, et al. Epidemiology of Munchausen syndrome by proxy, non-accidental poisoning, and non-accidental suffocation. *Arch Dis Child.* 1996;75:57-61

Surveillance over a 26-month period from 1992 to 1994 in the United Kingdom and Republic of Ireland identified 128 formal case conferences held to discuss MSBP, nonaccidental poisoning, or nonaccidental suffocation. The majority of children were younger than 5 years, and the mother was identified as the perpetrator in 85% of cases. Most pediatricians (85%) considered their diagnoses virtually certain prior to calling a conference. The combined annual incidence of these conditions is reported as at least 0.5 per 100,000, and in children younger than 1 year was 2.8 per 100,000.

Porter GE, Heitsch GM, Miller MD. Munchausen syndrome by proxy: unusual manifestations and disturbing sequelae. *Child Abuse Negl.* 1994;18:789-794

This brief report describes and confirms that truly bizarre and even more complicated cases of MSBP continue to be identified. This report identifies esophageal perforation (by vigorous deep suctioning), retrograde intussusception, and tooth loss. Bradycardia may have been induced by carotid artery massage.

Skau K, Mouridsen SE. Munchausen syndrome by proxy: a review. *Acta Paediatr.* 1995;84:977-982

The authors review the literature on epidemiology, perpetrators, family dynamics, recognition, management, and prognosis. They synthesize well many of the articles reviewed in this work. They identify MSBP as a borderline diagnosis between pediatrics and psychiatry that requires a lot of teamwork. The presentation of symptoms encompasses a huge range from slight exaggeration to physical abuse in both boys and girls. More than one child in the family may be affected. Mothers are most often the perpetrators; fathers are often described as distant or emotionally uninvolved.

A long latency from onset to diagnosis is common. Warning signals are identified as (1) unexplained, prolonged, and/or extraordinary illness; (2) signs and symptoms that are incongruous, inappropriate, or occur only when the mother is present; (3) ineffective or poorly tolerated treatments; (4) children alleged to be allergic to a great variety of foods and drugs; (5) mothers who appear inappropriately less concerned than health providers, will not leave the child, and form unusually close relationships on the ward, and (6) families with a history of sudden or unexplained infant deaths or many family members with serious medical disorders. Team case conferences are suggested as the best approach to determine further action. Management strategies include involvement of child protection services, protection of the child, confronting the family with the knowledge of what is happening, and the involvement of psychiatric services. Mistreatment is likely to continue if the child is not removed.

Diagnostic Considerations

Donald T, Jureidini J. Munchausen syndrome by proxy, child abuse in the medical system. *Arch Pediatr Adolesc Med.* 1996;150:753-758

This manuscript examines the current dilemmas in diagnosis and labeling of cases of MSBP. A clear discussion giving consideration to handling MSBP cases more in line with the handling of other forms of child abuse is presented. There has been inconsistency in how the term is applied— to the victim or perpetrator. The authors present a very enlightening and thought-provoking section on the role of the medical system. They suggest that the extent and quality of medical involvement is the most useful basis on which to differentiate MSBP from other forms of child abuse. They support the approach of diagnosing the medical condition of the abused child and, when possible, the psychiatric condition of the perpetrator. This can potentially avoid compromise by disputes about the appropriateness of an MSBP label. The implications for management of suspected MSBP cases are discussed.

Fisher GC, Mitchell I. Is Munchausen syndrome by proxy really a syndrome? *Arch Dis Child.* 1995;72:530-534

A review of MSBP is provided, with a discussion of issues in classification, comparing and contrasting the classification scheme of Libow and Schrier (active inducers, help seekers, doctor addicts) with the dimensional model (level of agreement between parent and physician on the need for consultation) of Eminson and Postlethwaite (Eminson DM, Postlethwaite RJ. Factitious illness: recognition and management. *Arch Dis Child.* 1992;67:1510-1516). The dilemma of MSBP as a pediatric or psychiatric diagnosis is discussed. The terms "MSBP" and "factitious illness" that have created trouble are discussed and recommendations for describing the observed situation rather than labeling are made.

Foreman DM, Farcides C. Ethical use of covert videoing techniques in detecting Munchausen syndrome by proxy. *BMJ.* 1993;307:611-613

The authors discuss the ethical issues in covert videotaping and suggest that the breach of trust by covert videotaping makes it unethical in most circumstances. In light of the Children's Act in Britain, they argue sufficient information should be obtained by separation of the parent and child or videotaping with consent. In some cases, however, it is considered ethical if the information obtained is not otherwise available.

Jones DP. Commentary: Munchausen syndrome by proxy - is expansion justified? *Child Abuse Negl.* 1996;20:983-984

In response to the following article by Schreier, this author takes issue for various reasons with the suggestion made by Schreier to expand the term MSBP to encompass broader forms of fabrication. Not enough is currently known about the causes and origins of MSBP. Use of the terminology in nonmedical settings could result in a significant diminution of its present meaning. Jones, like many other authors, prefers describing the harm to the child over picking a label.

Meadow R. What is, and what is not, 'Munchausen syndrome by proxy'? *Arch Dis Child.* 1995;72:534-538

This article begins to delineate clearly the diagnostic difficulties being confronted with MSBP and suggests that many forms of child abuse are being mislabeled as MSBP. Some of these other conditions that are "not quite" MSBP include unrecognized physical abuse (poisoning, suffocation), failure to thrive (when the mother lies about the circumstances), overanxious parent, mothers with delusional disorders, masquerade syndrome, hysteria by proxy, doctor shopping, and mothering to death. Meadow recognizes the inherent difficulty in restricting the definition to conditions in which the mother's motivation is to assume the sick role for herself, but does recommend the term MSBP be reserved for those cases. It is suggested that the way in which the child is abused must be carefully detailed and is more important than the nonspecific label.

Morley CJ. Practical concerns about the diagnosis of Munchausen syndrome by proxy. *Arch Dis Child.* 1995;72:528-530

This paper describes concerns about the difficulties and pitfalls in diagnosing MSBP. The use of the label is charged with emotion and is not as useful as a statement of the exact nature of the problem. The nonspecific nature of previously proposed criteria for diagnosis is discussed. The initial histories may not have been accurately heard, the frequency of seeking health care is not known; and sick children will go to the doctor more often, and denial of a role in the child's illness may be real. An illness that clears upon separation of the child and parent may simply be following the natural course of the illness and timing is coincidental. Concerns about interpreting histories as indicating fabrication, labeling exaggeration as MSBP, and inadequate history taking in general are also discussed. This paper reflects some of the general concern about issues in diagnosis of MSBP, pointing to the value of a careful multidisciplinary evaluation.

Reece RM, ed. *Child Abuse: Medical Diagnosis and Management*. Malvern, PA: Lea & Febiger; 1994.

The chapter on Munchausen Syndrome by Proxy in this textbook offers an excellent overview of the presentation, diagnosis, and management of this difficult condition. Particularly helpful may be the recommendations for approaches to establishing the diagnosis and protecting the child in the process.

Schreier HA. Repeated false allegations of sexual abuse presenting to sheriffs: when is it Munchausen by proxy? *Child Abuse Negl.* 1996;20:985-991

This report describes law enforcement as the primary "target" for a dependent relationship in a case with false allegations of child sexual abuse. The apparent need for relationships with powerful transferential people makes school psychologists, social workers, and lawyers the professionals other than physicians who might become involved in MSBP cases. The author offers some guidelines in assessing motives of parents to help differentiate MSBP from a custody battle. The author suggests expansion of the term MSBP to include behaviors beyond the medical sphere.

Southall DP, Plunkett MCB, Banks MW, Falkov AF, Samuels MP. Covert video recordings of life-threatening child abuse: lessons for child protection. *Pediatrics.* 1997;100:735-760

The authors report results of in-hospital covert video surveillance (CVS) of 39 children (median age 9 months, range 2 to 44 months) with apparent life-threatening events (ALTE). Representing about 15% of children with ALTE seen at national center hospitals in the United Kingdom, those undergoing CVS were generally selected through multi-agency planning meetings. Duration of CVS averaged 29 hours, with the middle half range being 5 to 60 hours.

In 33 cases surveillance identified abuse, often attempted suffocation while asleep. Many of the proffered explanations might have been plausible were it not for the video. Some parents repeatedly pinched or otherwise injured their children prior to a suffocation attempt. The authors reviewed the mechanisms of ALTE in apparently healthy infants and children and identified several associations with child abuse as the cause, including bleeding from the nose or mouth, having a sibling who died suddenly and unexpectedly, abuse of a sibling, and petechial hemorrhage of the face. Premature birth was less common, and ALTE occurred somewhat later on average in this population when compared with infants suffering ALTE from a respiratory mechanism. Personality disorder among the parents was relatively more common, although the authors did not obtain adequate information in many of the cases. The authors noted that attention-seeking behavior seemed to be important to many of the parents. They suggest that dramatic presentations, episodes occurring during times of parental stress, the absence of independent observers at the onset, and ceasing of episodes following parental separation may also be associated with similar cases elsewhere.

The authors recommend new strategies for assessing infants with ALTE, including a "low threshold" for obtaining skeletal survey, retinal exam, and brain imaging studies; evaluation of siblings and their medical histories; and reviews of child abuse registries. In cases with bleeding from the nose or mouth or histories of sudden death of siblings in childhood, they call for "a full and forensic analysis." They note that in 30% of the positive CVS cases, the referring pediatrician offered no hint that ALTE might have been due to abuse. They believe that CVS provided critical information necessary to protect children in a majority of the cases. They recommend CVS as standard practice. Finally, they discuss strategies for identifying and protecting children from abuse at the hands of deceptive and sadistic parents. In an accompanying editorial (*Pediatrics.* 1997;100:890-891), Krugman notes that CVS may not be required of all pediatricians, but he exhorts us all to "overcome our professional and societal denial" of abuse and neglect by supporting relevant research (eg, a "nurturing defect" in mice associated with a single gene) and working harder in diagnosis. (DS)

Follow-Up and Outcome

Bools CN, Neale BA, Meadow SR. Follow-up of victims of fabricated illness (Munchausen syndrome by proxy). *Arch Dis Child.* 1993;69: 625-630

The authors report on 54 children followed 1 to 14 years after a diagnosis of fabricated illness. Ten children suffered from further fabrications. Almost half (49%) had outcomes that were considered unacceptable, including conduct and emotional disorders.

Kinscherff R, Famularo R. Extreme Munchausen syndrome by proxy: the cases for termination of parental rights. *Juvenile Fam Court J.* 1991;42:41-53

This article reviews the syndrome and discusses extreme MSBP in the context of the law. It is argued that the system fails in these cases because of ignorance, convincing denial by the parent, and shifting players in the child protection and legal systems. The authors describe practical inefficiencies of juvenile and child protective systems and the nature of the risks posed to children by extreme MSBP that may form the basis of the argument for termination in some cases. This article can be helpful in educating legal colleagues because of the legal framework placed on some of the issues.

Libow JA. Munchausen syndrome by proxy victims in adulthood: a first look. *Child Abuse Negl.* 1995;19:1131-1142

Libow reports on 10 adults who were self-identified victims of illness fabricated by a parent. Posttraumatic stress symptoms, avoidance of medical treatment, and insecurity in adulthood were reported. Some parents continued to attempt to abuse (eg, poison) even when their children were adults. Some adults have continued to fabricate their own illnesses.

Acknowledgment

This section and its annotations were prepared by Roberta A. Hibbard, MD; selected annotations were written by Gerald E. Porter, MD, and David P. Schor, MD, MPH. Section review was by Gerald E. Porter, MD.

Neglect

See Also:
Failure to Thrive

Any one definition of neglect is problematic. In general, neglect involves inattention to a developing child's needs by parent(s) or caregiver with respect to physical care, health care, education, nutrition, stimulation, discipline, safety, and emotional nurture.

An explanation of what a "reasonable" or "prudent" parent or guardian must do is helpful (American Professional Society on the Abuse of Children, 1994). The duties are to provide, supervise, and to intervene; failure to do so may result in the child's serious illness or death.

Clinical Principles

▼ Failure to provide for basic needs—nutrition, clothing, and shelter—is most common and most apt to cause morbidity.

▼ Failure to provide stimulation, emotional support, and nurturance can lead to developmental and behavioral disturbances later in life.

▼ Failure to provide appropriate and timely medical and/or dental care in acute and/or chronic conditions may lead to serious illness or death, (eg, failure to provide necessary prescription medications to an asthmatic or diabetic).

▼ Failure to provide support for appropriate educational programs, including special education, may hinder the establishment of life skills.

▼ Failure to supervise, attend, guide, or protect children from dangerous situations (eg, fire, falls, extreme cold or heat, drownings, ingestions, poisonings, kidnapping, or dehydration) may result in injury or fatality.

▼ Failure to intervene, protect, or seek medical treatment for a child abused or neglected by another caretaker is neglect.

Other Comments

▼ Neglect is the most common form of child maltreatment, constituting nearly 60% of all reported cases of child abuse and neglect, and causing significant morbidity and mortality.

▼ Child neglect has severe negative consequences for its victims due to maltreatment, including fatalities (1.5 deaths per day) and severe deficits in cognitive or psychosocial functioning.

▼ Child neglect is strongly associated with poverty and female-headed households. It is often linked to physical and/or sexual abuse and differs across cultures and ethnicities.

▼ Factors that may predispose to child neglect include the following: mother's history of sexual abuse, mother's young age at first birth, number of children, mother's education, early failure to thrive, prematurity/LBW, lower levels of social support, perception of difficult infant temperament, child younger than 3 years of age, low-functioning parent(s), parental stressors, parental lack of skill, and problems with respect to parental roles and relationships.

▼ Neglect accelerates the cycle of morbidity and stress associated with chronic illness. "Chaotic" families fail to cope with chronic illness, or the medical and psychosocial demands that accompany chronic illness stress families beyond their capacity to cope.

Bibliography

Boxer GH, Carson J, Miller BD. Neglect contributing to tertiary hospitalization in childhood asthma. *Child Abuse Negl.* **1988;12:491-501**
This report substantiates the extent to which neglect and family dysfunction contribute to the need for hospitalization, and it discusses asthmatic children at imminent risk if returned to their home environment. The process of seeking alternative placements such as day treatment and home outreach programs are discussed.

Brayden BM, Altemeier WA, Tucker DD, Dietrich MS, Vietze P. Antecedents of child neglect in the first two years of life. *J Pediatr:* **1992;120:426-429**
This is a prospective study of low-income mothers in one urban hospital determined to be at high risk prenatally for maltreatment. Neglectful mothers

were less likely to have completed high school, had more children younger than 6 years, and scored poorer on the parenting skills and support systems scales. Neglected children were lower in birth weight, were rated more difficult temperamentally, and had poorer mental and motor developmental scores.

Drake B, Pandey S. Understanding the relationship between neighborhood poverty and specific types of child maltreatment. *Child Abuse Negl.* 1996;20:1003-1018

A comprehensive analysis of maltreatment types (physical abuse, sexual abuse, and neglect) by level of poverty was performed. Child neglect was most powerfully associated with neighborhood poverty status, while sexual abuse substantiation rates were invariant across poverty levels, but only moderately associated with poverty.

Johnson CF. Physicians and medical neglect: variables that affect reporting. *Child Abuse Negl.* 1993;17:605-612

Many factors affect the physician's decision to report medical neglect. There are no guidelines for determining medical neglect of specific diseases, and there is a need for definition. The wide range of responses to a survey of 52 physicians in a children's hospital were influenced by variables in physicians, caregivers, and 46 specific diseases such as leukemia and seizure disorder. Health care providers may need to identify the parents at high risk for medical neglect and target them for intensive training and assistance.

Jones ED, McCurdy K. The links between types of maltreatment and demographic characteristics of children. *Child Abuse Negl.* 1992;16:201-215

Utilizing a national sample from the second National Incidence Study of Child Abuse and Neglect (NIS-2), this article reports on four types of child maltreatment: physical abuse, sexual abuse, emotional maltreatment, and physical neglect. Physical neglect is the most predictable type, distinguishable and common (55% of cases reported), and most clearly related to economics, such as low income and AFDC status, regardless of race. Individuals who neglect their children most likely represent a fairly distinct group from those who sexually abuse their children. Children younger than age 3 years face the greatest likelihood of neglect.

Margolin L. Fatal child neglect. *Child Welfare.* 1990;69:309-319

This article isolates circumstances in Iowa surrounding fatal neglect, and differentiates them from those circumstances involved in (intentional) fatal abuse and those from (inadvertent) non–life-threatening neglect. Fatal neglect victims were younger (65% <2 years), male (71%), and from larger (4.9 members) single-parent families, and died as a result of neglect by a biological relative (88%) who was not there at a critical moment.

Sedlak AJ, Broadhurst DD. *Third National Incidence Study of Child Abuse and Neglect: Final Report.* US Dept of Health & Human Services; 1996

Substantial and significant increases in the child abuse and neglect incidence were found to have occurred since 1986, when the previous study was conducted. There was an 85% increase in the total number of children neglected—an estimated 879,000 during 1993. The majority (57%) of children countable under the Harm Standard were neglected, 48% were abused. Large, low-income families headed by a single parent are at highest risk.

Wolock I, Horowitz B. Child maltreatment as a social problem: the neglect of neglect. *Am J Orthopsychiatry.* 1984;54:530-543

This is a sociological analysis of issues related to both child abuse and child neglect—the latter occurring much more frequently, but the former receiving almost all the attention. Historical factors and the relationship between child neglect and poverty are viewed as the major reasons for the de-emphasis of neglect relative to abuse. This article provides a good summary of research on both.

Acknowledgment
This section and its annotations were prepared by Paula K. Jaudes, MD, and were reviewed by Kent P. Hymel, MD.

Photographic Documentation of Child Abuse

See Also:
Cutaneous Manifestations of Child Abuse

Clinical Principles

▼ The child should have a clear understanding of what is about to be done. It may be helpful to let the patient try out the camera and flash.

▼ Children should be allowed to assume a comfortable position. Better a cooperative, quiet subject in a less than optimal photographic position than an awkwardly positioned, moving child.

Technical/Mechanical Aspects

▼ No particular photographic system is best. A quality lens, adequate flash, and proper technique are far more important than the brand or type of equipment.

▼ Color photographs are recommended, with an object of reproducible pure color and a small metric scale inserted in the photograph.

▼ Physical abuse can be adequately documented with anything from a simple instant or self-developing camera to a sophisticated 35-mm close-up system.

▼ The colposcope has obvious advantages when documenting magnified examination of the sexually abused child, but all situations do not require such expensive equipment. Macro lenses or standard lenses with close-up adapters attached to a 35-mm camera can produce fine anatomic detail. Less expensive instant or self-developing camera systems can also provide adequate evidence.

Other Comments

▼ Photographs of abused children should provide a fair and accurate representation of the scene.

▼ Photographs to be submitted as legal evidence must be properly verified and relevant.

▼ The photographer or physician must be able to testify as to how the pictures were taken, and to verify that they accurately represent the physical findings.

Bibliography

Finkel MA, Ricci LR. Documentation and preservation of visual evidence in child abuse. *Child Maltreatment.* 1997;2:322-330
This article discusses documentation technologies, such as still and video cameras, colposcopes, and computer-based imaging. It presents the justification for such equipment and explores options for processing, storage, duplication, and computer transmission.

Ricci LR. Photodocumentation of the abused child. In: Reece RM, ed. *Child Abuse: Medical Diagnosis and Management.* **Philadelphia, PA: Lea and Febiger; 1994:248-265**
This chapter includes descriptions of the types of cameras and lenses, macrophotography, colposcopic photography, lighting, film, and composition. Legal issues are summarized.

Ricci LR. Photographing the physically abused child: principles and practice. *Am J Dis Child.* 1991;145:275-281
Physicians who examine sexually abused children should have ready access to an adequate photographic system, as well as basic knowledge of camera operation, film procedures, planned composition, and medicolegal implications.

Southall DP, Plunkett MCB, Banks MW, Falkov AF, Samuels MP. Covert video recordings of life-threatening child abuse: lessons for child protection. *Pediatrics.* 1997;100:735-760
The authors report results of in-hospital covert video surveillance of 39 children. In 33 cases, abuse was identified, often attempted suffocation while asleep.

Woodling BA, Heger A. The use of the colposcope in the diagnosis of sexual abuse in the pediatric age group. *Child Abuse Negl.* 1986;10:111-114

Acknowledgment

This section and its annotations were prepared by Lawrence R. Ricci, MD, and Jerry G. Jones, MD.

Poisoning as Child Abuse

See Also:
Homicide
Munchausen Syndrome by Proxy
Substance Use Disorders

Clinical Principles

▼ Most cases of intentional poisoning in children are undetected because of failure to consider the diagnosis or to order appropriate laboratory tests.

▼ Children have been poisoned by over-the-counter medications, eg, laxatives or ipecac; prescription drugs, eg, insulin, thyroxine, or furosemide; illicit drugs, eg, marijuana or cocaine; and common household compounds, eg, water, salt, pepper, or alcohol.

▼ Poisoning is suggested by unexplained vomiting, diarrhea, hypoglycemia, skeletal or cardiac myopathies, lethargy, apnea, seizures, ataxia, or other neurologic symptoms or signs.

Other Comments

▼ With intentional poisoning, the mother is most often responsible (Munchausen syndrome by proxy), and the poisoning frequently continues while the child is hospitalized.

▼ Other types of abuse and especially neglect should be considered in these children.

Bibliography
Review Article

Bays J. Child abuse by poisoning. In: Reece R, ed. *Child Abuse: Medical Diagnosis and Management*. Malvern, PA: Lea & Febiger; 1993
In this extensive, comprehensive reference on intentional poisoning in children, the author reviews 100 cases and provides 143 references.

Cocaine Exposure

Dinnies JD, Darr CD, Saulys AJ. Cocaine toxicity in toddlers, letter. *Am J Dis Child.* 1990;144:743-744

Mott SH, Packer RJ, Soldin SJ. Neurologic manifestations of cocaine exposure in childhood. *Pediatrics.* 1994;93:557-560

Shannon MW, Lacouture P, Roa J, Woolf A. Cocaine exposure in pediatrics, abstracted. *Am J Dis Child.* 1988;142:385
Young children may be passively intoxicated by crack cocaine smoked in their environments, or they may accidentally ingest or be fed cocaine powder. Children younger than 5 years of age exposed to cocaine demonstrate seizures and obtundation, while older children exhibit adult-type symptoms (delirium, dizziness, drooling, and lethargy). Cocaine may lower the seizure threshold in patients already prone to seizures. Urine screening for cocaine metabolites should be performed in children with new-onset seizures (febrile or nonfebrile, focal or generalized). Of 1,429 consecutive serum and urine toxicology screens at a children's hospital, 3.4% were positive for cocaine (mainly unsuspected).

Endocrine/Metabolic Disorders

D'Avanzo M, Santinelli R, Tolone C, et al. Concealed administration of furosemide simulating Bartter syndrome in a 4½ year old boy. *Pediatr Nephrol.* 1995;9:749-750
The patient had recurrent episodes of dehydration and polyuria with hypochloremia, hypokalemia, metabolic alkalosis, and impaired ability to concentrate the urine. A renal biopsy failed to reveal juxtaglomerular hyperplasia, and the urine was found to contain furosemide. The child did well after separation from the mother. Urines should be screened for diuretics in children with findings consistent with Bartter syndrome.

Ginies JL, Cascarigny F, Bouygues D, Limal JM: Syndrome de Munchausen par procuration: suite. *Arch Pediatr.* 1996;3:193 (in French)

Factitious hyperthyroidism was produced by a mother giving thyroxine to an 11-month-old. The child presented with failure to thrive and irritability. The mother had previously induced gastrointestinal symptoms in an older sibling.

Marks V. Hypoglycemia–real and unreal, lawful and unlawful: the 1994 Banting Lecture. *Diabetic Med.* 1995;12:850-864

Induced hypoglycemia has been reported in at least 10 cases. In all cases of hypoglycemia, serum or plasma should be frozen for subsequent sulfonylurea, insulin, C-peptide, and proinsulin assays. Postmortem blood glucose levels may be either spuriously high or low but insulin, C-peptide, and proinsulin are stable if collected within 24 hours after death.

Ipecac Poisoning

Goebel J, Gremse DA, Artman M. Cardiomyopathy from ipecac administration in Munchausen syndrome by proxy. *Pediatrics.* 1993;92:601-603

Schneider DJ, Perez A, Knilans TE, et al. Clinical and pathologic aspects of cardiomyopathy from ipecac administration in Munchausen's syndrome by proxy. *Pediatrics.* 1996;97:902-906.

Children with ipecac ingestion presented with recurrent vomiting and diarrhea, frequently producing dehydration requiring hospitalization. Many went on to develop cardiomyopathy (may be fatal) and skeletal muscle hypotonia. In this form of poisoning, muscle enzymes may be elevated. Rehydration may induce cardiac failure. Routine blood and urine drug screens will not detect emetine and cephaline (ipecac metabolites), and these must be sought in blood, urine, and gastric secretions at very specialized reference laboratories (listed in articles). Ipecac metabolites accumulate in the kidneys and may be found in the urine weeks after administration ceases. The myopathies may develop several weeks after cessation of ipecac administration. Electron microscopy of cardiac and skeletal muscle tissue may show characteristic abnormalities.

Sodium Poisoning

Carlson J, Fernlund P, Ivarsson S-A, Jakobsson I, et al. Munchausen syndrome by proxy: an unexpected cause of severe chronic diarrhoea in a child. *Acta Paediatr.* 1994;83:119-121

The poison in this case was sodium sulfate. The patient had high serum and urine sodium levels, suggesting high sodium intake. Stool analysis showed high sodium and sulfate levels. Other agents that may cause diarrhea include other sodium salts, eg, sodium phosphate, magnesium salts, phenolphthalein, and ipecac. Routine toxicology screens may not demonstrate many of these agents, and special laboratory tests must be ordered.

Meadow R. Non-accidental salt poisoning. *Arch Dis Child.* 1993;68:448-452

These children usually present in the first 6 months of life with unexplained hypernatremia and associated illness (vomiting, diarrhea, lethargy and other neurologic findings, and failure to thrive). If not vomiting or comatose, they are frequently very thirsty, as they are usually also fluid restricted. The urine sodium concentrations were 150 to 360 mmol/L (usually 200-230), making salt ingestion the most likely diagnosis. When tested, some children had exceedingly high sodium levels in their gastric contents. (Gastric content sodium is usually 50-60 mmol/L and levels above 200 are highly suggestive of salt ingestion.) Two children had abnormal sweat tests while in the care of their mothers, and one mother submitted a breast milk sample with a very high sodium concentration. These salt-poisoned children usually have normal bicarbonate and creatinine levels compared with acidotic and uremic patients with hypernatremic dehydration. Results of renal, endocrinological, and other investigations are normal. Their sodium levels should be corrected gradually. They may have better prognoses than children with hypernatremic dehydration. Many of the children were repeatedly poisoned.

Other Poisoning

Gieron-Korthals MA, Westberry KR, Emmanuel PJ. Acute childhood ataxia: 10 year experience. *J Child Neurol.* 1994;9:381-384

Thirty-five of 40 cases of acute ataxia in children 0 to 18 years of age (85% younger than 12 years) had drug screening and 17 were positive. Patients with positive screens frequently had changes in mental status. Drugs found included benzodiazepines, phenytoin, phenobarbital, carbamazepine, and phenothiazines. In cases of acute ataxia, in addition to a thorough history and physical exam, a drug screen should be performed before admission and before ordering more expensive and invasive tests.

Gotschlich T, Beltran RS. Poisoning of a 21-month-old child by a baby-sitter. *Clin Pediatr.* 1995;34:52-53

A baby-sitter gave a child muriatic acid, and she probably also had done this to an older sibling. Baby-sitters may poison children for amusement, to sedate the children, or because of the sitter's mental illness.

McClure RJ, Davis PM, Meadow SR, Sibert JR. Epidemiology of Munchausen syndrome by proxy, non-accidental poisoning, and non-accidental suffocation. *Arch Dis Child.* 1996;75:57-61

Over a 2-year period, 44 intentional poisonings of children were diagnosed in the United Kingdom and the Republic of Ireland. The commonest drugs were anticonvulsants, opiates, benzodiazepines, tricyclic antidepressants, acetaminophen, salt, and antihistamines.

Additional Resource

Hanzlick R. National Association of Medical Examiner's Pediatric Toxicology (PedTox) Registry. *Toxicology.* 1996; 107:153-158

This registry has been established to collect both fatal and nonfatal case reports of drugs and substances in children. The registry's purpose is to provide additional information to those who must interpret observed concentrations of drugs and substances in children. Contact Randy Hanzlick, 916 Cumberland Rd NE; Atlanta, GA 30306; phone, 404/616-6621.

Acknowledgment

This section and its annotations were prepared by Gerald E. Porter, MD, and reviewed by Roberta A. Hibbard, MD.

Prevention of Child Abuse

See Also:
Corporal Punishment

Clinical Principles

▼ The incidence of child abuse and neglect in this country is too high.

▼ In several parts of the world, the goal of child protection is achieved by providing support services to the general population and by increasing the intensity of those services for those who have greater needs, leaving the court-mandated interventions for the highest risk cases.

▼ There is growing awareness that the reactive and adversarial nature of this country's child protection system is a serious impediment to achieving the goal of preventing abuse.

Assessment of the effectiveness of prevention programs is complicated by a number of factors. In determining the effectiveness of *physical abuse prevention,* the most significant problem in controlled trials is the detection bias that exists between the control and intervention groups, resulting in better detection of abuse in the intervention groups than in the control groups. An aspect of family functioning generally unrecognized by physicians has been spousal violence and its accompanying risk of potentially preventable child abuse.

The strategies to prevent sexual abuse are different from those required to prevent physical abuse. In determining the effectiveness of *sexual abuse prevention efforts,* several studies have provided evidence that educational programs can improve safety skills and children's knowledge about sexual abuse. However, no study has demonstrated that education actually reduces the occurrence of sexual abuse. Anecdotal evidence suggests an increased disclosure of ongoing abuse following educational programs about sexual abuse. An aspect of prevention education programs that has not been explored well is the fear and anxiety that the programs may cause.

Bibliography

General

The US Advisory Board on Child Abuse and Neglect: *Neighbors Helping Neighbors: A New National Strategy for the Protection of Children. Executive Summary.* US Department of Health and Human Services, Administration for Children and Families, Washington, DC: Sept 1993

> The bottom line is that the child maltreatment crisis in this country is not being alleviated. It is worsening. We will not reverse current trends until (1) we recognize the inherent failure in a child protection system driven by investigation; (2) we engage in careful analysis and research to better understand the causes of child maltreatment; (3) we acknowledge and begin to change the conditions that permit the occurrence of child abuse and neglect; and (4) we realize that this is a problem that affects society as a whole and, therefore, an effective solution must be broad based in nature.

The suggested new national strategy must be comprehensive, neighborhood based, child centered, and family focused.

Prevention of Physical Abuse

Leventhal JM. Twenty years later: we do know how to prevent child abuse and neglect. *Child Abuse Negl.* 1996;20:647-653

Behrman RE (ed). Home visiting. *The Future of Children.* 1993;3:1-214
This publication of the David and Lucille Packard Foundation may be ordered at no charge (www.Futureofchildren.org).

MacMillan HL, et al. Primary prevention of child physical abuse and neglect: a critical review, Part I. *J Child Psychol Psychiatry*. 1994;35:835-856

Primary prevention is the prevention of the first event of abuse or neglect, rather than prevention of its recurrence. This article reviews the effectiveness of interventions aimed at primary prevention. While many of these programs did not show a reduction in physical abuse or neglect, there is evidence that extended home visitation can prevent physical abuse and neglect among disadvantaged families.

Olds DL, Eckenrode J, Henderson CR, et al. Long-term effects of home visitation on maternal life course and child abuse and neglect. *JAMA*. 1997;278:637-643

This is a remarkable 15-year follow-up of the children in the previous study. The author found that their program of prenatal and early childhood home visits by nurses can reduce child abuse and neglect, the number of subsequent pregnancies, use of welfare, and criminal behavior by low-income, unmarried mothers for up to 15 years after the birth of the first child.

Olds DL, Henderson CR, Kitzman H. Does prenatal and infancy nurse home visitation have enduring effects on qualities of parental caregiving and child health at 25 to 50 months of life? *Pediatrics*. 1994;93:89-98

This was a randomized study of 400 generally low-income or young primiparous women in semirural upstate New York. The authors concluded that, "The program does have enduring effects on certain aspects of parental caregiving, safety of the home, and children's use of the health care system, but it may be necessary to extend the length of the program for families at highest risk to produce lasting reductions in child abuse and neglect."

Roberts I, Kramer MS, Suissa S. Does home visiting prevent childhood injury? a systematic review of randomized controlled trials. *BMJ*. 1996;312:29-33

Ross S. Risk of physical abuse to children of spouse abusing parents. *Child Abuse Negl*. 1996;20:589-598

The risk of child physical abuse is high in situations of family violence, often not addressed in the context of pediatric care. This study showed that the greater the amount of violence against a spouse, the greater the probability of physical child abuse by the physically aggressive spouse. This relationship is stronger for husbands than for wives.

Prevention of Sexual Abuse

Daro DA. Prevention of child sexual abuse. *The Future of Children*. 1994;4:198-223

This is a good review article. The author examined 17 randomized trials and concluded that prevention programs overall have beneficial impacts, which are strongest for children 7 to 12 years old. (See Behrman entry for ordering information).

Elliott M, Browne K, Kilcoyne J. Child sexual abuse prevention: what offenders tell us. *Child Abuse Negl*. 1995;19:579-594

Results of interviews with acknowledged child sex offenders indicated that they gained access to children through caretaking; targeted children by using bribes, gifts, and games; used force, anger, threats, and bribes to ensure their continuing compliance; and systematically desensitized children through touch, talk about sex, and persuasion. Nearly half the offenders in this study had no bad feelings about sexually abusing children. This article provides suggestions about the prevention of child abuse. However, most of these prevention strategies focus on strangers, while most abuse occurs within the context of family and close contacts.

Acknowledgment

This section and its annotations were prepared by Mary M. Carrasco, MD, assisted by David P. Schor, MD, MPH.

Psychological Impact of Child Maltreatment

See Also:
Emotional Abuse
Sibling Studies
Substance Use Disorders

Clinical Principles

Physical Abuse

▼ Physical child maltreatment appears to affect a child's functioning in many areas, but particularly in terms of social and peer relationships and behavioral adjustment.

▼ The impact of physical maltreatment on a child is likely to be influenced by other child and family characteristics.

▼ The severity of physical injury does not appear to predict the severity of developmental dysfunction.

▼ For adults who were victims of physical child maltreatment, several different methodologies have demonstrated a strong relationship between physical abuse and nonfamilial and familial violence. Groups of adult substance abusers report higher rates of childhood physical abuse than those of the general population.

▼ Physical abuse has been associated with self-injurious and suicidal behaviors, as well as emotional problems such as somatization, anxiety, depression, dissociation, and psychosis in adult female inpatient and community samples.

Psychological Abuse

▼ Psychological maltreatment commonly co-occurs with physical maltreatment. However, there is evidence of adverse outcomes for children suffering psychological maltreatment without accompanying physical abuse.

▼ More research is needed before a good delineation of specific effects is available.

Neglect

▼ The developmental impact of neglect remains poorly understood despite data indicating that neglect is the most frequently reported category of child maltreatment (46%).

▼ Current findings suggest neglected children show deficits on measures of language ability and intelligence. They also suggest some qualitative differences in social cognition, delays in intellectual and linguistic abilities noted from infancy through adolescence, and behavioral difficulties and aggression in preschool and school-age children. Neglected children experience more negative affective states such as unhappiness and anger, as well as increased coping difficulties such as poor problem-solving ability.

▼ While males experiencing childhood neglect and/or physical abuse were at increased risk of engaging in subsequent violent criminal activity, the majority of neglected and physically abused children do not engage in later criminal activity.

Sexual Abuse

▼ Sexual abuse has been associated with a very wide variety of psychiatric and behavioral symptomatology, although no abuse-specific syndrome has been identified and not all victims develop apparent symptomatology. While methodological problems in existing research limit the ability to draw firm conclusions about abuse-specific sequelae, the symptoms that are most consistently cited in abused children and adolescents are sexualized behaviors and posttraumatic stress.

▼ Increased symptomatology appears to be related to the co-existence of family dysfunction and to several abuse-specific factors, such as increased severity of the abuse experience, greater frequency and duration of abuse, the use of force, and perpetration by a father figure.

▼ Adults sexually abused as children seem more commonly to experience sexual dysfunctions, anxious and depressive symptomatology, and revictimization experiences.

▼ Treatment intervention for management of the abuse experience appears to facilitate recovery, but the mechanism of such effect and the optimal therapeutic approach is not yet known.

Bibliography

Physical and Psychological Maltreatment and Neglect

Claussen AH, Crittenden PM. Physical and psychological maltreatment: relations among types of maltreatment. *Child Abuse Negl.* 1991;15:5-18
This study explored reasons for negative developmental outcome in child maltreatment. It was hypothesized that psychological maltreatment would be present in almost all cases of physical maltreatment and that psychological maltreatment would be more related to adverse outcomes than would severity of injury. Potentially adverse outcomes in children were assessed by trained interviewers' ratings regarding the effects of any type of maltreatment. Subjects were between the ages of 2 and 6, and included 175 maltreated children, 39 children in mental health treatment, and 176 normative children. Each child was assessed for type and severity of maltreatment. Support was found for both hypotheses. Furthermore, findings suggested that psychological maltreatment can occur alone, and that parental psychological maltreating behavior and negative child outcomes are highly correlated. Results also supported that age and gender in young children are not related to maltreatment, but that family income is related. Children from lower income families suffered more physical and cognitive neglect, which may be attributable to the family's lack of resources.

Cohen J, Mannarino A. Interventions for sexually abused children: initial treatment outcome findings. *J Child Maltreatment.* 1998;3:17-26
This study compared treatment outcomes for 49 recently sexually abused children ages 7 to 14. Subjects were randomly assigned to participate in sexual abuse-specific cognitive behavioral therapy or nondirective supportive therapy. Each child and his or her nonoffending parent participated in 12 individual treatment sessions. Sessions were monitored for compliance with the essential elements of the assigned treatment modality. Data were available from standardized assessment instruments completed by both the children and their parents before and after treatment. Children in the sexual abuse-specific cognitive behavioral therapy group were found to improve more on the Children's Depression Inventory and the Child Behavior Checklist Social Competence Scale than did children in the nondirective supportive therapy group. Clinical observation suggested that the sexual abuse-specific cognitive behavioral therapy may be more effective than nondirective supportive therapy for treatment of sexually inappropriate behaviors. This study gives support for the short-term outcome of a time-limited sexual abuse-focused cognitive behavioral treatment approach, especially in alleviating depressive symptoms.

Crouch JL, Milner JS. Effects of child neglect on children. *Crim Just Behav.* 1993; 20:49- 65
Research on the effects of child neglect on children's development is reviewed in this article. Methodological challenges caused by the nature of neglect are identified and discussed with respect to how these difficulties affect interpretation and generalizability of current findings. Empirical findings are explored regarding physical, intellectual, social, behavioral, and affective developmental domains. A developmental perspective is recommended throughout the review in order to conceptualize neglect and perceive its impact on child development.

Kolko DJ. Characteristics of child victims of physical violence. *J Int Viol.* 1992;7:244-276
Recent literature on empirical studies of short- and long-term outcomes of physical child maltreatment is reviewed according to impact on children's development and psychosocial functioning. Medical and cognitive factors

are examined with regard to development. Failure to thrive in infancy is primarily identified as a physical effect, while delays in intellectual and language development are frequently identified findings in the intellectual domain. Behavioral, interpersonal, academic, and affective outcomes and psychiatric disorders are explored in the domain of psychosocial functioning. Some studies of social and behavioral development in neglected children suggest that some children experience early passivity, isolation, and withdrawal, which gives way to later aggressive and/or delinquent behavior; this may vary according to gender. Research regarding affective and psychological adjustment for neglected children suggests difficulties with more negative than positive mood states and poorer coping skills.

Malinosky-Rummel R, Hansen DJ. Long-term consequences of childhood physical abuse. *Psychol Bull.* 1993;114:68-79
Empirical research on long-term consequences of childhood physical abuse examined potential outcomes for physical abuse and identified moderator variables. The seven potential areas include aggressive and violent behavior, nonviolent criminal behavior, substance abuse, self-injurious and suicidal behavior, emotional problems, interpersonal problems, and academic and vocational difficulties. The studies reviewed generally focus on adult populations with brief summaries of child and adolescent literature with relevant findings. The relationship of physical child maltreatment and nonfamilial and familial violence was a consistent finding with multiple methodologies yielding significant results. Also examined were moderator variables such as maltreatment characteristics, individual factors, family factors, and environmental factors that impact the relationship between physical abuse and long-term consequences.

Moore E, Armsden G, Gogerty P. A twelve year follow-up of maltreated and at-risk children who received early therapeutic child care. *J Child Maltreatment.* 1998;3:3-16.
Early intervention programs for abused and neglected children are increasingly being shown to report short-term positive results for children and parents, but long-term studies are not yet available. This study follows a randomized controlled clinical trial of a therapeutic child care program for maltreated or at-risk infants and toddlers 12 years after the original study. The original sample of children was randomly assigned to either an ecological-model therapeutic child care program or to standard community services. Thirty-five children considered representative of the original sample were assessed in early adolescence. Information about these youngsters was provided by the youths themselves, caregivers and teachers, home observation, and school and court records. The youth receiving standard community services showed significantly more behavior problems according to caregivers, earlier arrest and more frequent violent delinquency, and increasing school disciplinary problems. For youth who had experienced therapeutic child care, their groups were not found to differ on self-perception or school-related measures. The results support the long-term benefit of early intervention for maltreated and at-risk children.

Silverman AB, Reinherz HZ, Giaconia RM. The long-term sequelae of child and adolescent abuse: a longitudinal community study. *Child Abuse Negl.* 1996;20:709-723
The authors proposed to investigate the relationship between childhood and adolescent physical and sexual abuse before the age of 18 years and psychosocial functioning in mid-adolescence (age 15 years) and early adulthood (age 21 years) in a community sample of young adults. These data were available as part of an ongoing 17-year longitudinal study in which 375 subjects participated.

As young adults, almost 11% of the sample reported physical or sexual abuse prior to age 18 years. According to the results of assessments based on DSM-III-R criteria with the National Institute of Mental Health Diagnostic Interview Schedule, about 80% of the abused young adults met current criteria for at least one psychiatric disorder. These abused subjects showed significant impairments in functioning at both mid-adolescence and young adulthood when compared with nonabused subjects at the same ages. Impairments consisted of depressive symptomatology, anxiety, psychiatric disorders, emotional-behavioral problems, suicidal ideation, and suicide attempts. In addition to poorer overall functioning among abused subjects compared to nonabused subjects at 15 and 21 years of age, gender differences and distinct patterns of impaired functioning were apparent. Discussion of these findings pointed to the need for early intervention and prevention approaches to minimize the serious long-term sequelae of child abuse.

Sexual Abuse

Beitchman JH, Zucker KJ, Hood JE, DaCosta GA, Akman D. A review of the short-term effects of child sexual abuse. *Child Abuse Negl.* 1991;15:537-556
These authors conducted a critical evaluation of 42 previously published empirical studies on the impact of child sexual abuse. Many methodological weaknesses were identified in the review, thus limiting the ability to draw firm conclusions regarding sequelae specific to abuse. However, the authors nevertheless concluded victims of abuse have a greater likelihood than nonvictims to develop sexualized behavior problems and to come from more dysfunctional families. Additionally, they summarized findings that more severe symptomatic outcomes tend to be associated with greater frequency and duration of abuse, the use of force and/or penetration in the acts of abuse, and abuse perpetrated by a father or father figure.

Beitchman JH, Zucker KJ, Hood JE, DaCosta GA, Akman D, Cassavia E. A review of the long-term effects of child sexual abuse. *Child Abuse Negl.* 1992;16:101-118
Examining some 32 studies in the existing literature on the long-term sequelae of child sexual victimization, primarily conducted with samples of adult females, this review concluded that methodological inadequacies, to date, limit the ability to infer direct relationships between a history of child sexual abuse and the existence of adult emotional/behavioral symptomatology. However, the authors identify recurrent themes in the literature that suggest women with a history of child sexual abuse more commonly experience sexual dysfunctions, homosexual experiences, anxious and depressive symptomatology and suicidality, and revictimization experiences. The effects of the abuse-specific factors noted in

the Beitchman et al 1991 review (see previous review) of short-term abuse impact appear to persist and influence long-term outcomes as well.

Friedrich WN. Sexual victimization and sexual behavior in children: a review of recent literature. *Child Abuse Negl.* 1993;17:59-66
The author reviewed empirical research relating to sexual behavior in sexually abused children. Generally, sexual behavior was reported significantly more often in sexually abused children than in nonabused children, although clearly not all sexually abused children were found to exhibit elevated levels of sexual behavior. The significance of findings varied according to assessment methodology, with the most consistent differences in sexual behavior noted in studies relying upon direct behavioral observation of the child subjects, parent report, child self-report, and record review. In contrast, studies employing the use of projective drawings yielded somewhat mixed findings. When increases in sexual behavior were noted, such behaviors often appeared related to abuse-specific dimensions, such as the number of abuse perpetrators, abuse frequency and duration, available family support, the use of force, and overall abuse severity.

Kendall-Tackett KA, Williams LM, Finkelhor D. Impact of sexual abuse on children: a review and synthesis of recent empirical studies. *Psychol Bull.* 1993;113:164-180
These authors conducted a review of 45 empirical studies of child victims of sexual abuse, aged 1 to 18 years, reporting an overall finding that sexually abused children have greater psychiatric symptoms than nonsexually abused children, with 15% to 45% of the variance accounted for by the abuse history. Across these studies, the impact of sexual abuse manifested itself in a wide variety of symptoms and pathological behaviors, with essentially no domain of psychiatric symptoms not associated with a sexual abuse history. The most frequently cited symptoms were posttraumatic stress and sexualized behaviors.

No one symptom was found to characterize the majority of sexually abused children, and approximately one third of victims demonstrated no symptomatology. The absence of a specific sexual abuse syndrome suggests there is no single traumatization process. The development of some symptoms appeared age-related, and the intensity of symptoms was felt to be related to abuse-specific factors such as the occurrence of penetration, abuse duration and frequency, use of force, the relationship between the offender and victim, and the level of maternal support. Good recovery from abuse trauma was demonstrated for about two thirds of the victims during the first 12 to 18 months.

The authors provide a number of suggestions for improved future research, particularly arguing that studies need to be undertaken to develop and confirm theories as to what causes victimized children to be symptomatic.

McLeer SV, Deblinger E, Henry D, Orvaschel H. Sexually abused children at high risk for post-traumatic stress disorder. *J Am Acad Child Adolesc Psychiatry.* **1992;31:875-879**
Studying 92 sexual abuse victims, aged 3 to 16 years, these researchers reported 43.9% of their subjects met posttraumatic stress disorder (PTSD) diagnostic criteria. When the authors included children who met partial criteria for PTSD, the percentage of subjects with PTSD symptoms increased to as much as 86.5%, with greater PTSD symptomatology noted among children who were victims of incest or sexual abuse by a trusted adult than among youngsters abused by strangers. This study did not identify correlations between the presence of PTSD or development of different PTSD symptoms and elapsed time since the last incident of abuse or the seriousness of the abuse.

Mian M, Marton P, LeBaron D. The effects of sexual abuse on 3- to 5-year-old girls. *Child Abuse Negl.* **1996;20:731-745**
Forty-two intrafamilial and 28 extrafamilial female victims of sexual abuse, assessed within 6 weeks of the disclosure of the abuse, were compared with a control group of 42 nonabused children. The study found evidence that abuse was associated with at least short-term adverse emotional and behavioral effects, particularly with respect to increased sexual behaviors and increased internalizing problem behaviors such as affective or anxiety disorders. Symptom ratings were based primarily on maternal behavioral report, although the children were also directly observed. Increased severity of symptoms was associated

with more dysfunctional and problematic family environments (especially the presence of alcohol abuse by the father, poorer education of the mother, and a history of maternal sexual victimization), repeated abuse, and a more invasive abuse history.

Incest victims evidenced slightly more symptomatology, but such was not sufficient to differentiate them from the extrafamilial abuse victims. Incest victims were also found to have poorer social competence in peer interactions and to receive less maternal support, although the latter factor did not itself predict a poorer symptom outcome.

Treatment Outcome

Becker JV, Alpert JL, BigFoot DS, et al. Empirical research on child abuse treatment: report by the Child Abuse and Neglect Treatment Working Group, American Psychological Association. *J Clin Child Psychol.* **1995;24(suppl):23-46**
The empirical research on short- and long-term outcomes for sexual abuse, physical abuse, psychological abuse, and neglect is discussed separately. Research on treatment outcomes indicates various treatment approaches with child victims and adults victimized as children appear to be effective. However, methodological issues and the limited scope of current studies point out the need for further investigation. Outcome of treatment of parents and caregivers for each of these types of abuse is also examined, again concluding that there is empirical support for the effectiveness of treatment, but the generalizability of these studies is limited.

Finkelhor D, Berliner L. Research on the treatment of sexually abused children: a review and recommendations. *J Am Acad Child Adolesc Psychiatry.* **1995;34:1408-1423**
Twenty-nine treatment outcome studies of interventions with sexually abused children and adolescents were reviewed to determine the efficacy of therapy. Most of the studies were pre-post designs, although several were quasi-experimental with group comparisons but no assignment of treatment type; a few were small-scale experimental designs with group comparisons and treatment assignment,

although the review was generally limited by the lack of good long-term follow-up or large-scale randomized studies that compare treated and control subjects.

The studies generally noted improvement in sexually abused children participating in treatment, although methodological weaknesses make it difficult to determine if such change resulted directly from therapy or was due to the passage of time or factors external to treatment. In spite of treatment, some children showed no improvement, and externalizing and sexualized behavior symptoms appeared the most resistant to change.

The authors noted a number of complicating factors and other methodological considerations to be taken into account when doing research with this population. These include the distinction that treating sexual abuse involves treating an experience rather than a disorder or syndrome, the over-all diversity of responses to the abuse, the presence of some victims who appear asymptomatic and others who develop apparently delayed problems secondary to the abuse, the importance of family and community contexts in understanding the impact of abuse, the need to compare abuse-focused treatment with other more generic interventions and symptom-specific targeted approaches, identifying an optimal length of treatment, managing treatment dropouts, and development and utilization of abuse-specific measures to determine initial and outcome symptomatology.

Acknowledgment

This section and its annotations were prepared by Janice K. Church, PhD, and Karen Boyd Worley, PhD.

Reabuse (Revictimization)

Clinical Principles

- ▼ Reabuse refers to the occurrence of a substantiated incidence of abuse or neglect in a child who has been abused or neglected previously.

- ▼ A victim-based definition of reabuse considers a child to have been reabused regardless of whether the subsequent abuse is the same as the initial type of abuse and/or whether the perpetrator of the reabuse is the same.

- ▼ The risk of reabuse appears to be greatest during the period immediately following the initial diagnosis of abuse or neglect, and diminishes over time.

- ▼ Family structure and limited resources appear to influence the frequency of reabuse more than characteristics such as gender and/or ethnic origin.

- ▼ Children, between infancy and 6 years of age, exhibit the greatest vulnerability for reabuse.

- ▼ Children with initial maltreatment diagnoses of physical abuse or neglect are at slightly greater risk for reabuse than children with an initial diagnosis of sexual abuse.

- ▼ Regardless of the initial type of abuse, neglect appears to be the most frequent type of substantiated reabuse.

Other Comments

Reporting bias and the lack of consistent case follow-up demonstrate the systemic problems that have hampered reabuse research. Current knowledge about the characteristics that predispose children to repeated abuse and the data required to determine the most effective intervention is in its adolescence. Notwithstanding the need for additional research in these areas, the likelihood of an intervention's success will be dependent on the promptness with which it is instituted.

Bibliography

Boney-McCoy S, Finkelhor D. Prior victimization: a risk factor for child sexual abuse and for PTSD-related symptomatology among sexually abused youth. *Child Abuse Negl.* 1995;19:1401-1421

Prior victimization was found to increase the risk for subsequent child sexual abuse (CSA) in a national random sample of 2,000 American children (10-16 years). Previous victimization predicted subsequent CSA, even when background variables (gender, race, age, geographic location, quality of relationship with parents, and relative level of violence in the home) were controlled for. In addition, the prior victimization of a family member also predicted later CSA. Among children who experienced CSA, prior victimization increased the level of posttraumatic stress disorder symptomatology, even after demographic factors and characteristics of the CSA episode (eg, severity of the assault, severity of injury, fear of death, or serious injury) were included in the model.

DeParifillis D, Zuravis SJ. Rates, patterns and frequency of child maltreatment recurrences among families know to CPS. *J Child Maltreatment.* 1998;3:27-42

The authors provide a comprehensive review of the available research on the rates, patterns, and frequency of child maltreatment recurrences. A comparison of the differences in the populations, purposes, definitions of recurrence, the lengths of follow-up, and recurrence rates across 45 studies (1978-1995) are discussed.

This review stresses the need for prospective research using survival analysis techniques as well as a need for greater accountability by child protection services in delivering services to families at risk for future maltreatment.

Ferleger N, Glenwick DS, Gaines RR, Green AH. Identifying correlates of reabuse in maltreating parents. *Child Abuse Negl.* 1988;12:41-49

A sample of 45 abusive parents being treated at an urban medical center's child abuse program were compared on 22 parent, child, and treatment variables thought to bear on reabuse. No single variable was strongly associated with reabuse, but findings indicate that interactions involving several variables (income source, marital status, and the abuser's personal abuse history) differentiated between reabusers and non-reabusers.

Fryer GE, Miyoshi TJ. A survival analysis of the revictimization of children: the case of Colorado. *Child Abuse Negl.* **1994;18:1063-1071**
This study addresses the patterns of revictimization in a sample of children known to have been previously maltreated. Using survival analysis, the authors analyzed data on 24,507 children obtained from the Colorado Child Abuse and Neglect Registry. Fryer and Miyoshi conclude that the likelihood of revictimization is highest immediately after an initial incident of abuse or neglect. A greater risk of revictimization is noted for younger children and for females. Relationships were strongly influenced by the form of maltreatment. Revictimization rates of neglected children exceeded those for other major types of maltreatment.

Jellinek MS, Little M, Benedict K, et al. Placement outcomes of 206 severely maltreated children in the Boston Juvenile Court system: a 7.5-year follow-up study. *Child Abuse Negl.* **1995;19:1051-1064**
This study examines placement outcomes of 206 severely maltreated children 7.5 years after arraignment in Boston Juvenile Court on Care and Protection (C&P) petitions. Sixty-seven percent (n = 138) of the sample had been permanently removed from their parents, and 33% (n = 68) had their cases dismissed in the Boston Juvenile Court. At follow-up, 21% of the sample (n = 44) were still in temporary custody awaiting permanent placement and 4% (n = 8) of children had "drifted" back to their abusive/neglectful parents despite prior permanent removal. The average time children spent in probate proceedings (awaiting permanent placement) had increased substantially to 2.1 years since a study of this sample 4 years previously.

The rate of court referral for incidences of reabuse or delinquency was significantly lower among children who had been permanently placed (P<.003). Rates of court-referral for reabuse charges were the same (16%) for children

who were in temporary custody at the time of follow-up and children who had been dismissed back to the parent for whom the original Care and Protection petitions had been filed.

Results stress the urgent need to restructure time limits in juvenile court proceedings, integrate adequate tracking of child abuse and neglect cases through and across court and agency boundaries, and use standardized assessments of abused and neglected children as a tool in the adjudication process.

Jones DP. The untreatable family. *Child Abuse Negl.* **1987;11:409-420**
The author reviews the risk to children who have been abused and who are permitted to remain in the homes of families identified as resistive to treatment. Studies of recidivism in these families have shown that abused children who continue to reside in the home are at risk for physical reabuse (16%-60%) and sexual reabuse (16%). Similarly, treatment failure rates for physically abusing families (20%-87%) and sexually abusing families (16%-38%) have been well documented. Parental factors associated with poor outcomes include a parental history of severe childhood abuse, persistent denial of abusive behavior, refusal to accept help, severe personality disorders, mental handicaps complicated by personality disorders, psychoses, substance abuse, and commission of the most severe forms of abuse. It is suggested that early identification of these families might allow a redirection of valuable resources to families for whom there is relatively more hope.

Levy HB, Markovic J, Ahart S, Torres H, Chaudhry U. Reabuse rates in a sample of children followed for 5 years after discharge from a child abuse inpatient assessment program. *Child Abuse Negl.* **1995;19:1363-1377**
This study analyzes the frequency of reabuse over a 60-month period in a sample of children following their discharge from a hospital-based child abuse program. Results demonstrate that the risk of reabuse in this sample was greatest during the first 2 years following a diagnosis of maltreatment and subsequently diminished progressively over time. Although more than 77% of the subjects were followed up for 61 to 72 months, no reabuse incidents were reported after the 60th month, suggesting a period of relatively low risk for reabuse.

Family structure and limited resources appeared to influence the frequency of reabuse more than characteristics such as age, gender, and/or ethnic origin. While no particular initial maltreatment diagnosis was found to have statistically significant utility as a predictor of the likelihood or type of reabuse, an initial maltreatment diagnosis of physical abuse was predictive of reabuse at a statistically suggestive level (P<.1). Neglect was the most frequent reabuse type regardless of the initial maltreatment diagnosis. The authors suggest that the lower than expected cumulative reabuse rate (16.8%) over 60 months may reflect the benefit of early intervention with a comprehensive multidisciplinary assessment.

Murphy JM, Bishop SJ, Jellinek MS, Quinn D, Poitrast JF. What happens after the care and protection petition? Reabuse in a court sample. *Child Abuse Negl.* 1992;16:485-493

This study reviews the course of 206 cases of serious child mistreatment brought before a metropolitan juvenile court on Care and Protection petitions. Initial court dispositions of these cases are compared with their outcome at the end of a 2-year follow-up period. Study findings show that while 63 (31%) of the 206 cases initially presenting to the court were dismissed, 18 (29%) of these cases became the subjects of substantiated abuse reports and 10 (16%) subsequently returned to court on another Care and Protection petition. Families who had been to court for a Care and Protection petition previously, and families in which a parent was diagnosed as psychotic or character disordered, were significantly more likely to return to court. In addition, 8 (6%) of the 130 children ordered permanently removed from parental custody also returned to court. The study highlights the necessity for ongoing follow-up of individual cases into the court process, and suggests that it may be possible to identify cases with a very high probability of reinjury and return to court.

Rivara FP. Physical abuse in children under 2: a study of therapeutic outcomes. *Child Abuse Negl.* 1985;9:81-87

This study addresses the prognosis of the family, compliance with treatment recommendations, and the long-term outcome of physically abused children (<2 years of age). Data were collected from a multidisciplinary evaluation team and the Department of Human Services' records on 71 children. Although nearly all families were referred for mental health counseling and parent training, only 33% complied. Half of the children were abused more than once; 30% were abused after referral for counseling. The incidence of reabuse was unrelated to compliance with counseling. The majority of children had some out-of-home placement (mean time in foster care of 11 months and in care of relatives for 24.4 months). In 69% of the families, more than one child was abused. At follow-up, 41% of children and 47% of siblings were not living with either parent. Half of the families were judged to be functioning poorly and only nine had made good progress in counseling.

Acknowledgment

This section and its annotations were prepared by Howard B. Levy, MD.

Retinal Hemorrhages

See Also:
Falls
Fractures
Head Injury
Shaken Impact/Shaken Baby Syndrome

Clinical Principles

▼ Retinal hemorrhages are rare in severe head trauma due to accidents, do not occur in mild-to-moderate trauma, and are frequent in inflicted head injuries such as shaken baby syndrome.

▼ Retinal hemorrhages found after attempted resuscitation can usually be explained by predisposing medical conditions or traumatic injuries.

▼ More severe ocular pathology (eg, vitreous hemorrhage) is linked to deeper intracranial injury and more severe cranial trauma.

Bibliography

Annable WL. Ocular manifestations of child abuse. In: Reece RM, ed. *Child Abuse: Medical Diagnosis and Management.* Malvern, PA: Lea & Febiger; 1994:138-149.
This overview manuscript provides a thorough discussion of direct and indirect traumatic ocular injuries, including a very complete description of retinal findings in abusive head trauma and an exceptional review of the relevant literature linking ocular injuries to child abuse (through 1991). Differential diagnosis considerations are very well presented.

Betz P, Puschel K, Miltner E, Lignitz E, Eisenmenger W. Morphometric analysis of retinal hemorrhages in the shaken baby syndrome. *Forensic Sci Int.* 1996;78:71-80

Budenz DL, Farber MG, Mirchandami HG, Park H, Rorke LB. Ocular and optic nerve hemorrhages in abused infants with intracranial injuries. *Ophthalmology.* 1994;101:559-565

Buys Y, Levin A, Enzenauer R, Elder J, Morin D. Retinal findings after head trauma in infants and young children. *Ophthalmology.* 1992;99:1718-1723
In this prospective study at The Children's Hospital for Sick Children, all children ages 4 weeks to 36 months who sustained head trauma within the preceding 48 hours were eligible for study inclusion (N = 200). A dilated fundoscopic examination was performed on 79 children (39.5%) (mean age, 16.1 months). The children were separated into two groups: accidental or nonaccidental head injury. The children with retinal hemorrhages were automatically referred.
    Purpose: The purpose was to assess the medicolegal significance of retinal hemorrhages caused by head trauma.
    Accidental: Data on 75 children who incurred head injuries due to accidental falls from an average height of 4.4 feet showed that all had normal dilated fundoscopic examination results.
    Indeterminate: One child with skull fracture of indeterminate cause and a normal retinal examination was excluded from statistical analysis.
    Nonaccidental: Three children had retinal hemorrhages. In all three, the mechanism of injury was presumed to be shaken baby syndrome.
    Computed tomography was available in eight patients who showed evidence of intracranial abnormalities. It was determined that three of these children had been abused, while five were injured accidentally. Most of the literature supports the conclusion that retinal hemorrhages occur very rarely after severe head trauma in children and are seen most frequently in nonaccidental injuries. Unfortunately, the literature does not explain mechanism of injury.

Conclusion: Retinal hemorrhages rarely occur in children younger than 3 years of age after severe head trauma and not at all after mild-to-moderate head trauma. When a child presents with a head injury and retinal hemorrhage in the absence of obvious cause, child abuse should be strongly considered. (CL/KM)

Gayle MO, Kissoon N, Hered RW, Harwood-Nuss A. Retinal hemorrhage in the young child: a review of etiology, predisposed conditions, and clinical implications. *J Emerg Med.* 1995;13:233-239

Gilliland MGF, Luckenbach MW. Are retinal hemorrhages found after resuscitation attempts? a study of the eyes of 169 children. *Am J Forensic Pathol.* 1993;14:187-192
The authors reviewed 169 cases of pediatric deaths in children (age range, 26 weeks, gestation to 9 years 11 months) in which postmortem ocular examination was performed. One hundred thirty-one received cardiopulmonary resuscitation for 30 minutes or more before death. Thirty-eight patients were not resuscitated.

Retinal hemorrhages were found in 70 of 169 children, 61 of whom had been resuscitated. The authors demonstrated that the retinal hemorrhages in these 61 children could be explained by their pre-existing pathology. Sixty of 61 demonstrated conditions known to be associated with retinal hemorrhages (56/61 had craniocerebral trauma; 3/61 had central nervous system [CNS] tumor or infection; and 1/61 died of sepsis). One died of undetermined etiology. No retinal hemorrhages were found in 99 of 169 children, 70 of whom had been resuscitated. The authors concluded that no study case revealed evidence that retinal hemorrhages were caused solely by resuscitation attempts before death. (KH)

Gilliland MG, Luckenbach MW, Chenier TC. Systemic and ocular findings in 169 prospectively studied child deaths: retinal hemorrhages usually mean child abuse. *Forensic Sci Int.* 1994;68:117-132

Green MA, Lieberman G, Milroy CM, Parsons MA. Ocular and cerebral trauma in nonaccidental injury in infancy: underlying mechanisms and implications for paediatric practice. *Br J Ophthalmol.* 1996;80:282-287
These authors forensically analyzed 23 infant fatalities clearly linked to nonaccidental trauma.

Sixteen of 23 infants died due to head injury (70%). The remaining seven infants died of non-accidental trauma other than head injury, including asphyxia and abdominal injuries. The mean age at time of death was 6.9 months (range, 5-24 months). By ranking patients in order of severity, the authors sought to link trauma severity with specific cranial and eye injuries. Forensic autopsies and thorough gross and microscopic pathological examination of the eyes was completed in all cases.

Pathological examination of the eyes of each victim verified the presence/absence of retinal detachment, vitreous, subhyaloid, intraretinal, choroidal, and perineural (optic nerve) hemorrhages, allowing computation of an "eye trauma score." In the central nervous system, examiners documented the presence/absence of subdural, subarachnoid, and intracerebral hemorrhage(s); primary axonal injury and cerebral laceration(s), allowing computation of an "intracranial trauma score."

Eighty-one percent of the 16 infants with abusive head trauma injuries revealed ocular abnormalities, revealing a strong association between CNS trauma and ocular pathology. The children dying of CNS trauma had a significantly higher "eye trauma score." Careful examination revealed pathological evidence that subdural optic nerve sheath hemorrhages were not simply an extension of intracranial subdural hemorrhage.

By comparing eye and intracranial lesions, these authors revealed an apparent association between deeper intracranial lesions, more severe ocular pathology (eg, vitreous hemorrhage), and greater overall trauma severity. More specifically,

> with increasing trauma to the head, an infant is likely to develop subdural hemorrhage first, followed by (at slightly higher levels of trauma) subhyaloid and intraretinal hemorrhages and subdural optic nerve sheath hemorrhage. Slightly more trauma will produce retinal detachment, and only the most severe trauma will cause choroidal and vitreous hemorrhages which coincide with the development of subarachnoid and intracerebral hemorrhage and/or cerebral lacerations. (KH)

Johnson DL, Braun D, Friendly D. Accidental head trauma and retinal hemorrhage. *Neurosurgery.* 1993;33:231-235

The authors examined the incidence of retinal hemorrhages in accidental pediatric head injuries resulting from forces sufficient to cause skull fracture and/or intracranial hemorrhage. In total, 200 of 525 children admitted consecutively for head injuries met the criteria.

Thirty of the 200 children were excluded because of suspected child abuse or gunshot wounds. An ophthalmologist evaluated 140 of the remaining 170 children for retinal hemorrhage. Two children, both of whom had been involved in side-impact car accidents, sustained retinal hemorrhages associated with severe head injury. The authors concluded that retinal hemorrhage occurs rarely in accidental injury and is associated with extraordinary force. (CL/KM)

Matthews GP, Das A. Dense vitreous hemorrhages predict poor visual and neurological prognosis in infants with shaken baby syndrome. *J Pediatr Ophthalmol Strabismus.* 1996;33:260-265

Five cases of shaken baby syndrome (ages, 3 to 8 months) were reviewed to explore the relationship between vitreous hemorrhage and neurological outcome. The three infants who revealed dense vitreous hemorrhages had poor visual outcome due to significant retinal and visual cortical pathology. Conversely, the two infants with only intraretinal or subhyaloid hemorrhage demonstrated a much better visual outcome, with less noted injury to intraocular and intracranial structures. Although limited in size, this study also suggests a relationship between cranial trauma severity and more severe ocular pathology. (KH)

Munger CE, Peiffer RL, Bouldin TW, Kylstra JA, Thompson RL. Ocular and associated neuropathologic observations in suspected whiplash shaken infant syndrome. *Am J Forensic Med Pathol.* 1993;14:193-200

Odom A, Christ E, Kerr N, et al. Prevalence of retinal hemorrhages in pediatric patients after in-hospital cardiopulmonary resuscitation: a prospective study. *Pediatrics.* 1997;99:E31-E35

The authors sought to determine the prevalence of retinal hemorrhages after inpatient cardiopulmonary resuscitation in pediatric patients hospitalized for nontraumatic illnesses in an intensive care unit. Forty-three pediatric patients (mean age 23 months, range 1 month to 15.8 years) who underwent at least 1 minute of chest compressions (mean duration 16.4 minutes) and survived long enough for retinal examination were prospectively studied. Patients were excluded in the presence of traumatic injuries, documented retinal hemorrhages before cardiac arrest, suspicion of child abuse, or diagnosis of near-drowning or seizures. Although a significant percentage of study patients demonstrated evidence of coagulopathy, small punctate retinal hemorrhages were found in only 1 patient. This 1-month-old girl underwent 60 minutes of open chest cardiac massage and manifested activated coagulation (PT 22.9 seconds, PTT 78 seconds, and platelet count 91K). Her retinal hemorrhages were morphologically different from retinal hemorrhages typically described in the Shaken Baby Syndrome. The authors concluded that chest compressions do not result in retinal hemorrhages in children with a normal coagulation profile and platelet count.

Acknowledgment

This section and its annotations were prepared by Kent Hymel, MD. Selected annotations from the first edition were written by Carolyn Levitt, MD, and Kim Martinez, RN, CPNP, MPH.

Sexual Abuse of Children

See Also:
Sexually Transmitted Diseases and Child Sexual Abuse
AAP Statements *Guidelines for the Evaluation of Sexual Abuse of Children*
and *Sexual Assault and the Adolescent,* **which follow**

Clinical Principles

▼ Many people mistakenly believe that a medical examination can routinely determine when and how often a child has been molested, and whether or not sexual abuse has taken place or penetration has occurred.

▼ Those who are responsible for medical evaluation of the sexually abused child must recognize the critical importance of a thorough history.

▼ Positive diagnostic findings of sexual abuse are very low: 3% to 16% of child victims.

▼ A normal or nonspecific physical examination is common in victims of sexual abuse.

▼ The child's clear statement that he/she was sexually abused is the most important evidence of molestation.

▼ A remarkable healing process may quickly obscure the evidence of perianal and genital injuries, which serve as clues of sexual abuse.

▼ This is a rapidly expanding and changing field; caution must be exercised in attributing unusual genital findings to abuse.

Bibliography

Overview

Bays J, Chadwick D. Medical diagnosis of the sexually abused child. *Child Abuse Negl.* 1993;17:91-110

This is a very comprehensive review article, which seeks to define sexual abuse and place it in the context of the history and physical evaluation. A normal physical examination is common in victims of sexual abuse; diagnostic findings of sexual abuse are very low (3% to 16% of child victims).

There are several reasons for the lack of physical findings. A delay in seeking medical attention affects the clarity of physical evidence, which is subject to rapid tissue healing and hymenal elasticity.

Conditions that mimic sexual abuse include lichen sclerosis, congenital hemangiomas, streptococcal infection, straddle injuries, urethral caruncles or prolapse, and congenital vaginal and anal anomalies. Anal findings may be the result of Crohn's disease, hemolytic-uremic syndrome, postmortem anal dilatation, chronic constipation, or neurogenic patulous anus and anal fissures or dilation.

In the absence of multiple congenital anomalies, all girls are born with hymens, and normal hymens have different configurations. The appearance of the hymen can be altered by trauma or by a variety of nontraumatic factors. Accidents, masturbation, and tampons are not likely to cause injury to the hymen or internal genital structures. Hymen size increases with age, and examination method and child tension level affect hymenal diameter. Transmission of sexually transmitted diseases outside the perinatal period by nonsexual means is rare.

Previous research on physical findings associated with abuse is summarized and contrasted with normative data. The spectrum of physical findings produced with molestation, including erythema, narrowing of the hymenal rim, mounds, notches, and hymenal disruption, are noted; most injuries are found from the 3 o'clock to 9 o'clock positions.

The 1985 Child Sexual Abuse Summit Meeting identified three findings that strongly indicate abuse: (1) clear-cut hymenal damage or disruption; (2) injuries in the area of the posterior fourchette; and (3) anal dilatation greater than 15 mm transverse with gentle buttock traction.

Diagnostic findings of sexual abuse include presence of semen, sperm, or acid phosphatase; pregnancy; fresh genital/anal injuries without accidental history; positive syphilis/gonorrhea results or infection with human immunodeficiency virus (not acquired perinatally); and a markedly enlarged hymenal opening with associated findings. (CL, KM)

Kerns DL, Terman KL, Larson CS. The role of physicians in reporting and evaluating child sexual abuse cases. In: *The Future of Children: Sexual Abuse of Children.* **The David and Lucile Packard Foundation; 1994;4:119-134**
This article reviews the current role of physicians in reporting and evaluating child sexual abuse, identifies where improvement is needed, and makes specific recommendations for the medical community. The article summarizes the history of development of medical knowledge in the area of sexual abuse with references to some of the published landmark articles and books, existing written guidelines, and the development of societies for child abuse professionals. Problems associated with training of physicians are outlined. Despite the nationwide growth of interdisciplinary teams, and, in some areas, the regionalization of medical expertise, gaps in the medical community's response to sexual abuse remain a significant problem.

The article discusses current issues surrounding reporting and medical evaluation. The conflict of the physician's legal responsibilities as a mandated reporter and the physician's traditional relationship with the family are explored. The article reviews and summarizes articles that examine reasons why many physicians do not follow state mandates to report. Other difficulties facing many physicians include lack of knowledge concerning identification of anogenital abnormalities, lack of experience in child disclosures of or interviews for sexual abuse, and minimal knowledge of legal issues such as recording of evidence and court testimony. The lack of standardization in referral patterns for medical examinations is discussed.

The article defines the need for physician involvement, beyond just collection of forensic evidence. For example, physicians may be needed for treatment of trauma and sexually transmitted diseases, collection of history and documentation of utterances made or behaviors exhibited during the course of the exam, and aiding the department of social services or law enforcement agencies.

Recommendations include adding child sexual abuse discussions in medical school curricula, pediatric residencies, and continuing education programs. The authors also recommend more detailed protocols for child sexual abuse medical examinations, greater assistance in coordinating interdisciplinary team approaches, and increased reimbursement for these exams. (AB)

Anogenital Anatomy in Nonabused Children

Berenson A, Heger A, Hayes J, Bailey R, Emans B. Appearance of the hymen in prepubertal girls. *Pediatrics.* **1992;89:387-394**
This study documents the anatomy of 211 girls aged 1 month through 7 years with no history of abuse. The population was 36% black, 33.6% white, 29.9% Hispanic, and 0.5% Asian; the mean age was 21 months. Examiners divided subjects into age-group cohorts (younger than 12 months, 1-2 years, 2-4 years, and 4-7 years). The subjects were positioned supine on an examination table with their legs flexed for colposcopic examination and photography.

Labial agglutination is a common finding in prepubertal girls. It was seen most frequently in this study among those younger than 12 months. Labial agglutination sufficient to obscure the entire hymen was evident in 10 girls; partial posterior agglutination not obscuring the hymen was documented in 35. No significant cohort distinctions were found in the prevalence of notches, external hymenal ridges, or longitudinal intravaginal ridges. When notches were found, they were generally located in the annular hymens between the 11 o'clock and 1 o'clock positions. Longitudinal intravaginal ridges appeared in 25% of the subjects. Less frequent findings included hymenal tags and bumps. When the colposcopic photographs successfully visualized the vestibular area, vestibular bands or ligaments were usually evident. Midline sparing and the vascular hymenal pattern were noted when present; in 95% of these, examiners found a lacy pattern with multiple fine vessels on the hymen.

Three major hymenal configurations were noted: annular, fimbriated, and crescentic; significant distinctions were age related. A fimbriated hymen predominated among those younger than 12 months; most girls over 2 years had a crescent- shaped hymen. The crescentic hymen with an absence of tissue from the 11 o'clock to 1 o'clock position was not observed in the newborn population.

The mean horizontal hymenal diameter utilizing labial traction was 2.5 mm + 0.8 among those aged 1 to 12 months; 2.9 mm + 1.2 among those 13 to 24 months; 2.9 mm + 1.0 among those 25 to 48 months; and 3.6 mm + 1.2 among those 49 to 81 months.

The authors conclude that the absence of any scarring in 201 girls and presence of transection in only one subject support the significance of these findings for sexual abuse. They also note that notches between the 4 o'clock and 8 o'clock positions were not observed in the normal pediatric population. Hymenal bumps, notches between the 9 o'clock and 3 o'clock positions, tags, vestibular bands, longitudinal intravaginal ridges, and external ridges were all sufficiently common to be considered normal findings in the pediatric population. (CL, KM)

Berenson AB. A longitudinal study of hymenal morphology in the first 3 years of life. *Pediatrics*. 1995;95:490-496

This study was conducted to document the effects of aging on hymenal morphology during the first 3 years of life in a cohort of nonabused girls. Using a longitudinal design, the author examined and photographed the external genitalia of 134 girls at 2 months of age or less and near 3 years of age. Forty-two of these girls were also examined near 1 year of age. The prevalence of each hymenal characteristic was calculated at each time, and differences were analyzed using the z statistic and McNemar change tests. Measurements of transhymenal diameters and the inferior rim were compared using a paired T test.

Hymenal configuration in 65% (87/134) of the subjects changed between birth and 3 years, usually from annular or fimbriated to crescentic. External ridges observed at birth usually resolved by 3 years, whereas intravaginal ridges were observed more often in 3-year-olds ($P=.00$). Analysis by race showed that the prevalence of both superior and lateral notches decreased in whites, whereas the prevalence of intravaginal ridges changed only in blacks ($P=.00$). Sixty-eight percent (15/22) of the tags present at birth were not observed at 3 years, while nine tags appeared during this period. Changes observed between 1 and 3 years included in-

creases in the mean horizontal ($P=.00$) and vertical ($P=.02$) transhymenal diameters and in the prevalence of the crescentic configuration ($P=.04$).

The author concluded that changes in hymenal morphology, which may vary by race, occur in the first 3 years of life. Alterations are more pronounced in the first year than in years 2 and 3. Physicians should understand the effects of aging on the hymen's appearance to differentiate normal development from posttraumatic or infectious changes. (DK)

McCann J, Wells R, Simon M, Voris J. Genital findings in prepubertal girls selected for non-abuse: a descriptive study. *Pediatrics*. 1990;86:428-439

Ninety-three female subjects, aged 10 months to 10 years, were selected for nonabuse. Children were examined in supine position with labial separation, the supine position with labial traction, and the prone knee-chest position. In this normal population, 56% had erythema of the vestibule, 50% had periurethral bands, 39% had labial adhesions, 34% had lymphoid follicles of the fossa navicularis, 26% had posterior fourchette midline avascular areas, and 15% had urethral dilation with labial traction.

Mounds of the hymen were present in 33.8%, projections in 33.3%, and septal remnants or midline hymenal tags in 18.5%. Internal vaginal ridges and rugae were found in 90.2% and 88.7%, respectively. Horizontal and vertical hymenal orifice measurements were included for labial separation and labial traction, as well as supine and knee-chest positions, for three age groups. Horizontal measurements (mm) of hymenal orifice by traction method:

Age	Mean, mm	Range, mm
2 - 4 11/12 y	5.2 + 1.4 (8.0)	2.0 - 8.0
5 - 7 11/12 y	5.6 + 1.8 (9.2)	1.0 - 9.0
8 - Tanner II	6.9 + 2.0 (10.9)	2.5 - 10.5

(CL, KM)

Anatomic Findings With Child Sexual Abuse

Adams JA, Harper K, Knudson K, Revilla J. Examination findings in legally confirmed child sexual abuse: it's normal to be normal. *Pediatrics.* **1994;94:310-317**

This study was designed to determine the frequency of abnormal findings in a population of children with legal confirmation of sexual abuse, using a standardized classification system for colposcopic photographic findings. Case files and colposcopic photographs of 236 children with perpetrator conviction for sexual abuse were reviewed. The photos were reviewed blindly by a team member other than the examiner, and specific anatomical findings were noted and classified as normal to abnormal on a scale of 1 to 5. Historical and behavioral information, as well as legal outcome, was recorded, and all data were entered into a dbase III program. Correlations were sought between abnormal findings and other variables.

The mean age of the patients was 9.0 years (range, 8 months to 17 years, 11 months), with 63% reporting penile-genital contact. Genital examination findings in girls were normal in 28%, nonspecific in 49%, suspicious in 9%, and abnormal in 14% of cases. Abnormal anal findings were found in only 1% of patients. Using discriminant analysis, the two factors that significantly correlated with the presence of abnormal genital findings in girls were the time since the last incident and a history of blood being reported at the time of the molestation.

The authors concluded that abnormal genital findings are not common in sexually abused girls, based on a standardized classification system. More emphasis should be placed on documenting the child's description of the molestation and on educating prosecutors that for children alleging abuse, "It's normal to be normal." (DK)

Kerns D, Ritter M, Thomas R. Concave hymenal variations in suspected child sexual abuse victims. *Pediatrics.* **1992;90:265-272**

Of 1,383 suspected sexual abuse victims, 174 (12.5%) were found to have concave hymenal variations. Concavities were defined as indentations in the hymenal tissue that persisted regardless of subject position and examiner technique and were not formed by redundant folds or asymmetric anterior rim insertions in a crescentic hymen. Five experienced, "blinded" examiners diagnostically evaluated colposcopic photographs.

All concavity types were associated with significantly larger mean hymenal openings than hymens without concavities. The 174 concavities included 61 anterior, 100 posterior/lateral and 13 multiple. Two thirds of the anterior concavities and one third of the posterior/lateral concavities were curved and smooth. In contrast, one third of the anterior concavities and two thirds of the posterior/lateral concavities were angular or irregular. The characteristics most strongly associated with a clinical impression of trauma were posterior location and angular contour with rim irregularity.

Posterior/lateral location was associated with penile-vaginal contact, penetration, stranger perpetrator, hymenal rim narrowing, and posterior fourchette abnormality. Angular and/or irregular features were associated with penile contact, vaginal contact, penile/vaginal contact, penetration, abnormal general physical examination, and hymenal rim narrowing. (CL, KM, DK)

McCann J, Voris J, Simon M. Genital injuries resulting from sexual abuse: a longitudinal study. *Pediatrics.* **1992;89:307-317**

Three of 14 girls with genital injuries caused by sexual assault were selected for longitudinal study of anatomical changes. Victim ages ranged from 4 months to 9 years; follow-up periods were from 14 months to 3 years.

Colposcopic examinations were carried out with a multimethod approach; the article features many of the resulting color photographs.

Results revealed rapidly resolving physical findings, which included erythema, edema, submucosal hemorrhage, abrasions, lacerations, and hymenal transections. Follow-up examinations revealed sharp, jagged hymenal edges, uneven margins with "V-shaped" irregularities, narrow hymenal rims, rolled edges, mounds/projections, intravaginal ridges, and variations in the size of the vaginal introitus.

Healing was by regeneration and repair. The most persistent finding was a narrow hymenal rim. There was little evidence of scar tissue; one of the most notable transformations was the "smoothing off" of irregular edges of damaged tissues. (CL, KM)

McCann J, Voris J. Perianal injuries resulting from sexual abuse: a longitudinal study. *Pediatrics.* **1993;91:390-393**

This article, which features a number of color colposcopic photographs, serves to remind clinicians of the remarkable healing process that takes place in a sexually abused child. Four children with perianal injuries were followed longitudinally to document anatomical changes over time. The subjects, aged 4 months to 12 years, were examined in the supine and knee-chest positions using a colposcope fitted with a 35-mm camera.

On initial examination, all four children showed erythema and lacerations. Three of the four had edematous perianal tissues with thickened or flattened folds as well as venous congestion. Two victims had slightly dilated anal sphincters. Healing of perianal injury caused by child sexual abuse is rapid and occurs through regeneration and repair. Regeneration wound healing is complete within 48 to 72 hours; normal tissue restoration occurs within 6 weeks. Tissue healing through repair, which involves tissue granulation and scar tissue formation, takes about 60 days.

Evidence of perianal injury becomes increasingly difficult to detect over time. By the eighth day, acute signs of trauma had disappeared in all but one victim, who suffered persistent avulsion of a perianal skin tag. The authors also offer estimates for laceration healing time. They estimate 1 to 11 days without residual effects for superficial injuries and 1 to 5 weeks with residual narrow bands of scar tissue for second-degree lacerations. Third-degree lacerations heal in 12 to 14 months with residual evidence gradually fading into surrounding tissues. (CL, KM)

Behavioral Issues

Dubowitz H, Black M, Harrington D, Verschoore A. A follow-up study of behavior problems associated with child sexual abuse. *Child Abuse Negl.* **1993;17:743-754**

The objectives of this study were to examine the behaviors of children evaluated for sexual abuse, the stability of their behaviors over 4 months, and the relationships between aspects of the abuse and the children's behaviors. Sexually abused children had significantly more behavior problems than comparison children, including depression, aggression, sleep and somatic complaints, hyperactivity, and sexual problems. At the time of follow-up, only those children who initially had externalizing behavior in the clinical range improved significantly. During the initial evaluation, behavior problems were associated with the child's disclosure of abuse. At the time of follow-up, behavior problems were associated with abnormal physical findings. However, they were not related to characteristics of the abuse or perpetrator, likelihood of abuse, or therapeutic services. The persistence of behavior problems suggests that children suspected of having been sexually abused should receive an assessment of their psychological status and careful follow-up.

Friedrich WN, Grambsch P, Broughton D, Kuiper J, Beilke RL. Normative sexual behavior in children. *Pediatrics.* **1991; 88:456-464**

A large-scale, community-based survey was done to assess the frequency of a wide variety of sexual behaviors in normal preadolescent children and to measure the relationship of these behaviors to age, gender, socioeconomic, and family variables. A sample of 880 children (ages 2-12 years), screened to exclude those with a history of sexual abuse, were rated by their mothers using several questionnaire measures. The frequency of different behaviors varied widely, with more aggressive sexual behaviors and behaviors imitative of adults being rare. Older children (both boys and girls) were less sexual than younger children. The Child Sexual Behavior Inventory yielded the following behavior frequencies for all age groups combined (ranked from least to most frequent):

0.1%	puts mouth on sex parts
0.4%	asks to engage in sex acts
0.8%	masturbates with object
0.9%	inserts object in vagina/anus
1.1%	imitates intercourse
1.3%	touches animal sex parts
1.4%	sexual sounds
2.5%	French kisses
2.6%	undresses other people
2.6%	mouth on mother's breast
2.7%	asks to watch explicit television
3.2%	imitates sexual behavior with doll
4.9%	wants to be opposite sex
5.7%	talks about sexual acts

5.8%	dresses like opposite sex
6.0%	touches others' sex parts
6.7%	rubs body against people
7.1%	overly friendly with strange men
7.3%	hugs strange adults
8.1%	shows sex parts to children
8.8%	uses sexual words
10.4%	overly aggressive, overly passive
10.6%	talks flirtatiously
11.6%	stands too close
13.0%	pretends to be opposite sex
15.3%	masturbates with hand
15.5%	looks at nude pictures
16.0%	shows sex parts to adults
19.7%	touches sex parts in public
23.0%	interested in opposite sex
28.5%	tries to look at people
30.7%	touches breasts
33.9%	kisses nonfamily children
36.2%	kisses nonfamily adults
36.4%	sits with crotch exposed
38.7%	shy about undressing
41.2%	undresses in front of others
41.9%	walks around nude
45.8%	touches sex parts at home
52.2%	scratches crotch
52.9%	walks around in underwear
53.9%	boy-girl toys
64.5%	shy with strange men

Sexuality was found to be related to the level of general behavior problems, as measured by the Achenbach Internalizing and Externalizing T scores and to a measure of family nudity. It was not related to socioeconomic variables. (DK)

Supplemental Bibliography

General/Review

Bays J, Jenny C. Genital and anal conditions confused with child sexual abuse trauma. *Am J Dis Child.* 1990;144:1319-1322

Dubowitz H, Black M, Harrington D. The diagnosis of child sexual abuse. *Am J Dis Child.* 1992;146:688-693

Feldman W, Feldman E, Goodman JT, et al. Is childhood sexual abuse really increasing in prevalence? an analysis of the evidence. *Pediatrics.* 1991;88:29-33

Gibbons M, Vincent E. Childhood sexual abuse. *Am Fam Physician.* 1994;49:125-136

Hampton HL. Care of the woman who has been raped. *N Engl J Med.* 1995;332:234-237

Heger AH. Twenty years in the evaluation of the sexually abused child: has medicine helped or hurt the child and the family? *Child Abuse Negl.* 1996;20:893-897

Jaudes PK, Martone M. Interdisciplinary evaluations of alleged sexual abuse cases. *Pediatrics.* 1992;89:1164-1168

Kivlahan C, Kruse R, Furnell D. Sexual assault examinations in children: the role of a statewide network of health care providers. *Am J Dis Child.* 1992;146:1365-1370

Lafferty PM, Lawson GM, Orr JD, Scobie WG. The role of the paediatric surgeon in alleged child sexual abuse. *Pediatr Surg.* 1990;25:434-437

Lamb ME. The investigation of child sexual abuse: an interdisciplinary consensus statement. *Child Abuse Negl.* 1994;18:1021-1028

Levitt CJ. Medical evaluation of the sexually abused child. *Primary Care.* 1993;20:343-354

Paradise JE. The medical evaluation of the sexually abused child. *Pediatr Clin North Am.* 1990;37:839-862

Reinhart MA. Medical evaluation of young sexual abuse victims: a view entering the 1990's. *Med Sci Law.* 1991;31:81-86

Wells RD, McCann J, Adams J, Vories J, Ensign J. Emotional, behavioral, and physical symptoms reported by parents of sexually abused, nonabused, and allegedly abused prepubescent females. *Child Abuse Negl.* 1995;19:155-163

Anatomic Findings

Adams JA, Harper K, Knudson S. A proposed system for the classification of anogenital findings in children with suspected sexual abuse. *Adolesc Pediatr Gynecol.* 1992;5:73-75

Adams J, Harper K, Wells R. How pediatricians interpret genital findings in children? Results of a survey. *Adolesc Pediatr Gynecol.* 1993;6:203-206

Adams JA, Knudson S. Genital findings in adolescent girls referred for suspected sexual abuse. *Arch Pediatr Adolesc Med.* 1996;150:850-857

Adams JA, Phillips P, Ahmad M. The usefulness of colposcopic photographs in the evaluation of suspected child sexual abuse. *Adolesc Pediatr Gynecol.* 1990;3:75-82

Adams JA, Wells R. Normal versus abnormal genital findings in children: how well do examiners agree? *Child Abuse Negl.* 1993;17:663-675

Bays J, Chewning M, Keltner L, et al. Changes in hymenal anatomy during examination of prepubertal girls for possible sexual abuse. *Adolesc Pediatr Gynecol.* 1990;3:42-46

Berenson AB. Appearance of the hymen at birth and 1 year of age: a longitudinal study. *Pediatrics.* 1993;91:820-825

Berenson AB. The prepubertal genital exam: what is normal and abnormal. *Cur Opin Obstet Gynecol.* 1994;6:526-530

Berenson A, Heger A, Andrews S. Appearance of the hymen in newborns. *Pediatrics.* 1991;87:458-465

Berenson AB, Heger AH, Andrews SE. Morphology of the hymen in twins. *Adolesc Pediatr Gynecol.* 1991;4:82-84

Berenson AB, Somma-Garcia A, Barnett S. Perianal findings in infants 18 months of age or younger. *Pediatrics.* 1993;91:838-840

Berkowitz CD, Elvik SL, McCann J, Reinhart MA, Strickland S, Chikuma J. Septate hymen: variations and pitfalls in diagnosis. *Adolesc Pediatr Gynecol.* 1991;4:194-197

Bond GR, Dowd MD, Landsman I, Rimsza M. Unintentional perineal injury in prepubescent girls: a multicenter prospective report of 56 girls. *Pediatrics.* 1995;95:628-631

Brayden RM, Altemeier WA, Yeager T, et al. Interpretations of colposcopic photographs: evidence for competence in assessing sexual abuse? *Child Abuse Negl.* 1991;15:69-76

Chacko MR, Mishaw CO, Kozinetz CA, Bermudez A. Examination of the hymen in prepubertal children with suspected sexual abuse: interobserver agreement. *Adolesc Pediatr Gynecol.* 1991;4:187-193

Connon AF, Davidson GP, Moore DJ. Anal size in children: the influence of age, constipation, rectal examination and defaecation. *Med J Aust.* 1990;153:380-383

Dowd MD, Fitzmaurice L, Knapp JF. The interpretation of urogenital findings in children with straddle injuries: proceedings of the National Conference on Pediatric Trauma, Indianapolis—September 1992). *Pediatr Emerg Care.* 1993;9:182

Emans SJ. Sexual abuse in girls: what have we learned about genital anatomy? *J Pediatr.* 1992;120:258-260

Emans SJ, Woods ER, Allred EN, Grace E. Hymenal findings in adolescent women: impact of tampon use and consensual sexual activity. *J Pediatr.* 1994;125:153-160

Gardner JJ. Descriptive study of genital variation in healthy, nonabused premenarchal girls. *J Pediatr.* 1992;120:251-257

Heger A, Emans SJ. Introital diameter as the criterion for sexual abuse. *Pediatrics.* 1990;85:222-223

Hostetler BR, Muram D, Jones CE. Sharp injuries to the hymen. *Adolesc Pediatr Gynecol.* 1994;7:94-96

Irons TG. Documenting sexual abuse of a child. *Emerg Med.* 1993;25:57-75

Jones J, Lawson L, Rickert C. Use of optical glass binocular magnifiers in the examination of sexually abused child. *Adolesc Pediatr Gynecol.* 1990;3:146-148

Kellogg ND, Parra JM. Linea vestibularis: a previously undescribed normal genital structure in female neonates. *Pediatrics.* 1991;87:926-929

Kellogg ND, Parra JM. Linea vestibularis: follow-up of a normal genital structure. *Pediatrics.* 1993;92:453-456

McCann J. How to perform a genital exam in the prepubertal girl. *Med Aspects Human Sexuality.* 1990(Nov); 24:36-41

McCann J. Use of the colposcope in childhood sexual abuse examinations. *Pediatr Clin North Am.* 1990;37:863-880

McCann J, Reay D, Siebert J, Stephens BG, Wirtz S. Postmortem perianal findings in children. *Am J Forensic Med Pathol.* 1996;17:289-298

McCann J, Voris J, Simon M, et al. Comparison of genital examination techniques in prepubertal girls. *Pediatrics.* 1990;85:182-187

Muram D, Gale C. Acquired vaginal occlusion. *Adolesc Pediatr Gynecol.* 1990;3:141-145

Muram D, Jones C. Genital injury in a child with an imperforate hymen: a case report. *Adolesc Pediatr Gynecol.* 1992;5:201-202

Muram D, Speck PM, Gold SS. Genital abnormalities in female siblings and friends of child victims of sexual abuse. *Child Abuse Negl.* 1991;15:105-110

Murnane ML. Child sexual abuse; I: pictorial essay. *Aust Fam Physician.* 1990;19:603-606

Murnane ML. Child sexual abuse; II: pictorial essay. *Aust Fam Physician.* 1990;19:788-790

Sanfilippo JS. Sexual abuse: to colposcope or not? *Adolesc Pediatr Gynecol.* 1990;3:63-64

Sweet C, Galle P, McRae A, Denley J, Edwards M. Transverse vaginal septum: a diagnosis at 3 months of age. *Adolesc Pediatr Gynecol.* 1990;3:35-38

Yordan EE, Yordan RA. The hymen and Tanner staging of the breast. *Adolesc Pediatr Gynecol.* 1992;5:76-79

Children's Drawings

Hibbard RA, Hartman G. Genitalia in human figure drawings: child rearing practices and child sexual abuse. *J Pediatr.* 1990;116:822-828

Children's Responses to Anogenital Examinations

Berson NL, Herman-Giddens ME, Frothingham TE. Children's perceptions of genital examinations during sexual abuse evaluations. *Child Welfare League of America.* 1993; 72:41-49

Lazebnik R, Zimet GD, Ebert J, et al. How children perceive the medical evaluation for suspected sexual abuse. *Child Abuse Negl.* 1994;18:739-745

Peterson LW, Meservy Z, Furth SE, Morris X, Peele K, Cortese A. The stress of child sexual abuse examinations. *J Clin Forensic Med.* 1994;1:13-19

Steward MS, Schmitz M, Steward DS, Joye NR, Reinhart M. Children's anticipation of and response to colposcopic examination. *Child Abuse Negl.* 1995;19:997-1005

Evidentiary Issues

Aiken M, Muram D, Keene P, Mamelli J. Evidence collection in cases of child abuse. *Adolesc Pediatr Gynecol.* 1993;6:86-90

Annas GJ. Scientific evidence in the courtroom: the death of the Frye rule. *N Engl J Med.* 1994;330:1018-1021

Annas GJ. Setting standards for the use of DNA-typing results in the courtroom—the state of the art. *N Engl J Med.* 1992;326: 1641-1644

Gabby T, Winkleby MA, Boyce T, Fisher DL, Lancaster A, Sensabaugh GF. Sexual abuse of children: the detection of semen on skin. *Am J Dis Child.* 1992;146:700-703

Whitelaw JP. Clue to child sexual abuse. *N Engl J Med.* 1992;326:957

Interviews

Coulborn-Faller K, Corwin DL. Children's interview statements and behaviors: role in identifying sexually abused children. *Child Abuse Negl.* 1995;19:71-82

DeJong AR, Rose M. Legal proof of child sexual abuse in the absence of physical evidence. *Pediatrics.* 1991;88:506-511

Merritt KA, Ornstein PA, Spicker B. Children's memory for a salient medical procedure: implications for testimony. *Pediatrics.* 1994;94:17-23

Lichen Sclerosis et Atrophicus

Loening-Baucke V. Lichen sclerosus et atrophicus in children. *Am J Dis Child.* 1991;145:1058-1061

Young SJ, Wells DLN, Ogden EJD. Lichen sclerosus, genital trauma and child sexual abuse. *Aust Fam Physician.* 1993; 22:729-733

Maternal Perpetrators

Elliott AJ, Peterson LW. Maternal sexual abuse of male children: when to suspect and how to uncover it. *Postgrad Med.* 1993;94:169-180

Medical Photography

Ricci LR. Photographing the physically abused child: principles and practice. *Am J Dis Child.* 1991;145:275-281

Miscellaneous

Anveden-Hertzberg L, Gauderer MWL, Elder JS. Urethral prolapse: an often misdiagnosed cause of urogenital bleeding in girls. *Pediatr Emerg Care.* 1995;11:212-214

Famularo R, Fenton T, Kinscherff R. Child maltreatment and the development of post-traumatic stress disorder. *Am J Dis Child.* 1993;147:755-760

Feldman KW. Patterned abusive bruises of the buttocks and the pinnae. *Pediatrics.* 1992;90:633-636

Finkelhor D, Wolak J. Nonsexual assaults to the genitals in the youth population. *JAMA.* 1995;274:1692-1697

Herman-Giddens ME. Vaginal foreign bodies and child sexual abuse. *Arch Pediatr Adolesc Med.* 1994;148:195-200

Hibbard RA, Zollinger TW. Medical evaluation referral patterns for sexual abuse victims. *Child Abuse Negl.* 1992;16:533-540

Jenny C, Roesler TA, Poyer KL. Are children at risk for sexual abuse by homosexuals? *Pediatrics.* 1994;94:41-44

Krugman S, Mata L, Krugman R. Sexual abuse and corporal punishment during childhood: a pilot retrospective survey of university students in Costa Rica. *Pediatrics.* 1992;90:157-161

Krugman RD. Sexual politics and child protection: they don't mix. *Pediatrics.* 1994;94:45-46

Levine V, Sanchez M, Nestor M. Localized vulvar pemphigoid in a child misdiagnosed as sexual abuse. *Arch Dermatol.* 1992;128:804-806

Lynch JM, Gardner MJ, Albanese CT. Blunt urogenital trauma in prepubescent female patients: more than meets the eye! *Pediatr Emerg Care.* 1995;11:372-375

Paradise JE, Rose L, Sleeper LA, Nathanson M. Behavior, family function, school performance, and predictors of persistent disturbance in sexually abused children. *Pediatrics.* 1994;93:452-459

Pokorny SF. Long-term intravaginal presence of foreign bodies in children: a preliminary study. *J Reprod Med.* 1994;39:931-935

Resnick MD, Blum RW. The association of consensual sexual intercourse during childhood with adolescent health risk and behaviors. *Pediatrics.* 1994;94:907-913

Silber TJ. False allegations of sexual touching by physicians in the practice of pediatrics. *Pediatrics.* 1994;94:742-745

Socolar RRS, Champion M, Green C. Physicians' documentation of sexual abuse of children. *Arch Pediatr Adolesc Med.* 1996;150:191-196

Stanton B, Li X, Black MM, Ricardo I, Galbraith J. Anal intercourse among pre-adolescent and early adolescent low-income urban African-Americans. *Arch Pediatr Adolesc Med.* 1994;148:1201-1204

Yanovski JA, Nelson LM, Willis ED, Cutler GB. Repeated, childhood vaginal bleeding is not always precocious puberty. *Pediatrics.* 1992;89:149-151

Whitelaw JP. Clue to child sexual abuse. *N Engl J Med.* 1992;326:957

Postcoital Contraception

Glasier A, Thong KJ, Dewar M, Mackie M, Baird DT. Mifepristone (RU 486) compared with high-dose estrogen and progestogen for emergency postcoital contraception. *N Engl J Med.* 1992;327:1041-1044

Grimes DA, Cook RJ. Mifepristone (RU 486)—an abortifacient to prevent abortion? *N Engl J Med.* 1992;327:1088-1089

Acknowledgment

This section and its annotations were prepared by David L. Kerns, MD, and reviewed by Ann Botash, MD and V. Denise Everett, MD. Selected annotations from the first edition were written by Carolyn Levitt, MD, and Kim Martinez, RN, CPNP, MPH.

AMERICAN ACADEMY OF PEDIATRICS

Committee on Child Abuse and Neglect

Guidelines for the Evaluation of Sexual Abuse of Children (RE9202)

There are few areas of pediatrics that have so rapidly expanded in clinical importance in recent years as sexual abuse of children. What Kempe referred to in 1977 as a "hidden pediatric problem"[1] is certainly less hidden. Recent incidence studies, while imperfect, suggest approximately 1% of children will experience some form of sexual abuse each year.[2] Children may be sexually abused either in intrafamilial or extrafamilial settings and are more frequently abused by males. Boys may be victimized nearly as often as girls. Adolescents are perpetrators in at least 20% of reported cases,[2] and women may be perpetrators, especially in day-care settings.[3] Pediatricians will encounter these cases in their practices and will be asked by parents and other professionals for their opinions. These guidelines are prepared for use by the primary care pediatrician. Pediatricians who "specialize" in the area of child abuse or child sexual abuse have generally developed their own protocols for their referral practices. In addition, specific American Academy of Pediatrics guidelines for the evaluation of rape of the adolescent are published and should be used for this age-group.[4]

Because a pediatrician has unique skills and a trusted relationship with patients and families, he or she will often be in a position to provide essential support and gain information not readily available to others involved in the investigative, evaluative, or treatment processes. By the same token, the pediatrician may feel inadequately prepared to perform a medical examination of a sexually abused child. The pediatrician should think about these issues when determining how best to utilize his or her skills while avoiding actions that may obstruct the collection of essential evidence. The pediatrician should know what resources are available in the community and should identify these in advance, including a consultant with special expertise in evaluating sexually abused children.

DEFINITION

Sexual abuse can be defined as the engaging of a child in sexual activities that the child cannot comprehend, for which the child is developmentally unprepared and cannot give informed consent, and/or that violate the social and legal taboos of society. The sexual activities may include all forms of oral-genital, genital, or anal contact by or to the child, or nontouching abuses, such as exhibitionism, voyeurism, or using the child in the production of pornography.[1] Sexual abuse includes a spectrum of activities ranging from violent rape to a gentle seduction.

Criminal statutes define and classify sexual abuse as misdemeanors or felonies, depending on whether varying degrees of penetration of body orifices occurred or whether physical or psychological force was used.

Sexual abuse can be differentiated from "sexual play" by assessing the frequency and coercive nature of the behavior and by determining whether there is developmental asymmetry among the participants. Thus, when young children are mutually looking at or touching each other's genitalia, and they are at the same developmental stage, no coercion is used, and there is no intrusion of the body, this should be considered normal (ie, nonabusive) behavior. However, when a 6-year-old coercively tries to have anal intercourse with a 3-year-old, this is not normal behavior, and the health and child protective systems should respond to it whether or not is is legally considered an assault.

This statement has been approved by the Council on Child and Adolescent Health.
PEDIATRICS (ISSN 0031 4005). Copyright © 1991 by the American Academy of Pediatrics.

Reaffirmed 6/94

PRESENTATION

Sexually abused children will be seen by pediatricians in a variety of circumstances: (1) They may be brought in for a routine physical examination or for care of a medical illness, behavioral condition, or physical finding that would include child sexual abuse as part of the differential diagnosis. (2) They have been or are thought to have been sexually abused and are brought by a parent to the pediatrician for evaluation. (3) They are brought to the pediatrician by social service or law enforcement professionals for a "medical evaluation" as part of an investigation.

In the first instance, the diagnosis of sexual abuse and the protection of the child from further harm will depend on the pediatrician's willingness to consider abuse as a possibility. There are many ways sexual abuse can present,[5] and because children who are sexually abused are generally coerced into secrecy, a high index of suspicion is required to recognize the problem. On the other hand, the presenting symptoms are often so general in nature (eg, sleep disturbances, enuresis, encopresis, phobias) that caution must be exercised because these behaviors may be indicators of physical or emotional abuse or other nonabuse-related stressors. Among the more specific signs and symptoms of sexual abuse are rectal or genital pain, bleeding, or infection; sexually transmitted diseases; and developmentally precocious sexual behavior. Pediatricians evaluating children who have these signs and symptoms should at least consider the possibility of abuse and, therefore, should complete a report (see below).

Pediatricians who suspect sexual abuse as a possibility are urged to inform the parents of their concerns in a neutral and calm manner. It is critical to realize that the individual who brought the child to the pediatrician may have no knowledge of, or involvement in, the sexual abuse of the child. The physician may need to reinforce this point with office, clinic, or hospital staff. Children spend many hours in the care of people, other than the parents, who may be potential abusers. A complete history, including behavioral symptoms and associated signs of sexual abuse, should ensue. In some instances, the pediatrician may need to protect the child and, therefore, may delay informing the parent(s) until a report is made and an expedited interview with law enforcement and child protective services agencies can be conducted.

TAKING A HISTORY/INTERVIEWING THE CHILD

In many states, the suspicion of child sexual abuse as a possible diagnosis requires a report to the appropriate law enforcement or child protective services agency. All physicians should know what their state law requires and where and when to file a written report. The diagnosis of sexual abuse has both civil (protective) and criminal ramifications. Investigative interviews should be conducted by the designated agency or individual in the community to minimize repetitive questioning of the child. This does not preclude physicians asking relevant questions needed for a detailed pediatric history, including a review of systems. Occasionally children will spontaneously describe their abuse and indicate who it was who abused them. When asking 3- to 6-year-old children about abuse, the use of line drawings,[6] dolls,[7] or other aids[8] may be helpful. The American Academy of Child and Adolescent Psychiatry has guidelines for interviewing sexually abused children.[9] Children may also describe their abuse during the physical examination. It is desirable for those conducting the interview to use nonleading questions; avoid demonstrations of shock, disbelief, or other emotions; and maintain a "tell me more" or "and then what happened" approach. If possible, the child should be interviewed alone.

A behavioral review of systems may reveal events or behaviors relevant to sexual abuse, even in the absence of a clear history of abuse in the child.[5] The parent may be defensive or unwilling to accept the possibility of sexual abuse. This unwillingness is not of itself diagnostic, but it also does not negate the need for investigation.

In the second situation, where children are brought to physicians by parents who suspect abuse, the same behavioral history and approach is warranted.

In the third instance, when children are brought by protective personnel, little or no history may be available, other than that provided by the child. The pediatrician should try to obtain an appropriate history in all cases before performing a medical examination. The child may spontaneously give additional history during the physical examination as the mouth, genitalia, and anus are examined. When children are brought in by professionals, the history should focus on whether the symptoms are explained by sexual abuse, physical abuse to the genital area as a response to toileting accidents, or other medical conditions.

PHYSICAL EXAMINATION

The physical examination of sexually abused children should not lead to additional emotional trauma for the child. The examination should be explained to the child and conducted in the presence of a supportive adult not suspected of being party to the abuse. Many children are anxious about giving a history, being examined, or having proce-

145

dures performed. Enough time must be allotted to relieve a child's anxiety.

When the alleged sexual abuse has occurred within 72 hours, and the child provides a history of sexual abuse including ejaculation, the examination should be performed immediately. In this acute situation, rape kit protocols modified for child sexual assault victims should be followed to maintain a "chain of evidence." Adult rape kits have been adapted and standardized in some states (Florida, Indiana). These are available in emergency rooms, rape treatment centers, or law enforcement agencies. When more than 72 hours has elapsed, the examination usually is not an emergency, and therefore, the evaluation should be scheduled at the earliest convenient time for the child, physician, and investigative team.

The child should have a thorough pediatric examination, including assessments of developmental, behavioral, and emotional status. Special attention should be paid to the growth parameters and sexual development of the child. In the rare instance when the child is unable to cooperate and the examination must be performed because of the likelihood of trauma, infection, and/or the need to collect forensic samples, consideration should be given to performing the examination with the child under general anesthesia. Instruments that can magnify and illuminate the genital and rectal areas may be used if available, but they are not required. Any signs of trauma should be carefully documented. Specific attention should be given to the areas involved in sexual activity—the mouth, breasts, genitals, perineal region, buttocks, and anus. Any abnormalities should be noted.

In female children, the genital examination should include inspection of the medial aspects of the thighs, labia majora and minora, clitoris, urethra, periurethral tissue, hymen, hymenal opening, fossa navicularis, and posterior fourchette. Findings that are consistent with, but not diagnostic of, sexual abuse include (1) chafing, abrasions, or bruising of the inner thighs and genitalia; (2) scarring, tears, or distortion of the hymen; (3) a decreased amount of or absent hymenal tissue; (4) scarring of the fossa navicularis; (5) injury to or scarring of the posterior fourchette; (6) scarring or tears of the labia minora; and (7) enlargement of the hymenal opening. The volume of published literature is expanding quickly in this area.[10-15]

Various methods for visualizing the hymenal opening in prepubertal children have been described. Published studies are not uniform in their approach. The degree of relaxation of the child; the degree of separation, traction (gentle, moderate) on the labia majora, and the position of the child (supine, lateral, knee-chest); and the time taken will all influence the size of the orifice and the exposure of the hymen and the internal structures.[16] The technique used is less important than maximizing the view and recording the method and results (see below for discussion of significance of findings). Invasive procedures (eg, speculum or digital) are generally not necessary in the prepubertal child.

In male children, the thighs, penis, and scrotum should be examined for bruises, scars, chafing, bite marks, and discharge.

In both sexes, the anus can be examined in the supine, lateral, or knee-chest position. As with the vaginal examination, position may influence the anatomy. The presence of bruises around the anus, scars, anal tears (especially those that extend into the surrounding perianal skin), and anal dilation are important to note. Laxity of the sphincter, if present, should be noted, but digital examination is not always necessary. (See below for discussion of significance of findings.) Note the child's behavior and demeanor during the examination, and ask the child to demonstrate what, if anything, happened. Care should be taken not to suggest answers to questions.

LABORATORY DATA

In the examination occurring within 72 hours of acute sexual assault or sexual abuse with ejaculation, forensic studies should be performed. Routine cultures and screening of all sexually abused children for gonorrhea, syphilis, human immunodeficiency virus, or other sexually transmitted diseases are not recommended. The yield of positive cultures is very low in asymptomatic prepubertal children, especially those whose history indicates fondling only. When epidemiologically indicated, or when the history and/or physical findings suggest the possibility of oral, genital, or rectal contact, appropriate cultures and serologic tests should be obtained. The Centers for Disease Control and American Academy of Pediatrics Committee on Infectious Diseases also provide recommendations on laboratory evaluation.[17,18] The implications of the diagnosis of a sexually transmitted disease for the reporting of child sexual abuse are listed in Table 1.

Pregnancy prevention guidelines have been published by the Committee on Adolescence,[4] and the American Academy of Pediatrics Task Force on Pediatric AIDS has developed guidelines for human immunodeficiency virus testing for assailants.

DIAGNOSTIC CONSIDERATIONS

The diagnosis of child sexual abuse is made on the basis of a child's history. Physical examination alone is infrequently diagnostic in the absence of a history and/or specific laboratory findings. The physician, the multidisciplinary team evaluating the child, and the courts must establish a level of certainty about whether a child has been sexually abused. Table 2 as prepared by the AAP Committee on Child Abuse and Neglect provides suggested guidelines for making the decision to report sexual abuse of children based on currently (November 1990) available information.

As indicated in Table 2, the presence of semen/sperm/acid phosphatase, a positive culture for gonorrhea, or a positive serologic test for syphilis makes the diagnosis of sexual abuse a medical certainty, even in the absence of a positive history (congenital forms of gonorrhea and syphilis excluded).

TABLE 1. Implications of Commonly Encountered Sexually Transmitted Diseases (STDs) for the Diagnosis and Reporting of Sexual Abuse of Prepubertal Infants and Children

STD Confirmed	Sexual Abuse	Suggested Action
Gonorrhea*	Certain	Report†
Syphilis*	Certain	Report
Chlamydia*	Probable‡	Report
Condylomata acuminatum*	Probable	Report
Trichomonas vaginalis	Probable	Report
Herpes 1 (genital)	Possible	Report§
Herpes 2	Probable	Report
Bacterial vaginosis	Uncertain	Medical follow-up
Candida albicans	Unlikely	Medical follow-up

* If not perinatally acquired.
† To agency mandated in community to receive reports of suspected sexual abuse.
‡ Culture only reliable diagnostic method.
§ Unless there is a clear history of autoinoculation.
Prepared by the American Academy of Pediatrics Committee on Child Abuse and Neglect (November 1990).

TABLE 2. Guidelines for Making the Decision to Report Sexual Abuse of Children

Data Available			Response	
History	Physical	Laboratory	Level of Concern About Sexual Abuse	Action
None	Normal examination	None	None	None
Behavioral changes	Normal examination	None	Low (worry)	± Report*; follow closely (possible mental health referral)
None	Nonspecific findings	None	Low (worry)	± Report*; follow closely
Nonspecific history by child or history by parent only	Nonspecific findings	None	Possible (suspect)	± Report*; follow closely
None	Specific findings	None	Probable	Report
Clear statement	Normal examination	None	Probable	Report
Clear statement	Specific findings	None	Probable	Report
None	Normal examination, nonspecific or specific findings	Positive culture for gonorrhea; positive serologic test for syphilis; presence of semen, sperm, acid phosphatase	Definite	Report
Behavioral changes	Nonspecific changes	Other sexually transmitted diseases	Probable	Report

* A report may or may not be indicated. The decision to report should be based on discussion with local or regional experts and/or child protective services agencies.
Prepared by the American Academy of Pediatrics Committee on Child Abuse and Neglect (November 1990).

Other physical signs or laboratory findings may be "suggestive of" or "consistent with" a child's history of sexual abuse. In the absence of a positive history, these findings are, at the least, worrisome or suspicious and require a complete history. If the history is negative, the physician may wish to observe the child closely to monitor changes in behavior or physical findings. If the history is positive, sexual abuse is more than a worry, and a report should be made to the agency authorized to receive reports of sexual abuse.

The differential diagnosis of genital trauma also includes accidental injury and physical abuse. This differentiation may be difficult and may require a careful history and multidisciplinary approach. There are many congenital malformations and infectious or other causes of anal-genital abnormalities that may be confused with abuse. Familiarity with these is important.[19]

After the examination, the physician should provide appropriate feedback and reassurance to the child and family.

RECORDS

Because the likelihood of civil or criminal court action is high, detailed records, drawings, and/or photographs should be kept. The submission of written reports to county agencies and law enforcement departments is encouraged. The more detailed the reports and the more explicit the physician's opinion, the less likely the physician may need to testify in civil (juvenile) court proceedings. Testimony will be likely, however, in criminal court where records alone are not a substitute for personal appearance. In general, the ability to protect a child may often depend on the quality of the physician's records.[20]

TREATMENT

All children who have been sexually abused should be evaluated by competent mental health providers to assess the need for treatment. Unfortunately, treatment services for sexually abused children are not universally available. The need for treatment will vary with the type of sexual molestation (intrafamilial vs extrafamilial), the length of time the molestation has gone on, and the age and symptoms of the child. In general, the more intrusive the abuse, the more violent the assault, the longer the sexual molestation has occurred, and the closer the relationship of the perpetrator to the victim, the worse the prognosis and the greater the need for long-term treatment. Whether or not the parents are directly involved, the parents may also need treatment and support in order to cope with the emotional trauma of the child's abuse (as in the instance when the child has been the victim of extrafamilial molestation).

LEGAL ISSUES

The legal issues confronting pediatricians in evaluating sexually abused children include mandatory reporting with penalties for failure to report; involvement in the civil, juvenile, or family court systems; involvement in divorce/custody proceedings in divorce courts; and involvement in criminal prosecution of defendants in criminal court. In addition, there are medical liability risks for pediatricians.

All pediatricians in the United States are required under the laws of each state to report suspected as well as known cases of child sexual abuse. These guidelines do not suggest that a pediatrician who sees a child with an isolated behavioral finding (nightmares, enuresis, phobias, etc) or an isolated physical finding (eg, a hymenal diameter of 5 mm) must feel obliged to report these cases as suspicious. If additional historical, physical, or laboratory findings suggestive of sexual abuse are present, the physician may have an increased level of suspicion and then should report. Pediatricians are encouraged to discuss cases with their local or regional child abuse consultants as well as with their local child protective services agency. In this way, agencies may be protected from being overburdened with large numbers of vague reports, and physicians may be protected from potential prosecution for failure to report.

Civil courts in most states will intervene protectively if it is more likely than not that child abuse or neglect has occurred. The court should be acting in the best interest of the child to try to determine the safety of the child's environment and should be less concerned with "who did it" than with how recurrence can be prevented. These courts should order evaluations and/or treatment, appoint a guardian ad litem and/or therapist for the child, and monitor the family during a treatment plan.

Pediatricians and children are faced with increasing numbers of cases in which parents who are in the process of separation or divorce are alleging that one or the other (or both) is sexually abusing the child during custodial visits. These cases are generally more difficult for the pediatrician, the child protective services system, and law enforcement agencies. They require more time and should not be unsubstantiated or dismissed simply because a custody dispute exists. Allegations of abuse that occur in the context of divorce proceedings should be reported to the child protective services agency.

A juvenile court proceeding may ensue to determine whether the child needs protection. The pediatrician should act as an advocate for the child in these situations and should encourage the appointment of a guardian ad litem by the court to represent the child's best interests. It should be noted that the American Bar Association indicates that the majority of divorces do not involve custody disputes, and relatively few custody disputes involve allegations of sexual abuse.[20]

In criminal proceedings, the standard of proof is the highest—"beyond a reasonable doubt" or "to a reasonable degree of medical certainty." For many physicians, this level of certainty may be a focus of concern because, in this setting, the pediatrician's testimony is part of the information used to ascertain the guilt or innocence of an alleged abuser. Physicians should be aware of the specificity of their findings and their diagnostic significance.[21]

Pediatricians may find themselves involved in civil malpractice litigation. The failure of a physician to recognize and diagnose sexual abuse in a timely manner may lead to liability suits if a child has been brought repeatedly to the physician and/or a flagrant case has been misdiagnosed. With approximately 50% of American children in some form of out-of-home care, the risk of sexual abuse outside the family is substantial (about half that of intrafamilial abuse)[3] and increases the importance of making the diagnosis in a timely manner. The possibility of a suit being filed for "false reports" by physicians exists. Statutes generally provide immunity as long as the report is done in good faith. We are unaware of any successful suits as of this writing.

Civil litigation suits may be filed by parents against institutions or individuals who may have sexually abused their children. The physician may be asked to testify in these cases. In the civil litigation cases, the standard of proof is "a preponderance of the evidence."

CONCLUSION

The evaluation of sexually abused children is increasingly a part of general pediatric practice. The pediatrician will be part of a multidisciplinary approach to the problem and will need to be competent in the basic skills of history taking, physical examination, selection of laboratory tests, and differential diagnosis. An expanding clinical consultation network is available to assist the primary care physician with the assessment of difficult cases.

COMMITTEE ON CHILD ABUSE
AND NEGLECT, 1990–1991

Richard D. Krugman, MD, Chairman
Judith Ann Bays, MD
David L. Chadwick, MD
Carolyn J. Levitt, MD
Margaret T. McHugh, MD
J. M. Whitworth, MD

Liaison Representatives
Thomas Halversen, MD, American Academy of Child and Adolescent Psychiatry
Marshall D. Rosman, PhD, American Medical Association

Section Liaison
Robert H. Kirschner, MD, Section on Pathology

REFERENCES

1. Kempe CH. Sexual abuse, another hidden pediatric problem: the 1977 C. Anderson Aldrich lecture. *Pediatrics,* 1978; 62:382–389
2. *National Study on The Incidence of Child Abuse and Neglect.* Washington, DC: US Dept of Health and Human Services; 1988
3. Finkelhor D, Williams LM. *Nursery Crimes: Sexual Abuse in Daycare.* Newbury Park, CA: Sage Publications; 1988
4. American Academy of Pediatrics, Committee on Adolescence. Rape and the adolescent. *Pediatrics.* 1988;81:595–597
5. Krugman RD. Recognition of sexual abuse in children. *Pediatr Rev.* 1986;8:25–30
6. Hibbard RA, Roghmann K, Hoekelman RA. Genitalia in children's drawings: an association with sexual abuse. *Pediatrics.* 1987;79:129–137
7. Boat BW, Everson MD. *Using Anatomical Dolls: Guidelines for Interviewing Young Children in Sexual Abuse Investigations.* Chapel Hill, NC: Dept of Psychiatry, University of North Carolina; 1986
8. Jones DPH, McQuiston M. *Interviewing the Sexually Abused Child.* 2nd ed. Denver CO: C. Henry Kempe National Center for the Prevention and Treatment of Child Abuse and Neglect; 1986
9. Guidelines for the clinical evaluation of child and adolescent sexual abuse: position statement of the American Academy of Child and Adolescent Psychiatry. *J Am Acad Child Adolesc Psychiatry.* 1988;27:655–657
10. McCann J, Voris J, Simon M, Wells R. Perianal findings in prepubertal children selected for nonabuse: a descriptive study. *Child Abuse Negl.* 1989;13:179–193
11. Muram D. Child sexual abuse: relationship between sexual acts and genital findings. *Child Abuse Negl.* 1989;13:211–216
12. White ST, Ingram DL, Lyna PR. Vaginal introital diameter in the evaluation of sexual abuse. *Child Abuse Negl.* 1989;13:217–224
13. Hobbs CJ, Wynne JM. Sexual abuse of English boys and girls: the importance of anal examination. *Child Abuse Negl.* 1989;13:195–210
14. Heger A, Emans SJ. Introital diameter as the criterion for sexual abuse. *Pediatrics.* 1990;85:222–223
15. Krugman RD. The more we learn the less we know 'with reasonable medical certainty'? *Child Abuse Negl.* 1989;13:165–166
16. McCann J, Voris J, Simon M, Wells R. Comparison of genital examination techniques in prepubertal girls. *Pediatrics.* 1990;85:182–187
17. Centers for Disease Control. 1989 sexually transmitted diseases treatment guidelines. *MMWR.* September 1, 1989;38(suppl S-8):1–43
18. American Academy of Pediatrics, Committee on Infectious

Diseases. Sexually transmitted diseases. In: *Report of the Committee on Infectious Diseases, 1988.* 21st ed. Elk Grove Village, IL: American Academy of Pediatrics; 1988:79–89

19. Chadwick DL, Berkowitz CA, Kems DA, et al. *Color Atlas of Child Sexual Abuse.* Chicago, IL: Year Book Medical Publishers, Inc; 1989

20. Nicholson EB, Bulkley J, eds. *Sexual Abuse Allegations in Custody and Visitation Cases: A Resource Book for Judges and Court Personnel.* Washington, DC: American Bar Association, National Legal Resource Center for Child Advocacy and Protection; 1988

21. Paradise JE. Predictive accuracy and the diagnosis of sexual abuse: a big issue about a little tissue. *Child Abuse Negl.* 1989;13:169–176

AMERICAN ACADEMY OF PEDIATRICS

Sexual Assault and the Adolescent

Committee on Adolescence   (RE9433)

ABBREVIATION. STD, sexually transmitted disease.

Rape is a significant and serious crime in our society. The Uniform Crime Report for 1991 published by the US Department of Justice listed over 100 000 reported rapes nationwide, but this report excluded statutory rape, rape against men, and unreported sexual assaults.[1] The National Victim Center estimates that almost 700 000 women are raped each year, and that 61% of the rape victims are under the age of 18.[2]

The American Academy of Pediatrics last published a policy statement on rape and the adolescent in 1988,[3] and in 1991 the Committee on Child Abuse and Neglect addressed the evaluation of the sexually abused child.[4] Current definitions of rape, new data on date rape and acquaintance rape, and new suggested protocols for rape management mandate an updated knowledge base for the pediatrician who may need to care for the patient who has been sexually assaulted.

Sexual assault in childhood and adolescence includes incest, acquaintance rape, and stranger rape. As incest has been discussed in the statement on childhood sexual abuse,[4] this statement will focus on a discussion of stranger and acquaintance rape.

DEFINITIONS

There is often confusion among legal definitions, medical terminology, and lay usage of terms related to sexual assault. Rape has historically been defined under standard common law as "the unlawful carnal knowledge of a woman by a man, forcible and against her will, or without her consent."[5] In general, the ability to consent to an act is an essential concept in defining sexual assault. Current legal and medical definitions are included in Tables 1 and 2. When legal definitions are reviewed, it is important to note that, in first-degree sexual assault, lack of consent does not necessarily require physical resistance or verbal refusal. For example, someone who is intoxicated may be unable to give consent. Age alone defines third-degree sexual assault (formerly called statutory rape)—lack of consent and the elements of force and resistance are not required.[6] The age of consent in the United States varies from state to state from 14 to 18 years of age.

DATE AND ACQUAINTANCE RAPE

There is the common perception that rape is perpetrated by strangers, although about half of adolescent sexual assaults are committed by acquaintances. "Date rape" in the context of the assailant and the victim knowing one another has received attention in the literature only recently. In a survey of middle school and high school students, 12% of the males and 18% of the females reported a history of unwanted sexual activity, with the majority of these episodes occurring between 13 and 16 years of age. Female adolescents overwhelmingly reported being forced into sexual situations against their will, and male adolescents reported being socially pressured into sexual situations before they were ready for them.[8] In addition, large surveys of college students in both the United States and New Zealand have documented that over 50% of women in college had experienced unwanted sexual activity in the past, and up to 25% of all college women and 6% of college men reported having been the victims of assaults that met the legal definition of rape. Virtually none of these episodes had been reported to the authorities.[9–12] Several studies show that there is confusion among youth about what constitutes sexual consent,[6,9] and educational programs for adolescents are now being developed to clarify these issues. The law is currently unclear on issues of male rape by a female.

Of those women surveyed and described in the studies, the highest incidence of acquaintance rape appeared to occur in grade 12 and the freshman year of college. These data were collected from college students and did not include those women who had dropped out of high school. Of the 25% of college women surveyed who reported having had unwanted sexual intercourse, 84% knew their assailant, 57% of the episodes occurred on dates, and 41% of the women stated they were virgins at the time of the assault.[9] Between 25% and 47% of date rape occurred on the first date, with an increased risk of rape if the male had initiated the date, driven the car, and paid for the date. Several studies have also documented that both males and females believe that forced sex may be legitimate and acceptable in certain circumstances.[7,10]

Male victims represent about 5% of the total number of sexual assault cases reported.[13] The actual number of males assaulted is probably much higher than statistics indicate because of the low incidence

This statement has been approved by the Council on Child and Adolescent Health.

The recommendations in this statement do not indicate an exclusive course of treatment or procedure to be followed. Variations, taking into account individual circumstances, may be appropriate.

TABLE 1. Legal Definitions of Sexual Assault

Every state has statutory definitions of sexual assault. This example from Rhode Island is representative of current statutes:

First-degree sexual assault—sexual penetration by a part of a person's body or by any object into the genital, oral, or anal openings which occurs when there is a) force or coercion or b) mental or physical inability to communicate unwillingness to engage in an act.

Second-degree sexual assault—sexual contact without penetration that could include intentional touching of a person's sexual or intimate parts or the intentional touching of the victim's clothing covering these intimate parts when there is a) force or coercion or b) mental or physical unwillingness to engage in such an act.

Third-degree sexual assault—sexual penetration by a person 18 years or older of a person under the age of consent.[6]

TABLE 2. Medical Terminology of Sexual Assault

Molestation—noncoital sexual activity between a child and an adolescent or an adult, which may include viewing, genital or breast fondling, or oral-genital contact.

Sexual assault—any contact of an offender with the genitalia of a nonconsenting victim.

Rape—a sexual assault in which the penis of an assailant is introduced into the victim's genitalia, either without consent or by threat of force or compulsion.

Acquaintance or date rape—rape in which the assailant and the victim know one another.[7]

of reporting by men. A majority of male victims knew their attackers, and the use of weapons and multiple assailants were more common in male rape than in female rape.[14,15]

Victims of rape have a difficult adjustment to the assault, as they tend to blame themselves, may suffer diminished self-esteem, and may have difficulty establishing trust in future relationships.[16] Date rape usually occurs in the context of a relationship between two people in a social setting before the assault, with subsequent betrayal of trust.[17] The date rapist tends to be sexually promiscuous, to have a hostile attitude toward women, and to use verbal coercion and alcohol to facilitate the sexual assault.[8] In contrast, rapes by strangers usually involve more violence, trauma, and the display or use of a weapon.[18] Little is known about men who rape men, although there is some information about men who are victims of rape.[13,14]

An association exists between the high incidence of alcohol and other drug abuse on college campuses and date rape.[6,10] Up to 20% of college students are considered problem drinkers,[19] and many surveys have shown a link between impairment of judgment in sexual relationships and the use of alcohol. In a large college study, 73% of the assailants and 55% of the victims had used drugs, alcohol, or both immediately before a sexual assault.[20] College officials are beginning to address the problem of date rape by establishing written policy on date/acquaintance rape, providing educational programs for students on both rape and alcohol, training staff on how to manage sexual assault situations, and providing appropriate counseling and support for the victims.[10]

Pediatricians need to provide both information and counseling about acquaintance rape and its association with alcohol and other drug abuse as part of an annual adolescent health visit. This preventive counseling is especially important during the precollege physical examination.

MANAGEMENT OF THE RAPE VICTIM

Rape is a serious medical and psychological emergency. The pediatrician has an obligation to the adolescent patient who has been the victim of sexual assault to provide optimal medical care and to support that patient and his or her family. The goals of rape intervention include identification and treatment of injury and infection, pregnancy prevention, evidence collection, and psychological assessment with referral for counseling. Findings need to be carefully and accurately documented in the medical record. State legal mandates may require parental notification of the minor's sexual assault that may supersede confidentiality issues.

RAPE PROTOCOL

The pediatrician may be the first professional consulted about the sexual assault. Some pediatricians may prefer to perform this type of evaluation themselves, while others may wish to refer the victim to an assessment team.[21] Some metropolitan areas have trained rape teams and crisis centers that can respond immediately to the sexual assault victim, but many rapes occur in communities where no such services exist. If a pediatrician is consulted about a possible sexual assault within 72 hours of the event, the best course is for an evaluation by a pediatrician knowledgeable in forensic procedures or referral to a rape crisis center or to the emergency room. State laws and guidelines dictate the content of the legal forensic evaluation and "rape kits" are available for the collection of forensic evidence that may be needed in a criminal investigation. It is essential that a forensic examination include careful documentation and an unbroken chain of evidence of specimens.

If the sexual assault took place greater than 72 hours before the report to the pediatrician, the physical assessment of the patient can appropriately be performed in the pediatrician's office, as this type of examination would not require forensic legal documentation. An example of a nonforensic protocol is included in the appendix.

New technologies are being applied to sexual assault assessment, including DNA testing and colposcopy. The recent availability in some centers of DNA testing (fingerprinting) on semen specimens may help to aid in the identification of the perpetrator.[22] The use of the colposcope is not mandatory in the assessment of a sexual assault victim since almost all findings can be seen without magnification or with a hand-held lens.[23,24] The use of these new technologies has not yet become the standard of care.

A major role of pediatricians is to make certain that an adequate rape protocol exists, and each community needs to have written guidelines outlining the local management of the sexual assault victim. Regardless of which professional conducts the exam, the pediatrician needs to remain available and supportive to the patient.

MANAGEMENT OF SEXUALLY TRANSMITTED DISEASES

There is some controversy about appropriate screening and prophylactic treatment of sexually transmitted diseases (STDs) for victims of sexual assault. The risk of acquiring an STD after a rape is indeterminate, as the prevalence of STDs in rape victims is similar to that of the population at large. It is difficult to be certain which infections were already present and which ones were the result of the sexual assault.[25-27] The types of STDs that are commonly found in rape victims include gonorrhea, *Trichomonas vaginalis*, genital warts, *Chlamydia trachomatis* infection, herpes simplex virus infection, and pediculosis.[28-30] Human immunodeficiency virus (HIV) infection and syphilis, although uncommon, have also been reported in child and adolescent assault victims.[31-34] Although there is the theoretical risk of transmission of hepatitis B infection following rape, no cases have yet been reported.

Although the incidence of STD acquisition following sexual assault is not completely known at this time, the American Academy of Pediatrics advises the following evaluation for victims of acute sexual assault.

1. Cultures from appropriate sites for *Neisseria gonorrhoeae* and *C trachomatis*. If vesicles or ulcers exist, a culture for herpes simplex virus can be obtained. A wet mount can be examined for sperm and trichomonads.
2. A baseline urine pregnancy test.
3. A serum specimen drawn and frozen so that serostatus for hepatitis B, syphilis, and HIV at the time of the assault can later be determined, if needed. With appropriate informed consent, the victim can be offered testing for HIV infection with counseling before and after testing. (This testing, however, only indicates baseline status because the incubation period for HIV is 3 to 6 months.)
4. Follow-up examination and blood tests for incubating syphilis, HIV, and hepatitis B (at 6 weeks), and repeat HIV (at 3 to 6 months) should be done when indicated. Even though the medical risk of bloodborne infection is low, the victim may obtain significant psychological relief from negative test results.[35]

In view of the unknown incidence of STDs acquired following rape and the potential for serious long-term consequences to the adolescent, including sterility, the American Academy of Pediatrics currently recommends that prophylaxis be offered to prevent incubating syphilis, gonorrhea, and chlamydia. Current recommendations from the Centers for Disease Control and Prevention (CDC, 1993) are outlined in Table 3.[36]

TABLE 3. STD Prophylaxis for Acute Sexual Assault* (CDC Guidelines, 1993)

Ceftriaxone, 125 mg intramuscularly, in a single dose

plus

Metronidazole, 2 g orally, in a single dose

plus

Doxycycline, 100 mg orally, two times a day for 7 days

* For patients requiring alternative treatments, see the appropriate sections of the CDC Guidelines.

PREGNANCY PREVENTION

Since the overall risk of conception following a rape is approximately 2% to 4%, most experts recommend offering postcoital contraception to the female victims of rape. The possible (but low) failure rate of postcoital contraception and options for pregnancy management in case of failure should be discussed. The current recommended treatment within 72 hours of the rape is Ovral (50 μg of ethinyl estradiol and 0.5 mg of norgestrel per tablet)—two tablets immediately, followed by two tablets 12 hours later or Lo-Ovral (35 μg ethinyl estradiol and 0.5 mg of norgestrel)—four tablets immediately, followed by four tablets 12 hours later. Mild side effects are not uncommon, but if nausea or vomiting occur after the first dose, the patient can be given an antiemetic such as prochlorazine, 5 to 10 mg orally, before the second dose.[37] Recently, mifepristone (RU 486) has been shown to be more effective than Ovral treatment for postcoital contraception,[38,39] and, if RU 486 becomes available in the United States, it may become a treatment option. Regardless of the prophylaxis given, a urine pregnancy test should be done 2 to 3 weeks later to detect treatment failures.

PSYCHOLOGICAL REACTIONS

In addition to managing the physical needs of the adolescent sexual assault victim, the pediatrician should be sensitive to the psychological needs of both the adolescent and the parents. Some parents become angry or feel guilty, and they may blame the adolescent for the sexual assault. Parents can require as much support as the victim, and they need help and counseling to remain supportive to their teenager during this time of crisis.[1]

The majority of adolescent rape victims report concerns about safety, self-blame and shame, irrational fears of bodily damage (infertility, STDs, and abnormal genital function), and fear of pregnancy.[40] During the early stages of the patient's psychological reaction to the rape, referral to a rape crisis team, when available, may be an important adjunct to treatment. Many studies have documented a long term reaction to rape that has the characteristics of a posttraumatic stress disorder.[41-43] This disorder is thought to affect at least 80% of all adolescent rape victims. This syndrome is characterized by the following four symptoms: (1) re-experiencing the traumatic event by intrusive thoughts, dreams, or flashbacks; (2) an avoidance of previously pleasurable activities; (3) an avoidance of the place or circumstances in which the rape occurred; and (4) an increased state of psychomotor arousal leading to difficulties with sleep and memory.[44] Counseling for the adolescent with posttraumatic stress disorder as a result of rape is usually directed toward helping the victim deal with the trauma as well as encouraging the avoidance of self-blame and guilt that often result from the rape.[44] The pediatrician needs to develop referral sources for this type of counseling in the community.

During the period of recovery after a rape, the adolescent may present to the pediatrician with psychophysiologic symptoms, depression, and multiple phobias. Acting out behaviors including running away, truancy, and promiscuity may also occur during this time.[13]

RAPE PREVENTION

One study on both adolescent and adult female rape victims suggests that strong physical resistance by an adult-sized victim during a sexual assault will decrease the incidence of completed rape while increasing the chance of physical injury.[45,46] Overall, about 1% of injuries during a rape require hospitalization and about 0.1% of rape injuries are fatal.[47]

Epidemiologic studies of rape include one report of 63 adolescent male rapists, most of whom committed the sexual assault as an unprovoked and unanticipated act of violence that occurred while the rapist was intoxicated.[48] Another study reported on more than 100 adolescent female rape victims and found that most sexual assaults occurred at night with three factors involved: (1) a teenage girl voluntarily agreeing to go to the house, apartment, or car of a young man she had known for less than 24 hours, (2) impairment of the victim by drugs or alcohol, and (3) hitchhiking.[49,50] The pediatrician can alert the adolescent patient to this information and can direct the patient to community resources, including police self-protection classes and self-defense courses, that may be available through community centers such as the YWCA/YMCA. School programs for middle school, high school, and college students and programs for out-of-school youth need to offer similar educational and practical advice.

RECOMMENDED COURSE OF ACTION

The American Academy of Pediatrics recommends that pediatricians:

1. be knowledgeable about the incidence of stranger and acquaintance sexual assault;
2. participate in the establishment of rape protocols;
3. understand the legal aspects of the forensic examination; and
4. be prepared to offer preventive counseling, immediate medical referral, and psychological support to the adolescent patients in their practices who may be the victims of a sexual assault.

Anticipatory guidance about sexual assault needs to be given to adolescent patients at annual health visits and in school settings during middle school and high school. The pediatrician also needs to be aware of community resources for both the management of the examination and the counseling of the patient after the rape. The pediatrician should remain a member of the team that provides the ongoing medical and psychological support to the adolescent sexual assault victim.

APPENDIX: SEXUAL ABUSE AND RAPE PROTOCOL

This protocol is adapted from The Children's Hospital Rape Protocol, Boston, MA.

A. General Information
   • Name, DOB, race, parent and sibling information
   • Alleged perpetrator and relationship to victim
B. Pertinent History
   • Chief complaint or description of event in victim's own words
   • Description of event from caretaker's report of victim's statement
C. Pertinent Medical History
   • If pubertal female-menarche age, last menstrual period, use of tampons, history of vaginitis, previous sexual activity, use of birth control
   • Pre-existing physical injuries
   • Pertinent medical history of ano-genital injuries, surgeries, diagnostic procedures, or medical treatment
   • History of child abuse
D. Summary of Acts Described by Patient and/or Historian
   • Genital contact (with penis, finger, foreign object, etc)
   • Anal contact (with penis, finger, foreign object, etc)
   • Oral copulation of genitals (of victim by assailant, or of assailant by victim)
   • Oral copulation of anus (of victim by assailant, or assailant by victim)
   • Physical symptoms (ie, pain, urinary retention, enuresis, bleeding, discharge)
   • Behavioral symptoms (eg, sleep, aggressiveness, sexual acting out)
E. Physical Examination
   • Vital signs, general physical examination, documentation of physical injuries by diagram
   • Genital examination, female
      • Document Tanner stage of breasts and genitalia
      • Indicate method used for genital examination—direct visualization, colposcope, hand held magnifier
      • Examination position used—supine, knee chest, stirrups
      • Describe labia majora, clitoris, labia minora, urethral meatus, periurethral tissue
      • In prepubertal female, careful examination of external genitalia, including hymen
      • In postpubertal female, speculum pelvic examination if atraumatic, otherwise external examination with cotton-tipped swab samples
   • Female/male anus
      • Describe buttocks, perianal skin, anal tone, tags, anal spasm, fissures, anal laxity, stool in vault
      • Document method of examination (observation, digital, anoscopic, proctoscopic) and position used (supine, prone, lateral recumbent)
   • Genital examination, male
      • Document Tanner/genital or sexual maturation staging
      • Describe method of examination (direct visualization, colposcope, hand-held magnifier)
      • Diagram any lesions on genitalia, anus, perineum, or buttocks
F. Laboratory Collection
   • Cultures for N gonorrhoeae and C trachomatis from appropriate sites—vagina, cervix, rectum, urethra, pharynx
   • Blood for RPR, HIV, hepatitis B, frozen serum
   • Wet mount, pregnancy test, sperm studies
G. Treatment (see text of statement for STD and postcoital contraception discussion)
H. Follow-up Appointments
   • Counseling at 2- and 6-week follow-up appointments, with testing then for pregnancy, syphilis, HIV, hepatitis, and other STDs as indicated

REFERENCES

1. US Dept of Justice, FBI. *Crime in the United States: Uniform Crime Reports 1990.* Washington, DC, US Government Printing Office; 1991:23–26
2. National Victim Center, and Crime Victims Research and Treatment Center. *Rape in America: A Report to the Nation.* Arlington, VA; 1992:1–16
3. American Academy of Pediatrics, Committee on Adolescence. Rape and the adolescent. *Pediatrics.* 1988;81:595–597
4. American Academy of Pediatrics, Committee on Child Abuse and Neglect. Guidelines for the evaluation of sexual abuse of children. *Pediatrics.* 1991;87:254–260
5. Silberstang E. *American Jurisprudence.* Jurisprudence Publishers, Inc; 1972
6. Simon T, Harris CA. Using high school peer groups to reduce sex without consent. In: *School Intervention Report.* Holmes Beach, FL: Learning Publications, Inc; 1992;6:7–9
7. Hibbard RA. Sexual abuse. In: McAnarney ER, Kreipe RE, Orr DP, Comerci GD, eds. *Textbook of Adolescent Medicine.* Philadelphia, PA: WB Saunders Co; 1992:1123–1127
8. Erickson PI, Rapkin AJ. Unwanted sexual experiences among middle and high school youth. *J Adolesc Health.* 1991;12:319–325
9. Koss MP, Gidycz CA, Wisniewski N. The scope of rape: incidence and prevalence of sexual aggression and victimization in a national sample of higher education students. *J Consult Clin Psychol.* 1987;55:162–170
10. Simon T. Violence and sexual assault on college campuses. In: *Principles and Practices of Student Health, Volume Three: College Health.* Oakland, CA: Third Party Publishing Co; 1992: Chap 20
11. Gavey N. Sexual victimization prevalence among New Zealand university students. *J Consult Clin Psychol.* 1991;59:464–466
12. Tanzman ES. Unwanted sexual activity: the prevalence in college women. *J Am College Health.* 1992;40:167–171
13. Greydanus DE, Shaw RD, Kennedy EL. Examination of sexually abused adolescents. *Semin Adolesc Med.* 1987;3:59–66
14. Lacey HB, Roberts R. Sexual assault on men. *Int J STD AIDS.* 1991;2:258–260
15. Mezey G, King M. The effects of sexual assault on men: a survey of 22 victims. *Psychol Med.* 1989;19:205–209
16. Katz BL. The psychological impact of stranger versus nonstranger rape on the victims' recovery. In Parrot A, Bechhofer L, eds. *Acquaintance Rape: The Hidden Crime.* New York: John Wiley and Sons; 1991:251–269
17. Malamuth NM, Sockloskie RJ, Koss MP, Tanaka JS. Characteristics of aggressors against women: testing a model using a national sample of college students. *J Consult Clin Psychol.* 1991;59:670–681
18. Bownes I, O'Gorman E, Sayers A. Rape—a comparison of stranger and acquaintance assaults. *Med Sci Law.* 1991;31:102–109
19. Abbey A. Acquaintance rape and alcohol consumption on college campuses: how are they linked? *J Am College Health.* 1991;39:165–169
20. Warshaw R. *I never called it rape: The Ms. Report on Recognizing, Fighting, and Surviving Date and Acquaintance Rape.* New York: Harper and Row; 1988
21. Wilde JA, McDonald D, Pedsoni T, Wissow L. Managing acute sexual abuse. *Contemp Pediatr.* 1994;11:52–63
22. McCabe ER. Applications of DNA fingerprinting in pediatric practice. *J Pediatr.* 1992;120:499–509
23. Heger A, Emans SJ, Jenny C, et al. *Evaluation of the Sexually Abused Child: A Medical Textbook and Photographic Atlas.* New York: Oxford University Press; 1992
24. Muram D, Elias S. Child sexual abuse - genital tract findings in prepubertal girls. II. Comparison of colposcopic and unaided examinations. *Am J Obstet Gynecol.* 1989;160:333–335
25. Ross JD, Scott GR, Busuttil A. Rape and sexually transmitted diseases: patterns of referral and incidence in a department of genitourinary medicine. *J R Soc Med.* 1991;84:657–659
26. Estreich S, Forster GE, Robinson A. Sexually transmitted diseases in rape victims. *Genitourin Med.* 1990;66:433–438
27. Jenny C, Hooton TM, Bowers A, et al. Sexually transmitted diseases in the victims of rape. *N Engl J Med.* 1990;322:713–716
28. Glaser JB, Schachter J, Benes S, et al. Sexually transmitted diseases in postpubertal female rape victims. *J Infect Dis.* 1991;164:726–730
29. Murphy SM. Rape, sexually transmitted diseases and human immunodeficiency virus infection. *Int J STD AIDS.* 1990;1:79–82
30. Lacey HB. Sexually transmitted diseases and rape: the experience of a sexual assault centre. *Int J STD AIDS.* 1990;1:405–409
31. Murphy S, Kitchen V, Harris JR, Forster SM. Rape and subsequent seroconversion to HIV. *Br J Med.* 1989;299:718
32. Siqueira LM, Barnett SH, Kass E, Gertner M. Incubating syphilis in an adolescent female rape victim. *J Adol Health Care.* 1991;12:459–461
33. Gutman LT, St Claire KK, Weedy C, et al. Human immunodeficiency virus transmission by child sexual abuse. *AJDC.* 1991;145:137–141
34. Gellert GA, Durfee MJ, Berkowitz CD, Higgins KV, Tubiolo VC. Situational and sociodemographic characteristics of children infected with human immunodeficiency virus from pediatric sexual abuse. *Pediatrics.* 1993;91:39–44
35. Emans SJH, Goldstein DP. *Pediatric and Adolescent Gynecology.* Boston: Little, Brown & Co; 1990
36. Centers for Disease Control. Sexually Transmitted Diseases—Treatment Guidelines. *MMWR.* 1993;42:1–102
37. Hatcher RA, Trussell J, Stewart F, et al, eds. *Contraceptive Technology: Sixteenth Revised Edition.* New York: Irvington Publishers, Inc; 1994
38. Webb AM, Russell J, Elstein M. Comparison of Yuzpe regimen, Danazol, and Mifepristone (RU 486) in oral postcoital contraception. *Br Med J.* 1992;305:927–931
39. Glasier A, Thong KJ, Dewar M, Mackie M, Baird DT. Mifepristone (RU 486) compared with high-dose estrogen and progestogen for emergency postcoital contraception. *N Engl J Med.* 1992;327:1041–1044
40. Mann EM. Self-reported stresses of adolescent rape victims. *J Adolesc Health Care.* 1981;2:29–33
41. Moscarello R. Posttraumatic stress disorder after sexual assault: its psychodynamics and treatment. *J Am Acad Psychoanal.* 1991;19:235–253
42. Bownes IT, O'Gorman EC, Sayers A. Assault characteristics and post-traumatic stress disorder in rape victims. *Acta Psychiatr Scand.* 1991;83:27–30
43. Dahl S. Acute response to rape—a PTSD variant. *Acta Psychiatr Scand Suppl.* 1989;80:56–62
44. Pynoos RS, Nader K. Post-traumatic stress disorder. In: McAnarney ER, Kreipe RE, Orr DP, Comerci GD, eds. *Textbook of Adolescent Medicine.* Philadelphia, PA: WB Saunders Co; 1992:104:1003–1009
45. Marchbanks PA, Lui KJ, Mercy JA. Risk of injury from resisting rape. *Am J Epidemiol.* 1990;132:540–549
46. Siegel JM, Sorenson SB, Golding JM, Burnam MA, Stein JA. Resistance to sexual assault: who resists and what happens? *Am J Public Health.* 1989;79:27–31
47. American College of Obstetricians and Gynecologists. *Sexual Assault.* Technical Bulletin Number 172, September 1992
48. Vinogradov S, Dishotsky NI, Doty AK, Tinklenberg JR. Patterns of behavior in adolescent rape. *Am J Orthopsychiatry.* 1988;58:179–187
49. Jenny C. Adolescent risk-taking behavior and the occurrence of sexual assault. *AJDC.* 1988;142:770–772
50. Renshaw DC. Treatment of sexual exploitation: rape and incest. *Psychiatric Clin North Am.* 1989;12:257–277

Sexually Transmitted Diseases and Child Sexual Abuse

See Also:
AAP Statements *Sexually Transmitted Diseases* and
Gonorrhea in Prepubertal Children, which follow

Clinical Principles

▼ Sexually transmitted disease (STD) is a major health problem worldwide. Sexually transmitted diseases are used by physicians, social service departments, and the criminal justice system as a marker to identify children who may have been sexually abused.

▼ Sexually transmitted diseases occur in 2% to 15% of sexually abused children. The rate of STDs in children is proportional to the rate in the general population of adults where the child lives. Many of the STDs may have a long incubation period and/or asymptomatic carriage rate, which may lead to delay in presentation.

▼ There are two documented modes of transmission in children: (1) perinatal acquisition or (2) sexual contact. Detailed histories and complete physical examinations are required to discern the etiology in each individual case.

▼ There are at least 20 different STDs of concern; the most likely to be considered clinically are:

Human papilloma virus (HPV)
Neisseria gonorrhoeae
Chlamydia trachomatis
Herpes simplex virus
Syphilis
Trichomonas vaginalis
Gardnerella vaginalis
Ureaplasma urealyticum
Human immunodeficiency virus (HIV)

Bibliography

Overview

Estreich S, Forster G. Sexually transmitted diseases in children: introduction. *Genitourin Med.* 1992;68:2-8
This article provides a broad overview of STDs, with historical perspective and information about modes of transmission and treatment. Incidence and prevalence are presented by age group from birth to adolescence. Infectious agents discussed are syphilis, *N gonorrhoeae, C trachomatis,* vulvovaginitis, HPV, herpes simplex virus, HIV, and hepatitis B.

Any STD in children (if not perinatally acquired) should be investigated for sexual abuse as a mode of transmission. Cultures for *N gonorrhoeae* and *C trachomatis* should be obtained from appropriate sites, sometimes even if there is no history of exposure to those areas. Children may not disclose all types of assault because they are embarrassed, fearful, or do not understand the questions. Because of legal implications, all STDs should be confirmed by a regional reference laboratory. Many questions remain unanswered due to the multiple suggested modes of transmission. Further investigation is needed. (STS, JJ)

Ingram D, Everett D, Lyna P, White S, Rockwell L. Epidemiology of adult sexually transmitted disease agents in children being evaluated for sexual abuse. *Pediatr Infect Dis J.* 1992;11:945-950
This is a prospective study describing the prevalence of STDs in 1,538 children aged 1 to 12 years who were alleged victims of sexual abuse. Reports from children old enough to verbalize a history of sexual contact were matched against laboratory findings of sexually transmitted disease. *N gonorrhoeae* was found in 2.8% (41/1,469); *C trachomatis* in 1.2% (17/1,473); HPV (condylomata acuminata) in 1.8% (28/1,538); *Treponema pallidum* (syphilis) in 0.1% (1/1,263); and herpes simplex virus in 0.1% (2/1,538). Vaginal discharge was found in 245 children. Only 141 children were tested for trichomoniasis; 3 were positive. Of the 99 children evaluated for bacterial vaginosis, 7 were positive by whiff test and clue cells.

History of sexual contact was present in 83% of children who were positive for *N gonorrhoeae;* 94% of those with *C trachomatis;* 43% of those with condylomata acuminata; 0% of those with syphilis (numbers extremely small); 50% of those with herpes simplex virus; 33% of those with *T vaginalis;* and 28% of those with bacterial vaginosis.

Of the 1,538 children evaluated, 4 had at least two diseases: 3 with both *N gonorrhoeae* and *C trachomatis,* and one with both *C trachomatis* and condylomata acuminata.

Overall, children with *C trachomatis* infection were older. Those with condylomata acuminata were younger than those with *N gonorrhoeae* or *C trachomatis.* The prevalence of these diseases did not vary significantly by age group, except for a finding that children with condylomata acuminata were younger in the 1 to 3 year age group than those with *N gonorrhoeae.*

The authors conclude that *N gonorrhoeae,* syphilis, and *C trachomatis* are highly associated with sexual abuse. Condylomata acuminata, *T vaginalis,* herpes simplex virus, and bacterial vaginosis are associated with sexual abuse, but further studies are needed to determine the extent of that association. (STS, JJ)

Ingram DL, Everett D, Flick LAR, Russell TA, White-Sims ST. Vaginal gonococcal cultures in sexual abuse evaluations: evaluation of selective criteria for preteenaged girls. *Pediatrics* (Electronic Abstracts). 1997; 99:863-864
Accurate selective criteria could limit the number of vaginal cultures for *N gonorrhoeae* performed on preteenaged girls as part of their sexual abuse evaluations. This study was performed to determine whether the published selective criteria of the AAP Committee on Child Abuse and Neglect (a copy is enclosed in the section Sexual Abuse of Children) and of Siegel et al (the next annotation) would have accurately detected all cases of vaginal gonococcal infections in our large study population.

Cultures for *N gonorrhoeae* were performed on 2,731 preteenaged girls. There were 84 girls with gonococcal infections, 80 of whom had a vaginal discharge. The four girls without a vaginal discharge included two with a history of having vaginal intercourse with an alleged perpetrator with gonorrhea, one with *N gonorrhoeae* isolated from a urine culture, and one whose preteenaged sister had gonorrhea. All of the 84 girls would have been identified using the selective culturing criteria of the AAP Committee on Child Abuse

and Neglect: culturing when epidemiologically indicated (interpreted as the girl having another STD, a child sibling, child household member, a close child associate or a perpetrator with a known STD) or when the history and/or physical findings suggest the possibility of oral, genital, or rectal contact; or Siegel et al's more selective criteria: only culturing prepubertal girls for *N gonorrhoeae* if there is a vaginal discharge at the time of presentation or if there is a high risk for STD acquisition, defined as having an STD diagnosed, a sibling with an STD, contact with a perpetrator known to have an STD, contact with multiple perpetrators, or Tanner stage III or above.

Whether the results of this and the following article are applicable to other geographic areas is unclear.

Siegel RM, Schubert CJ, Myers PA, Shapiro RA. The prevalence of sexually transmitted diseases in children and adolescents evaluated for sexual abuse in Cincinnati: rationale for limited STD testing in prepubertal girls. *Pediatrics.* 1995;96:1090-1094
This prospective study was designed to determine the prevalence of *C trachomatis, N gonorrhoeae, T vaginalis,* syphilis, and HIV infection in sexually abused children and to develop selective criteria for STD testing in these children in the Cincinnati, OH, area. All children evaluated for sexual abuse at the regional children's hospital were eligible. Eight hundred fifty-five children were evaluated over a 1-year period. The study included 704 girls and 151 boys. Children ranged in age from 3 weeks to 18 years old.

Standard STD testing (AAP recommendations) was defined as serum rapid plasma reagin test, examination for *Trichomonas; N gonorrhoeae* culture of the throat, rectum, and genitalia; and *C trachomatis* culture of the rectum and genitalia. STD testing in this study was recommended in children with (1) a history of genital discharge or contact with the perpetrator's genitalia, (2) examination findings of genital discharge or trauma, and (3) all adolescents. Human immunodeficiency virus testing was obtained in children with risk factors for HIV infection, those with contact with a perpetrator with HIV risk factors, or if the family was concerned about HIV acquisition.

A total of 423 children were tested for *N gonorrhoeae,* 415 for *C trachomatis,* 275 for syphilis, 208 for *Trichomonas,* and 140 for HIV. Twelve children were determined to have *N gonorrhoeae* infection, 11 had *C trachomatis* infection, and four had *Trichomonas* infection. Overall, the prevalence of STDs in prepubertal girls was 3.2% and 14.6% in pubertal girls. The prevalence of *N gonorrhoeae* in prepubertal girls with vaginal discharge was 11.1% and 0% in prepubertal girls without discharge (*P*<.001). *C trachomatis* infection was ' diagnosed in 0.8% of prepubertal girls compared with 7.0% of pubertal girls (*P*< .001). None of the children tested positive for syphilis or HIV, and no males had an STD.

It was concluded that (1) in this particular community, *N gonorrhoeae* testing in prepubertal girls can be limited to those with a vaginal discharge on examination unless other risk factors are present; (2) the prevalence of *C trachomatis* and *Trichomonas* in prepubertal girls was low and screening for these pathogens may be omitted from routine evaluations; and (3) all pubertal girls evaluated for sexual abuse should be tested for STDs because of the high prevalence of asymptomatic infection in this patient population.

These findings emphasize the importance of tailoring screening recommendations to the STD epidemiology of a particular locality. (DK)

Specific Agents and Issues

Boyd L. Condylomata acuminata in the pediatric population. *Am J Dis Child.* 1990;144:817-824

The incidence of condylomata acuminata, caused by HPV, has steadily increased among adults and children. The author reviews the English literature for well-documented cases addressed in terms of five criteria: age, sex, how the warts were acquired, areas of the body involved, and method of treatment. A total of 74 children, aged birth to 17 years, were included.

The anatomical appearance of condylomata acuminata lesions in children may be different from that seen in adults. Only 1 of 31 male children had evidence of wart lesions on the penile shaft, while 52% of men displayed lesions on the glans, frenulum, and corona, 33% on the prepuce, and 18% on the shaft. Urethral meatal involve-

ment, 16% in male children, was 23% in adult men. There are far fewer differences in females. Adult labial involvement is higher, at 30% for women and 16% for children. Adult women have urethral and anal lesions, 8% and 18%, respectively, while 2% and 19% of girls display lesions in those respective areas.

The virus for condylomata acuminata is transmitted by (1) infected birth canal at time of delivery; (2) routine nonsexual familial contact; and (3) sexual contact. Additional possible methods of transmission include sexual play in children and autoinoculation.

There is a growing incidence of condylomata acuminata in patients who are positive for the Human immunodeficiency virus, HIV testing may need to be considered.

A critical analysis of treatment in the pediatric age group is limited by a lack of long-term follow-up. Treatment failures have been reported for surgery, cryotherapy, podophyllum resin, fulguration, and carbon dioxide laser. Complete eradication may be impossible; close follow-up is necessary. (STS, JJ)

Gellert G, Durfee M, Berkowitz C, Higgins K, Tubiola V. Situational and sociodemographic characteristics of children infected with human immunodeficiency virus from pediatric sexual abuse. *Pediatrics.* 1993;91:39-44

A survey was sent to medical professionals, social service departments, and members of the judicial system across the United States and Canada, to delineate the prevalence of HIV manifestation in sexually abused children. A total of 2,147 letters were sent. The results revealed 113,198 sexual abuse assessments. A total of 5,622 HIV tests were performed, and 41 children tested positive. Thirteen cases were excluded because acquisition had occurred via another source; 28 children were evaluated according to the protocol.

According to the survey, children were to be evaluated for HIV if the perpetrator was known to be infected, had signs and symptoms suggesting HIV infection, or engaged in high-risk activities or lifestyle habits. The article delineates family situations of the child victim and a profile of the perpetrator.

In conclusion, there is infrequent transmission of HIV from sexual abuse, but as the rate of HIV in the adult population increases, so will the rate among children. The children who became HIV positive reported five or fewer episodes of abuse, which is of great concern. Further surveillance and a standard protocol are needed to be able to identify these children. (STS,JJ)

Gutman LT, Herman-Giddens ME, Phelps WC. Transmission of human genital papillomavirus disease: comparison of data from adults and children. *Pediatrics.* 1993;91:31-38

A substantial body of evidence has demonstrated that the primary means of transmission of genital warts in sexually active adults is through sexual contact. However, the epidemiology and social significance of anal-genital warts in prepubertal children is controversial. Debate continues regarding the frequency with which these lesions have resulted from sexual abuse or transmission by other means. An accurate understanding of the dominant means of transmission of anal-genital warts in children is of particular importance because that understanding influences the extent to which child protective services may become involved following a diagnosis. This paper reviews the evolution of the data on the means of transmission of HPV of the genital tract of adults and compares those data with the information available concerning the transmission of anal-genital HPV-related disease in children. Methods for the diagnosis of child sexual abuse that have developed in the past decade form one of the bases for the evaluation of studies of the transmission of anal-genital HPV-related diseases to children.

Ingram D, White S, Lyna P, et al. *Gardnerella vaginalis* **infection and sexual contact in female children.** *Child Abuse Negl.* 1992;16:847- 853

Gardnerella vaginalis is reported to be sexually transmitted, and has been proposed as a marker to identify sexually abused children. This prospective study investigated 366 female children between the ages of 1 and 12 years. The ethnicity of the group was 47% black and 53% white.

The children were placed in one of three groups. Group I included 191 children with a history of sexual contact and/or infection with *N gonorrhoeae* or *C trachomatis*. The 144 children in group II were those with no history of abuse, gonorrhea, or chlamydial infection. In

group III, the authors placed 31 children who were friends of the authors and had no history of abuse.

Gardnerella vaginalis was found not to be statistically different in all three groups: 5.3% of group I, 4.9% of group II, and 6.4% of group III. *Gardnerella vaginalis* was only found to be associated with increase in age in white children. Therefore, *G vaginalis* is not a good identifying marker for sexual abuse. (STS, JJ)

Supplemental Bibliography

Chlamydia

Aronson MD, Phillips RS. Screening young men for chlamydial infection. *JAMA.* 1993;270:2097-2098

Bell TA, Stamm WE, Wang SP, Kuo CC, Holmes KK, Grayston JT. Chronic *Chlamydia trachomatis* **infections in infants.** *JAMA.* 1992;267:400-402

Genc M, Ruusuvaara L, Mardh P. An economic evaluation of screening for *Chlamydia trachomatis* **in adolescent males.** *JAMA.* 1993;270:2057-2064

Goh BT, Forster GE. Sexually transmitted diseases in children: chlamydial oculo-genital infection. *Genitourin Med.* 1993;69:213-221

Hammerschlag MR, Golden NH, Oh MK, et al. Single dose of azithromycin for the treatment of genital chlamydial infections in adolescents. *J Pediatr.* 1993;122:961-965

Shafer M, Schachter J, Moncada J, et al. Evaluation of urine-based screening strategies to detect Chlamydia trachomatis among sexually active asymptomatic young males. *JAMA.* 1993;270:2065-2070

Workowski KA, Lampe MF, Wong KG, Watts MB, Stamm WE. Long-term eradication of Chlamydia trachomatis genital infection after antimicrobial therapy: evidence against persistent infection. *JAMA.* 1993;279:2071-2075

Gardnerella

Emans SJ. Significance of *Gardnerella vaginalis* in a prepubertal female. *Pediatr Infect Dis J.* 1991;10:709-710

Genital Flora

Gardner JJ. Comparison of the vaginal flora in sexually abused and nonabused girls. *J Pediatr.* 1992;120:872-877

Genital Mycoplasmas

Ingram DL, White ST, Lyna P, et al. Ureaplasma urealyticum and large colony mycoplasma colonization in female children and its relationship to sexual contact, age, and race. *Child Abuse Negl.* 1992;16:265-272

Gonorrhea

Handsfield HH, McCormack WM, Hook EW, et al. A comparison of single-dose cefixime with ceftriaxone as treatment for uncomplicated gonorrhea. *N Engl J Med.* 1991;325:1337-1341

Geidinghagen DH, Hoff GL, Biery RM. Gonorrhea in children: epidemiologic unit analysis. *Pediatr Infect Dis J.* 1992;11:973-974

Portilla I, Lutz B, Montalvo M, Mogabgab WJ. Oral cefixime versus intramuscular ceftriaxone in patients with uncomplicated gonococcal infections. *Sex Transm Dis.* 1992;19:94-98

Herpes Simplex

Amir J, Straussberg R, Harel L, Smetana Z, Varsano I. Evaluation of a rapid enzyme immunoassay for the detection of Herpes Simplex Virus antigen in children with Herpes gingivostomatitis. *Pediatr Infect Dis J.* 1996;15:627-629

Do AN, Green PA, Demmler GJ. Herpes simplex virus type 2 meningitis and associated genital lesions in a three-year-old child. *Pediatr Infect Dis J.* 1994;13:1014-1016

HIV

Fost N. Ethical considerations in testing victims of sexual abuse for HIV infection. *Child Abuse Negl.* 1990;14:5-7

Gellert GA, Durfee MJ, Berkowitz CD. Developing guidelines for HIV antibody testing among victims of pediatric sexual abuse. *Child Abuse Negl.* 1990;14:9-17

Gutman LT, St Claire KK, Weedy C, et al. Human immunodeficiency virus transmission by child sexual abuse. *Am J Dis Child.* 1991;145:137-141

Gutman LT, St. Claire KK, Weedy C, Herman-Giddens M, McKinney RE. Sexual abuse of human immunodeficiency virus-positive children: outcomes for perpetrators and evaluation of other household children. *Am J Dis Child.* 1992;146:1185-1189

Gutman LT, Herman-Giddens ME, McKinney RE. Pediatric acquired immunodeficiency syndrome: barriers to recognizing the role of child sexual abuse. *Am J Dis Child.* 1993;147:775-780

Murtagh C, Hammill H. Sexual abuse of children: a new risk factor for HIV transmission. *Adolesc Pediatr Gynecol.* 1993;6:33-35

Rimsza ME. Words too terrible to hear: sexual transmission of human immunodeficiency virus to children. *Am J Dis Child.* 1993;147:711-712

Siegel R, Christie C, Myers M, Duma E, Green L. Incest and pneumocystis carinii pneumonia in a twelve-year-old girl: a case for early human immunodeficiency virus testing in sexually abused children. *Pediatr Infect Dis J.* 1992;11:681-682

Yordan EE, Yordan RA. Sexually transmitted diseases and human immunodeficiency virus screening in a population of sexually abused girls. *Adolesc Pediatr Gynecol.* 1992;5:187-191

Human Papillomavirus

Cripe TP. Human papillomaviruses: pediatric perspectives on a family of multifaceted tumorigenic pathogens. *Pediatr Infect Dis J.* 1990; 9:836-844

Franger AL. Condylomata acuminata in prepubescent females. *Adolesc Pediatr Gynecol.* 1990;3:38-41

Gutman LT, Herman-Giddens M, Prose NS. Diagnosis of child sexual abuse in children with genital warts (letter). *Am J Dis Child.* 1991;145:126-127

Gutman LT, St Claire K. Prevalence of sexual abuse in children with genital warts (letter). *Pediatr Infect Dis J.* 1991;10:342-343

Gutman LT, St Claire K, Herman-Giddens ME, Johnston WW, Phelps WC. Evaluation of sexually abused and nonabused young girls for intravaginal human papillomavirus infection. *Am J Dis Child.* 1992;146:694-699

Koutsky LA, Holmes KK, Critchlow CW, et al. A cohort study of the risk of cervical intraepithelial neoplasia grade 2 or 3 in relation to papillomavirus infection. *N Engl J Med.* 1992;327:1272-1278

Pacheco BP, DiPaola G, Mendez Ribas JM, Vighi S, Rueda NG. Vulvar infection caused by human papilloma virus in children and adolescents without sexual contact. *Adolesc Pediatr Gynecol.* 1991;4:136-142

Padel AF, Venning VA, Evans MF et al. Human papillomaviruses in anogenital warts in children: typing by in situ hybridisation. *B M J.* 1990;300:1491-1494

Smith McCune KK, Horbach N, Dattel BJ. Incidence and clinical correlates of human papillomavirus disease in a pediatric population referred for evaluation of sexual abuse. *Adolesc Pediatr Gynecol.* 1993;6:20-24

Sexually Transmitted Diseases - General

Abramowicz M, ed. Drugs for sexually transmitted diseases. *The Medical Letter.* 1994;36:1-6

Argent AC, Lachman PI, Hanslo D, Bass D. Sexually transmitted diseases in children and evidence of sexual abuse. *Child Abuse Negl.* 1995;19:1303-1310

Chief Editor. 1989 Sexually transmitted diseases treatment guidelines: extracted from the Centers for Disease Control guidelines. *Pediatr Infect Dis J.* 1990;9:379-382

Embree JE, Lindsay D, Williams T, Peeling RW, Wood S, Morris M. Acceptability and usefulness of vaginal washes in premenarcheal girls as a diagnostic procedure for sexually transmitted diseases. *Pediatr Infect Dis J.* 1996;15:662-667

Hammerschlag MR, Rawstron SA, Bromberg K. A commentary on the 1989 sexually transmitted diseases guidelines. *Pediatr Infect Dis J.* 1990;9:382-384

Jenny C, Hooton TM, Bowers A, et al. Sexually transmitted diseases in victims of rape. *N Engl J Med.* 1990;322:713-716

Shafer MB. Sexually transmitted diseases in adolescents: prevention, diagnosis, and treatment in pediatric practice. *Adolescent Health Update, AAP Section on Adolescent Health.* 1994;6:1-8

Sturm JT, Carr ME, Luxenberg MG, et al. The prevalence of *Neisseria gonorrhoeae* and *Chlamydia trachomatis* in victims of sexual assault. *Ann Emerg Med.* 1990;19:587-590

Syphilis

Bays J, Chadwick D. The serologic test for syphilis in sexually abused children and adolescents. *Adolesc Pediatr Gynecol.* 1991;4:148-151

Horowitz S, Chadwick DL. Syphilis as a sole indicator of sexual abuse: two cases with no intervention. *Child Abuse Negl.* 1990;14:129-132

Lande MB, Richardson AC, White KC. The role of syphilis serology in the evaluation of suspected sexual abuse. *Pediatr Infect Dis J.* 1992;11:125-127

Siqueira LM, Barnett SH, Kass E, Gertner M. Incubating syphilis in an adolescent female rape victim. *J Adolesc Health Care.* 1991;12:459-461

Vulvovaginitis

Bacon JL. Pediatric vulvovaginitis. *Adolesc Pediatr Gynecol.* 1989;2:86-93

Straumanis JP, Bocchini JA. Group A beta-hemolytic streptococcal vulvovaginitis in prepubertal girls: a case report and review of the past twenty years. *Pediatr Infect Dis J.* 1990;9:845-848

Shapiro RA, Schubert CJ, Myers PA. Vaginal discharge as an indicator of gonorrhea and chlamydia infection in girls under 12 years old. *Pediatr Emerg Care.* 1993;9:341-345

Vandeven AM, Emans SJ. Vulvovaginitis in the child and adolescent. *Pediatr Rev.* 1993;14:141-147

Acknowledgment

This section and its annotations were prepared by David L. Kerns, MD, and reviewed by Ann S. Botash, MD, and V. Denise Everett, MD. Selected annotations from the first edition were written by Susanne Tropez-Sims, MD, MPH, and Jerry G. Jones, MD.

AMERICAN ACADEMY OF PEDIATRICS

Sexually Transmitted Diseases*

Committee on Adolescence   (RE9428)

Major social and behavioral changes have occurred in the pediatric population since the Academy published its first statement more than 20 years ago concerning the pediatrician's role in the diagnosis and treatment of sexually transmitted diseases (STDs).[1] As we approach the year 2000, adaptation to these changes requires greater vigilance and expertise by the practitioners who care for children and adolescents. Of the 20 000 000 cases of STDs reported annually, one third occur in adolescents.[2] Although a few sexually transmitted diseases have been known since biblical times, the current recognized spectrum has expanded to more than 20 potential pathogens (Table).[3] In the last 10 years the recognition of human immunodeficiency virus (HIV) and acquired immunodeficiency syndrome (AIDS) has added even greater urgency to the need for pediatricians to address the management and prevention of STDs.

Asymptomatic STDs contribute to a reservoir of potential infection that allows unknowing transmission to a succession of partners, challenging the physician to be alert in history taking, to use appropriate diagnostic techniques, and to treat patients promptly and appropriately. Sexually transmitted diseases can be transmitted horizontally, ie, to sexual partners, or vertically, ie, from mother to infant.

WHAT ARE THE RISKS?

In addition to the few traditionally recognized STDs, the sexually active adolescent may now be faced with a multitude of other STDs that have serious long-term implications and are more resistant to treatment. These STDs include herpes simplex, which can result in recurrent painful episodes and subsequent neonatal infection; human papilloma virus (HPV) infection, which has led to an increased prevalence of cervical neoplasia in adolescents; hepatitis B and C, which can result in cirrhosis and carcinoma; and HIV infection, which can lead to AIDS.

Human immunodeficiency virus infection is usually a sexually transmitted disease. It can also be transmitted via contaminated blood and needles. The incubation period may be more than a decade. As the incidence of AIDS is increasing among the young

adult population, it is inferred that many newly recognized cases were acquired during adolescence.

Prevalence studies among military recruits and job corps applicants have shown HIV seropositivity of 1.31 per 1000 to 3.6 per 1000, respectively.[4,5] In a study of inner city adolescents, seropositivity has increased from 4.03 per 1000 to 19.44 per 1000 during the past 5 years.[6] Although the virus can be transmitted via heterosexual vaginal intercourse, anal heterosexual or homosexual intercourse puts the adolescent at even greater risk. Thus, the specifics of sexual practices may be important in suggesting a diagnosis in those adolescents who are sexually active.

Sexually active adolescents are at risk for contracting hepatitis B if they have not been properly immunized. Since most children and teenagers have not received the currently recommended Academy schedule of three doses of hepatitis B vaccine, high-risk adolescent groups should receive the vaccine to prevent this disease. Gay youth, teenagers who abuse intravenous drugs, and those with multiple sex partners are at highest risk. However, more than one third of infected persons do not have a readily identifiable risk factor.

To accomplish universal vaccination most rapidly, immunization of all children during or before adolescence is necessary and recommended. If resources are insufficient to allow concurrent immunization of both infants and adolescents or preadolescents, infants should be preferentially immunized before all adolescents are routinely vaccinated. However, resources should be sought so that immunization of all children before or at adolescence can be accomplished. Immunization of adolescents can be accomplished by vaccination at an earlier age than 11 years, which has the advantage of less cost because of the lower recommended dose.

There has also been a recent resurgence of syphilis. Infection rates for 15- to 19-year-olds have risen from 15 per 100 000 in 1985 to 30 per 100 000 in 1990.[7] Rates for African-Americans and Hispanics are higher than those for whites.[8] The number of cases of congenital syphilis has risen as the number of cases of syphilis has increased in women of childbearing age. An increase in the number of syphilis cases also appears to be concomitant to the increase in sexually transmitted HIV infections.[9]

Human papilloma virus is now the most common sexually transmitted disease in the United States.[10] Types 16, 18, 31, 33, and 35 have the highest potential for producing cervical cancer, and it is these serotypes that are most frequently found in adolescents.

TABLE 1. Sexually Transmitted Diseases in Adolescents

Agent	Clinical Syndrome
A) Bacterial	
Neisseria gonorrhoeae	Urethritis, prostatitis, epididymitis, cervicitis, PID, perihepatitis, disseminated gonococcal infections (DGI)
Chlamydia trachomatis	Urethritis, epididymitis, cervicitis, PID, perihepatitis, conjunctivitis, lymphogranuloma venereum
Treponema pallidum	Syphilis
Ureaplasma urealyticum	Urethritis
Mycoplasma hominis	PID
Haemophilus ducreyi	Chancroid
Gardnerella vaginalis	Bacterial vaginosis
Calymmatobacterium granulomatis	Granuloma inguinale
B) Viral	
HIV	AIDS
Herpes simplex virus	Genital ulcers
Human papillomavirus (HPV)	Condylomata, cervical intraepithelial neoplasia
Hepatitis A	Acute hepatitis A
Hepatitis B	Acute hepatitis B, chronic active hepatitis
Hepatitis C (non-A, non-B)	Non-A, non-B hepatitis
Cytomegalovirus	Mononucleosis-like syndrome
C) Protozoal	
Trichomonas vaginalis	Vaginitis
Entamoeba histolytica	Gay bowel syndrome
Giardia lamblia	Gay bowel syndrome
D) Parasites	
Sarcoptes scabiei	Scabies
Phthirus pubis	Pediculosis pubic

WHO IS AT RISK?

Half of all adolescents are sexually active by age 17 and are therefore at risk for STDs. It has been estimated that as many as 25% of adolescents may develop an STD before graduating from high school. Adolescents are more likely to have asymptomatic infections than adults and to suffer long-term consequences such as chronic infection, spontaneous abortions, and infected offspring. Sexually active adolescents have the highest rates of gonorrhea, syphilis, and pelvic inflammatory disease of any age group, and, the younger the teenager, the greater the risk of acquiring an STD.[11] Pelvic inflammatory disease in adolescent women is a cause of chronic pelvic pain and infertility and is an important predisposing factor in the development of an ectopic pregnancy.

Behavioral and developmental differences that affect STD exposure and put adolescents at greater risk of disease acquisition include the following.

Immature Biological Defenses

The adolescent cervix, with its larger area of exposed columnar epithelium (ectropion), is especially susceptible to *Chlamydia trachomatis* and *Neisseria gonorrhoeae* invasion. In addition, the active squamous metaplasia at the transformation zone increases the susceptibility to HPV infection.

Limited Access to Services

Adolescents may be uncomfortable discussing sensitive issues of sexuality with pediatricians or other providers. Services for adolescents may not be "user friendly," which discourage some adolescents from seeking care. Financial and transportation barriers limit health care access for many poor teenagers.

Number of Partners

Age at first intercourse is variable and in early adolescence tends to be correlated with perceived norms of the peer group, gender (males still tend to engage in intercourse at an earlier age than do females[12]), race, ethnicity, and socioeconomic status, although the influence of these demographic variables tends to disappear by late adolescence. Early onset of sexual activity leads to increased risk of multiple sexual partners and to decreased discrimination of partner selection, both of which contribute to a higher risk for acquiring an STD. Other risk behaviors such as alcohol and other drug experimentation, which impair judgment, can contribute to increased adolescent vulnerability to STDs. Adolescents at particularly high risk for STDs and AIDS include homosexual males, street youth, incarcerated adolescents, and teens engaged in prostitution. Pregnant adolescents are more likely to have an STD than are nonpregnant adolescents.

Unprotected Sexual Intercourse

Unprotected sexual activity is clearly a risk factor for the development of an STD at any age. Programs aimed at promoting sexual abstinence may reduce STDs in adolescents. There is some evidence that comprehensive skills-based education on postponing sexual intercourse is most effective in younger adolescents,[13] and may reduce risk-taking behaviors. For sexually active adolescents, correct and consistent use of latex condoms is recommended for STD prevention even though the protection is not absolute. Educational efforts at promoting responsible sexual decision making and more convenient availability of condoms for those who choose to engage in sexual intercourse, rather than postponing it, may foster greater and more consistent use of barrier contraception.

DIAGNOSIS

History

Teenagers are entitled to a confidential interview, and it is imperative to make the confidentiality explicit at the time the history is taken. In the United States, there are no legal barriers to confidentiality (except in situations of potential sexual abuse) in the diagnosis or treatment of any child or adolescent for an STD. A detailed sexual history is necessary, including information on gender preference, number and medical history of partners, frequency of intercourse, contraceptive and condom use, consensuality of the encounters, route of penetration, frequency of urination, and presence of any symptoms of pain, discharge, skin lesions, or pruritus. Adolescents who have exchanged sex for drugs or money, who have had anal intercourse, or have a history of previous STDs are particularly at risk for STDs.

More than one STD may be present in an individual patient at any time. The potential for reinfection should also be kept in mind during follow-up visits and interval history taking. Treatment of partners must be aggressively attempted to decrease the reinfection rate. The physician should be nonjudgmental while working to educate and correct misconceptions of the adolescent.

Physical Examination

When an STD is suspected, a complete examination of the adolescent is generally indicated. The entire body should be visualized. The provision of appropriate draping and the presence of a chaperone may add to the comfort of the patient. The skin should be carefully examined for rashes and bruises. Examination of the throat, joints, abdomen, genitalia, and rectal area may reveal evidence of an STD. When an STD is suspected, male genitalia should be examined by inspection, palpation, attempt at expression of urethral discharge, and notation of adenopathy or any visible lesions. A rectal examination should be done for evidence of prostatitis in symptomatic patients. Discharges collected by using a urethral swab can be microscopically examined, cultured on appropriate medium, or evaluated by indicated diagnostic tests. Unexplained abdominal pain in sexually active female adolescents requires a pelvic examination for appropriate assessment of possible pelvic inflammatory disease.

Even when sexually active adolescents do not complain of an infection, they should be routinely screened for STDs. The frequency of screening for STDs depends on the sexual practices of the individual and associated risk factors, such as a previous STD. Annual screening is recommended for all sexually active adolescents. Some high-risk teenagers may need more frequent examinations.

All sexually active males can easily be screened for the presence of gonorrhea or chlamydia urethritis by utilizing a urine leukocyte esterase analysis (urine dipstick for white blood cells).[14] For sexually active females, the periodic examination includes a Papanicolaou (Pap) smear, screening tests for gonorrhea and chlamydia, and a microscopic examination of vaginal secretions.

Laboratory Assessment

The diagnosis of most STDs can be made by observing the infecting organism on a smear, culturing the organism, or by the use of newer diagnostic techniques such as enzyme immunoassay, DNA probes, and immunofluorescent antibody screening. Office-based pediatricians may need to determine specific testing techniques of their referral laboratory.

Gonorrhea

Gram-negative intracellular diplococci can be seen on an appropriately stained smear of the urethral discharge in males. Gram staining is a less accurate diagnostic test in females, because of the presence of Gram-negative diplococci in normal vaginal flora. *Neisseria gonorrhoeae* is a fastidious organism. Special culture media, therefore, such as Thayer-Martin or other appropriate media, and immediate placement of the culture plate in an oxygen-poor CO_2-rich environment, are necessary. Sensitivities need to be obtained in order to determine the presence of penicillinase-producing *N gonorrhoeae*. Gen-Probe is a newer DNA probe assay test that indicates the presence of gonorrhea, but culture confirmation is required.

Chlamydia

Both culture and nonculture detection techniques for chlamydia are available. Culture remains the "gold standard," but direct fluorescent antibody tests, enzyme immunoassay, and DNA hybridization assays have acceptable sensitivity and specificity for use on clinical specimens. Yields are highest in high prevalence populations and in symptomatic subjects rather than asymptomatic carriers.

Human Papilloma Virus

Most HPV infections in women are demonstrated by direct visualization of lesions or dysplastic changes seen on the Pap smear. Human papilloma virus-DNA probes are being used more frequently to detect the presence of HPV infection. Specific probes are available, such as Virapap, that provide information regarding the presence of subtypes associated with cancerous transformation. Abnormal sites visualized on colposcopy may be associated with a high incidence of cancer-producing HPV subtypes. Human papilloma virus infections may also be suspected by finding warts on the vulva, vagina, penis, or perianal area.

Herpes Simplex Virus

Viral culture of the base of a new lesion is the definitive diagnostic method for herpes simplex virus.[15] Older lesions can be diagnosed by monoclonal antibody staining. A Tzanck preparation (stained ulcer smear) may be examined for evidence of multinucleated giant cells, but is not a highly sensitive or specific test. Serologic tests for herpes simplex virus are not generally helpful in acute disease diagnosis.

Vaginitis

Any vaginal discharge should be suspended in saline solution and examined under a microscope for the presence of trichomoniasis, bacterial vaginosis, or both. *Trichomonas* is diagnosed by the presence of motile pear-shaped flagellated organisms seen on the wet mount preparation. A greenish, frothy, foul-smelling discharge may be present.

Although not technically an STD, bacterial vaginosis is seen at greatly increased rates in sexually active adolescents. The diagnosis is made when the vaginal discharge has a pH > 4.5 and releases a fishy odor when mixed with 10% potassium hydroxide (KOH) ("whiff test"). "Clue cells" (epithelial cells dotted with adherent bacteria) are seen on saline wet mount.

Vaginal candidiasis is diagnosed when hyphae are seen on a slide prepared with a drop of KOH added to the discharge. However, approximately half of culture-positive candidiasis will not be detected by a wet mount preparation.

HIV Infection/AIDS

Human immunodeficiency virus infection is usually diagnosed serologically. In most laboratories the initial test, enzyme-linked immunosorbent assay, is followed by Western blot studies for confirmation. Tests for the presence of the specific virus are available in some research laboratories. Testing for HIV should be done with informed consent and appropriate counseling before and after testing. Any teenager diagnosed with an STD needs to be evaluated for HIV risk factors (multiple sex partners, intravenous drug abuse, homosexual contact, etc) and screening needs to be offered to those at risk or done on request.

Hepatitis B

Hepatitis is diagnosed by serologic patterns. Detection of the hepatitis B surface antigen indicates acute infection with hepatitis B or the chronic carrier state. Antibody to core antigen indicates previous infection. The presence of IgM core antibody indicates a recent infection. Antibody to surface antigen indicates recovery from infection or past immunization.

Syphilis

The chief serologic tests for syphilis remain the VDRL and RPR. Direct visualization of the treponema on dark field examination can be demonstrated by examining the fluid of primary ulcerated lesions. Confirmatory specific treponemal tests such as the FTA-ABS must be done after a screening serology is positive to eliminate false-positive results. An annual screening serologic test for syphilis is recommended for those who live in an endemic area, have had other STDs, have had more than one sexual partner in the last 6 months, have exchanged sex for drugs or money, or for males who have had sex with other males.

Special Considerations

In cases of suspected sexual abuse or rape, the practitioner must be careful to fulfill the state's legal requirements for permissible court evidence.[16] Many emergency departments have special rape kits available that assist in the proper collection of evidence. In general, for legal purposes, cultures are preferable to immunological detection methods for gonorrhea, chlamydia, and herpes. The presence of one STD should always alert the practitioner to the probable presence of other STDs.

TREATMENT

The Centers for Disease Control and Prevention guidelines[17] and the current *Report of the Committee on Infectious Diseases* (*Red Book*) of the American Academy of Pediatrics are appropriate resources for the most recent treatment guidelines for an identified STD. It should be remembered, however, that optimal treatment of the child or adolescent may differ from that of the adult. The treatment of pelvic inflammatory disease in the adolescent is of special concern, because of their long reproductive period and the need to optimize future fertility. While many adults with pelvic inflammatory disease can be treated as outpatients, most adolescents with the disease should be hospitalized to ensure adequate therapy. The physician may also have to modify treatment in pubertal teenagers because of altered metabolism and excretion of a particular drug, which can affect dose and dose intervals.

Effective single-dose regimens are now available for the treatment of uncomplicated gonococcal and chlamydial genital infection and vaginitis. To improve compliance, single-dose treatment is preferred to multiple-dose regimens and, when possible, the drug is administered directly to the patient and partner(s) under supervision.

All drug treatment protocols require concurrent counseling appropriate to the cognitive developmental maturity of the child, adolescent, and parent, if indicated.

CONCLUSION

Sexually transmitted diseases are a critical public health concern, and adolescents are at particular risk. The pediatrician must play a primary role in the prevention, diagnosis, and treatment of STDs. Anticipatory guidance for all youth and explicit education on safer sex practices for sexually active adolescents are central principles for office management. Adolescents should be counseled that abstinence from sexual intercourse is the most effective way to prevent STDs. The importance of barrier contraceptives (eg, latex condoms) in the reduction of HIV transmission cannot be overemphasized. Physicians should actively promote condom use in their sexually active patients, not only for AIDS prevention but for prevention of all STDs and unintended pregnancy. Pediatricians should be active participants in collaborative community-based approaches to promote responsible sexual behavior and healthy life-style choices for all youth.

REFERENCES

1. American Academy of Pediatrics, Committee on Youth. Venereal disease and the pediatrician. *Pediatrics*. 1972;50:492–496
2. Shafer M. Sexually transmitted disease syndromes. In: McAnarney ER, Kreipe RE, Orr DP, Comerci GD, eds. *Textbook of Adolescent Medicine*. Philadelphia, Pa: WB Saunders Co; 1992, p 696
3. Golden N. Sexually transmitted diseases in adolescents. In: Shenker IR, ed. *Monographics in Clinical Pediatrics, Adolescent Medicine*. Switzerland: Harwood Academic Publishers; 1994:37–38
4. Brundage JT, Burke DS, Gardner LI, et al. Tracking the spread of the HIV infection epidemic among young adults in the United States: results of the first four years of screening among civilian applicants for U. S. military service. *J Acquired Immune Defic Syndr*. 1990;3:1168–1180
5. St. Louis ME, Conway GA, Hayman CR, Miller C, Peterson LR, Dondero TJ. Human immunodeficiency virus infection in disadvantaged adolescents. *JAMA*. 1991;266:2387–2391
6. D'Angelo LJ, Getson PR, Brasseux BA, Stallings E, Guagliardo M, Shaffer N. The increasing prevalence of human immunodeficiency virus infection in urban adolescents: a five year study. *J Adolesc Health Care*. 1993;14:46
7. Centers for Disease Control. Primary and secondary syphilis—United States, 1981–1990. *MMWR*. 1991;40:314–315, 321–323
8. Rolfs RT, Nakashima AK. Epidemiology of primary and secondary syphilis in the United States, 1981 through 1989. *JAMA*. 1990;264: 1432–1437
9. Kipke M, Hein K. Acquired immunodeficiency syndrome and human immunodeficiency virus-related syndromes. In: McAnarney ER, Kreipe RE, Orr DP, Comerci GC, eds. *Textbook of Adolescent Medicine*. Philadelphia, Pa: WB Saunders Co; 1992;76:713
10. Rosenfeld WD, Vermund SH, Wertz ST, Burk RD. High prevalence rate of human papilloma virus infection and association with abnormal papilloma smears in sexually active adolescents. *AJDC*. 1989;1443–1447
11. Cates W, Jr. The epidemiology and control of sexually transmitted diseases in adolescents. *Adolesc Med: State of the Art Rev*. 1990;1:409–427
12. Biro FM. *Adolescents and Sexually Transmitted Diseases*. Washington, DC: Maternal and Child Health Technical Information Bulletin; 1992. US Dept of Health and Human Services (PHS) publication
13. Kirby D. School based programs to reduce sexual risk-taking behavior. *J Sch Health*. 1992;62:280–287
14. Adger H, Shafer MA, Sweet RL, Schachter J. Screening for *Chlamydia trachomatis* and *Neisseria gonorrhoeae* in adolescent males: value of first catch urine examination. *Lancet*. 1984;2:944–945
15. Bryson YJ. Genital herpes in adolescents and young adults. *Adolesc Med: State Art Rev*. 1990;1:471–496
16. American Academy of Pediatrics, Committee on Adolescence. Sexual assault and the adolescent. *Pediatrics*. 1994. In press
17. Centers for Disease Control. Sexually transmitted diseases treatment guidelines. *MMWR*. 1993;42:1–102

AMERICAN ACADEMY OF PEDIATRICS

Committee on Child Abuse and Neglect

Gonorrhea in Prepubertal Children (RE9803)

ABSTRACT. This statement updates a 1983 statement on this topic and reminds physicians that sexual abuse should be strongly considered when a gonorrheal infection is diagnosed in a child after the newborn period and before the onset of puberty.

Sexual abuse should be strongly considered when a gonorrheal infection (ie, genital, rectal, oral, or ophthalmologic) is diagnosed in a child after the newborn period and before the onset of puberty. A sexually transmitted disease may be the only physical evidence of sexual abuse in some cases.[1] Sexually abused children may deny that abuse has occurred. The Centers for Disease Control and Prevention provides the following guideline: "The identification of a sexually transmissible agent from a child beyond the neonatal period suggests sexual abuse."[2] This statement does not address gonorrheal infection in adolescents, which may result from sexual abuse or consensual sexual activity. The Committee on Adolescence statement on sexually transmitted diseases provides additional guidance for the pediatrician evaluating adolescents.[3]

EPIDEMIOLOGIC FACTORS

The risk of acquiring sexually transmitted diseases as a result of sexual abuse during childhood is unknown. Reported rates of gonococcal infection range from 3% to 20% among sexually abused children.[4,5] The incidence of *Neisseria gonorrhoeae* in a given population of children who may have been sexually abused is determined by the type and frequency of sexual contact, the age of the child, the regional prevalence of sexually transmitted diseases in the adult population, and the number of children referred for evaluation of possible sexual abuse.[6] The presence of *N gonorrhoeae* infection in a child is diagnostic of abuse with very rare exception.[7]

CLINICAL FINDINGS

A gonococcal infection may be diagnosed in the course of an evaluation of a medical condition such as conjunctivitis, in which no suspicion of abuse existed, or it may be diagnosed during an assessment for possible sexual abuse. In the prepubertal child, gonococcal infection usually occurs in the lower genital tract, and vaginitis is the most common clinical manifestation. Pelvic inflammatory disease and perihepatitis can occur, but are uncommon. Infections of the throat and rectum typically are asymptomatic and may go unrecognized. If no source of the infection is identified, a conclusion that the transmission was perinatal or nonsexual in nature is unacceptable.

LABORATORY FINDINGS

Laboratory confirmation of *N gonorrhoeae* is essential before sexual abuse is reported to the local child protective services agency solely on the basis of a positive *Neisseria* culture. However, an immediate report should be made if other compelling indicators of abuse are evident. A carefully structured laboratory protocol must be used to ensure identification of the organism.[7] An accurate diagnosis of gonococcal infection can be made only by using Thayer–Martin or chocolate blood agar-based media. Positive cultures must be confirmed by two of the following methods: carbohydrate utilization, direct fluorescent antibody testing, or enzyme substrate testing.[1,8,9] A culture reported as *N gonorrhoeae* from the pharynx of young children can be problematic because of the high number of nonpathogenic *Neisseria* species found at this site. To prevent an unwarranted child abuse investigation, confirmatory tests must be performed to differentiate *N gonorrhoeae* from organisms such as *Neisseria meningitidis*, *Neisseria lactamica*, and *Neisseria cinerea* that may be normal flora.[9] Currently, the use of nonculture methods (ie, DNA probes or enzyme-linked immunosorbent assay) for the documentation of *N gonorrhoeae* is investigational. If a nonculture method is used, a positive result *must* be confirmed by culture. No current data are available for the pediatric population, but studies of adults have shown a significant incidence of false-positive indirect tests compared with the incidence obtained by culture methods.[10,11]

By law, all known cases of gonorrhea in children must be reported to the local health department. A report also should be made to a child protective services agency. An investigation should be conducted to determine whether other children in the same environment who may be victims of sexual abuse are also infected. A child in whom a culture is positive for *N gonorrhoeae* should be examined for the presence of other sexually transmitted diseases such as syphilis, chlamydia infection, hepatitis B, and human immunodeficiency virus infection.

This statement has been approved by the Council on Child and Adolescent Health.

The recommendations in this statement do not indicate an exclusive course of treatment or serve as a standard of medical care. Variations, taking into account individual circumstances, may be appropriate.

PEDIATRICS (ISSN 0031 4005). Copyright © 1998 by the American Academy of Pediatrics.

REFERENCES

1. Ingram DL. Controversies about the sexual and nonsexual transmission of adult STDs to children. In: Krugman RD, Leventhal JM, eds. *Child Sexual Abuse. Report of the Twenty-Second Ross Roundtable on Critical Approaches to Community Pediatric Problems.* Columbus, OH: Ross Laboratories; 1991

2. Centers for Disease Control and Prevention. 1993 Sexually transmitted diseases treatment guidelines. *MMWR.* 1993;42(RR-14):99

3. American Academy of Pediatrics. Committee on Adolescence. Sexually transmitted diseases. *Pediatrics.* 1994;94:568–572

4. Ingram DL. *Neisseria gonorrhoeae* in children. *Pediatr Ann.* 1994;20:341–345

5. Siegel RM, Schubert CJ, Myers PA, Shapiro RA. The prevalence of sexually transmitted diseases in children and adolescents evaluated for sexual abuse in Cincinnati: rationale for limited STD testing in prepubertal girls. *Pediatrics.* 1995;96:1090–1094

6. American Academy of Pediatrics, Committee on Child Abuse and Neglect. Guidelines for the evaluation of sexual abuse of children. *Pediatrics.* 1991;87:254–260

7. Neinstein LS, Goldenring J, Carpenter S. Nonsexual transmission of sexually transmitted diseases: an infrequent occurrence. *Pediatrics.* 1984;74:67–76

8. Whittington WL, Rice RJ, Biddle JW, Knapp JS. Incorrect identification of *Neisseria gonorrhoeae* from infants and children. *Pediatr Infect Dis J.* 1988;7:3–10

9. Alexander ER. Misidentification of sexually transmitted organisms in children: medicolegal implications. *Pediatr Infect Dis J.* 1988;7:1–2

10. Stary A, Kopp W, Zahel B, Nerad S, Teodorowicz L, Horting-Muller I. Comparison of DNA-probe test and culture for the detection of *Neisseria gonorrhoeae* in genital samples. *Sex Transm Dis.* 1993;20:243–247

11. Vlaspolder F, Mutsaers JA, Blog F, Notowics A. Value of a DNA probe (Gen-Probe) compared with that of culture for the diagnosis of gonococcal infection. *J Clin Microbiol.* 1993;31:107–110

Shaken Impact/Shaken Baby Syndrome

See Also:
Falls
Fractures
Head Injury
Retinal Hemorrhages
AAP Statement *Shaken Baby Syndrome: Inflicted Cerebral Trauma,* **which follows**

Clinical Principles

▼ Initial findings may include the following: retinal hemorrhage, subdural and/or subarachnoid hemorrhage, interhemispheric blood visible on computed tomography (CT), supra- and infra-tentorial subdural hematoma, cerebral edema, bilateral chronic subdural hematoma, profound neurological impairment, seizures and encephalopathy, injuries at the cervicomedullary junction of spinal cord, hematomas of the cervical spinal cord with proximal spinal cord contusions, tense or bulging fontanelle, head circumference greater than 90th percentile for age, respiratory alterations despite normal pulmonary exam, galeal and cortical contusions, skull fractures, associated fractures of ribs or long bones, and altered consciousness.

▼ Shaken impact syndrome has some characteristics in common with other head injuries from child abuse. Because these children often have no obvious external sign of injury, they are often initially misdiagnosed.

▼ The typical victim is less than 1 year old, and often younger than 3 months.

Other Comments

▼ It is estimated that 80% of deaths from head trauma among children under age 2 are non-accidental.

▼ Brain injury due to child abuse should be suspected in any infant presenting with altered consciousness of unknown etiology.

▼ CT scan is recommended for initial management; both MRI and serial CTs provide increased accuracy in diagnosis.

▼ Victims may sustain severe whiplash-shake injuries to brain and spinal cord without direct cranial trauma. Conversely, external evidence of cranial impact may be lacking (though discovered at autopsy). Subdural and subarachnoid hemorrhage, as well as contusions of the high cervical spinal cord, may contribute to the morbidity and mortality associated with classic injuries of shaken baby syndrome (SBS).

▼ Shaking or cranial impact is not usually an isolated event. It is most often preceded by other abuse, and suggests risks to siblings.

▼ Limited long-term outcome studies reveal very frequent and severe neurological, developmental, and/or behavioral sequelae in victims of SBS, even among infants who appeared clinically normal 2 months post-injury.

▼ Apnea frequently triggers the "pathophysiologic cascade of events" secondary to shaking and/or impact and the duration of hypoxia is related to the severity of the brain injury.

Bibliography

Overview

Bonnier C, Nassogne MC, Evrard P. Outcome and prognosis of whiplash shaken infant syndrome: late consequences after a symptom-free interval. *Dev Med Child Neurol.* 1995;37:943-956
This paper is the first published long-term outcome report of victims of whiplash shaken infant syndrome (WSIS). The selected 13 cases all displayed intraocular hemorrhage, intracranial lesions, and absence of other traumatic or non-traumatic injury mechanisms at the time of their initial clinical presentations with signs/symptoms of WSIS (mean age, 5.5 months). One of 13 infants died acutely. The remaining 12 infants were followed up annually for a period of time between 4 and 14 years, with general, neurologi-

cal, psychological, and social evaluations, including standardized developmental testing. The results of these evaluations were compared to those of 10 age-matched children (controls) diagnosed with non-WSIS abusive trauma (ie, fractures, bruises, and failure to thrive).

Detailed descriptions of the injuries sustained by these 12 infants at the time of their clinical presentations suggest significant abusive head trauma mechanisms. Long-term outcome was divided into two groups: those with and without a sign-free interval after the acute injury. Those without a sign-free interval remained severely damaged after their acute injury and one died. Those children who were initially without clinical signs after their acute injury (n=6) recovered fully and were normal on examination 2 months post-injury. However, all but one of these children displayed later disabilities after 6 months to 5 years, including hemiparesis (n=2/6), psychomotor retardation (n=1/6), mental retardation (n=5/6), severe behavior problems (n=3/6), severe anxiety disorder (n=1/6), pervasive developmental disorder (n=2/6), and severe hyperkinetic behavior (n=1/6). Only one of the six children who appeared clinically normal at 2 months post-injury remained clinically normal through age 5 years on annual evaluation.

The authors noted that declining cranial growth (in the presence of retinal hemorrhages and intracranial lesions) was the most reliable predictor of permanent deficits. The authors concluded that long-term outcome is poor in almost all cases of WSIS. Finally, they cautioned that final favorable prognosis should be withheld minimally until 5 years after the injury event. (KH)

Bruce D, Zimmerman R. Shaken impact syndrome. *Pediatr Ann.* 1989;18:482-494

This is an excellent review article that is descriptive, comprehensive, and easy to read. It reports on the mechanism, diagnosis, and treatment of shaken impact syndrome (shaken baby syndrome). The authors point out that 4 out of 5 deaths from head trauma among children less than 2 years old at Children's Hospital, Philadelphia, during 1981–1982 were the result of non-accidental injury. They provide data which should encourage clinicians to suspect abuse whenever a child under 1 year of age presents with brain injury and altered consciousness.

These infants present without a history of severe trauma; evidence of other trauma is rare and the physical examination can be easily misinterpreted in infants. Many SBS infants will be unconscious or comatose with involuntary movements/posturing, a full fontanelle with already splitting sutures, and inadequate respiratory effort. Intracranial bleeding, especially subdural hematoma and subarachnoid hemorrhage, are common. Retinal hemorrhages occur in 50% to 100% of infants with shaken impact syndrome and rarely occur in accidental trauma of infants. Non-accidental trauma must be included in the differential diagnosis whenever an infant without a history of seizures presents with their sudden onset.

Obtaining a CT scan is recommended for first-line diagnosis. Most commonly, it will reveal a parafalcine subdural hematoma in the parietal and occipital regions. Abnormal brain tissue involving one or both cerebral hemispheres may also be seen, along with loss of grey/white matter differentiation.

The magnetic resonance imaging (MRI) studies may detect thin layers of methemoglobin within the subdural space. (Methemoglobin is formed about 3 days after clot formation, when oxidation occurs.) About 1 week after bleeding, most of the hematoma is high-intensity extracellular methemoglobin. Later (3-6 months after injury), MRI can distinguish bilateral chronic subdural hematomas surrounding a brain that has atrophied.

Autopsies of infants who die from shaken impact syndrome reveal significant numbers of galeal and cortical contusions and skull fractures. Based on the research by Duhaime, et al (see next entry), Bruce and Zimmerman point out that simply shaking a model of a 1-month-old baby produced maximum acceleration and deceleration forces less than or equal to 10 G. However, forces of up to 300 G were recorded when the head was impacted against even a soft mattress. The authors speculate that a shaking episode is likely to be followed by some type of impact, as frustrated and angry custodians are not likely to lay the infant down gently. Because the most severe injuries may be caused when children are roughly discarded onto a sofa or into a crib, the authors feel that "shaken impact injury" is more accurate than "shaken baby syndrome." (CL/KM)

Duhaime AC, Gennarelli TA, Thibault LE, Bruce DA, Margulies SS, Wiser R. The shaken baby syndrome. A clinical, pathological, and biomechanical study. *J Neurosurg.* 1987;66: 409-415

This study reviewed cases of 48 babies with shaken baby syndrome aged 1 month to 2 years (mean age 7.85 months), 13 (27%) of whom died. All of the babies had a history suspicious for abuse. Retinal hemorrhages plus subarachnoid hemorrhages or subdural hematomas were seen in 81% of the babies, while 13% had subarachnoid hemorrhages and/or subdural hematomas without retinal hemorrhages. Bilateral chronic subdural hematoma was seen in 6%.

Evidence of blunt head trauma was seen in all of the 13 children who died, including 7 in whom impact injury had not been documented prior to autopsy. Soft tissue contusions were seen in eight, and contusions and skull fractures were present in the remaining five. The authors distinguished between focal injuries (those resulting from impact and contact) and diffuse injuries (those caused by acceleration/deceleration). Shaken babies suffer from both types of injuries; the initial shaking is likely compounded by rough discarding, based on the research presented in this paper with models of 1-month-old infants to measure gravitational forces with various acceleration/deceleration. The authors conclude that in a normal infant, shaking alone will not cause severe injuries of the SBS. (CL/KM)

Fischer H, Allasio D. Permanently damaged: Long-term follow-up of shaken babies. *Clin Pediatrics.* 1994;33:696-698

Hadley M, Sonntag V, Rekate H, Murphy A. The whiplash-shaken injury syndrome. A clinical and pathological study. *Neurosurgery.* 1989;24:536-540

The authors report on 13 infants with a mean age of 3 months, who sustained primary neurological injury from non-accidental trauma. Subjects were selected from a pool of 36 infants when (1) a perpetrator admitted to shaking the infant, and (2) there was no historical, clinical, or radiographic evidence of direct cranial impact.

All 13 infants presented with profound neurological impairment, seizures, retinal hemorrhages, and intracranial subarachnoid and/or subdural hemorrhages. None had a skull fracture; only one had an extracalvarial contusion. Of the 13 babies, 8 died, and the remaining 5 had a clinical pattern of profound encephalopathy. Five of the six autopsies performed revealed injuries at the cervicomedullary junction (subdural or epidural hematomas of the cervical spinal cord with proximal spinal cord contusions). Cranial subdural hemorrhages were seen in all six babies who were autopsied; only one autopsy suggested extracalvarial contusion.

The authors conclude that young patients may sustain severe whiplash-shake injuries without direct cranial trauma. They point out that hemorrhages and contusions of the high cervical spinal cord may contribute to the morbidity and mortality associated with the classic injuries in shaken baby syndrome. (CL/KM)

Johnson DL, Boal D, Baule R. Role of apnea in nonaccidental head injury. *Pediatr Neurosurg.* 1995;23:305-310

The authors hypothesize that apnea plays a major pathophysiologic role in the poor outcome associated with pediatric shaking and/or cranial impact. Twenty-eight children with confirmed abusive head trauma were retrospectively studied. Neuroimaging and clinical findings were compared between two groups: shaken/impact patients with external signs of impact trauma and/or skull fracture (mean age, 6 months), and shaken patients without clinical or radiologic signs of impact trauma (mean age, 4 months).

The authors were struck by the frequent history of apnea prior to hospitalization (57%), requirement for endotracheal intubation upon admission (82%), hypotension with initial blood pressure less than 80 mmHg (50%), and acidosis with pH less than 7.3 (54%). They predict:

> The pathophysiologic cascade of events which culminate in SBS is likely triggered by crying. Persistent crying …provokes shaking or shaking with impact. The shaking stops when the perpetrator's frustration and anger dissipates or when the crying ends. The crying ends when the infant becomes apneic or loses consciousness. The duration of the hypoxic injury is proportional to the severity of the brain injury and is a major determinant of clinical outcome. (KH)

Ludwig S, Warman M. Shaken baby
syndrome: a review of twenty cases.
Ann Emerg Med. 1984;13:104-107
These authors reviewed records for 20 children
aged 1 month to 15 months (mean age, 5.8
months) with a diagnosis of shaken baby
syndrome. Of the 20 infants, 3 died and 10
sustained significant morbidity. The authors
point out that the signs and symptoms of SBS
are nonspecific, often mimicking infection or
metabolic disease.

Shaken baby syndrome should be suspected in
young infants with abnormal respiratory patterns
despite a normal pulmonary examination. Three
further findings strengthen a diagnosis of shaken
baby syndrome: tense or bulging fontanelle, head
circumference greater than 90th percentile for age,
and retinal hemorrhage (revealed in 67% of these
cases).

Intracranial hemorrhage was diagnosed on
the basis of lumbar or subdural puncture showing
blood in the cerebral spinal fluid. Lumbar puncture
identified intracranial hemorrhage in 10 of 12
cases, and subdural taps enabled the same diagnosis in 8 of 10 cases. A CT scan can confirm shaking when it shows acute interhemispheric subdural
hematoma or cerebral contusion in the absence of
external trauma. (CL/KM)

Nachelsky MB, Dix JD. The time interval
between lethal infant shaking and onset
of symptoms. *Am J Forensic Med Pathol.*
1995;16:154-157

Implications for Siblings

Alexander RC, Crabbe L, Sato Y, Smith W,
Bennett T. Serial abuse in children who are
shaken. *Am J Dis Child.* 1990;144:58-60
This study of 24 children diagnosed with shaken
baby syndrome determined that shaking is not
usually an isolated event, and is often preceded
by other types of abuse. Half the victims showed
co-existing evidence of direct, external trauma.
Seventeen (71%) evidenced prior abuse or neglect
and 8 (33%) had multiple intracranial hemorrhages, indicating previous shaking. Three of
the 9 families with more than one child had
other siblings with SBS, and one had other
siblings who suffered abuse or neglect. (CL)

Acknowledgment

This section and its annotations were prepared by
Kent Hymel, MD. Selected annotations from the
first edition were written by Carolyn Levitt, MD,
and Kim Martinez, RN, CPNP, MPH.

AMERICAN ACADEMY OF PEDIATRICS

Shaken Baby Syndrome: Inflicted Cerebral Trauma (RE9337)

Committee on Child Abuse and Neglect

Physical abuse is the leading cause of serious head injury in infants.[1] While physical abuse has in the past been a diagnosis of exclusion, data regarding the nature and frequency of head trauma consistently support a medical presumption of child abuse when a child younger than 1 year of age has intracranial injury.

Shaken baby syndrome is a serious form of child maltreatment, most often involving infants younger than 6 months of age.[2,3] It occurs commonly, yet it is frequently overlooked in its most subtle form and underdiagnosed in its most serious expression. Caretakers may misrepresent or have no knowledge of the cause of the brain injury. There is often an absence of externally visible injuries. Given the initial difficulty of identifying a shaken infant and the variability of the syndrome itself, the physician must be extremely vigilant regarding any brain trauma in infants and be familiar with the radiologic and clinical findings that support the diagnosis of the shaken baby syndrome.

HISTORICAL

In 1972, pediatric radiologist John Caffey[4] popularized the term "whiplash shaken baby syndrome" to describe a constellation of clinical findings in infants, which included retinal hemorrhages, subdural and/or subarachnoid hemorrhages, and little or no evidence of external cranial trauma. One year earlier, Guthkelch[5] had postulated that whiplash forces caused subdural hematomas by tearing cortical bridging veins. While many have added breadth to Caffey's findings, a challenge to the presumption that the shaking alone is the sole source of the trauma has come from Duhaime et al,[6] who found in laboratory settings that the force of rapid deceleration of a shaken head hitting any surface, such as a bed or pillow, may be the basis for most of these serious injuries. The investigators found evidence on autopsy to support the shake-plus-impact model of injury. This statement relates to children with signs of having undergone shaking, whether or not additional injuries are present.

ETIOLOGY

While caretakers may be unaware of the specific injuries they may cause by shaking, the act of

shaking/slamming is so violent that competent individuals observing the shaking would recognize it as dangerous. Shaking may seem to be a proportionate response to the tension and frustration frequently generated by a baby's incessant crying or irritability.[7] Caretakers at risk for abusive behavior generally have unrealistic expectations of their children and may exhibit a role reversal, whereby the parents expect their needs to be met by the child.[8] Additionally, parents with psychiatric difficulties or those who are experiencing stress as a result of environmental, social, biologic, or financial situations may also be more prone to impulsive and aggressive behavior. In some cases it is not clear whether there was an intent to inflict serious harm on the infant by shaking or a desire to stop the crying. In other cases, the careless disregard for the child's safety and the force required to account for the intracranial and extracranial injuries suggest an intent by the caretaker to severely injure, if not kill, the infant or child.

UNINTENTIONAL VERSUS INFLICTED INJURIES

Homicide is the leading cause of injury-related deaths in infants (those younger than 1 year of age).[9] Serious injuries in infants, particularly those that result in death, are rarely unintentional unless there is another clear explanation, such as trauma from a motor vehicle crash. Billmire and Myers[1] found that when uncomplicated skull fractures were excluded, 95% of serious intracranial injuries and 64% of all head injuries in infants younger than 1 year of age were due to child abuse. Bruce and Zimmerman[3] document that 80% of deaths from head trauma in infants and children younger than 2 years of age were the result of nonaccidental trauma. In large groups of physically abused children, brain trauma has represented from 7% to 44% of the injuries.[10]

CLINICAL FEATURES AND EVALUATION

Shaken baby syndrome is characterized as much by what is obscure or subtle as by what is immediately clinically identifiable. A shaken infant may suffer only mild ocular or cerebral trauma. The infant may have a history of poor feeding, vomiting, lethargy, and/or irritability occurring intermittently for days or weeks prior to the time of initial health care contact. The subtle symptoms are often minimized by physicians or attributed to mild viral illnesses, feeding dysfunction, or infant colic. Most often one caretaker is aware of the true etiology of the injuries and the others are not. There appears to be a spectrum of the shaken baby syndrome in infancy, and mild cases may never be diagnosed.

The caretaker who violently shakes a young infant, causing unconsciousness, may put the infant to bed, hoping that the baby will later recover.[3] Thus the opportunity for early therapeutic intervention is often lost.[11] When brought to medical attention, the shaken infant typically is convulsing or comatose, not sucking or swallowing, unable to follow movements, and not smiling or vocalizing. The comatose state may be unrecognized by caretakers and even by some medical providers who may assume that the infant is sleeping or lethargic. Such infants often have respiratory difficulty, progressing to apnea or bradycardia, requiring cardiorespiratory resuscitation.[2,3]

There should be a meticulous search for evidence of other injuries such as bruises. Any such injuries should be documented with photographs and examined sequentially, looking for progression of these bruises or the delayed appearance of other bruises. In 75% to 90% of the cases, unilateral or bilateral retinal hemorrhages are present but may be missed unless the child is examined by a pediatric ophthalmologist or experienced physician who is familiar with the hemorrhages, has the proper equipment, and dilates the child's pupils.[2,3,12] The number, character, and size of retinal hemorrhages following shaking injury vary from case to case. Retinal and vitreous hemorrhages and nonhemorrhagic changes including retinal folds and traumatic retinoschisis are characteristic of shaken baby syndrome.[12,13]

At times the diagnosis is confused with meningitis and a spinal tap yields bloody cerebrospinal fluid.[2] Centrifuged spinal fluid that is xanthochromic should be interpreted to be the result of past cerebral trauma. Because of confusing respiratory symptoms, chest roentgenograms often are obtained, and they may be normal or show unexplained rib fractures. Because blood is lost to the intracranial space, the shaken infant is typically mildly to moderately anemic.[14] Clotting dysfunction should be assessed initially and followed up. Hemorrhagic disease of the newborn due to vitamin K deficiency can present as intracranial bleeding in infants older than 1 month.[15] Elevated transaminase levels may indicate occult liver injury.[16]

RADIOLOGY

Computed tomography (CT) has assumed the first-line role in the imaging evaluation of the brain-injured child. It adequately demonstrates those injuries needing urgent intervention, although some false-negative studies occur, particularly early in the evolution of cerebral edema.[17] The initial CT evaluation should be performed without intravenous contrast and should be assessed by using bone as well as soft tissue windows. Computed tomography is generally the method of choice for demonstrating subarachnoid hemorrhage, mass effect, and large extraaxial hemorrhages.[17] It may need to be repeated after a time interval or if the neurologic picture changes rapidly.[18]

Magnetic resonance imaging (MRI) is of great value as an adjunct to CT in the evaluation of brain injuries in infants.[19] Owing to the lack of universal availability of the technology, the physical limitations of access to

MRI when life support is required for the critically ill infant or child, and insensitivity to subarachnoid blood and fractures, MRI is considered complementary to CT. Sato et al[17] have demonstrated a 50% improvement in detection of subdural hematoma using MRI as compared with CT. The ability to detect and define intraparenchymal lesions of the brain is substantially improved by the use of MRI. In Sato and coworkers' study[17] CT did not miss any surgically treated injuries that were detected by MRI. Magnetic resonance imaging and CT can date injuries and substantiate repeated injuries by documenting changes in the chemical states of hemoglobin in the affected areas.[17]

A skeletal survey including the long bones, skull, spine, and ribs should be obtained as soon as the infant's medical condition permits. Skull films are complemented by the CT bone windows in the detection of skull fractures. In one retrospective series of abused children, skull films were slightly more sensitive and improved the confidence of diagnosis of skull fracture as compared with CT.[17] Skull fractures that are multiple, are bilateral, or cross suture lines are more likely to be nonaccidental.[20] Single or multiple fractures of the midshaft or metaphysis of long bones or rib fractures may be associated findings. Specialized views coned down may be needed to delineate subtle fractures.[19] A skeletal survey should be repeated in 2 weeks to better delineate new fractures that may not be apparent until they begin to heal (a process that does not begin for 7 to 10 days).[19]

PATHOLOGY

The cranial cerebral injuries documented in abused children depend on the force or severity of the shake or shake plus impact and the time elapsed from the injury. Subdural hemorrhage caused by shearing forces disrupting small bridging veins over the surface of the brain is a common result of shaking.[4,5] Such hemorrhage may be most prominent in the interhemispheric fissure and minimal over the convexities of the hemispheres.[3,10] However, cerebral edema with or without subarachnoid hemorrhage may be the only finding. Visible cerebral contusions are unusual, but diffuse axonal injury is probably frequent.[21] Isolated or concomitant hypoxic-ischemic damage may result in mild to severe cerebral edema initially and cerebral atrophy and/or infarction as a later finding. Extracerebral fluid collections over the surface of the brain, cerebral atrophy, and cystic encephalomalacia are common late sequelae.[18] Previous reports of benign subdural effusions remain unsubstantiated since multidisciplinary evaluations in those cases were lacking.[22]

OUTCOME/CONSEQUENCES

There is an extraordinarily high incidence of morbidity and mortality among infant victims of shaking.[14,18] In one series, of those infants who were comatose when initially examined, 60% died or had profound mental retardation, spastic quadriplegia, or severe motor dysfunction. Others who initially had seizures, irritability, or lethargy with no lacerations or infarctions of brain tissue, who did not have severe intracranial pressure increases, had subtle neurologic sequelae or persistent seizures.[18] When these severely injured children survive, they may be blind or have chronic subdural fluid collections, enlarging ventricles, cerebral atrophy, encephalomalacia, or porencephalic cysts.[18] The consequence of shaking to infants who do not come to medical attention is presently unknown.

CLINICAL/COMMUNITY MANAGEMENT OF NONACCIDENTAL HEAD INJURIES

Suspicion of serious head injury as a result of maltreatment must be reported immediately to the appropriate authorities to provide for a thorough investigation before the issues become clouded by time and comparison of explanations by caretakers. The clinical team should include a physician who can immediately resuscitate and stabilize the baby while diagnostic radiologic studies are being done. Specialists in pediatric radiology, neurology, neurosurgery, and ophthalmology, as well as a pediatrician specializing in child abuse, should form the diagnostic team. In rural or medically underserved areas where one or more of these specialists are not available, a regional consultation network for child abuse cases should be developed. Careful follow-up by this same team is necessary to document and treat ocular and neurologic sequelae of the trauma. A pediatrician who works with a Child Protection Team should be available to take a broad but detailed history from the caretakers. Information regarding symptom onset, as well as information regarding the chain of caretakers, needs to be quickly passed on to mandated law enforcement and child protection investigators. Physicians can provide interpretation of the likely scenario, timing, and nature of the injuries involved. If notified promptly, investigators may be able to provide reciprocal service by exploring the probable scene of the injury and eliciting information from the caretaker prior to the time that defensive reactions have developed. A psychosocial assessment of the caretakers should be a part of this comprehensive team approach. Siblings or other children, when abuse occurs in settings outside of the home, may have findings of inflicted trauma or repeated shaking.[23] Therefore, child protection assessments need to be available immediately to ensure the current and future safety of these children.

PREVENTION

As a part of anticipatory guidance, the pediatrician should ask about parental stress and their response to the crying infant as well as advise parents regarding the risks of shaking. The efficacy of home visitation programs in preventing intrafamilial physical abuse is established. Nationwide home visitation programs have been recommended by the US Advisory Board on Child Abuse and Neglect.[24] Showers[25] has evaluated "Don't Shake the Baby" cards, and others have developed flyers and used billboard displays to increase public awareness of "The Shaking Shocker." Whether or not these educational efforts will prevent stressed adults from shaking babies needs to be evaluated. The prevention of extrafamilial abuse in out-of-

home settings is more problematic. Careful checking of references, frequent unannounced visits, and conversations with others using the same caretaker may be valuable, but there are no data available to verify the efficacy of these preventive measures as there are for home visitation programs.

SUMMARY

The shaken baby syndrome is a clearly definable medical condition. It requires integration of specific clinical management and community intervention in an interdisciplinary fashion.

COMMITTEE ON CHILD ABUSE AND NEGLECT, 1993 TO 1994
Richard D. Krugman, MD, Chair
Judith Ann Bays, MD
David L. Chadwick, MD
Mireille B. Kanda, MD
Carolyn J. Levitt, MD
Margaret T. McHugh, MD, MPH

Liaison Representatives
Marilyn Benoit, MD, American Academy of Child and Adolescent Psychiatry
Kenneth E. Powell, MD, MPH, Centers for Disease Control and Prevention
Marshall D. Rosman, PhD, American Medical Association

Section Liaison
Robert H. Kirschner, MD, Section on Pathology

REFERENCES

1. Billmire ME, Myers PA. Serious head injury in infants: accident or abuse. *Pediatrics*. 1985;75:340–342
2. Ludwig S, Warman M. Shaken baby syndrome: a review of 20 cases. *Ann Emerg Med*. 1984;13:104–107
3. Bruce DA, Zimmerman RA. Shaken impact syndrome. *Pediatr Ann*. 1989;18:482–494
4. Caffey J. On the theory and practice of shaking infants: its potential residual effects of permanent brain damage and mental retardation. *AJDC*. 1972;124:161–169
5. Guthkelch AN. Infantile subdural haematoma and its relationship to whiplash injury. *Br Med J*. 1971;2:430–431
6. Duhaime AC, Gennerelli TA, Thibault LE, Bruce DA, Margulies SS, Wiser R. The shaken baby syndrome: a clinical, pathological, and biomechanical study. *J Neurosurg*. 1987;66:409–415
7. Dykes LJ. The whiplash shaken infant syndrome: what has been learned. *Child Abuse Negl*. 1986;10:211–221
8. Steele BF, Pollock CB. A psychiatric study of parents who abuse infants and small children. In: Helfer RE, Kempe CH, eds. *The Battered Child*. 2nd ed. Chicago, IL: University of Chicago Press; 1974:89–133
9. Waller AE, Baker SP, Szocka A. Childhood injury deaths: national analysis and geographic variations. *Am J Public Health*. 1989;79:310–315
10. Merten DF, Osborne DR. Craniocerebral trauma in the child abuse syndrome. *Pediatr Ann*. 1983;12:882–887
11. Chadwick DL, Chin S, Salerno C, Landsverk J, Kitchen L. Deaths from falls in children: how far is fatal? *J Trauma*. 1991;31:1353–1355
12. Levin AV. Ocular manifestations of child abuse. *Ophthalmol Clin North Am*. 1990;3:249–264
13. Greenwald MJ, Weiss A, Oesterle CS, Friendly DS. Traumatic retinoschisis in battered babies. *Ophthalmology*. 1986;93:618–625
14. Hadley MN, Sonntag VKH, Rekate HL, Murphy A. The infant whiplash-shake injury syndrome: a clinical and pathological study. *Neurosurgery*. 1989;24:536–540
15. Lane PA, Hathaway WE. Vitamin K in infancy. *J Pediatr*. 1985;106:351–359
16. Coant PN, Kornberg AE, Brody AS, Edwards-Holmes K. Markers for occult liver injury in cases of physical abuse in children. *Pediatrics*. 1992;89:274–278
17. Sato Y, Yuh WT, Smith WL, Alexander RC, Kao SC, Ellerbroek CJ. Head injury in child abuse: evaluation with MR imaging. *Radiology*. 1989;173:653–657
18. Sinal SH, Ball MR. Head trauma due to child abuse: serial computerized

tomography in diagnosis and management. *South Med J*. 1987;80: 1505–1512

19. American Academy of Pediatrics, Section on Radiology. Diagnostic imaging of child abuse. *Pediatrics*. 1991;87:262–264
20. Meservy CJ, Towbin R, McLaurin RL, Myers PA, Ball W. Radiographic characteristics of skull fractures resulting from child abuse. *Am J Roentgenol*. 1987;149:173–175
21. Vowles GH, Schultz CL, Cameron JM. Diffuse axonal injury in early infancy. *J Clin Pathol*. 1987;40:185–189

22. Aoki N, Masuzawa H. Infantile acute subdural hematoma: clinical analysis of 26 cases. *J Neurosurg*. 1984;61:273–280
23. Alexander R, Crabbe L, Sato Y, Smith W, Bennett T. Serial abuse in children who are shaken. *AJDC*. 1990;144:58–60
24. US Advisory Board on Child Abuse and Neglect. *Creating Caring Communities: Blueprint for an Effective Federal Policy on Child Abuse and Neglect*. Washington, DC: US Government Printing Office; 1991;141–146
25. Showers J. Don't shake the baby: the effectiveness of a prevention program. *Child Abuse Negl*. 1992;16:11–18

Sibling Studies

Clinical Principles

▼ Homes in which one child has been abused confer increased risk to siblings, including risk of fatal abuse. Sibling vulnerability demands aggressive investigation, as well as intervention when appropriate.

▼ A generational effect of physical abuse has been demonstrated in siblings as young as 2 years old, in that the siblings interacted with the victims in a manner similar to their mothers.

▼ Siblings of sexual abuse victims, and other children closely associated with the victims and exposed to the perpetrator, should be interviewed and medically evaluated to determine whether they have been abused.

▼ Sexual activity between siblings commonly involves use of force (about one-third) or a large age disparity between the perpetrator and victim (about three-fourths). If a contact between siblings is not typical of sexual experimentation, the case should be managed as one of suspected child abuse.

Bibliography

Physical abuse

Alexander RC, et al. Serial abuse in children who are shaken. *Am J Dis Child.* 1990;144:58-60
Nine infants diagnosed with shaken baby syndrome had siblings. Three of the infants had siblings with shaken baby syndrome, and one had other siblings who had suffered abuse or neglect. (JJ)

Crittenden PM. Sibling interaction: evidence of a generational effect in maltreating infants. *Child Abuse Negl.* 1984;8:433-8
The authors evaluated the videotaped interactions of 36 infants 6 to 11 months of age with siblings between 2 and 10 years of age, their mothers, and a second adult. At each sibling age, one abused, one neglected, one problematic, and one normally reared infant were evaluated. Siblings were found to interact with the infant in a manner similar to that of their mothers, suggesting that they had learned their style of interaction from their mothers. Although adequately reared siblings increased in sensitivity with age, maltreated siblings did not. The effect did not appear to be attributable to infant temperament. These data provide evidence of a generational effect in the learning of parenting styles appearing as early as the third year of life. (JJ)

Halperin SM. Family perceptions of abused children and their siblings. *Child Abuse Negl.* 1985;7:107-115
This study compared the family perceptions of 20 abused children and their non-abused siblings with one another and with a matched group of 29 control children and their siblings. In semistructured interviews conducted by the investigator, each child was asked to describe parents and siblings. Verbatim transcripts were subject to content analysis. The results indicated a statistically significant difference between abused and control children. While the abused children tended to perceive family members less positively and more negatively than did the control children, no such differences were found between abused children and their siblings. Statistically significant differences were also found between the siblings of the abused children and the siblings of the control children. Siblings from abused families tended to perceive family members less positively than siblings from control families. (LRR)

Herrenkohl EC, Herrenkohl RC. Comparison of abused children and their non-abused siblings. *J Am Acad Child Adolesc Psychiatry.* 1979;18:260-269
When 295 targets of abuse were compared to 284 non-abused siblings with reference to birth record data and maternal perceptions of the birth and subsequent development, certain characteristics emerged. Prematurity, Apgar scores, age of mother at child's birth, and maternal reports of postpartum depression were significant. Maternal perceptions that the child had emotional difficulties, was stubborn, and exhibited negative characteristics reminiscent of others were related to certain types of abuse and gross neglect. Explanatory hypotheses

included weakened attachment bonds and maternal projection of negative attributes and feelings of helplessness.

Previous investigators have noted that children may provoke abuse because they are unwanted or difficult to care for. Other issues that have been noted include problems with prematurity, physical handicaps, mental retardation, congenital factors, and parental perceptions that the child is "different." There is, however, a dearth of good research. (LRR)

Hicks RA, Gaughan DC. Understanding fatal child abuse. *Child Abuse Negl.* **1995;19:855-863**
The authors reviewed 14 cases of fatal child abuse and neglect involving children from 24 days to 3 years of age. Six families had prior protective services involvement, four of them initiated because of reports involving a sibling rather than the fatally injured child. The safety of all children in a home must be considered in child abuse investigations. (JJ)

McClure RJ, Davis PM, Meadow SR, Sibert JR. Epidemiology of Munchausen syndrome by proxy, non-accidental poisoning, and non-accidental suffocation. *Arch Dis Child.* **1996;75:57-61**
A total of 128 cases of child maltreatment were identified: 55 suffered Munchausen syndrome by proxy alone; 15, poisoning; 15, suffocation; and 43, more than one type of abuse. In 42% of families with more than one child, a sibling had previously suffered some form of abuse. In child abuse investigations, the safety of all children in the home must be considered. (JJ)

Merrick J. Child abuse and the lack of care: An epidemiologic and social pediatric study of fatal child abuse and neglect in Denmark in 1970-1979. *Ugeskr Laeger.* **1989;151:874- 877**
This retrospective study of 38 victims of fatal child abuse and neglect in Denmark revealed that at least 11% of their siblings had been subjected to past abuse. (JJ)

Nakou S, et al. Health status of abused and neglected children and their siblings. *Child Abuse Negl.* **1982;6:279-284**
The cases of 50 Greek children who had been neglected or physically abused by one or both parents were studied, along with their families.

Of these, 18 were from single-child families. The other 32 children in the study, including two sets of twins, had a total of 53 siblings. In comparison with their siblings, the abused children were more frequently the result of an unplanned or unwanted pregnancy, had a higher incidence of perinatal problems, and more illness in the first year of life. Almost half had feeding problems. Their nutritional status was often poorer than that of their siblings, and they were characterized by their parents as more difficult than other children. In some cases, there was evidence of a lesser degree of neglect or abuse in the siblings. More than twice as many boys as girls were abused, although there were more girls than boys among the siblings. This probably reflects the higher value and resultant higher expectations the Greek culture places on male children. (LRR)

Rivara FP. Physical abuse in children under two: A study of therapeutic outcomes. *Child Abuse Negl.* **1985;9:81-87**
This study of physical abuse to children under the age of 2 addresses family prognosis, compliance with treatment recommendations, and long-term outcome. Data were collected from multidisciplinary evaluation teams and from Department of Human Services' records of 71 children. Generally, all families were referred for mental health counseling and parent training, but only 33% complied. Half of the children were abused more than once; 30% were abused after referral for counseling. The incidence of re-abuse was unrelated to compliance with counseling. The majority of children had some out-of-home placement, with a mean of 11 months in foster care and 24.4 months in care of relatives. *In 69% of families, more than one child was abused. At the time of follow-up, 41% of children and 47% of siblings were not living with either parent.* Half of the families were judged to be functioning poorly, and only nine had made good progress in counseling. (LRR)

Sinal SH, Ball MR. Head trauma due to child abuse: Serial computerized tomography in diagnosis and management. *South Med J.* **1987;80:1505-1512**
The authors reviewed clinical features and CT scans for 24 children who had acute head trauma as a result of child abuse. All but one child was

less than 1 year old. Whiplash shaken infant syndrome was diagnosed in 17 of the children. Two siblings of these children died of child abuse, which reinforces the necessity of evaluating the safety of other children in the same environment and continuing intervention to prevent additional abuse. (JJ)

Sexual Abuse

DeJong AR. Sexual interactions among siblings and cousins: Experimentation or exploitation? *Child Abuse Negl.* **1989;13:271-279**

Among 831 children less than 14 years of age evaluated at a hospital-based sexual assault center, 35 cases of sibling incest were identified. Twenty-five perpetrators were natural brothers and 10 were half brothers or stepbrothers. The mean age of the victims was 7.4 years, and the mean age of the perpetrators was 15.5 years.

The author assessed whether the incest was abusive or normal sexual experimentation. Four factors were considered indicative of abusive behavior: (1) age difference of 5 years or more between the victim and perpetrator; (2) the use of force, threat, or authority by the abuser; (3) attempted or completed penile-vaginal or penile-anal penetration; and (4) documented physical injury in the victim. When any one or more of these four factors were present, the contact was considered abusive or exploitative. If all four factors were absent, the contact was considered consistent with normal sexual exploration or experimentation. In this study, no clear case of normal sexual exploration was found among the victims. Only 9% of the victims were less than 5 years younger than the assailants. About one-third of the perpetrators threatened or used force, and 4 pressured victims with their authority relationship. Most of the victims gave histories of attempted anal and/or vaginal penetration. Two presented with sexually transmitted diseases.

If a sexual contact between siblings is determined to be typical of sexual experimentation, the physician should discuss normal child sexual behaviors with the parents and steps to be taken to minimize inappropriate sexual stimulation at home. If the contact is not typical of exploratory behavior, a medical examination should be performed, the case reported to the appropriate agencies as required by state laws, and the family should be referred for counseling. (JJ)

Finkelhor D. Sex among siblings: A survey on prevalence, variety, and effects. *Arch Sex Behav.* **1980;9:171-194**

In a survey of 796 students at six colleges, 15% of the females and 10% of the males reported some type of sexual experience involving a sibling. Fondling and touching of the genitals were the most common activities in all age categories. Seventy-three percent of the experiences occurred when at least one of the partners was older than age 8. One-fourth of the experiences could be considered exploitative either because force was used or because there was a large age disparity between the partners. Reactions to the experiences were equally divided among those who considered them positive and those who considered them negative. Females were more likely than males to have been exploited and feel badly about it. (JJ)

Muram D, Speck PM, Gold SS. Genital abnormalities in female siblings and friends of child victims of sexual abuse. *Child Abuse Negl.* **1991;15:105-110**

The authors evaluated medically 247 girls age 12 or younger who were closely associated with victims of sexual assault, even if these children denied being victims themselves. They found that 188 girls were primary victims of sexual abuse and 59 were secondary victims, associates of victims of abuse. When compared with primary victims, secondary victims were more likely to demonstrate genital abnormalities suggestive of sexual abuse. Of the 50 secondary victims who were later interviewed by the state social agency, 24 girls (48%) reported that they were also victims of assault. The authors recommended that siblings of sexual abuse victims, as well as other children who are closely associated with them and exposed to the perpetrator, be evaluated to determine whether they have abnormalities suggestive of sexual assault. (JJ)

Acknowledgment

This section and its annotations were prepared by Jerry G. Jones, MD, and reviewed by David P. Schor, MD. Selected annotations from the first edition were written by Lawrence R. Ricci, MD.

Statistics of Child Abuse

Clinical Principles

▼ There were an estimated 3.1 million child abuse reports in the United States in 1996, of which nearly 1 million were substantiated. About 60% of the substantiated cases involved neglect; 23%, physical abuse; 9%, sexual abuse; 4%, emotional maltreatment; and 5%, other. The number of sexual abuse cases has decreased slightly, while the neglect cases have increased slightly.

▼ The actual number of child abuse cases is estimated to be three to four times these amounts, with tens of millions of adults who have been the victims of childhood abuse.

▼ About 2,000 children die from child abuse each year, averaging about 5 1/2 children per day. They die of neglect and physical abuse in roughly equal measures. Most die under 4 years of age, with head or abdominal injuries. About 40% of the fatal cases have had prior involvement with child protective services and 60% are new cases at the time of the child's death. Most physical abuse fatalities are caused by males, and most neglect fatalities are caused by females.

▼ Child abuse causes an estimated 18,000 cases of serious disabilities and over 140,000 cases of serious injury each year. Billions of dollars are spent in the investigation and treatment of child abuse.

Bibliography

Petit MR, Curtis PA. *Child Abuse and Neglect: A Look at the States (1997 CWLA Stat Book)*. Washington, DC: CWLA Press, 1997
This comprehensive book, a publication of the Child Welfare League of America, provides summaries and state statistics on the following subjects: child abuse and neglect; child abuse fatalities; out-of-home care; adoption; finance and administration; family preservation and support; and risk factors, conditions, and trends related to child well-being. It may be ordered from the CWLA Publication Department, 440 First St, NW, Third Floor, Washington, DC 20001-2085.

Sedlak, AJ, Broadhurst D. The Third National Incidence Study of Child Abuse and Neglect (NIS-3). Washington, DC: US Department of Health and Human Services, September, 1996
This study contains extensive statistics about child abuse obtained from child protective services, but also from community professionals. Child abuse has increased significantly since the last national survey in 1986. Children in single-parent families were found to have a greater risk of harm when compared to their counterparts living with both parents: a 77% greater risk of physical abuse, 87% greater risk of physical neglect, 74% greater risk of emotional neglect, 220% risk of educational neglect, and a 120% greater risk of being endangered by some type of child abuse. Low socioeconomic status was significantly related to higher risks of all forms of child abuse. Nearly 80% of all abuse was committed by birth parents.

US Advisory Board on Child Abuse and Neglect. *A Nation's Shame: Fatal Child Abuse and Neglect in the United States*. Washington, DC: US Government Printing Office; 1995
This publication provides an overview of child abuse fatalities in the United States with policy recommendations for Congress, federal and state governments, and the general public. Twenty-six recommendations include development of state and regional child death review teams, increased education and research, better data gathering of child abuse statistics, and support for child abuse prevention programs such as home visitation. A free copy of this report can be obtained from the National Clearinghouse on Child Abuse and Neglect (1-800/394-3366) or accessed through the Internet (www.calib.com/nccanch).

Wang CT, Daro D. *Current Trends in Child Abuse Reporting and Fatalities: The Results of the 1996 Annual Fifty State Survey*. Chicago, IL: National Committee to Prevent Child Abuse; 1997
This is a source for the most current statistics known to state child protective services agencies. Child abuse rates remain high. Neglect may be

increasing somewhat, but a positive finding is that sexual abuse reporting has decreased 7% from the previous year.

State Child Death Review Team Reports are available through team coordinators (eg, Arizona, California, Colorado, Iowa, Oklahoma, Missouri). Refer to Resources section of this manual for addresses.

Acknowledgment

This section and its annotations were prepared by Randell C. Alexander, MD, PhD.

Substance Use Disorders and Child Abuse

See Also:
Homicide
Poisoning as Child Abuse

Note: Substance abuse is a term no longer accepted in DSM-IV or ICD-10, which refer to "substance use disorders" (intoxication, hazardous use, withdrawal, abusive use, and dependence; the last being most often associated with child maltreatment of all types). However, the phrase "substance abuse" continues to have great acceptance among current practitioners and, indeed, is used in many titles and texts of papers abstracted in this section.

Clinical Principles

▼ Substance use disorders are common in adolescents and adults, and they are associated with dramatic alterations in parenting. These disorders lead to increased child maltreatment and require specific actions by health and human service personnel caring for maltreated children or their alcohol- or drug-dependent parents.

▼ Parental alcohol and drug consumption adversely affect children across the life cycle, beginning with exposure in utero. Nearly 40% of pregnant women use illegal drugs during pregnancy. The amount of alcohol ingested during pregnancy is unknown. These substances may produce both anatomical and behavioral abnormalities in exposed offspring, which may make them particularly susceptible to child abuse and neglect.

▼ Estimates based on 1989 data are that at least 1 in 10 children were being raised by addicted parents and 675,000 children were seriously mistreated by a substance-abusing caretaker. These numbers are increasing. Crack cocaine is the most frequent illicit drug used by women of child-bearing age and its use has skyrocketed. Crack users often binge for days or weeks at a time. All children of chemical abusing caretakers are neglected to some degree; at the extreme, children are simply abandoned.

▼ Parental substance abuse is associated with a higher risk of recurrent child abuse and neglect. Child protective agencies must assess abusive families for drug and alcohol problems in their initial investigations. Similarly, substance abuse counsellors should seek information on child abuse and neglect and address such problems. Denial is common in substance-abusing parents. Unless the problem of drug and alcohol abuse is successfully addressed, efforts to improve the parenting of abusing and neglecting caretakers will not be successful.

▼ Few substance abuse programs make provisions for child care, and those which do are very costly. Lack of available child care is a frequent barrier to initiating or completing treatment. When child abusing or neglecting parents fail to comply with drug and alcohol treatment programs, early termination of parental rights should be considered.

▼ A history of child abuse or neglect has been implicated as a factor in the development of substance use disorders during adulthood.

Bibliography

General

Bays J. Substance abuse and child abuse—impact of addiction on the child. *Ped Clin North Am.* 1990;37:881-904 (A Review) Chemically dependent and abuse/neglect prone families have the following characteristics in common: diversion of resources (money, time, energy, and emotional support) from children to drug habits; criminal activity; other physical and mental illnesses in the parents; poor parenting skills; and family violence. In addition, many drugs make adults more violent, paranoid, and prone to injure, molest, or neglect their children.

Recognition

Dore MM, Doris JM, Wright P. Identifying substance abuse in maltreating families: a child welfare challenge. *Child Abuse Negl.* 1995;19:531-543

Incidence of Dual Abuse

Bijur PE, Kurzon M, Overpeck MD, Scheidt PC. Parental alcohol use, problem drinking, and children's injuries. *JAMA.* 1992;267: 3166-3171

This randomized household survey of 12,360 parents and children demonstrated that the offspring of women who were problem drinkers had 2.1 times the risk of serious injury as children of non-drinking mothers. Children with two parents who were problem drinkers were at even higher risk. Primary prevention of childhood injury might be enhanced if physicians elicited information about parental drinking, helped secure appropriate treatment, and participated in public health efforts to reduce the deleterious effects of alcohol.

Famularo R, Stone K, Barnum R, Wharton R. Alcoholism and severe child maltreatment. *Amer J Orthopsychiat.* 1986;56:481-485

Fifty parents whose children were removed by courts because of physical or sexual abuse or neglect (or combinations thereof) were compared to 38 control parents. A history of alcoholism (either current or past) was 4.5 times as frequent in the study parents. Even the past history of alcoholism may be a risk factor for severe child maltreatment and warrants prospective study.

Hernandez JT. Substance abuse among sexually abused adolescents and their families. *J Adolescent Health.* 1992;13:658-662

A statewide survey of 3,179 9th-grade students showed that adolescents who had self-reported sexual abuse were more likely to report substance abuse for themselves and for their family members than those not reporting sexual abuse. These findings suggest that screening adolescents for personal and family histories of substance abuse and sexual abuse should be performed whenever they give histories of either type of abuse. Such screening will identify large numbers of individuals in need of effective and available services.

Kelleher K, Chaffin M, Hollenberg J, Fischer E. Alcohol and drug disorders among physically abusive and neglectful parents in a community-based sample. *Am J Pub Health.* 1994;84:1586-1590

A community study of 11,622 parents/child care-takers showed 1.4% self-reporting physical abuse of a child, and 1.8% self-reporting neglect. After controlling for confounding factors, adults with substance abusing/dependent problems were 2.7 times more likely to abuse and 4.2 times more likely to neglect children than nonsubstance-abusing/dependent controls. Forty percent of physically abusing adults and 56% of neglecting adults met criteria for substance abuse during their lifetimes.

Murphy JM, Jellinek M, Quinn D, et al. Substance abuse and serious child mistreatment: prevalence, risk, and outcome in a court sample. *Child Abuse Negl.* 1991;15:197-211

A prospective study was conducted of 206 families in which urban courts were considering removal from the parents of seriously physically abused or neglected children. In 50% of the families, at least one parent had an alleged substance abuse problem, including 43% with at least one parent with substantiated substance abuse. Alcohol, cocaine, and heroin were the most frequently abused substances. When compared to nonsubstance-abusing parents, substance abusers had 50% more previous reports of child abuse and neglect, presented greater risk to their children, rejected court-ordered services more frequently, and were more apt to have their children permanently removed. Maternal rather than paternal substance abuse appeared more related to these observations, but the vast majority of the families were headed by single parents (mothers).

Williams-Petersen MG, Myers BJ, Degen HM, et al. Drug-using and nonusing women: potential for child abuse, child-rearing attitudes, social support, and affection for expected baby. *Int J of the Addictions.* 1994;29:1631-1643

A questionnaire measuring child-rearing attitudes was administered to 25 substance using and 55 nonusing pregnant women with similar demographic characteristics. The mean score on the Child Abuse Potential Inventory for substance users was 214 and for nonusers was 156. (A score of 215 or higher is considered an elevated abuse potential score; persons scoring this high exhibit characteristics similar to persons who are known, active physical child abusers.) Over 50% of users and 25% of nonusers had scores exceeding 215. This risk for abuse was the greatest in women with low social support (both substance users and nonusers).

Substance Use in Survivors of Child Abuse

Bennett EM, Kemper KJ. Is abuse during childhood a risk factor for developing substance abuse problems as an adult? *J Dev Behav Pediatr.* **1994;15:426-429**

A survey was conducted of 733 mothers of children younger than 6 years of age being seen for routine pediatric care. After controlling for family histories of substance abuse and socioeconomic factors, physical abuse was found to be a significant risk factor for later substance abuse in the women interviewed. Substance abuse prevention programs may be important in the treatment of child abuse victims.

Widom CS, Ireland T, Glynn PJ. Alcohol abuse in abused and neglected children followed-up: are they at increased risk? *J. Studies on Alcohol.* **1995;56:207-217**

A group of 609 adults, who had been physically or sexually abused or neglected as children, were interviewed 20 years after the official reports of abuse/neglect. They were matched with 457 controls. After controlling for many confounding factors, there was no overall relationship between the history of abuse/neglect and subsequent development of alcohol problems. However, women had a significant relationship between the history of childhood neglect and the number of alcohol symptoms. Children of parents with alcohol problems are at increased risk of developing alcohol problems themselves; neglect may be an additive factor in girls and they may need special treatment to prevent the development of alcohol abuse.

Treatment

Metsch LR, Rivers JE, Miller M, et al. Implementation of a family-centered treatment program for substance-abusing women and their children: barriers and resolutions. *J Psychoactive Drugs.* **1995;27:73-83**

Acknowledgment

This section and its annotations were prepared by Gerald E. Porter, MD. Review of the manuscript by Michael S. Jellinek, MD, and Kelly J. Kelleher, MD, is gratefully acknowledged.

The following are considered to be of interest to health-care professionals. The lists are not exhaustive, however, and materials of interest are available from other resources.

Textbooks

Briere J, Berliner L, Bulkley JA, Jenny C, Reid T. *The APSAC Handbook on Child Maltreatment.* Thousand Oaks, CA: SAGE Publications; 1996

Brodeur AE, Monteleone JA. *Child Maltreatment: A Clinical Guide & Reference.* St Louis, MO: G.W. Medical Publishing, Inc; 1994

Giardino A, Christian C, Giardino E. *A Practical Guide to the Evaluation of Child Physical Abuse and Neglect.* Thousand Oaks, CA: Sage Publications; 1997

Giardino A, Finkel M, Giardino E, Seidl T, Ludwig S. *A Practical Guide to the Evaluation of Sexual Abuse in the Prepubertal Child.* Newbury Park, CA: Sage Publications; 1993

Heger A, Emans SJ. *Evaluation of the Sexually Abused Child: A Medical Textbook and Photographic Atlas.* New York, NY: Oxford University Press; 1992

Kleinman PK. *Diagnostic Imaging of Child Abuse.* Baltimore, MD: Williams & Wilkins; 1987

Ludwig S, Kornberg AE. *Child Abuse: A Medical Reference.* New York, NY: Churchill Livingstone; 1992

Monteleone, JA. *Child Maltreatment: A Comprehensive Photographic Reference Identifying Potential Child Abuse.* St Louis, MO: G.W. Medical Publishing, Inc; 1994

Monteleone JA. *Child Abuse: Quick Reference for Medical and Allied Health Practitioners.* St Louis, MO: G.W. Medical Publishing, Inc; 1997

Reece RM, ed. *Child Abuse: Medical Diagnosis and Management.* Malvern, PA: Lea & Febiger; 1993

Journals and Periodicals

The journals listed below are devoted to child maltreatment subjects. However, high-quality articles appear in a wide variety of journals including *Pediatrics,* published by the American Academy of Pediatrics.

APSAC Advisor. Chicago, IL: American Professional Society on the Abuse of Children; (407 South Dearborn St, Suite 1300; Chicago, IL 60605)

Child Abuse & Neglect: The International Journal. New York, NY: Pergamon/Elsevier Science

Child Maltreatment: Journal of the American Professional Society on the Abuse of Children. Thousand Oaks, CA: Sage Periodicals Press/SAGE Publications, Inc

Journal of Child Sexual Abuse. Binghamton, NY: Haworth Maltreatment and Trauma Press

The Quarterly Child Abuse Medical Update. Boston, MA: Institute for Professional Education/Massachusetts Society for the Prevention of Cruelty to Children (399 Boylston St; Boston, MA 02116)

SCAN. Chicago, IL: Section on Child Abuse and Neglect of the American Academy of Pediatrics (Charles Felzen Johnson, MD, Editor)

Audiovisual/Computer Resources

ABC News. *Shaken Babies.* 1997
This videotape, presented on the television program *20/20* on August 15, 1997, is 25 minutes in length. It may be ordered by calling 1-800/913-3434. Potentially misleading is that a prison interviewee demonstrates he shook the deceased child gently.

American Academy of Pediatrics and C. Henry Kempe National Center on Child Abuse & Neglect. *Visual Diagnosis of Child Physical Abuse.* Elk Grove Village, IL: American Academy of Pediatrics; 1994
This package features a study guide and 150 slides. It can be ordered from the AAP Department of Marketing and Publications; PO Box 747; Elk Grove Village, IL 60009-0747 (1-800/433-9016; www.aap.org).

American Academy of Pediatrics. *Focus on Child Abuse: Resources for Prevention, Recognition, and Treatment.* Elk Grove Village, IL: American Academy of Pediatrics; 1996
This CD-ROM includes all 150 slides from *Visual Diagnosis of Child Physical Abuse* with narrative component, an extensive collection of relevant articles from *Pediatrics* 1990-1995, all related AAP policy statements, parent information that can also be used as handouts, visual self-assessment with more than 60 previously unpublished slides, and other references and resources. It can be ordered from the AAP Department of Marketing and Publications; PO Box 747; Elk Grove Village, IL 60009-0747 (1-800/433-9016; www.aap.org).

American Academy of Pediatrics. *Portraits of Promise-Preventing Shaken Baby Syndrome.* St Paul, MN: The Junior League of St Paul, Inc, and Midwest Children's Resource Center at Children's Health Care - St Paul; 1995
This 11-minute video comes with 100 parent fact sheets. It can be ordered from the AAP Department of Marketing and Publications; 141 Northwest Point Blvd, PO Box 927; Elk Grove Village, IL 60009-0927 (1-800/433-9016).

Indiana State Department of Health SIDS Project. *Finding Answers with Compassion (Infant Death Investigation Guide).*
This videotape with four supplemental pamphlets is available from the Indiana State Department of Health (Attn: Cashier's Office); 1330 W Michigan St, PO Box 1964; Indianapolis, IN 46206).

National Clearinghouse on Child Abuse and Neglect Information. *Child Abuse and Neglect 1965-July 1995.* Baltimore, MD: National Information Services Corporation
This CD-ROM program, available free, contains an extensive collection of references and abstracts.

It is currently being updated. Some of the information is available through the Clearinghouse site on the Internet, at http://www.calib.com/nccanch (National Clearinghouse on Child Abuse and Neglect Information; PO Box 1182; Washington, DC 20013-1182; 1-800/394-3366).

Booklets/Pamphlets

For Professionals

American Medical Association; Division of Health Science; 515 N State St; Chicago, IL 60610 (312/464-5000)
Diagnostic and Treatment Guidelines on Child Physical Abuse and Neglect
Diagnostic and Treatment Guidelines on Child Sexual Abuse
Diagnostic and Treatment Guidelines on Domestic Violence
Mental Health Effects of Family Violence
Strategies for the Treatment and Prevention of Sexual Assault

National Clearinghouse on Child Abuse and Neglect Information; PO Box 1182; Washington, DC 20013-1182 (1-800/394-3366; http://www.calib.com/nccanch)
User Manual Series, each one covering an aspect of child abuse or neglect: Statistical Information; Diagnostic Imaging and Child Abuse: Technologies, Practices, and Guidelines; etc. Catalog available.

For Nonprofessionals

American Academy of Pediatrics, Department of Marketing and Publications; 141 Northwest Point Blvd, PO Box 927; Elk Grove Village, IL 60009-0927 (1-800/433-9016)
Prevent Shaken Baby Syndrome
Child Sexual Abuse
Child Sexual Abuse: What It Is and How to Prevent It: Guidelines for Parents

Channing L. Bete Co, Inc; 200 State Rd; South Deerfield, MA 01373 (1-800/628-7733)
Numerous booklets relating to child maltreatment.

National Committee to Prevent Child Abuse; 332 S Michigan Ave, Suite 1600; Chicago, IL 60604 (312/663-3520)
Numerous pamphlets on child maltreatment, stress management, and poverty.

North Carolina Pediatric Society Committee on Child Abuse and Neglect; PO Box 27617; Raleigh, NC 27611

This pamphlet was designed to increase awareness of the potential detrimental effects of advertising that characterizes children in a sexually vulnerable or sexualized manner.

Prevent Child Abuse-Illinois; 528 S 5th St, Ste 211; Springfield, IL 62701

Never Shake a Baby

Spokane Sexual Assault Center ACT for Kids; Symons Building, Suite 200; 7 S Howard St; Spokane, WA 99204

How to Survive the Sexual Abuse of Your Child. This 40-page booklet provides information in the following sections: Coping after Disclosure, Therapy and Recovery, Legal Involvement, Offender Information, and Resources.

Winters Communications, Inc; 14740 Lake Magdalene Circle; Tampa, FL 33613 (1-813/264-7618)

Numerous booklets relate to child maltreatment.

Acknowledgment

This section was prepared by Jerry G. Jones, MD.

Thoracic Trauma

See Also:
Fractures (Rib)
(AAP Statement *Diagnostic Imaging of Child Abuse*)

Clinical Principles

▼ Rib fractures are the most frequent thoracic injury, especially in infants.

▼ Other injuries occur but are much less common. These include pulmonary contusion, hemothorax, pneumothorax, cylothorax, and cardiac contusion/laceration.

▼ Pharyngeal injuries may be manifest by thoracic abnormalities.

Other Comments

▼ As thoracic injuries are often occult, a high index of suspicion is required for diagnosis.

▼ Abuse-related thoracic injuries result from application of substantial force.

Bibliography

Cohle SD, Hawley DA, Berg KK, Kiesel EL, Pless JE. Homicidal cardiac lacerations in children. *J Forensic Sci* 1995;40:212-218
The authors present six cases of fatal cardiac laceration involving children between ages 9 weeks and 2.5 years. In five of the cases, the right atrium was lacerated with a left ventricle injury discovered in the last case. Confessions provided in three cases showed injuries were caused by stomping, punching, and drop kicking the children. At least two rib fractures were present in four of six cases, with five children sustaining concurrent abdominal injuries.

The article presents previous literature on cardiac lacerations, discussing the possible mechanisms and causes of blunt force cardiac injury including the following: a direct blow to the anterior chest, a blast injury, compression of the heart between the sternum and the vertebral column, increased cardiac hydrostatic pressure secondary to abdominal or leg compression, acceleration/deceleration injury, penetration by fractured ribs, and delayed rupture of a cardiac contusion. Various types of accidents involving these mechanisms are described, illustrating the large amount of force involved (eg, in a motor vehicle accident or being kicked by a horse).

Further literature review of injuries resulting from cardiopulmonary resuscitation in adults is provided with discussion of the role in children. The authors conclude their article by stating,

> Cardiac lacerations in infants and young children result from severe blunt trauma such as occurs in motor vehicle accidents or in violent assaultive injury. This injury does not result from cardiopulmonary resuscitation (CPR) or from minor accidents at home.

Garcia VF, Gotschall CS, Eichelberger MR, Bowman LM. Rib fractures in children: a marker of severe trauma. *J Trauma.* 1990;30:695-700
The significance of rib fractures in children admitted to a Level 1 pediatric trauma center with thoracic trauma was evaluated in this review of 33 children (0-14 years). Rib fractures represented about 30% of the total cases of thoracic trauma.

Children with rib fractures were more severely injured than those without. This was demonstrated by a 42% mortality in children with rib fractures as compared with 18% mortality in those with thoracic injury without rib fractures. A greater number of rib fractures was indicative of more severe injury and a 71% mortality was present in cases with both head injury and rib fractures.

The mechanism of injury included motor vehicle accidents (70%), child abuse (21%), and falls (9%). Sixty-three percent of the rib fractures in those less than 3 years of age were attributed to child abuse. The authors concluded that rib fractures were a marker of severe trauma with significant injurious force necessary to deform and fracture the inherently elastic chest wall of a child.

Reece RM, Arnold J, Splain J. Pharyngeal perforation as a manifestation of child abuse. *Child Maltreatment*. 1996;1:364-367

Inflicted perforations of the pharynx, while reported, are unusual in child abuse. Frequently these injuries are discovered because of thoracic abnormalities.

The authors present three cases of pharyngeal perforation, two of which manifest with thoracic abnormalities. In contrast to previous literature on abusive pharyngeal injuries (reviewed in the article), these cases involved recent medical procedures. Although pharyngeal injuries are recognized complications of the interventions, in these cases the acute appearance at endoscopy and surgery eliminated any relationship.

The typical physical findings in such cases are presented, including lesions of the palate and posterior pharyngeal anatomy. These are generally accompanied by radiologic signs that include retropharyngeal air, subcutaneous emphysema, pseudodiverticulum, pneumomediastinum, or a mediastinal abscess.

The authors provide insight into differentiating accidental and iatrogenic perforations from those inflicted, by clinical presentation and knowledge of typical iatrogenic injuries.

Spevak MR, Kleinman PK, Belanger PL, Primafk D, Richmond JM. Cardiopulmonary resuscitation and rib fractures in infants: a postmortem radiologic-pathologic study. *JAMA*. 1994;272:617-618

This brief report involved a retrospective review of the autopsy findings and postmortem radiographs of 91 infants who had undergone cardiopulmonary resuscitation prior to suffering death that was not related to child abuse.

CPR was administered to the infants (age, 26 hours to 8.5 months) by people with a variety of experience including parents or family members (21%), emergency medical technicians (82%), emergency department personnel (91%), police (9%) and other hospital personnel (1%). In 80% of the cases, personnel from more than one group performed CPR. The duration of CPR was determined in 64% of the cases, ranging from 10 to 120 minutes with a mean duration of 47.3 minutes.

Thorough evaluation of the autopsy findings and postmortem radiographs did not reveal rib fractures in any of the infants. The article discusses the previous literature on complications from CPR including a critical review of such literature related to children. The authors conclude "when rib fractures are encountered in an otherwise normal infant, abuse should be considered."

Specific Organ Injury

Dowd MD, Krug S. Pediatric blunt cardiac injury: epidemiology, clinical features and diagnosis. *J Trauma*. 1996;40:61-67

This multicentered retrospective study reviewed 184 cases of blunt cardiac injury over a 10-year period in children less than 18 years of age.

Accidental mechanisms were responsible in the vast majority of cases (181). Myocardial contusion was the diagnosis in 95% of occurrences. Cardiac injury was accompanied by other thoracic injuries, including pulmonary contusion (50%) and rib fractures (23%). Multisystem injury was common (87%), with head injuries present in 47% and abdominal injuries in 45%.

The clinical features, diagnostic testing utilized, and an approach to evaluation and management of blunt cardiac injury are presented.

Kleinman PK, Marks SC, Nimkin K, Rayder SM, Kessler SC. Rib fractures in 31 abused infants: postmortem radiologic-histologic study. *Radiology*. 1996;200:807-810

This article is one of a series published by Kleinman et al, relating to a database developed from study of 31 child abuse victims (Kleinman PK, Marks SC, Richmond JM, Blackbourne BD. Inflicted skeletal injury: a postmortem radiologic-histo-pathologic study in 31 infants. AJR. 1995;165:647-650).

Eighty-four (51%) of the total 165 fractures identified in the victims were rib fractures. These were isolated to 11 infants. Postmortem skeletal surveys revealed only 30 (36%) of the rib fractures, with pathologic analysis or specimen radiography required to detect the remainder.

The distribution of the fractures was rib head (28), costovertebral articulation (27), posterior arc (8), lateral arc (5), anterior arc (6), and costochondral junction (10). Important features contributing to fracture detection were location, age, orientation of the fracture line, and position and alignment of the fracture fragments.

Specific review of the fractures situated laterally and anteriorly (9 of 21 were detected by skeletal survey) demonstrated histological and radiologic evidence supporting a mechanism of thoracic compression.

Strouse PJ, Owings CL. Fractures of the first rib in child abuse. *Radiology*. 1995;197:763-765
Thirty-five children 2 years of age or less with radiologically detected rib fractures were retrospectively reviewed. Child abuse was causative in 12 of the children. The other causes were osteopenia in 13 (complication of prematurity and/or other medical diagnosis), unknown (3), motor vehicle accident (2), osteogenesis imperfecta (2), complication of medical procedure (2) and birth trauma (1).

Four of the 35 reviewed were found to have first rib fractures, 3 of which were related to child abuse; osteogenesis imperfecta was present in the other. Two other cases (outside of the study period) of child abuse related to first rib fractures were added to make a second study group of 5. In the absence of bone disease, first rib fractures were therefore specific for child abuse in this study.

The first rib fractures were isolated in four of five cases, suggesting specific causative mechanism. The authors postulated and expanded upon possible mechanisms. These involved a direct blow, significant direct compression of the first rib during forceful holding of the chest and indirect application of force transmitted through the neck muscles during violent shaking of a child.

Technical

Kleinman PK, Nimkin K, Spevak MR, et al. Follow-up skeletal surveys in suspected child abuse. *Am J Roentgenol*. 1996;167:893-896
Repeat skeletal surveys were performed 2 weeks after the initial survey in 23 children 1 to 35 months of age who were strongly suspected to be victims of child abuse. The follow-up skeletal surveys demonstrated 19 (27% increase) previously undetected fractures, which included metaphyseal fractures (8), rib fractures (8), and single fractures of a spinous

process, the sacrum and a metacarpal. Additional information about the age of 13 fractures was provided. Overall the follow-up surveys provided additional information regarding skeletal injury in 61% of the cases (14 of 23).

Smith FW, Gilday DL, Ash JM, Green MD. Unsuspected costo-vertebral fractures demonstrated by bone scanning in the child abuse syndrome. *Pediatr Radiol*. 1980;10:103-106
This article presents four cases with multiple costovertebral rib fractures detected by bone scintigraphy. While much has been written about the use of scintigraphy in child abuse since this 1980 article, the authors were the first to recommend such use in detection of the posteriorly located highly specific (for non-accidental injury) rib fractures.

Acknowledgment

This section and its annotations were prepared by Dirk Huyer, MD, and reviewed by David P. Schor, MD.

Part 2: Resources

Medical Diagnostic Child Abuse Programs in the United States and Canada

Compiled by
The American Academy of Pediatrics
Section on Child Abuse and Neglect

January 1994
Updated 1997

Introduction

The following listing was developed by the Section on Child Abuse and Neglect of the American Academy of Pediatrics in response to requests for medical diagnostic programs in the United States which practitioners can use for referral. Our wishes were to include programs that are multidisciplinary, accept referrals, and provide comprehensive forensic evaluations.

The Section on Child Abuse and Neglect offers no recommendations nor endorsements of any of these programs. Responsibility lies with the referent to see that a particular program matches their patients' needs.

We hope to update this listing yearly. Those medical programs wishing to be included should send a one-paragraph description of the program along with its name, address, phone number, and medical director to:

Tammy Piazza
Sections Manager, Section on Child Abuse and Neglect
American Academy of Pediatrics
141 Northwest Point Blvd
PO Box 927
Elk Grove Village, IL 60009-0927

Carole Jenny, MD
Chairperson 1994-1998
Section on Child Abuse and Neglect
American Academy of Pediatrics

Dept of Pediatrics, Rm Co-Op 140
Hasbro Children's Hospital
593 Eddy St
Providence, RI 02903

July 1, 1997

Alabama

Bessemer Cut-Off Child Advocacy Center
District Attorney Samuel Russell
Courthouse Annex
Bessemer, AL 35020-4907
205/481-4145
205/481-4254 (Fax)
Director: Harold Johnston

The Advocacy Center is housed in a renovated 75-year-old home. The house is set up with two interview rooms, where sexually and physically abused children are interviewed and provided direct services when necessary. The center is staffed with a director, assistant director, and a state licensed counselor under contract to provide counseling to child victims and non-offending parents. Medical examinations are provided primarily by CHIPS (Phone: (205) 254-5199) and The Children's Hospital of Alabama. The district attorney is the primary sponsor of the program and is president of the executive board, which consists of various community leaders.

The Child Advocacy Center of Mobile, Alabama
1351 Springhill Ave
Mobile, AL 36604
334/432-1101
Medical Director: John F. Shriner, MD

The Child Advocacy Center houses a multidisciplinary team which includes workers of the Department of Human Resources, law enforcement officers, counselors, an assistant district attorney, a medical director, and support personnel and child advocate volunteers. Twice weekly scheduled clinics are held in the University of South Alabama Pediatric Outpatient Clinic. Referrals are made by law enforcement officers, child protective workers of the Department of Human Resources, and physicians after reporting requirements have been met. Acute cases of child maltreatment are seen at the Child Evaluation Center at the University of South Alabama Women/Children's Hospital.

Children's Hospital Intervention and Prevention Services (CHIPS)
1510 - 5th Ave South
Birmingham, AL 35233
205/254-6199
205/975-9088 (Fax)
Medical Director: Michelle Amaya, MD, MPH
              mamaya@uab.edu (E-mail)

CHIPS is a multidisciplinary clinic offering outpatient medical and psychosocial evaluation services to child victims of suspected sexual abuse in a child-friendly atmosphere. The team of three physicians, three clinical counselors, and two nurses work with community professionals to assist the child through the system — from discovery to prosecution. When warranted, an Extended Assessment or Victim/Trauma Assessment may be offered for purposes of determining the extent and nature of the child's trauma, facilitating disclosure, and generating treatment recommendations. CHIPS also provides consultation and evaluation services for children admitted to Children's Hospital for possible physical abuse.

Tuscaloosa Children's Center
520 Martin Luther King, Jr Blvd
Tuscaloosa, AL 35401
205/752-7711
205/345-7297 (fax)
Director: Carol Somers
Medical Examiner: Michael A. Taylor, MD

The child advocacy center is home to a multidisciplinary team approach to child abuse evaluations. There are two sound proof interview rooms equipped with two-way mirrors and audiovisual recording capabilities. Workers from the Department of Human Resources and the Juvenile Division of the Tuscaloosa County Sheriff's Department interview most of their child witnesses and/or victims at the center. The assistant district attorney in charge of child abuse cases has an office on site as well as the director, her assistant, and a psychologist for evaluation and counseling. Dr Taylor performs the medical examinations. Team meetings are held every other Thursday at the center.

Arkansas

Program for Children at Risk
Arkansas Children's Hospital
800 Marshall St
Little Rock, AR 72202
501/320-1013
501/320-3939 (Fax)
Director: Jerry G. Jones, MD

Comprehensive programs for physically and sexually abused children and their families are under the Programs for Children at Risk. The Team for Children at Risk (TCAR), an evidentiary team, includes physicians, nurse practitioner, part-time psychologist, and master's level social workers. The physicians and nurse practitioner perform outpatient forensic evaluations of sexually abused children. Family assessments are provided by the social workers, and all the professionals provide crisis intervention. The TCAR also provides consultations on all hospitalized physically and sexually abused children. The Family Treatment Program provides long-term treatment of within-family child sexual abuse cases. Therapy is delivered by a multidisciplinary team of psychologists and social workers. The Adolescent Sexual Adjustment Project (ASAP) provides treatment for children and adolescents with sexual behavior disorders.

Arizona

The Child Abuse Assessment Center
124 W Thomas Road
Phoenix, AZ 85013
602/406-3621
Medical Director: Kay Rauth-Farley, MD
602/406-3716

This program provides clinical services which include videotaped forensic interviews of child victims, forensic medical exams for sexual and physical abuse, failure to thrive evaluations, and consultation on sexual exploitation cases. The child protection team provides multidisciplinary staffings weekly and upon request from other agencies as needed. The staff members of the center are from the Children's Justice Project training team, sponsored by the Arizona Governor's Division for Children. Free multidisciplinary trainings are available through this team for any community in the state upon request.

Maricopa Medical Center Child Advocacy Program
2601 E Roosevelt
PO Box 5099
Phoenix, AZ 85010
602/267-5404
602/267-5859 (Fax)
Director: Mary Rimsza, MD

This program is available to all children and adolescents in Maricopa County. Social service and psychology staff are also available. Multidisciplinary team consultations of complex cases which have had initial evaluations at other facilities can also be scheduled.

University of Arizona College of Medicine Dept of Pediatrics Evaluation Clinic
Tucson, AZ 85724
602/626-6303
Director: Anna Binkiewicz, MD

Twice weekly scheduled clinics for evaluation of physical or sexual abuse victims by a pediatrician and social worker are now conducted at the Southern Arizona Children's Advocacy Center (520/741-6931) at Kino Community Hospital. Emergency evaluations and inpatient consults are also performed.

California

Bates-Eldredge Clinic
Natividad Medical Center
PO Box 81611
Salinas, CA 93912-1611
408/769-8682
Director: Valerie Barnes, MD

This child sexual abuse clinic for Monterey County operates Monday through Friday and provides comprehensive evaluation and evidentiary interviewing of the child victim. Children are referred by the Multidisciplinary Interview Team (MDIT), which consists of social workers from the Department of Social Services-Family and Children's Services, investigators from the district attorney's office, and law enforcement officials. Consultation is also provided to community physicians. The program provides community and resident education, as well as expert witness services to the judicial process. Every effort is made to provide culturally sensitive, language appropriate services to the affected families.

Center for Child Protection
Children's Hospital Oakland
747 52nd St
Oakland, CA 94609
510/428-3742
Director: James Crawford, MD
          510/428-3885, ext 4644

The Center for Child Protection Clinic provides expert medical examination, case management and counseling to physically and sexually abused children. It is the designated facility in Alameda County for evaluation of all acute (<72 hours) and non-acute sexually abused children under the age of 15 years.

Center for Child Protection
Santa Clara Valley Medical Center
Department of Pediatrics
751 S Bascom Ave
San Jose, CA 95128
408/299-6460
408/885-5411 (Fax)
Director: David L. Kerns, MD
          408/858-5405
Coordinator: Mary Ritter, PA, CHA

A medical evaluation program focuses on comprehensive evaluation of suspected child sexual abuse victims. The principal features are "state of the art" medical exams, evidentiary interviewing, and a 24-hour response team. There is an active research component with analyzable data currently on 4,000 patients.

Child Abuse Crisis Center
Harbor/UCLA Medical Center
1000 W Carson St
Box 460
Torrance, CA 90509
310/222-3091
310/222-3567
Medical Directors: Carol Berkowitz, MD
                   James J. Williams, MD

This is a well-established program in child physical and sexual abuse and neglect. The team approach is utilized, and the staff includes physician and nurse practitioner examiners, psychologist, county child protection social workers, a

deputy district attorney, a program director, and clerical personnel. They work closely with law enforcement, the courts, mental health services, and the Department of Children and Family Services to provide high-quality interviews and evaluations. Extensive training in child maltreatment recognition and evaluation is also offered. Separate clinics provide for failing-to-thrive children, family support, and infants of substance abusing mothers. We are hoping to expand to include adult rape and family violence intervention.

Child Abuse and Neglect Team
Riverside General Hospital
9851 Magnolia Ave
Riverside, CA 92503
714/358-7561
Director: Rebecca Piantini, MD
          714/824-4304

A multidisciplinary team utilizes skills of physicians, social workers, occupational therapists, dieticians, and nurses in the evaluation of cases of suspected abuse. Cases are referred to the clinic from law enforcement agencies, child protective services, public health nurses, and occasional outside physicians. The clinic also provides referrals for ongoing counseling. Monthly meetings occur for training and educational purposes.

Child Abuse Services Team
401 City Dr South
Orange, CA 92668
714/935-6390
714/935-6171 (Fax)
Director: Cathy Singletary
          714/704-8100

CAST is a multidisciplinary child sexual abuse investigation team involving law enforcement, district attorney, child welfare services, medical examinations, child advocacy and victim services, and crisis intervention. Information and referral to community resources and professional education services are also an ongoing part of the program. Services are provided in a child friendly environment. As a public/private partnership, CAST receives funds from a variety of community groups and state grants. Law enforcement agencies pay for medical evaluations.

Child and Adolescent Sexual Abuse Referral Center (CASARC)

San Francisco General Hospital
1001 Potrero Ave
San Francisco, CA 94110
415/206-8386

Medical Director: Kevin Coulter, MD

CASARC performs medical interviews and examinations in suspected cases of sexual abuse.

Child Protection Center

Loma Linda University Medical Center
11262 Campus St, West Hall
Loma Linda, CA 92350
909/478-8242
909/824-4184 (Fax)

Director: Clare Sheridan, MD
Coordinator: Dodie Grovet, MSW

This hospital-based program has existed since 1981. Using a multidisciplinary approach, all forms of child abuse are evaluated. The team includes physicians, nurses, social workers, and therapists. There is a large treatment program, primarily funded through the Victims of Crime Program, providing therapy to children from ages three years and up. Referrals are primarily from law enforcement agencies, child protection services, and area physicians.

Child Protection Center

San Francisco General Hospital
1001 Potrero Ave
San Francisco, CA 94110
415/206-8772

Medical Director: Kevin Coulter, MD

All children in San Francisco County are sent to the Child Protection Center when there are concerns of physical and sexual abuse. When requested by law enforcement, physical examinations are performed to document cases of abuse.

Child Protection Center

University of California, Davis Medical Center
2521 Stockton Blvd
Sacramento, CA 95817
916/734-8396

Director: Marilyn Peterson, MSW, MPA
Medical Director: John McCann, MD
Associate Director: Angela Rosas, MD
916/734-3691

University of California, Davis Medical Center (UCDMC) is a primary, secondary, and tertiary care facility that serves Northern California. The child abuse program offers both medical and psychological consulting services for all forms of child abuse and neglect. As the medical training center for Northern California, the program offers training to health care providers, children protection service personnel, law enforcement officers, members of the District Attorney Association, and other members of the judicial system in child abuse; adult sexual assault evaluation, domestic violence identification and management, and the recognition and treatment of abused elders are included. Two major foci of the medical training center program will be the coordination of training efforts for the involved agencies and the establishment of telecommunication linkages with rural communities to provide consultative services along with educational programs.

Childhood Sexual Abuse Evaluation Program

University Medical Center
445 S Cedar Ave
Fresno, CA 93702
209/453-5758
209/453-3852 (Fax)

Director: Joan Voris, MD

The Childhood Sexual Abuse Evaluation Program provides comprehensive medical evaluations for children with suspected sexual abuse. A full-time coordinator, who is a pediatric nurse practitioner, is funded through a state program, child abuse prevention, intervention and treatment funds. The program currently conducts five one-half day clinics per week, with two physicians and two nurse practitioners as medical examiners. All patients are examined using a colposcope, and photos are taken and reviewed weekly.

The program provides community education, resident education, and expert witness testimony on sexual abuse cases for a six-county region. There is also an active research component.

Children's Hospital & Health Center
Center for Child Protection
3020 Children's Way
San Diego, CA 92123
619/576-5814, 619/576-5803
Director: Mark Horton, MD

This multidisciplinary health-based child abuse program has a professional staff of 30 and a well-developed program for assessment and treatment of abused children. Close ties to community agencies involved in child abuse work include social services, law enforcement, courts, prosecutors, county counseling, and others.

Children's Protection Center
Memorial Miller Children's Hospital
2801 Atlantic Ave
Long Beach, CA 90801-1426
213/595-2555
Director: Deborah Stewart, MD
213/595-2555

The Children's Protection Center is a multidisciplinary program. It is composed of the outpatient Children's Protection Center and the inpatient SCAN team. The center is charged with the investigation of suspected abuse and neglect of patients admitted to or referred to Miller Children's Hospital. A team is composed of a social worker, nurses, and representatives from psychiatry, dentistry, and medicine. It is also a police/DA/county counsel referral center for advice on cases of abuse already in the legal system.

Los Angeles County and University of Southern California Violence Intervention Program
Center for the Vulnerable Child
Sexual Assault Center
Domestic Violence Center
1240 N Mission Road, Trailer #11
Los Angeles, CA 90033
213/226-3961
Executive Director: Astrid H. Heger, MD

The LAC and USC Violence Intervention Program is a medically based program providing multidisciplinary interventions for all victims of child abuse and neglect, sexual assault, and domestic violence. Medical services are available seven days a week, 24 hours a day, given by professionals trained to provide appropriate diagnosis and treatment. Assessments are conducted in cooperation with social, legal, and mental health professionals and coordinated with community resources and shelters for follow-up care and safe housing. The Center for the Vulnerable Child (CVC), located at the Violence Intervention Program, is an internationally acclaimed child abuse intervention and prevention program. The CVC offers multidisciplinary medical/legal evaluations of suspected victims of child abuse with the capacity for a team approach coordinated with law enforcement, the district attorney's office, and the Department of Children's Services. Follow-up medical care, crisis intervention, and ongoing mental health services are also offered to the children and their parents. Since this program is based in a teaching hospital, extensive training in the area of the recognition, evaluation, documentation, and treatment of child sexual and physical abuse is also offered. The Sexual Assault Center Team provides quality clinical and forensic evaluations of all rape victims, regardless of age or gender. All patients are accompanied by a trained rape advocate and are provided with follow-up medical and mental health services. The Domestic Violence Center has introduced and implemented domestic violence protocols, training, treatment guidelines, a hospital hotline, medical outreach service for shelters, and a specialized follow-up clinic. Victims of domestic violence and their children are currently involved in individual and group counseling at the Violence Intervention Program.

Palomar Medical Center
555 E Valley Pkwy
Escondido, CA 92025
760/739-3800

Physician Director: Mary Spencer, MD

This is a multidisciplinary based child abuse program. Agencies involved are Child Protective Services, Escondido Police Department and other law enforcement offices, district attorneys, Escondido Youth Encounter, and other counseling programs. All sexual abuse patients are examined using a colposcope, and cases are reviewed monthly at a multidisciplinary meeting. The program also provides community education.

San Luis Obispo County Suspected Abuse Response Team
3433 S Higuera
PO Box 8119
San Luis Obispo, CA 93403-8113
805/781-1700
805/781-1701 (Fax)

Director: F. Schneider
            (805) 549-4896

The SART Program is responsible for the medical/legal evaluations of suspected victims of child abuse, adult sexual assault and forensic examinations of the alleged perpetrators. SART has been in existence for over ten years and serves as a model for the coordination and implementation of medical and support services to victims of abuse and assault. The team is composed of trained MDs and RNs who share a 24 hour on-call schedule and work together with law enforcement, child protective services, rape crisis volunteers, victim/witness personnel, the district attorney's staff, and the coroner's office. The services include identification, investigation, medical/legal examinations, treatment, and follow-up counseling. The examiners provide testimony in court and work closely with the judicial process. The services are performed expeditiously with consistency, objectivity, and compassion. The program is dedicated to the prevention of revictimization of the victims by the system's response.

SART Program
Pomerado Hospital
15615 Pomerado Rd
Poway, CA 92064
619/485-4455
619/485-4749 (Fax)

Clinical Coordinator: Diane Faugnau, RN
MD Consultant/Advisor: Mary Spencer, MD

The SART Program is responsible for the medical/legal evaluation of sexual assault victims 14 years and older and forensic examinations of the perpetrators. SART serves as a multidisciplinary model for the County of San Diego. This model program is staffed by forensic nurse examiners who provide the medical/legal examination, treatment, and follow-up examinations, as well as expert testimony in court. Video colposcopy is provided in this program. Annual training is conducted each January; call for information regarding these week-long seminars. Community education is also provided.

SART/SANE Program
Dominican Hospital
155 Soquel Dr
Room 1222
Santa Cruz, CA 95065
408/462-7744
408/462-7816 (Fax)

Director: Reggie Lopez, RN

The SART/SANE Program coordinates medical-legal exams on suspected child sexual abuse victims with law enforcement, Child Protective Services, and the district attorney's office. The team is comprised of a nurse examiner, law enforcement officer, an advocate, and a pediatrician as primary physical examiner. All physicians associated with the program are in private practice. Exams are usually scheduled and conducted at a special exam room in the hospital.

SCAN Team
Kaiser Walnut Creek
1425 S Main St
Walnut Creek, CA 94596
415/943-3491
Director: Walter Keller, MD

A child sexual abuse clinic meets one day each week. We perform medical interviews and medical examinations with colposcopic and photographic capabilities. Police, sheriff, and Children's Protective Service workers are responsible for the evidentiary interviews. Medical evaluations of acute cases are also performed. Mental health services are available for the victims and their families.

SCAN Team - Contra Costa Regional Medical Center
2500 Alhambra Ave
Martinez, CA 94553
415/370-5000 or 415/370-5490
Director: Jim Carpenter, MD, MPH
415/370-5000

The Contra Costa County SCAN Team has several functions. The SAM Clinic provides comprehensive evaluations of victims of child sexual abuse with interviews, review of accompanying records, medical exams with colposcopy, and screening for STDs. The SCAN Team conducts bimonthly meetings with physicians, social worker, and CPS supervisors to discuss cases referred by our hospital and clinics. SCAN Outreach provides education of hospital staff (MD, RN) in recognition, treatment, management, and reporting of child abuse/neglect. Affiliated programs:

1. Multidisciplinary Interview Center (MDIC) - Forensic interviews of child victims. Program in development.
2. SART (Sexual Abuse Response Teams) - Acute sexual abuse forensic examinations of children and adults by nurse examiners in community hospitals:

    SART Coordinator - Maria Ramirez
    510/307-4120
    Doctors Medical Center 510/235-7006
    Sutter Delta Hospital 510/779-7200

3. Contra Costa Child Death Review Team (DRT) - Multidisciplinary team reviews child deaths within Contra Costa County. 510/946-9961. Child Abuse Prevention Council.
4. Child Abuse Systems Review Committee - Multidisciplinary team reviews and investigates the child abuse system within Contra Costa County and reports on an annual basis to the county supervisors. Case review and consultation are provided. 510/946-9961. Child Abuse Prevention Council.

SCAN Team
Naval Medical Center San Diego
Department of Pediatrics
34800 Bob Wilson Dr
San Diego, CA 92134-5000
Consultants: Susan Horowitz, MD
619/532-6929
CDR Kathleen Dully
760/725-0390

This multidiscipline program offers extensive evaluation of children presenting with possible non-accidental trauma. We work closely with Navy Family Advocacy, as well as Child Protective Services and law enforcement.

Talbert Medical Group
818 W Alondra Blvd
Compton, CA 90220
310/537-1337
Director: Lillie M. Lewis Williams, MD
562/496-4900

The Compton Clinic, located in South Central Los Angeles, offers medical and counseling services, the latter provided by psychiatric social workers. Children Services workers or police are contacted when necessary.

UCLA Children's Hospital
10833 LeConte Ave
Los Angeles, CA 90095-1752
310/825-6301
Coordinator: Nancy Hayes, LCSW
Medical Director: Claudia Wang, MD
310/794-7259

A multidisciplinary consultation team provides interviews and medical evaluations of physical and sexual abuse cases, the latter with colposcopy. It is a resource to community agencies, with ongoing training for the Department of Children and Family Services, county counsel, legal counsel, and dependency court judges.

Canada

Child Protection Service Unit
BC Children's Hospital
4480 Oak St
Vancouver, BC V6H3V4
CANADA
604/875-2345
Director: Lois J. Hlady, MD
604/875-2130

This program provides medical and social diagnosis and assessment to professionals in cases of alleged child abuse and neglect. Hospital inpatient and outpatient referrals are accepted. Education is provided to physicians, other staff, and residents.

Hospital Child Abuse Committee
Sarnia General Hospital
220 Mitton St North
Sarnia, Ontario
CANADA
519/383-8180
Director: Kunwar R. Singh, MD, FRCP
519/336-6311

This program provides medical and other services to maltreated children and their families.

Suspected Child Abuse and Neglect (SCAN) Program
Hospital for Sick Children
555 University Ave
Toronto, Ontario M5G 1X8
CANADA
416/813-6275
416/813-5846 (Fax)
Web Page:
http://www.sickkids.on.ca/HSCWeb/SCAN/SCAN proHomepage.HTML
Medical Director: Marcellina Mian, MD, FRCPC
416/813-5794
marcellina.mian
@mailhub.sickkids.on.ca
(E-mail)

The Suspected Child Abuse and Neglect (SCAN) Program at the Hospital for Sick Children, affiliated with the University of Toronto, is one of the largest hospital-based child maltreatment programs in Canada. It is a multidisciplinary team whose members include pediatricians, a general practitioner, social workers, an art therapist, and a nurse. Team members provide care for children, from birth to 18 years of age, and their families when any form of child abuse or neglect is suspected. Services include medical and psychosocial assessment, as well as treatment. Program members provide consultation to the hospital staff, community health professionals, child protection agencies, law enforcement, legal personnel, and other community agencies. The program is also active in educational and policy development endeavors at the local, national, and international level. Clinicians are involved in research into various aspects of child maltreatment.

Child Advocacy and Assessment Program
Hamilton Health Sciences Corporation
1200 Main St West
Hamilton, Ontario L8N 3Z5
CANADA
Director: Harriet MacMillan, MD
905/521-2100, ext 3268

The program provides assessment, diagnosis and management to children and families when any aspect of child maltreatment is an issue. Inpatient and outpatient referrals are accepted. The overall aim of the program is to reduce the burden of suffering associated with child maltreatment through clinical, educational, and research activities. The program is affiliated with the Centre for Studies of Children at Risk.

Colorado

C. Henry Kempe National Center for the Prevention & Treatment of Child Abuse & Neglect
1825 Marion St
Denver, CO 80218
303/321-3963
303/329-3523 (Fax)
Director: Susan Hiatt, PhD

This multidisciplinary center has 30 staff members in pediatrics, psychiatry, law, developmental and clinical psychology, and social work, as well as volunteers and lay staff. It operates eight programs on local, statewide, national, and international levels. Activities include model program development, clinical consultation and training, research, and provision of services to children and families. It is also the site of the editorial offices of *Child Abuse & Neglect, The International Journal.* A program brochure is available on request.

Child Advocacy and Protection Team
The Children's Hospital
1056 East 19th Ave, B138
Denver, CO 80218
303/861-6919
303/837-2791 (Fax)
Director: Andrew Sirotnak, MD

A shared program of The Children's Hospital and The Kempe National Center, this multidisciplinary team is comprised of pediatricians, psychologist, physician's assistant, and hospital-based social workers. The team provides forensic medical evaluations and evidence collection for children with suspected physical and sexual abuse injuries, failure to thrive, and all forms of neglect. Colposcopy is performed in the outpatient child protection team clinic. An organized training program in child abuse exists for medical students and residents. A one- to two-year fellowship program

is offered for board certified or board eligible pediatricians. The team participates in local child fatality review, provides expert consultation to law enforcement, child welfare agencies, and courts in a three-state region, and is involved in research in many areas of child abuse and neglect.

Connecticut

DART Committee
Yale-University School of Medicine
Department of Pediatrics
333 Cedar St
New Haven, CT 06520-8065
203/785-2468
203/785-3932 (Fax)
Director: John M. Leventhal, MD

The DART Committee is a multidisciplinary hospital-based committee that meets weekly to review cases of child maltreatment and high risk social situations that are seen at Yale-New Haven Hospital. In addition, the sexual abuse clinic (pediatrician, two nurse practitioners, and three social workers) evaluates children suspected of having been sexually abused.

Hospital of Saint Raphael
Emergency Department
1450 Chapel St
New Haven, CT 06511
203/789-3464
203/789-3600 (Fax)
Director: Kenneth Fine, MD

The emergency department, in cooperation with the social service department, provides medical and psychosocial evaluations to victims of child abuse/neglect and their families. The medical team diagnoses and treats the physical signs of abuse/neglect and arranges medical follow-up upon discharge. The social worker assesses the family's strengths, stressors, and conflicts. In all cases of documented abuse/neglect, a report is made to DCYS for social follow-up. Other community referrals may be made, and continued contact with the hospital social worker is usually encouraged.

Milford Hospital Emergency Department
300 Sea Side Ave
Milford, CT 06460
203/876-4100
203/876-4128 (Fax)
Director: Jay Walshon, MD
        (Director, Emergency Medicine)

This community hospital emergency department is frequently the resource for first contact in cases involving abuse/neglect. Professionals assess patients who are abused/neglected and work with a state agency (DCYS) for disposition, utilizing a formalized protocol. All cases are referred to the hospital social services department and other community resources as appropriate.

District of Columbia

Children's National Medical Center
Division of Child Protection
111 Michigan Ave, NW
Washington, DC 20010
202/884-4100
202/884-6997 (Fax)
Acting Director: Lavdena Orr, MD

A multidisciplinary hospital-based team provides medical, psychological and psychosocial assessments; medical follow up; forensic exams; and mental health treatment. Court testimony and parenting education services are offered. Collaborative efforts are with the criminal and civil judicial system, as well as multijurisdictional child protective services.

Waterbury Regional Child Abuse
Investigation Team
56 Franklin St
Waterbury, CT 06779
203/575-7041
Medical Director: Cheryl Outland, MD
Coordinator: Linda Foster, MSW

This community-based investigation team consists of physician, social workers, psychologist, regional district of state DCF, local police departments, and regional prosecutor.

Florida

Brevard County Child Protection Team
1260 S US 1, Suite 203
Rockledge, FL 32903
407/632-7107
Director: Donald H. Arnold, MD
        Richard K. O'Hern, MD, FAAP
        407/636-3066

The Child Protection Team of Brevard County assists the Florida Department of Health and Rehabilitative Services (HRS) in the diagnosis and treatment of child abuse and neglect and development of coordinated services and treatment plans for children and their families. CPT also provides training and education for the community in all aspects of child abuse and neglect and actively participates in community efforts on behalf of abused children.

Center for Children in Crisis
1720 E Tiffany Dr
Suite 101
Mangonia Park, FL 33407-3223
407/863-1611
Director: Lawrence R. Leviton, MD
        407/832-1139

The program is divided into two separate components.
1. Case finding: four master's degree social workers evaluate cases and provide appropriate disposition or an investigation, staffing, etc.
2. Treatment program: four full-time and six part-time therapists treat victim, spouse, siblings, and perpetrators.

Child Protection Team
Children's Advocacy Center
344 S Beach St
Daytona Beach, FL 32114
904/238-3830
Director: Michael Bell, MD
        904/734-1824

The Child Protection Team utilizes a multidisciplinary approach to helping children who have been sexually abused. Victims are referred by law enforcement or the Department of Children & Families. Services include videotaped forensic interviews of the victims, medical exams and consultations, case coordination, and counseling referrals. This team also serves victims of severe physical abuse and failure to thrive.

Child Protection Team
2012 Lisenby Ave
Suite A
Panama City, FL 32405
904/763-8449

Director: Malcolm M. Traxler, MD
904/763-5413

Our Child Protection team is a multidisciplinary team established to protect children from abuse and help prevent abuse. It assists the state children-youth and families protective investigators by providing medical and psychological evaluations, as well as social evaluations by our case coordinators. Case coordinators do "one strike" videotaped interviews with the children, with representatives of other agencies present. Multidisciplinary staffings of cases, child abuse presentations, and educational work are provided.

Child Protection Team
1750 17th St
Sarasota, FL 34234
813/365-1277

Director: Hal Hedley

The CMS Child Protection Team of Sarasota and DeSoto Counties is a medical model team. The heart of the team is the multidisciplinary staffing model used to help to direct cases of child abuse and neglect toward an appropriate treatment plan. Case coordinators conduct video-taped interviews of children and perform social assessments. Team physicians provide medical D&Es, and contract psychologists perform evaluations.

Child Protection Team
820 E Park Ave, Building I
Tallahassee, FL 32301
850/487-2838

Director: Sam Moorer, MD
850/877-6119

Child Protection Team, Satellite 1A
4400 Bayon Blvd
Suite 21
Pensacola, FL 32503

Director: Neil McWilliams, MD

A multidisciplinary team provides services to abused and neglected children and their families.

Child Protection Team-District 6A
Manatee Children's Services
1101 Sixth Ave West
Bradenton, FL 34205
941/746-1904

Medical Director: Jerome H. Isaac, MD

A multidisciplinary team provides assessment activities to Department of Children and Families child abuse investigations. The team consists of a pediatrician, psychologist, attorney, and case coordinators. Services include medical evaluations, videotaped forensic interviews, staffings, psycho-social assessments, court testimony, case coordination and referrals. CPT also provides training and education for the community in aspects of child abuse and neglect.

Child Protection Team, District 7A
340 Beal Pkwy
Ft Walton Beach, FL 32548
850/833-3846

Director: Lynn M. Keefe, MD

A multidisciplinary team provides services to abused and neglected children and their families.

Child Protection Team-District 7A
Arnold Palmer Hospital
For Children & Women
92 West Miller St
Orlando, FL 32806
407/317-7430
407/843-9027 (Fax)

Director: Matthew Seibel, MD
407/317-7430

A multidisciplinary team provides services to abused and neglected children and their families, including physical and sexual abuse medical evaluations and psychological treatment of sexual abuse victims.

Child Protection Team - District VIII-B
3900 Broadway
Suite B-1
Fort Myers, FL 33901
941/939-2808
Medical Director: John Ritrosky, Jr, MD
J.W. Bartlett, MD

This multidisciplinary team provides services to abused and neglected children and their families.

Child Protection Team-District 10
(Sexual Assault Treatment Center)
400 Northeast 4th St
Fort Lauderdale, FL 33301
954/765-4159
Medical Director: Penny Grant, MD

The Broward County Child Protection Team is a medically directed multidisciplinary team. This team consists of a medical director, team supervisor, psychologist, nurse practitioner, lawyer, social worker, and six master's level mental health professionals. The program receives referrals from the Department of Children and Families, law enforcement, and the Dependency Court. It provides a variety of assessment activities to address the validity of abuse allegations and to identify risk factors and interventions for reducing the risk of further abuse and neglect. The assessment activities provided include medical examinations, medical consultations, specialized interviews, family assessments, psychological evaluations, multi-disciplinary team staffings, case review, and expert court testimony. The team also provides training on the dynamics, prevention, and treatment of child abuse/neglect.

Child Protection Team of the Children's Crisis Center, Inc University Medical Center
655 W Eighth St
Jacksonville, FL 32209
904/366-2444
Director: J. M. Whitworth, MD
904/366-2456
CPT Medical Director: Bruce McIntosh, MD
904/387-7373

This program utilizes a crisis-oriented, multidisciplinary team approach for assessment and evaluation of abused/neglected children and their families.

The team is composed of pediatricians, psychologist, attorney, and case coordinators with varying backgrounds. A team case coordinator and pediatrician are available 24 hours a day to provide crisis intervention, case coordination, family system evaluation, medical/forensic examination, and legal and psychological evaluation. The team remains involved with the family through resolution of the case.

Child Protection Team of Collier County
2500 Airport Rd
Suite 308
Naples, FL
813/263-2858
Director: Richard E. Marting, MD

Child Protection Team is a multidisciplinary crisis-oriented approach to the identification and treatment of child abuse and neglect. The team is composed of an executive director, three case coordinators, and a secretary. Services provided include, medical diagnosis and evaluation, evidentiary interviews of alleged victims, assessments of family dynamics, case staffings and written treatment plans, psychological evaluations, assessments and sexual abuse validation, crisis counseling, court testimony, case coordination, and referrals. Staff also provides training for professionals and the community at large in the dynamics, treatment, and prevention of child abuse and neglect.

Community Health of South Dade-Protection Team
10300 SW 216 St
Miami, FL 33190
305/252-4822
Director: Barbara Lew, MD
Phyllis Harriet

This program consists of one physician and three social workers. It provides medical and psychological evaluation of children involved in sexual abuse, physical abuse, medical and physical neglect, emotional abuse, and failure to thrive. It also provides family assessment. Lectures and workshops are given to schools and hospitals in the surrounding area. The program serves as liaison between the community and the Department of Health and Rehabilitation Services.

HRS-CMS District III, Child Protection Team
University of Florida
5700 SW 34th St
Suite 1310
Gainesville, FL 32608
904/392-7286
Director: F. Thomas Weber, MD, FAAP
904/392-5960

This medically based, multidisciplinary program provides consultative evaluations of children and families suspected of having abused and neglected children as well as children failing to thrive. Serving the 16 counties of HRS District 3 in North Central Florida, it is 1 of 22 such teams providing services throughout the state, linked by a common program, direction, and ongoing education. Professionals provide expert court testimony, psychological and medical evaluations, and family evaluations. The program is linked to a pediatric residency training program with continuous monthly pediatric resident rotations.

Pasco Family Protection Team
7619 Little Rd
Suite 325 Counsel Square
New Port Richey, FL 34654
813/848-4878
Director: Andrew Gellady, MD

Child protection team of Pasco County is one of many local teams set up by Child Protection Team of Florida. The team consists of medical directors, examining physicians, intake people, investigators, psychologists, etc.

Suncoast Child Protection Team, Inc
3601 34th St, North
St Petersburg, FL 33713
813/527-5955
813/526-4674 (Fax)
Director: Patricia Wallace

This multidisciplinary child abuse crisis program is administered by Suncoast Child Protection Team, Inc under a state appropriated grant through the Department of Health and Rehabilitative Services/Children's Medical Services. The grant provides funds for a medical director, social workers, and nurses on staff, as well as purchase of medical, psychological, psychiatric, and legal services. Another service provided is the Medical Placement Home Program, which provides short-term foster placements to children with medical needs.

University of Miami
Child Protection Team (District 11N)
1150 NW 14th St - Suite 212
Miami, FL 33136
305/243-7550
Director: Walter F. Lambert, MD

University of Miami
Child Protection Team (District 11S)
17400 SW 97th Ave
Miami, FL 33157
305/234-2298
Director: Walter F. Lambert, MD

University of Miami
Child Protection Team (District 11K)
175 Wren St
Tavernier, FL 33070
305/853-3526
Director: Walter F. Lambert, MD

The University of Miami Child Protection Team is an interdisciplinary team comprised of pediatricians, ARNP, nurses, psychologists, social workers, and case coordinators providing services in Dade and Monroe County. The program is divided into two separate components. The first component provides medical, psychological, and psychosocial assessments to children who are alleged victims of physical, sexual, and emotional abuse. The team is available 24 hours a day, seven days a week. The purpose of these assessments is to assist the Department of Children and Families in their investigation of the alleged abuse and to provide recommendations to minimize the risk of re-abuse. The second component provides medical and psychological assessments to children removed from their homes as a result of an abuse allegation. The purpose of these assessments is to identify the medical and psychological needs of the child and assist the Department of Children and Families in placement decisions.

State of Florida
Child Protection Teams

The Child Protection Team uses a crisis-oriented, multidisciplinary approach for the evaluation and treatment of the abused and neglected child and family. Teams act as a consultant resource to primary investigators of allegations of abuse. It is recognized that families in need of assistance must have access to resources from medical, social services, legal and psychological components to address the multifaceted problems they face, and to develop a broad and similarly multifaceted plan for appropriate treatment.

J. M. Whitworth, MD
Professor of Pediatrics
University of Florida

Medical Director
Child Protection Teams
State of Florida
PO Box 40279
Jacksonville, FL 32203-0279
904/549-4670

District 1A
Neil McWilliams, MD
Team Medical Director

Pam Schuster
Team Coordinator
Northwest Florida Comprehensive Services
    for Children, Inc
4400 Bayou Blvd, Suite 21
Pensacola, FL 32503
904/474-0244
904/474-0131 (Fax)

District 1B
Lynn M. Keefe, MD
Team Medical Director

Cathy Cheung
Team Coordinator
340 Beal Pkwy
Fort Walton Beach, FL 32548
904/833-3846
904/833-3848 (Fax)

District 2A
Ingrid Rachesky, MD
Team Medical Director

Vickie Olsen
Team Coordinator
Child Protection Team
229 Harrison Ave
Panama City, FL 32401

District 2B
Samuel H. Moorer, Jr, MD
Team Medical Director

Elizabeth Jackson
Team Coordinator
Child Protection Team, S 100
820 E Park Ave, Building I
Tallahassee, FL 32303
904/487-2838

Districts 3 and 13
Howard L. Rogers, MD
Team Medical Director

James G. Spencer
Team Coordinator
Child Protection Team
1701 SW 16th Ave
Gainesville, FL 32608
352/334-1300
352/334-1521 (Fax)

District 4
Bruce J. McIntosh, MD
Team Medical Director

Lisa Murphy
Team Coordinator
Children's Crisis Center, Inc
PO Box 40279
Jacksonville, FL 32203-0279
904/549-4670
904/549-4675 (Fax)

District 5A

Mark Morris, MD
Team Medical Director

Patsy Buker, EdS
Team Coordinator
Suncoast Child Protection Team, Inc.
3601 - 34th St N, Suite 200
St Petersburg, FL 33713
813/527-5955
813/526-4675 (Fax)

District 5B

Vacant
Team Medical Director

Richard Hess
Team Coordinator
Pasco Family Protection Team, Inc
7511 Little Rd, Building C
New Port Richey, FL 34654-5531
813/845-8080
813/848-1292

District 6

Laleh Bahar-Posey, MD
Team Medical Director

Sandra Herskowitz
Team Coordinator
Child Protection Team
1 Davis Blvd, Suite 404
Tampa, FL 33606
813/251-8007
813/254-5771 (Fax)

District 6A

Jerome H. Isaac, MD
Team Medical Director

Libby Maginness
Team Coordinator
Manatee Children's Services, Inc
1101 6th Ave West, Suite 218
Bradenton, FL 34205
941/476-1904
941/746-1684 (Fax)

District 7A

Matthew A. Seibel, MD
Team Medical Director

Marie Martinez
Acting Team Coordinator
Child Protection Team
1717 S Orange Ave, Suite 200
Orlando, FL 32806
407/317-7430, ext 102
407/843-9027 (Fax)

District 7B

Richard K. O'Hern, MD
Donald H. Arnold, MD
Team Medical Directors

Judy Wood
Team Coordinator
Child Protection Team
3101 Suntree Blvd
Rockledge, FL 32955
407/259-1883
407/259-1916 (Fax)

District 8A

Katherine Keeley, MD
Team Medical Director

Hal Hedley, PhD
Team Coordinator
Child Protection Center, Inc.
1750 - 17th St, BL
Sarasota, FL 34234
941/365-1277
941/366-1849 (Fax)

District 8B

John Bartlett, MD
Team Medical Director

Jill L. Turner
Team Coordinator
Child Protection Team
3900 Broadway, Suite B-1
Fort Myers, FL 33901
941/939-2808
941/939-4794 (Fax)

District 8C

Barbara Rumberger, MD
Team Medical Director

Jackie Stephens
Team Coordinator
Collier City Child Advocacy Council, Inc.
1034 - 6th Ave North
Naples, FL 33940
941/263-8383
941/263-7931 (Fax)

District 9

Philip Colaizzo, MD
Team Medical Director

Alison Hitchcock
Team Coordinator
2840 6th Ave South
Lake Worth, FL 33461
561/433-0060
561/357-9622 (Fax)

District 10

Penny Grant, MD
Team Medical Director

Maria Juarez
Team Coordinator
Child Protection Team
400 NE 4th St
Fort Lauderdale, FL 33301
954/765-4159
954/765-4075 (Fax)

District 11

Walter Lambert, MD
Team Medical Director

Silvia Torres
Team Coordinator
Child Protection Team
1150 NW 14th St, Suite 212
Miami, FL 33136
305/243-7550
305/243-7548 (Fax)

Phyllis Harriet
Team Coordinator
17400 SW 97th Ave
Miami, FL 33157
305/234-2298
305/234-2297 (Fax)

Elizabeth Logan
Child Protection Team
2796 Overseas Hwy
Marathon, FL 33050
305/289-2684
305/289-2686 (Fax)

District 12

Michael Bell, MD
Team Medical Director

Karen Vogt
Team Coordinator
Child Protection Team
PO Box 11109
Daytona Beach, FL 32120-1109
904/238-3830
904/238-3831 (Fax)

District 14

Pedro Montanez, MD
Team Medical Director

Michele Hewitt
Team Coordinator
1260 Golfview Ave
Bartow, FL 33830
941/299-7476
941/294-7101 (Fax)

District 15

Randall deB Bertolette, MD
Team Medical Director

Kerry Bartley
Team Coordinator
Child Protection Team
2274 N US Highway 1
Fort Pierce, FL 34946-8914
(561) 489-5601
(561) 489-5604 (Fax)

Georgia

**Backus Children's Hospital at
Memorial Medical Center, Inc**
4700 Waters Ave
PO Box 23089
Savannah, GA 31403-3089
912/350-8016
Medical Director: Edwin Sheppard, MD
Evaluators: Lynn A. Platt, MD
　　　　　　Donna L. Evens, MD

This program is housed in the outpatient center.
Children are referred by various county agencies
and physicians for outpatient evaluation of alleged
abuse. Children are evaluated by consultation in
the inpatient setting. The program uses Coastal
Children's Advocacy Center for videotaped interviews. Acute and chronic counseling is available
through the community education services.

The Child Advocacy Center
Scottish Rite Children's Medical Center
1001 Johnson Ferry Rd
Atlanta, GA 30342
404/250-2674
Medical Director: Terese M. DeGrandi, MD
Director: Laura Eubanks, LCSW

The Child Advocacy Center team specializes in
expert medical examination and forensic interview of possible child victims of sexual abuse in
which the incident occurred more than 72 hours
previously. The center serves the entire state of
Georgia and referrals are accepted from public
service authorities, physicians, and mental health
professionals. The center sees patients by appointment only. The team is comprised of three pediatricians, a social worker, two nurses, and child life
specialists. Referrals are coordinated with outside
agencies for psychological services. The Child
Advocacy Center provides education for health
care providers and the community in both
prevention and diagnosis.

Child Protection Program
Egleston Children's Hospital at Emory University
1600 Tullie Cir
Atlanta, GA 30329
404/638-1944
Director: Nancy N. Fajman, MD, MPH

Inpatient consultation on cases of suspected abuse
or neglect is offered. An outpatient referral clinic
is also provided for the evaluation of possible
maltreatment. Colposcopic exams are performed
in sexual abuse evaluations. Multidisciplinary
cooperation with law enforcement, Child Protective Services, and the local Child Advocacy Center
is a primary goal, and weekly team meetings are
organized by the Child Protection Program. Chart
review and court testimony are given as needed.
Training in abuse evaluation is provided for pediatric residents; a child abuse elective is offered.
Professional education is also provided to local
practitioners and other non-medical community
professionals.

**Crescent House - The Center for the
Prevention of Child Abuse**
Medical Center of Central Georgia
777 Hemlock St
Box 6000, Hospital Box 31
Macon, GA 31208
912/633-7044
912/633-2780
912/633-7043 (Fax)
912/633-5142 (Fax)
Medical Director: Lowell Clark, MD
Director: Dee Simms

Crescent House, a service of The Children's Hospital at the Medical Center of Central Georgia, is
a participating advocacy center within the Georgia
network of Children's Advocacy Centers. The
primary goal is to insure the safety and well-being
of the children in the community. Crescent House
provides a child-friendly environment for children
suspected of having been abused. Specially trained
medical personnel conduct colposcopic exams in
a much less traumatizing environment than the
typical emergency room, where these children
traditionally have been seen. Specially trained
forensic examiners conduct interviews with children suspected of having been sexually, physically,
or emotionally abused. Referrals for mental health

treatment are routinely made as a part of each case, because the total well-being of the child is of utmost importance. Crescent House is working with other members of the community to design and implement many child abuse prevention programs.

Dooly Medical Center
Union St
Vienna, GA 31092
912/268-4141
Director: Larry Anderson

Dooly Medical Center is capable of treating all types of sexual and/or physical abuse. Due to its small size, if an illness or injury is very severe, patients are transferred to a larger hospital in a larger city.

Family Protective Services
The Children's Medical Center
Medical College of Georgia
1120 15th St
Augusta, GA 30912
706/721-1433
Director: Maureen O. Claiborne, MD
706/774-8985

This is a comprehensive program for evaluation of all forms of child physical abuse and neglect.

University Hospital
1350 Walton Way
Augusta, GA 30910
706/774-8985
Educational Coordinator,
Pediatrics: Maureen O. Claiborne, MD

This inclusive program that covers evaluation and treatment of all forms of child abuse and neglect. It serves as a multi-county referral area for child sexual abuse evaluations.

Hawaii

Kapl'olani Child Protection Center
Kapiolani Medical Center for Women
and Children
55 Merchant St, 22nd Floor
Honolulu, HI 96813
808/535-7700
808/535-7722 (Fax)
Director: Steven J. Choy, PhD

The multidisciplinary center provides consultation for Hawaii's Department of Human Services, Child Protection Services Section. It provides medical, clinical nursing, psychological and social work consultation, and related services to the State CPS Child Welfare Services workers. It also provides mental health treatment services to victims of child maltreatment and their families and assists in coordinating medical and mental health services to children in foster care. The center services about 1,500 cases per year and assists in diagnosis, treatment recommendations, and coordination of necessary services for these cases. It is responsible for completing a diagnostic and discharge team conference for all children hospitalized due to suspected child maltreatment. The center also is the Pacific regional training center for pediatric residents, post- and pre-doctoral psychology residents, psychiatry residents, nursing and public health students, and social work students. Continuing educational services for community professionals are provided on all of the major islands of the Hawaiian chain.

Idaho

CARES Program
St Lukes R.M.C
190 E Bammock
Bosie, ID 83712
208/386-3063
208/381-3222
Director: Tom Cornwall, MD
Program Director: Julie Canthon

CARES provides comprehensive and credible evaluations of children of alleged sexual abuse by videotaped interviews and medical examinations with pelvic photocolposcopy. This service is provided for counties in southwest Idaho in a centralized and neutral manner. Children are referred by Child Protection caseworkers and/or detectives from law enforcement agencies. CARES evaluations are accepted as a standardized medical method for providing forensic evidence required for prosecution and court process in the Boise area.

Illinois

Child Protection Team - Carle Clinic
Carle Clinic
602 W University Ave
Urbana, IL 61801
217/337-3100
Director: Kathleen Buetow, MD
217/337-3100

Multidisciplinary evaluations for suspected abuse and neglect include interview of victims by physician and social worker, physical examination, and appropriate laboratory studies. Follow up is available. The program interacts with local Department of Children and Family Services, state attorney's office, and police departments.

Columbus Hospital Child Protection Center
An Affiliate of Catholic Health Partners
2520 N Lakeview
Chicago, IL 60614
773/388-5661
Director: Emalee G. Flaherty, MD

The Columbus Hospital Child Protection Center provides interdisciplinary services to child victims of sexual abuse and their families. These services include forensic medical examinations, psychosocial assessments, victim sensitive interviews, and follow-up services including mental health services. Children are referred to the center by law enforcement agencies, child protective services, and other professionals in the community. The center staff works in the community to promote prevention, identification, and awareness of child sexual abuse. The center is a full member of the National Network of Children's Advocacy Centers.

The Division of Child Protective Services at Cook County Children's Hospital
700 S Wood St
Chicago, IL 60612
312/633-7130
312/633-7649 (Fax)

The Division of Child Protective Services at Cook County Children's Hospital provides coordinated multidisciplinary evaluations to all children presenting to the hospital who are suspected of, or identified as being victims of child abuse and/or neglect. The division provides evaluations on both an inpatient and outpatient basis. Staff consists of pediatricians, social workers, child psychologists, pediatric developmental and nutritional professionals, and an administrative assistant. Children evaluated include but are not limited to those with physical abuse, neglect, failure to thrive, emotional abuse, and sexual abuse. The division maintains active liaisons with the Department of Children and Family Services, Chicago Police, Cook County States Attorney, and the Office of the Public Guardian. It is a member of the Victim Sensitive Interview Program Hospital Partnership, providing medical examinations and coordinated interviews to victims of child sexual abuse. In addition, Child Protective Services maintains a weekly follow-up clinic where ongoing medical, psychosocial, and developmental care of children evaluated by the program continues. Child Protective Services functions as an educational resource regarding issues of child abuse/neglect to other health care providers, law enforcement and legal professionals, social service providers, and the community.

Pediatric Ecology Program
Grant Hospital
550 W Webster St
Chicago, IL 60614
773/883-3555
773/883-3882 (Fax)
Director: Howard B. Levy, MD

This program consists of a pediatric Ecology Unit (child psychiatry, behavioral, developmental, inpatient pediatric assessment, and "short-term" treatment unit); Behavioral Guidance Center (child psychiatry, behavioral, developmental, outpatient pediatric assessment, treatment unit); and a Center for sleep disorders. Disorders/problems targeted include child abuse and neglect, school avoidance/performance problems, sleep disorders, eating disorders, enuresis/encopresis, developmental delays, mental retardation, anxiety, conduct and separation related disorders, divorce and custody issues, situational crises, home placement problems, thought and dissociative disorders, failure to thrive and other nutrition related disorders, psychosomatic disorders, and behavioral/psychological diseases associated with chronic illnesses and handicapping conditions.

Pediatric Resource Center
530 NE Glen Oak Ave
Peoria, IL 61637
Contact: Kay L. Saving, MD
309/655-3640

The center serves abused and neglected children through comprehensive medical examinations, complete medical documentation, case coordination, and staffings with other professionals. Staff includes a master's degree social worker and several pediatricians with special training in the examination of sexually abused children. The center staff has a commitment to provide comprehensive physical examinations to abused and neglected children. It has an equally important commitment to work with other professionals in combating and preventing child maltreatment through a joint effort to take ownership of cases, share information, combine resources, and cooperate when court intervention is necessary. The Pediatric Resource Center will also provide educational opportunities to the community on areas of child maltreatment through the sponsorship of conferences and seminars, as well as being responsive to individual inquiries.

Protective Service Team
Children's Memorial Hospital
2300 Children's Plaza, #16
Chicago, IL 60614
773/880-4322
773/281-4237 (Fax)
Director: Emalee G. Flaherty, MD

The Protective Service Team was established in 1970 to improve detection, evaluation, and intervention services for children who may have been abused or neglected. This multidisciplinary team includes pediatricians, radiologists, social workers, a child life therapist, a child protective services representative, and other medical specialists and professionals involved in the evaluation of a particular child. This team provides consultations on inpatients and outpatients. At twice weekly staff meetings, all children evaluated during the previous week are discussed in detail by the various disciplines. In collaboration with the Columbus Hospital Child Protection Center, children who may have been sexually abused receive a victim-sensitive interview and a forensic medical exam using colposcopy. This Protective Service Team provides training for medical students, residents, faculty, and other community professionals involved in the care of children. With strong hospital advocacy support, the team works for improved services and interventions for children. It is committed to researching different aspects of child abuse and neglect and contributing new information that will assist in the prevention, detection and care of children who have been abused or neglected.

University of Chicago:
The Combined LaRabida and University of Chicago Children's Hospital Child Abuse and Neglect Team

LaRabida Children's Hospital and Research Center
East 65th St at Michigan
Chicago, IL 60649
773/363-6700
Director: Paula K. Jaudes, MD

University of Chicago Children's Hospital
Child Protective Service Team
5839 S Maryland Ave
Chicago, IL 60637
773/702-3578 (Voice Mail)
773/702-9087 (Section of Emergency
Medicine Office)
773/702-4900 (Child Protective Service Office)
Medical Director: Jill Glick, MD

The Combined LaRabida-University of Chicago Children's Hospital Child Abuse and Neglect Team provides interdisciplinary services designed to address the multiple, often complex needs of abused and neglected children and their families

The program is comprehensive in that it provides care for acutely ill children requiring inpatient care at the University of Chicago Children's Hospital, and inpatient and outpatient specialized evaluative and treatment services based at LaRabida Children's Hospital and Research Center. Specific services based at LaRabida include the following: expert interviewing through the Victim Sensitve Interview Project (VSIP) and counseling services for victims and their families; a special medical and psychosocial clinic for sexually abused children; training for foster parents and community agencies working with foster parents; a Permanency Planning Program to promote stable foster care placements and to reunify children with their biological families; information, education, and training programs for professionals and community groups; consultation to health care professionals, social service agencies, schools and law enforcement agencies.

Indiana

Child Protection Program
Indiana University
Department of Pediatrics
1001 W 10th St; Bryce B2109
Indianapolis, IN 46202
317/692-2377
Director: Roberta Ann Hibbard, MD
      317/630-2617

Patient care is in the form of psychosocial and medical evaluations (with colposcopy) for alleged sexual abuse victims, seen by referral with scheduled and emergent visits. Psychiatry and gynecology consults are available. Medical evaluations are also provided for physical abuse and neglect. Court testimony is given when needed. Educational programs include community professional education and consultation and student and resident clinical rotations. Research includes ongoing studies of examination findings, behavioral and child-rearing issues, and health status.

Pediatric Advocates
285 W 12th
Peru, IN 46970
317/472-4356
317/471-4401 (Fax)
Director: Neil J. Stalker, MD
317/472-4356

A private practice site receives referrals from social services departments as well as private referrals. A clinical social worker (ASCW) provides counseling. Referrals come from an eight-county area.

Iowa

Child Protection Center
St Lukes Hospital
1026 A Ave NE
Cedar Rapids, IA 52402
319/369-7908
319/369-8726 (Fax)
Director: Kathleen Opdebeeck, MD, FAAP
      319/369-7908

The Child Protection Center is committed to the interdisciplinary evaluation and treatment of children suspected of having been abused, especially sexually abused. Children are seen at the request of Department of Human Services or law enforcement officers. The evidentiary interview is videotaped. Medical exam is done with the use of a colposcope. The team meets after each evaluation to determine if the child is protected, if treatment is necessary, and to discuss the evidentiary evidence. The main philosophy is to avoid revictimization of the child.

Children's Health Center
1212 Pleasant, Suite 300
Des Moines, IA 50309
515/241-4138
515/241-8728 (Fax)
Director: Rizwan Z. Shah, MD

Children's Health Center is a referral center for multidisciplinary evaluation and treatment of issues confronting families and children. Service areas include five interrelated program components: (1) B-Safe Clinic - sexual abuse forensic evaluation clinic provides comprehensive medical evaluation and treatment for sexually abused children; examination by colposcope is conducted; (2) CAIRE - Cocaine affected infant evaluation and rehabilitation services; this is the state's only such existing program; (3) HAPPY BEAR - Sexual abuse prevention education for preschool children; (4) Assessment of physical trauma; and (5) Foster care health appraisal evaluation and follow-up.

University of Iowa Child Abuse Program
University of Iowa
209 Hospital School
Iowa City, IA 52242
319/353-6136
Director: Randall Alexander, MD, PhD

The University of Iowa maintains a tertiary program in all aspects of child abuse. Children are evaluated through outpatient clinics and inpatient units, and a wide array of support services are offered including pediatric radiology, pediatric ophthalmology, nutrition, comprehensive developmental evaluations, pediatric orthopedics, and colposcopic examinations. Cases range from acute examination to court-ordered cases requiring developmental evaluations and placement recommendations. Acute medical care and ongoing tertiary developmental evaluations complement local service providers. In addition, extensive case consultation and teaching is provided throughout Iowa, and active research efforts are underway regarding a wide variety of child abuse concerns.

Kansas

Child Abuse Evaluation Clinic
c/o Pediatric Faculty Clinic
3243 E Murdock, Suite 200
Wichita, KS 67208
316/688-2080
316/688-2079 (Fax)
Medical Director: Katherine J. Melhorn, MD, FAAP

Referrals to the clinic are taken from social service agencies, law enforcement, court agencies, therapists, physicians, and other professionals. Self-referrals from patients and families are screened by the director before scheduling. Interviews and medical exams are performed for concerns of physical or sexual abuse or neglect. Visits are scheduled on Wednesday mornings, but can be

arranged more urgently if needed. The medical director also reviews all pediatric cases seen at Via Christi St Joseph Medical Center by the sexual assault nurse examiners with the Sexual Assault Response Team. Acute or emergent cases can be referred to SANE/SART c/o Diana Schunn, RN, at 316/689-5252.

University of Kansas Medical Center
Department of Pediatrics
39th & Rainbow
Kansas City, KS 66103
913/588-5908
913/588-6319 (Fax)
Director: Lynn K. Sheets, MD

Kansas University Children's Center's Sexual Abuse Program utilizes pediatricians, a nurse practitioner, and a social worker to conduct forensic medical sexual abuse evaluations. A colposcope is used in most exams. The program also provides expert court testimony, consultations, medical education, and community outreach. The Sexual Abuse Program is affiliated with the local Children's Advocacy Center, Sunflower House. Referrals are accepted from a variety of sources after reporting mandates have been fulfilled. Inpatient consultation on cases of suspected physical or sexual abuse is also available.

Kentucky

Child Advocacy Clinic
Family Health Services
Hazard Appalachian Regional Healthcare
Hazard, KY 41701
606/436-5572
Physicians: Artie Ann Bates, MD
Elizabeth Spencer-Allen, MD

The Child Advocacy Clinic of Family Health Services provides comprehensive medical services for child and adolescent victims of sexual and physical abuse. Mentally retarded adults have been examined for sexual abuse in selected cases. Services consist of confidential files; colposcopic examination; culturing for sexually transmitted diseases; collection of forensic data; consultation with social workers, law enforcement, and physicians; and expert court testimony. Patient referrals are from southeastern and south central Kentucky.

Department of Pediatrics/Kosair Children's Hospital
231 E Chestnut St
Louisville, KY 40202
502/629-7212

Director: Mary A. Smith, MD
502/629-7225

The Department of Pediatrics - University of Louisville School of Medicine, with the Kosair Children's Hospital, serves as the medical component for the surrounding region including metropolitan Louisville, central Kentucky, and southern Indiana in cases of physical abuse, sexual abuse, and neglect. The patients we see and evaluate are referred to the Crimes Against Children Program in Jefferson County which does the investigations, Department of Human Resources Social Services reports, police reports and court functions, with the assistance of the Department of Obstetrics/ Gynecology, Surgery and Psychiatry. The hospital gives total medical care for the child including follow-up and counseling. Some of these services are also provided by court order through the program, Family and Children's Agency. This is a program for sexual abuse counseling for family members only. In outlying counties and Southern Indiana, we do the medical component of the child abuse program in cooperation with their programs - Department of Human Resources and the police departments. The metropolitan area is serviced by a county program called Seven Counties which provides follow-up for the patient, family, and perpetrator.

Division of General Pediatrics
University of Kentucky
Department of Pediatrics
Kentucky Clinic
Lexington, KY 40536
606/323-6426

Director: Katherine L. Bright, MD
606/253-6699

The University of Kentucky Department of Pediatrics provides the medical component for child sexual abuse investigations for the eastern portion of Kentucky. Referrals come from primary care physicians, in cooperation with local child protective social workers and police. Patients are examined at the Child Advocacy Center of the Bluegrass. For local Fayette County cases, the advocacy center provides coordinated, comprehensive services, including investigative interviews, individual and group counseling, and referrals of children and families for other needed support services. UK pediatricians are available for consultation with other professionals involved in these cases and provide expert courtroom testimony when necessary. In addition, the physicians also conduct educational and training programs for physicians and other health care workers, as well as for non-medical professionals involved in child sexual abuse cases.

Lexington-Fayette County Health Department
650 Newtown Pike
Lexington, KY 40508
Director: Deborah Stanley, MD
606/288-2467

The Lexington-Fayette County Health Department provides medical evaluations for children suspected of having been sexually abused. Patient referrals come from social workers and police and are limited to Fayette and contiguous counties. Patients are examined at the Child Advocacy Center of the Bluegrass, which provides comprehensive services to child victims and their families. Physician consultation with other involved professionals and expert courtroom testimony are provided as needed.

St Claire Medical Center
222 Medical Circle
Morehead, KY 40351-1180
606/783-6813
606/783-6814
Director: Mary Jane Humkey, MD

Child sexual abuse examinations are conducted by Dr Humkey as part of the St Claire Medical Center's Primary Care System. Dr Humkey sees patients from the hospital's surrounding eleven county service area. Referrals come mostly via Department of Social Services, and occasionally from police or other physicians within the area. Court testimony is also provided.

Louisiana

Child Abuse Program
Children's Hospital
200 Henry Clay Ave
New Orleans, LA 70118
504/896-9237
504/896-9733 (Fax)
Director: Scott A. Benton, MD

Children's Hospital Child Abuse Program provides forensic medical evaluations of infants, children, and adolescents from birth to 21 years old. The clinic and consultation services are staffed by board-certified pediatricians who evaluate all aspects of child maltreatment (physical, sexual, and neglect). The program does not provide forensic psychology or psychiatry services at this time. Patients are seen by referral only. The referring agency will automatically receive a report of each child's evaluation.

Child Sexual Abuse Program
Ouachita Parish
102 Thomas Rd, Suite 111
West Monroe, LA 71291
318/329-8456
Director: Meade O'Boyle, MD

Medical evaluation of sexual abuse is performed with colposcopy. Interviews are provided, accompanied by law enforcement or social workers.

Massachusetts

Boston Medical Center Child Protection Program
818 Harrison Ave
Boston, MA 02118
617/534-7902
Director: Jan Paradise, MD, FAAP

The Child Protection Program of Boston Medical Center provides diagnostic and treatment services for children and adolescents with difficulties related to child abuse and neglect. Children are referred from area physicians, neighborhood health centers, nursing and social service agencies, state protective social workers, and the courts. Consultation is available for medical diagnosis and treatment, psychological assessment and referral, social service evaluation, and the clarification of legal issues. Patients are seen by appointment in Family Development Clinic and by consultation at other hospital sites including other outpatient programs, the pediatric emergency department, and the pediatric inpatient unit.

Brockton Children and Youth Project
Family Violence Consultation Group
680 Centre St
Brockton, MA 02402
508/583-2900
508/941-6402 (Fax)
Director: John J. McNamara, MD

The Family Violence Consultation Group is a consultation group, not a crisis intervention program, for abused children in the greater Brockton area. Referrals are received from physicians or agencies. No self-referrals are accepted.

Child Advocacy Team
University of Massachusetts Medical Center
55 Lake Ave, North
Worcester, MA 01655
508/856-6629
508/856-6740
Clinical Director: C. Susie King, LICSW
508/856-3281

The Child Advocacy Team is a multidisciplinary group including a child protective services representative, which provides clinical consultation and training to medical center personnel regarding issues of child maltreatment. The team meets weekly to review all mandated reports filed at the medical center, with follow-up discussion focusing on comprehensive treatment/services planning. The team also sponsors a physical findings diagnostic clinic for children who are victims of suspected sexual abuse.

Child Protection Program
Children's Hospital
Boston, MA 02115
617/735-7979
Director: Eli H. Newberger, MD

The program consists of research, training, and service activities. Clinical activities include an outpatient clinic (the Family Development Clinic) in which medical examinations are given to victims of child physical abuse and sexual abuse, and court ordered assessments, often in the context of custody conflicts, are conducted; a sexual abuse diagnostic and treatment clinic in the Department of Psychiatry; and a Child Protection Team which offers consultation on a 24-hour a day basis to all clinical units at the Children's Hospital. The program also includes an advocacy program for battered women (called AWAKE, for Advocacy for Women and Kids in Emergencies). AWAKE offers emergency consultation, liaison to community battered women's service agencies, access to specialized legal, social service, medical, and housing resources, and training.

Child Protection Program and CARE Clinic

The Floating Hospital at New England
Medical Center
750 Washington St, Box 351
Boston, MA 02111
617/636-5241
617/636-7719 (Fax)
Director: Robert M. Reece, MD

This multidisciplinary program offers consultation on cases of child maltreatment in all of its presentations. Consultation is available for cases on the inpatient services of the Floating Hospital for Children (NEMC) and in the Child Abuse Referral and Evaluation (CARE) Clinic, an outpatient diagnostic facility. The Floating Hospital offers comprehensive primary care and tertiary care services in pediatrics. The Child Protection Program can enlist the services of the pediatric subspecialty services in emergency medicine, neurology, neurosurgery, the Kiwanis Trauma Institute, general surgery, intensive care, orthopedics, dermatology, psychology and psychiatry, genetics and metabolic diseases, hematology, cardiology, gastroenterology, radiology, and gynecology. Referrals are received from other physicians, public and private social service agencies, the courts, district attorneys' offices, and law enforcement agencies.

Children's Advocacy Clinic

Framingham Union Campus
Columbia Metrowest Medical Center
115 Lincoln St
Framingham, MA 01702
508/383-1141
Director: Jan E. Paradise, MD

The Children's Advocacy Clinic at the Framingham Union Campus of Columbia Metrowest Medical Center provides comprehensive medical and forensic assessment for children and adolescents through the age of 18 years who have been, or may have been, abused or neglected. Children and adolescents are referred by area physicians, mental health providers, nursing and social service agencies, and the courts. Patients are seen by appointment.

Family Advocacy Project

Bay State Medical Center
2 Medical Center Dr, Suite 201
Springfield, MA 01199
413/784-5083
Director: Edward N. Bailey, MD
Shiri Katz, MD

The Family Advocacy Project includes an interdisciplinary team within a large medical center. Its primary goal is the evaluation and treatment of children who have been victimized by abuse or sexual assault. The team is composed of a physician, pediatric nurse practitioner, social worker, and psychologist who see children for medical comprehensive examinations and evaluations. Subsequently children and their families are enrolled for ongoing treatment as indicated.

Imaging Center for Child Abuse and Neglect

Department of Radiology
University of Massachusetts Medical Center
55 Lake Ave, North
Worcester, MA 01655
508/856-2153
Director: Paul K. Kleinman, MD

The Imaging Center for Child Abuse and Neglect (ICCAN) is dedicated to research, education, and service in the area of physical child abuse. The active research program focuses on the pathologic features present on diagnostic imaging studies in cases of abuse. The ICCAN team provides instruction to physicians and other professionals and serves as a national resource for individuals and institutions dealing with physical abuse.

Maryland

CARE Clinic
700 W Lombard St
Baltimore, MD 21201
301/328-5176
Director: Howard Dubowitz, MD
         301/328-5289

A multidisciplinary team for the evaluation of children alleged to have been sexually abused consists of pediatricians, a child psychologist, a nurse, and a social worker. The focus is on the function of the child and parents and clarification of whether abuse occurred. Feedback is provided to the family and a report is sent to the referral source. Recommendations for further treatment/therapy are facilitated. The evaluation is usually conducted in a single afternoon.

Child Protection Team
University of Maryland Medical System
700 W Lombard St
Baltimore, MD 21201
410/706-5176
410/706-0653 (Fax)
Director: Howard Dubowitz, MD

The Child Protection Team, an interdisciplinary team of professionals from UMMS and the community, ensures that children who may have been maltreated receive optimal care and attention. The team assists UMMS staff in the assessment and/or management of these cases by providing various levels of consultation, (including case conferences involving UMMS staff and community service providers), continuing education and training, and support to staff.

Maine

The Family Support Team
Eastern Maine Medical Center
489 State St
Bangor, ME 04401
207/973-7835
Medical Director: John Farquhar, MD

A hospital-based team with two full-time social workers and pediatric medical consultation provides evaluation and some services at the social service level. It provides and/or coordinates referral medical evaluations of physically and sexually abused children; and it provides regional telephone consultation to physicians, service providers, and community institutions such as schools. The team receives in excess of 800 annual referrals and provides 100 to 125 medical evaluations annually.

The Spurwink Child Abuse Program
17 Bishop St
Portland, ME 04103
207/879-6160
Director: Lawrence R. Ricci, MD

A full-time, fully staffed child abuse evaluation and treatment program is located primarily in Portland, but it has five satellite clinics throughout the state. Services include expert medical forensic evaluations, forensic social work interviews, and parenting capacity evaluations by psychologists. Individual component and full team evaluations are available. The program serves 600-700 children a year.

Michigan

Child Protection Team
St Joseph Mercy Hospital
900 N Woodward
Pontiac, MI 48341
248/858-3000
Director: Annamaria Church, MD
248/858-3020

The CPT's objectives are to identify children who have been abused and neglected; identify families who are at risk for child abuse and neglect; coordinate appropriate treatment interventions for child and family; and collaborate with physicians, hospital staff, and community agencies to reduce the risk of future abuse and neglect. The core team consists of the medical director, pediatric resident, pediatric clinical nurse specialist, and pediatric social worker. The CPT offers consultations, recommendations, advocacy, and follow-up on suspected child abuse and neglect cases; weekly parent education support group; paid child care while parents attend support groups; emergency funds for transportation, food, shelter, clothing, and medicine based on need; and continuing education programs for physicians, nurses, social workers, and other professionals within the community. In the Child Protection Team clinic, physical examination, evaluation, and medical testing is provided to children suspected of being abused or neglected.

Child Protection Team
Children's Hospital of Michigan
3901 Beaubien Blvd
Detroit, MI 48201
313/745-5281
313/993-7106 (Fax)
Coordinator: David Allasio, MSW, CSW
Medical Coordinator: Howard Fischer, MD
313/745-4323

This team provides medical and social diagnosis and assessment to professionals in cases of suspected abuse or neglect. Inpatient and outpatient referrals are taken. The team has an educational role for attending staff, house staff, and other personnel.

Child Protection Team
DeVos Children's Hospital at Butterworth
100 Michigan St, NE
Grand Rapids, MI 49503
616/391-1223
Director: Vincent J. Palusci, MD

The Child Protection Team provides comprehensive medical evaluations for children to facilitate the prevention, identification, diagnosis, and treatment of child abuse and neglect in west Michigan through education, clinical practice, and research. This is a multifaceted hospital-based program providing evaluation of physically and sexually abused children on an inpatient and outpatient basis with team members from pediatrics, adolescent medicine, critical care, neonatology, emergency medicine, radiology, law, social work, pastoral care, nursing, and administration. Other professionals participate in case review and are available for consultation using a team approach coordinated with law enforcement, district attorneys, and the Department of Social Services. Consultation is provided by appointment and the Child Protection Team serves as a resource to the hospital, community, and region for training, research, and patient evaluation.

Children's Health Care of Port Huron, P.C.
1321 Stone St
Port Huron, MI 48060
(810) 984-1000
Directors: John J. Zmiejko, MD
Sharon Johnston, CPNP

Members of the St Clair County Multidisciplinary Team have been providing physical and sexual abuse evaluations for county protective services and law enforcement since 1984. Referrals from medical professionals and phone consultations are welcome.

Grace Hospital Child Protection Program
6071 W Outer Dr, Suite L541
Detroit, MI 48235
313/966-3133
313/966-4567 (Fax)
Director: Ceres Morales, MD
Supervisor: Barbara Tanstill

This program provides medical and other services to maltreated children and their families.

**Michigan State University/
Kalamazoo Center for Medical Studies**
Department of Pediatrics
1000 Oakland Dr
Kalamazoo, MI 49008
616/337-6457
Director: Colette A. Gushurst, MD

The staff serves as consultant to Protective Services when a comprehensive medical examination of an abused child is necessary. Outpatient appointments are made for physical examinations, medical testing, diagnosis, and appropriate reporting. Acute care and emergency cases are not accepted at this setting. Colposcopy is available, if necessary, for sexual abuse evaluations. Experienced expert testimony is provided locally. An educational component is provided for residents in pediatrics, family practice, medicine/pediatrics, and emergency medicine, as well as medical students at this campus of Michigan State University.

Minnesota

Child Maltreatment Program
Hennepin County Medical Center
Department of Pediatrics
701 Park Ave South
Minneapolis, MN 55415
Contact: Karen Shannon, LCSW
612/347-2671

This multidisciplinary team is hospital based and evaluates children and adolescents of all ages for child maltreatment, including sexual abuse, physical abuse, and neglect. The team includes pediatricians, pediatric social workers, and nurses. It involves hospital and community professionals as needed.

Mayo Clinic Child Abuse Team
200 First St SW
Rochester, MN 55905
507/284-2511
507/255-9872 (Fax)
Director: Julia A. Rosekrans, MD
507/255-5388

The Mayo Clinic Child Abuse Team works closely with local and state social service agencies to identify and investigate children and families in which allegations have been made. Initial evaluations are available on an emergency or appointment basis. The team provides medical, social service, psychiatric, and psychological evaluations. It also participates in a community-based child protection team, developing treatment plans for children and families.

Midwest Children's Resource Center
360 Sherman St, Suite 200
St Paul, MN 55102
612/220-6750
612/220-6670 (Fax)

and

2525 Chicago Ave South
Room 5003
Minneapolis, MN 55404
612/813-6750
612/813-7720 (Fax)
Medical Director: Carolyn Levitt, MD
Consultant: Jud Reaney, MD
Consultant: Robert Segal, MD
Consultant: Ellen De Vries, MD

This multidisciplinary program provides expert consultation for parents and professionals working with abused children. The staff includes pediatricians, pediatric nurse practitioners, social worker, psychologists, and attorney. The center offers 24-hour telephone consultations and emergency medical services. Sexual abuse interviews are all videotaped. Forensic photographic documentation and diagnosis of physical abuse and neglect are provided. Over 1500 children are seen each year, with more than 2400 telephone consultations.

Missouri

The CARE (Children at Risk Evaluation) Team
Children's Mercy Hospital
2401 Gillham Rd
Kansas City, MO 64108
816/234-3691

Medical Director: Irene Walsh, MD
Additional Providers: Barbara Allphin, MD
Bruce Peters, DO
Katherine Smith, MD
Kathe Kraly, RN, MSN,
CPNP

The CARE Team provides medical evaluation and treatment for children and adolescents of all ages who are at risk of physical abuse, sexual abuse, and neglect. It has two main components: (1) the CARE clinic for scheduled outpatient evaluation, and (2) an inpatient consultative service for hospitalized children. The CARE team functions as a part of the Division of Pediatric Emergency Medicine and works collaboratively with multiple other disciplines within the hospital. Providers are members of the SAFE-CARE Network of the State of Missouri.

Child Protection Program & Sexual Abuse Management Clinic (SAM)
St Louis Children's Hospital
One Children's Place
St Louis, MO 63110
314/454-2879
314/454-2473 (Fax)

Program Coordinator: Lee Ann Taylor, MSEd,
MSW, LCSW
Nurse Practitioner: Nancy Duncan, RN, CPNP
SAM Clinic
Medical Director: Robert T. Paschall, MD
314/454-2341
314/454-4345 (Fax)

This hospital-based program provides evaluations for victims of child maltreatment. The scope of services includes both inpatient and outpatient evaluations. A Sexual Abuse Management Clinic provides comprehensive forensic evaluations encompassing the psychosocial and medical aspects of care. Interviewers are skilled in utilizing accepted forensic techniques. Most interviews are documented on videotape with facilities available for involved professionals to view the interview process through a two-way mirror. Physical examinations are conducted in a clinic setting by a pediatrician and/or nurse practitioner. Video colposcopy is utilized for purposes of documentation, case review, peer review, and education. Examiners are providers and trainers for the Missouri Sexual Assault Forensic Examination-Child Abuse Resources and Education (SAFE-CARE) Network.

Kathy J. Weinman Children's Advocacy Center
University of Missouri-St Louis
8001 National Bridge Rd
St Louis, MO 63121
314/516-6798
314/516-6624 (Fax)

Director: Jeffrey Wherry, PhD

Utilizing a multidisciplinary approach to the management of sexually abused children, disclosure interviews are performed, physical examinations are provided utilizing colposcopy, and treatment is implemented. The social and law enforcement agencies participate.

St Louis University
Division of Child Protection
Cardinal Glennon Children's Hospital
1465 S Grand
St Louis, MO 63104

Director: James Monteleone, MD
314/268-6406
Special Assessment and Management
(SAM) Clinic
314/577-5347

Children who are alleged victims of sexual or physical abuse are evaluated by a physician trained by the SAFE (Sexual Abuse Forensic Exam) Network of Missouri. The SAM Team of Cardinal Glennon Hospital provides physical and psychological evaluations of children and adolescents who are alleged victims of sexual abuse. All requests for examinations are reviewed by the SAM Team.

University of Missouri Child Abuse Evaluation Program
Department of Child Health
University of Missouri Hospital
Columbia, MO 65212
573/882-4141
573/884-5282 (Fax)
Director: Lori Frasier, MD

Children are evaluated under Missouri's SAFE program for sexual and physical abuse. The SAFE network requires formal education to become state approved, in order to receive full reimbursement for sexual abuse evaluations.

Child Protection Program
University of Missouri-Columbia Hospitals & Clinics
One Hospital Dr, DC 106
Columbia, MO 65212
573/882-3713

Medical Director: Lori Frasier, MD

This program is a medical center-based multidisciplinary team that serves as a resource for the hospital, surrounding local community hospitals and physicians, and other involved professionals in the mid-Missouri region. It provides evaluations of children for sexual abuse, physical abuse, and neglect. The team is beginning to utilize telemedicine and other technologies to better serve providers in outlying areas of the state.

New Hampshire

The Children at Risk Program and The C.A.R.E. Network
Dartmouth Hitchcock Medical Center
One Medical Center Dr
Lebanon, NH 03756-0001
603/650-5473
603/650-5458 (Fax)
Contact: Steven W. Kairys, MD

This is a multidisciplinary child protection program involved in diagnostic and treatment services and research in abuse and neglect. The team provides hospital and community-wide consultation in all aspects of physical abuse, neglect, and sexual abuse. In addition, the program is in its fourth year of a research project developing a model treatment approach for families already

reported for physical abuse. Another initiative is called the C.A.R.E. Network, C.A.R.E. standing for Child Abuse Referral and Evaluation program. This is a statewide program for pediatricians and family physicians who have agreed to meet regularly to develop standards in quality of care, in order for them to be considered regional experts in the evaluation of physical and sexual abuse. The team works cooperatively with the state Child Protection Agency and is used by the Child Protection Agency for evaluations of children who have entered their system. The team meets twice a year to review cases and information. The tertiary center for the team is located at Dartmouth, and difficult cases or second opinions are referred there as necessary.

New Jersey

Center for Children's Support
A Resource for the Evaluation and Treatment of Child Sexual Abuse
University of Medicine and Dentistry of New Jersey
School of Osteopathic Medicine
42 East Laurel Rd, Suite 3400
Stratford, NJ 08084-1504
609/566-7036
609/566-6108 (Fax)
Medical Director: Martin A. Finkel, DO
Clinical Director: Esther Deblinger, PhD

The Center for Children's Support is southern New Jersey's only dedicated facility providing diagnostic and treatment services for sexually and physically abused children. The center is a University Center of Excellence and a joint program of the Departments of Pediatrics and Psychiatry of the University of Medicine and Dentistry of New Jersey's School of Osteopathic Medicine. The center also provides expert testimony, professional training, legislative advocacy and conducts NIMH supported research. The comprehensive services include both medical and mental health diagnosis and treatment. Both individual and group therapy utilizing research-based cognitive behavioral therapy is provided to child victims and their non-offending parents. Center staff are active participants in county-based multidisciplinary child abuse teams. The center provides both formal pre- and post-doctoral training for psychology and social work students. The center staff includes six psychologists, two pediatricians, one research assistant, two MSW social workers, and three support staff.

Child Sexual Abuse Program

UMDNJ-Robert Wood Johnson Medical School
Department of Pediatrics
MEB 388
One RWJ Place-CN19
New Brunswick, NJ 08903-0019
732/235-6146
Director: Linda Shaw, MD, MSSW

and

Child Protection Center

St Peter's Medical Center
Department of Pediatrics
137 Guilden St
New Brunswick, NJ 08901
732/745-9449
Director: Cynthia Barabas, MD

The Child Sexual Abuse Program and the Child Protection Center serve central New Jersey as the regional consultation program for abused and neglected children. The regional center offers medical examinations and multidisciplinary medical consultations, psychological and psychosocial evaluations, and crisis counseling. Case consultations are provided to health, education, child protection, and legal professionals. Educational programs are offered for medical students/residents, child protection workers, law officers, hospital personnel, etc. The regional center participates in collaborative research projects on child abuse. Coordinating services for child abuse victims and their families, especially counseling, is another major role of the regional center.

Child Abuse Diagnostic Center

Jersey Shore Medical Center
c/o Social Work Department
1945 Route 33
Neptune, NJ 07754
908/776-4245
908/776-4690 (Fax)
Director: Joseph Bogdan, MD
908/776-4245

The Child Abuse Diagnostic Center at Jersey Shore Medical Center is a collaborative effort of the Division of Youth and Family Services (DYFS), the Monmouth County Prosecutor's Office, and the medical center. It is the first comprehensive child abuse diagnostic center in the state of New Jersey dealing with the broad spectrum of child abuse and neglect. Establishment of the center puts into place the mechanism for dealing with early intervention of the medical, social, and legal components that may be involved in suspected child abuse or neglect cases. The unique coordinated effort of the Child Abuse Diagnostic Center is designed to achieve the earliest possible identification, diagnosis, and treatment of the child. It also brings together the three major components in suspected child abuse and neglect cases; the social (DYFS), medical, and law enforcement. They can cooperatively intervene in a way that will minimize trauma to the child and expedite the appropriate disposition of the case. A team approach to care is utilized. The child abuse team includes the physician, nurse, clinical social worker, DYFS child protective services worker, as well as law enforcement, child evaluation, and mental health staff when needed. A complete range of professional services are given to safeguard the health and welfare of the child. All suspected cases of child abuse are evaluated, diagnosed, provided emergency treatment, and admitted to the hospital if necessary, or referred to a private physician, pediatric clinic, child evaluation center, or mental health center for continued care or treatment.

New York

Bellevue Hospital Center

First Ave at 27th St
New York, NY 10016
212/562-4141

Director: Margaret T. McHugh, MD, MPH

Child protection services at Bellevue Hospital are provided in an intradisciplinary program under the direction of Margaret T. McHugh, MD, MPH. This team provides assessments that are focused on the unique developmental needs of each child and adolescent. Specialized protocols for developmentally delayed and/or physically impaired children are utilized by staff members to insure a comprehensive evaluation in a child-focused environment. Each member of the team participates in the ongoing interdisciplinary training program designed to provide a meaningful clinical experience for health professionals in training. With this current program, a core of professionals with extensive training evaluates cases in which child sexual abuse is suspected. Evaluations are coordinated with Child Protection Services and criminal justice systems to minimize the number of professionals interacting with the child and family.

Brooklyn Child Advocacy Center

30 Main St
Brooklyn, NY 11201
718/260-6080

Director: Ms Jane Barker
Medical Directors: Stephen Ajl, MD
Richard Switzer, MD

The Brooklyn Child Advocacy Center is an independent multidisciplinary site for the evaluation of children reported to child welfare. At the center on a continuous basis are a sexual abuse unit of Administration for Children's Services, a sex crimes squad of the police department, an assistant district attorney, and victim's services. The physicians are there on a part-time basis.

Child Abuse Referral and Evaluation (CARE) Program

Pediatric Department
State University of New York Health Science
Center, University Health Care Center
90 Presidential Plaza
Syracuse, NY 13202
315/464-5420

Director: Ann S. Botash, MD
315/464-5831
315/464-2030 (Fax)
Botasha@vax.cs.hscsyr.edu (E-mail)

The CARE Program uses a team approach to provide medical evaluations of children suspected to have been abused. This team provides medical care, social and psychological assessments and evaluations, patient/family education and support, and child advocacy. There is a close working relationship with county social services and law enforcement agencies as evidentiary interviews are performed. Follow-up care is either directly provided or implemented by referral. The team is available for court testimony and educates other professionals by offering an Intensive Clinical Fellowship in Child Abuse. Referrals are received from a variety of sources from several surrounding counties, such as the Rape Crisis Center, sheriff and city police abused persons units, New York State police, district attorneys offices, and departments of social service child protective units, as well as from physicians, parents, counselors, and patients.

Child Advocacy Center

Columbia Presbyterian Medical Center
Department of General Pediatrics
622 W 168th St, VC4
New York, NY 10032
212/305-2393
212/305-6474
212/305-9742 (Fax)

Director: Jocelyn Brown, MD, MPH
JB58@columbia.edu (E-mail)

This hospital-based Child Advocacy Center receives referrals directly from community agencies, primary care physicians, city agencies, law enforcement, and child protection services. The center has a multi-disciplinary team and ongoing case management review. Joint investigative interviews are conducted at the center via two-way mirror with video capabilities. Pediatric residents and emergency room fellows are trained through the center.

The Child Protection Center

Montefiore Medical Center
3314 Steuben Ave
Bronx, NY 10467
718/920-5833
718/405-6149 (Fax)
Medical Director: Linda Cahill, MD
Executive Director: Mary L. Pulido, MAT, CSW

The Child Protection Center (CPC) is a critical component of the Montefiore Child Health Network, a broad-reaching, coordinated system of programs and resources focused on the needs of children in the Bronx and lower Westchester. Administered by Montefiore's Division of Community Pediatrics, the center provides critical emergency medical and psychosocial evaluation of child victims of sexual abuse, physical abuse, and neglect. The CPC also evaluates children at-risk for abuse who need comprehensive exams. These children have often been removed from their caretakers due to domestic violence, substance abuse, poverty, and inadequate medical attention and nutrition. Since 1984, over 9,000 children and their families have been treated at the CPC. During 1996, over 740 children received medical and social work services from the expert CPC team. After initial evaluation, each child is entered into the database and tracked by dedicated volunteers for as long as several years to monitor their progress.

Child Protection Team

Schneider Children's Hospital
269-01 76th Ave
New Hyde Park, NY 11042
713/470-3281
718/347-2415 (Fax)
Director: Bruce N. Bogard, MD

Evaluation of physical and sexual abuse is provided. Referrals for sexual abuse expertise are received from local child protection services (three counties) as well as county and local police. It is a community resource, the activities including education for lay and professional groups. Expert witnesses are available for court.

Child Sexual Abuse Program

The Child Health Clinics of NYC
Family Health Services Diagnostic and
Treatment HHC Center
346 Broadway
New York, NY 10013
Coordinator: Flora Ramirez-Hojohn, MD
212/442-4202

The Child Sexual Abuse Program provides consultation to the primary care providers of 40 Child Health Clinics in New York City. Referrals from community pediatricians, child advocacy groups, local Child Protective Services, foster care agencies, police, and district attorneys are also accepted. The consultants are board certified and trained to do sexual abuse assessments which include medical interview, physical examination, and appropriate laboratory examinations. Patients are seen by appointments only. Location and schedule of clinic sessions are as follows:

Manhattan: Riverside Health Center
160 West 100th St
New York, NY 10025
Fridays 8:30 am- 4:30 pm
Dr Carlos Rivera
212/280-0240

Queens: Corona Health Center
34-33 Junction Blvd
Queens, NY 11372
Tuesdays 8:30 am - 4:30 pm
Dr Flora Ramirez Hojohn
718/476-7654

Brooklyn: Crown Heights Child Health Clinics
1218 Prospect Place
Brooklyn, NY 11213
Wednesdays and Thursdays
8:30 am - 4:30 pm
Dr Flora Ramirez Hojohn (Wednesday)
Dr Richard Di Pasquale (Thursday)
718/735-5630

Children's Advocacy Center of Manhattan
330 E 70th St
New York, NY 10021
212/517-3012, Ext 24
212/517-6738 (Fax)
Medical Director: Katherine Teets Grimm, MD

The Children's Advocacy Center of Manhattan is a privately funded, non-profit agency affiliated with The Mount Sinai Medical Center. It provides crisis intervention and support to physically and sexually abused children and their families in cooperation with the NYC Police Department, Administration for Children's Services, and the Manhattan DA's office. The center also provides treatment for the non-offending parent(s) and the victimized child.

Erie County's Child Advocacy Center
560 Delaware Ave
Buffalo, NY 14222
716/886-KIDS

Family Advocacy Program
Jacobi Hospital
Pelham Pkwy
Bronx, NY 10461
718/918-4568
718/918-4580
Co-Directors: Kathleen Porder, MD
Jamie Rosenfeld, MD

The Family Advocacy Program consists of an interdisciplinary team of two physicians, one pediatric nurse practitioner, three social workers, and a social worker/child abuse coordinator. The team meets for two formal sessions per week, one devoted to case review and one devoted to direct patient care. In the patient care session all patients receive medical evaluations. Social work intervention is provided when indicated. All suspected cases receive social services ranging from telephone outreach to direct crisis intervention and referral for therapy. The team is available for inpatient and outpatient consultation of suspected cases. It also provides consultation and direct patient evaluations for local child protective services, schools, private physicians, and the courts.

Family Crisis Center
Crisis Nursery-New York Foundling Hospital
590 Ave of the Americas
New York, NY 10011
212/472-8555 - Parent Helpline
212/886-4041 (Fax)
Director: Vincent J. Fontana, MD
212/886-4050

A multidisciplinary team provides physical and sexual abuse evaluations, including medical evaluations, and psychological treatment of sexual abuse victims. Respite care of children is provided to families in crisis.

Family Support Program
Harlem Hospital Center
Department of Pediatrics
506 Lenox Ave
New York, NY 10037
212/939-2444
Director: Danielle Laraque, MD

The Family Support Program, located in northern Manhattan, is staffed by a multidisciplinary team of professionals skilled in the evaluation and treatment of children suspected of having been sexually or physically abused or neglected. The staff includes two pediatricians trained in sexual abuse evaluation, a pediatric surgeon, a clinical social worker, a pediatric psychologist, a caseworker, and a coordinator. Comprehensive medical and mental health services are provided. As needed, the team coordinates its efforts with the Administration for Children Services, the district attorney's office, and Special Victims. Community outreach and education are also provided.

Norman S. Ellerstein Child Abuse Center
Children's Hospital of Buffalo
219 Bryant St
Buffalo, NY 14222
716/878-7109
Director: Paula Mazur, MD

This center provides initial assessments of abused children, consultations to Child Protective Services and physicians, and expert witnesses for court. It centers on physical abuse although comprehensive sexual abuse evaluations are performed.

Special Victims Clinic
Downstate Medical Center
King's County Hospital
451 Clarkson Ave
Brooklyn, NY 11203
718/245-3612

Directors: Stephen Ajl, MD
          Richard DiPasquale, MD
          718/270-1475

This is a specialized clinic for the evaluation
of children who may have been sexually abused.
Referrals are accepted from physicians, foster
care agencies, and child welfare, as well as police.
Physicians, a nurse practitioner, and a social worker
are available for the evaluation. The team provides
inpatient consultation as well.

Task Force for Child Protection, Inc.
Child Advocacy Center Program
249 Hooker Ave
Poughkeepsie, NY 12603
914/454-0595
914/454-0129 (Fax)

Program Director: Sandra Banas
Medical Consultant: Rita Jaeger, MD

This is a facility for the forensic interviewing and
forensic medical examinations of alleged child
sexual abuse victims. Referrals are from Child
Protective Services and police agencies. The
facility serves the entire Dutchess County area,
and provides courtesy services to surrounding
counties.

North Carolina

Asheville Pediatric Association
77 McDowell St
Asheville, NC 28801
704/254-5326
704/251-5954 (Fax)

Director: Andrea Gravatt, MD

Asheville Pediatric Association is a general
pediatric office which is also interested in evaluating children in our community and surrounding
counties for evaluation of child abuse and neglect.
The office works closely with the WNC Regional
Child Abuse Center in Asheville.

**Center for Child and Family Health -
North Carolina**
Suite 100
3518 Westgate Dr
Durham, NC 27707
919/419-3474
919/419-9353 (Fax)
Medical
Director: Desmond K. Runyan, MD, DrPH
Mental Health
Director: Lisa Amaya-Jackson, MD, MPH
Family and Legal
Support Director: Cheryl Amana, JD, LLM

The Center for Child and Family Health -
North Carolina is a multidisciplinary collaboration of North Carolina Central University, Duke
University, and The University of North Carolina
at Chapel Hill. The center combines the medical
and mental health consultation activities of the
Duke and UNC Medical Schools in the area of
maltreatment with the Family Law Program from
North Carolina Central University. Services
include medical and mental health evaluations of
suspected physical and sexual abuse, mental health
treatment of trauma victims, family support and
legal services, and consultations on cases for medical and social work professionals across the state.
The center also provides continuing education for
social work, mental health, nursing, law, and
medical professionals.

Child Abuse Clinic
Southern Regional AHEC
1601 Owen Dr
Fayetteville, NC 28304
910/678-7221
910/678-7274 (Fax)
Medical Director: Howard H. Loughlin, MD

The Child Abuse Clinic at the Southern Regional Area Health Education Center provides outpatient medical evaluations for suspected physical, sexual, or emotional abuse and neglect. Referrals are accepted from regional DSS and law enforcement agencies as well as health care providers. Primary evaluations and second opinion examinations are available.

Child Medical Evaluation Program
Department of Pediatrics
CB#3415
University of North Carolina at Chapel Hill
Chapel Hill, NC 27599
Medical Director: Desmond K. Runyan, MD,
DrPH
919/962-1136
Program Coordinator: Joyce Moore, RN, MPH
919/419-7874

Established in 1976, the Child Medical Evaluation Program (CMEP) is a cooperative effort of the UNC School of Medicine's Department of Pediatrics, the North Carolina State Division of Social Services, the North Carolina Legislature, local departments of social services, and local medical and mental health providers. The CMEP staff has developed a statewide network of local providers who perform medical and psychological assessments of children referred by DSS agencies to help determine the presence or extent of abuse and neglect. Payment for the services is provided through a contract with the State Office of Social Services. There are approximately 350 medical providers and 200 psychological providers in the state, as well as referral clinics at the major medical centers. The CMEP of North Carolina has served as a model for the development of similar programs in other states in efforts to identify, treat, and prevent maltreatment of children.

Child Medical Evaluation Team
Brenner Children's Hospital
Medical Center Blvd
Winston-Salem, NC 27157-1179
Medical Director: Sara H. Sinal, MD
919/716-2538
910/716-7100 (Fax)
Contact: Cynthia Stewart, MA
919/716-7663

The Brenner Children's Hospital Child Medical Evaluation Team provides comprehensive in-patient and outpatient evaluations for suspected physical abuse, sexual abuse, emotional abuse, and neglect. There is a special hospital team for suspected Munchausen Syndrome by Proxy (MSBP) cases. The multidisciplinary medical evaluation team is comprised of three pediatricians and four hospital social workers. One social worker is a child interview specialist. Referrals are accepted from physicians, county social workers, law enforcement, the court, and mental health professionals. Telephone calls from the public are screened by a social worker to assess the need for evaluation or reporting of suspected abuse or neglect. Referrals are accepted for children and adolescents from birth to age 18. For sexual abuse evaluation, colposcopy is available. For all evaluations, court testimony is provided if necessary.

The Child Sexual Abuse Team
Wake Medical Education Institute
3024 New Bern Ave, Suite 307
Raleigh, NC 27610-1255
919/250-7810
919/250-8677 (Fax)
Director: V. Denise Everett, MD

This multidisciplinary team consists of two physicians, one sexual abuse interviewer, a research assistant, and an intake worker. CSAT evaluates children less than 13 years of age that are suspected of having been sexually abused. Referrals from 11 counties are received from physicians, social services, law enforcement, district attorney's offices, and parents. Evaluations consist of structured interviewing, videotaping of interviews, physical examination with use of colposcopy, and testing for sexually transmitted diseases.

Family Advocacy Program, US Navy
Naval Hospital, Dept of Pediatrics
Cherry Point, NC 28533
919/466-5751
Dept Head: LCDR. Anthony N. Mishik, MC,
          USNR
          919/466-0245

This US Navy Family Advocacy Program provides child abuse evaluations coordinated by the Department of Pediatrics of the local naval hospital. Active local programs include medicolegal interviews, comprehensive physical evaluations, emergency room consultations, and inpatient admissions. The program strives for active involvement of military base authorities and support programs, county department of social services, and area counseling/psychological resources. Research is focused on discipline and violence issues. The program is limited to active duty military, retired military, and their dependents.

TEDI BEAR Children's Advocacy Center
504B Dexter St
Greenville, NC 27834
Medical Director: Rebecca S. Coker, MD

TEDI BEAR CAC provides multidisciplinary diagnostic medical evaluations for over 300 children from 34 counties of eastern coastal North Carolina each year, including forensic interviewing, expert medical evaluation, and case conferencing. The community-based site is affiliated with East Carolina University School of Medicine and Pitt County Memorial Hospital, and equipped with closed-circuit video monitoring for interviewing and colposcopic medical examination in a child-friendly environment. Referrals are made through the Department of Social Services and law enforcement. Other services include nurturing sessions for victims and families, and counseling services.

Western North Carolina Child Advocacy and Prevention Services, Inc
PO Box 5861
Asheville, NC 28813
704/254-2000
704/254-2605 (Fax)
E-mail: childabusecenter.org
Medical Director: Cynthia J. Brown, MD
President: Ann Flynn

This program provides multidisciplinary team evaluations for Buncombe County children who are allegedly physically/sexually abused; provides primary and/or second opinions for children who are physically/sexually abused; offers prevention/educational programming for all civic, community, and medical persons; and offers consultation for establishment of abuse prevention programming.

Ohio

Child Abuse Program
Children's Hospital
700 Children's Dr
Columbus, OH 43205
614/461-2504
Director: Charles Felzen Johnson, MD

This internationally recognized program, which is involved in child abuse diagnosis, prevention, treatment, and research, works closely with a variety of state and community agencies. Child abuse encompasses physical and emotional abuse and neglect, non-organic failure to thrive, and sexual abuse. Standardized abuse reports are not made to the abuse team, but rather to Children's Services and/or the police department. Assessments of children suspected of having been abused, or who are at risk for abuse are made in Teenage Clinic, Family Development Clinic or Emergency Services, depending upon the age of the child, the type of abuse, and the urgency of the assessment. Appointments are necessary for assessments in all these areas. Medical, psychosocial, and nursing assessments, with recorded and photographic documentation, are routine and involve a physician, nurse, and social worker; depending on the needs of the child, psychological, nutritional, and medical specialty evaluations may also be needed. Appropriate information is transmitted to mandated agencies on standard forms. Medical follow-up and behavioral-emotional and family counseling are available through other programs. A special service, the Family Support Program, treats sexually abused children and their families. Mini-residencies are available to train practitioner physicians and nurse practitioners in abuse assessment. The state chapter of the National Center for the Prevention of Child Abuse is located at Children's Hospital.

Child Abuse Review and Evaluation Team and Clinic

The Children's Medical Center
One Children's Plaza
Dayton, OH 45404-1815
937/226-8403
937/463-5134 (Fax)
Director: Ralph A. Hicks, MD

The CARE Team is a multidisciplinary team developed to assist in the evaluation and treatment planning of cases of child abuse/neglect. Specific areas handled by the CARE Team include diagnostic evaluations (both medical and psychosocial), treatment planning, and coordination of community agencies. The team is hospital based and has permanent members that include a hospital social worker, hospital-based pediatrician, hospital psychologist, clinic nurse, liaison supervisor from Montgomery County (Ohio) Children Services Board, Montgomery County Sheriff's Department detective, Montgomery County Prosecutor's Office, and City of Dayton Police Department. The CARE Clinic provides outpatient diagnostic evaluation of child sexual abuse, physical abuse and neglect to referring community agencies and physicians. A Children's Advocacy Center opened in 1997.

Child Abuse Team/SAM Clinic

Children's Hospital Medical Center
Division of Emergency Medicine
3333 Burnet Ave, OSB-4
Cincinnati, OH 45229-2899
Medical Director: Robert Shapiro, MD
513/636-7966
513/636-7967 (Fax)
robert.shapiro@chmcc.org
(E-mail)
Associate Director: Patricia Myers, MSW
513/636-4711
513/636-3735 (Fax)
myerp0@chmcc.org (E-mail)

The Child Abuse Team of Children's Hospital Medical Center is active in child abuse diagnosis, treatment, education, research, and prevention. The team is composed of pediatricians from the Division of Emergency Medicine and social workers from the Department of Social Services. Child advocacy is closely coordinated with community organizations and agencies. Children can be scheduled for an appointment in the Social and Medical Clinic by calling 513/636-4711. Professional consultation is available by contacting Dr Shapiro or Ms Myers.

Child and Family Assessment Unit

Medical College of Ohio
Toledo, OH 43699
419/381-4487
Director: W. David Gemmill, MD, MS

This multidisciplinary team offers medical evaluations of victims to agencies in northwest Ohio. In addition, psychological evaluations are provided, with access to all medical specialties when indicated. The members, a pediatrician, clinical nurse specialist, social workers, and psychologist, provide court assistance when called.

Child Protection Program

Rainbow Babies and Children's Hospital
University Hospitals of Cleveland
11100 Euclid Ave
Cleveland, OH 44106
216/884-3761
216/884-5256
Medical Coordinator: Lolly McDavid, MD
Coordinator: Darlynn Constant

The Child Protection Program has three major components:

1. The Care Clinic is an outpatient evaluation and diagnostic center for child sexual abuse. Referrals come from such sources as medical and mental health care providers, social service agencies, legal and law enforcement units, and parents themselves. A multidisciplinary team provides evaluation services including psychosocial assessments, complete medical examinations, and referrals.

2. Consultation services are provided to hospital inpatient divisions. They include psychosocial assessments, medical evaluations, recommendations for additional tests, con-

ferring with divisions and clinics about cases of child abuse, coordinating with outside agencies, court appearances and other communications with the legal community, and educational activities about child abuse.

3. Telephone consultation services are provided to staff, community professionals, and parents on issues of abuse and neglect.

Children at Risk Evaluation (CARE) Center
Children's Hospital Medical Center of Akron
One Perkins Sq
Akron, OH 44308
330/379-8453 or 800/430-4060
Director: R. Daryl Steiner, DO

The CARE Center developed as an off-shoot of the Department of Emergency Services because of the need to establish a controlled care program for victims of abuse. The CARE Center provides a complete multidisciplinary team approach to the evaluation and treatment of these children. An active effort of interaction with the legal system affords strong lines of communication should treatment need to be expanded through the courts. The CARE Center provides services 5 days per week; when coupled with the Emergency Services, this gives 24-hour per day, 7 days per week expertise.

Oklahoma

Children's Hospital of Oklahoma
General Pediatric Department
Emergency Department
Special Pediatric Clinic (child abuse evaluations)
940 NE 13th Street, 1B-1306
Oklahoma City, OK 73104
405/271-4407 or 405/271-4518
Medical Director: John Stuemky, MD

Medical evaluations and treatment of physically and sexually abused children are provided through the outpatient facilities noted above and on the inpatient service of this university-based program. Multidisciplinary staffing of all cases of abuse and neglect seen or referred to Children's Hospital of Oklahoma are conducted weekly. The Center on Child Abuse and Neglect, a component of this program directed by Barbara L. Bonner, PhD, provides psychological assessment and treatment

for abused children and their parents. It also offers treatment of adolescent sex offenders, children with sexual behavior problems, and drug affected infants and parents. Professional and public education and research are also provided. The multiagency staff of a nearby facility conducts assessment interviews.

The University of Oklahoma College of Medicine-Tulsa
Tulsa Children's Justice Center
Department of Pediatrics
2815 S Sheridan
Tulsa, OK 74129
918/831-4599
Medical Director: Ed Gustavson, MD

The Justice Center is a child advocacy facility in which the Department of Pediatrics faculty perform child abuse medical evaluations as part of a multidisciplinary team approach to child abuse. Work at the center is coordinated by the executive director of the Child Abuse Network, Inc. (CAN), a not-for-profit community agency linking medical, investigation, treatment and prevention resources. Open during the traditional work week, the center provides medical assessments for all levels of physical and sexual abuse, including colposcopic examination and telemedicine consultation. The founding medical director, now chair of the Department of Pediatrics, Robert W. Block, MD, remains clinically involved with the center.

Oregon

Child Abuse Response and Evaluation Services (CARES) Program
Emanuel Hospital
2801 N Gantenbein St
Portland, OR 97227
503/280-4943
503/331-2410
Interim Medical Director: Leila Kelnter, MD, PhD

In a program founded in 1987, the staff of CARES Northwest provides medical evaluations with the use of photo/video colposcopes and specialized forensic videotaped interviews in the assessment of children for sexual abuse, physical abuse, and/or neglect. Over 1,200 children are seen annually at the community-based center, which is a collaborative effort of three health care organizations (Kaiser Permanente, Legacy Emanuel Children's Hospital and OHSU-Doernbecher's Children's Hospital). A multidisciplinary approach is utilized, with community partners of protective service workers and law enforcement officers present for evaluations; mental health therapists are on site to provide crisis intervention and follow-up treatment for those families with no other counseling resources. CARES Northwest staff provides local and regional consultations and training as well as participating in CRESAC (Collaboration for Research on the Sexual Abuse of Children).

Kids Intervention and Diagnostic Service (KIDS) Center
1375 NW Kingston Ave
Bend, OR 97701
541/383-5958
541/383-3016 (Fax)
Medical Director: Susan K. Reichert, MD

The KIDS Center is a community based program for medical assessments of child abuse. A full assessment includes medical and social history of caretaker, physical examination with photographic and colposcopic documentation of findings, a videotaped interview, and debriefing with the caretaker. (If the full assessment is conducted in the context of the examination, a videotaped interview in a separate room may not be conducted.) A physician or nurse practitioner and a licensed clinical social worker conduct the assessment as a team. Child protective service workers and law enforcement may observe the assessment through a video monitor to avoid multiple interviews. The KIDS Center also offers therapy, parent training, and advocacy services, and KIDS Center staff members coordinate the Child Abuse Multi-Disciplinary Team of Deschutes County.

Lane County Child Advocacy Center
2560 Frontier Dr
Eugene, OR 97401
541/682-3938
Medical Director: Scott Halpert, MD

This is a community-based program for forensic medical evaluations of child physical and sexual abuse. Evaluations include videotaped interviews, medical evaluations with videocolposcopy, and an advocacy program to aid victims.

Lincoln City Medical Center, P.C.
2870 W Devils Lake Rd
Lincoln City, OR 97367
503/994-9191
Director: Robert D. Sewell, MD
        503/994-9191

In a rural location on the Oregon coast, examinations are performed within a private pediatric practice setting, utilizing colposcope with photo capability. The physician in charge has performed more than 500 abuse evaluations, most of them sexual abuse in this "model" program. The physician lectures on conducting abuse assessments in the private practice setting.

Rosenfeld Abuse Center
Suspected Child Abuse and Neglect Team (SCAN)
Doernbecher Children's Hospital
Oregon Health Services University
14121 Sam Jackson Park Rd
Portland, OR 97201-3098
503/494-6513
Director: Joseph Zenel, MD

The Suspected Child Abuse and Neglect Team (SCAN) is a hospital-based multidisciplinary program that assesses suspected child abuse cases, both locally and referred, reports abuse episodes to the appropriate authorities, and educates students, medical residents, faculty, and community health professionals on legal, medical, and social aspects of child abuse. SCAN is a community partner with CARES, NW, based at Emanuel Hospital, Portland, OR.

Pennsylvania

The Child Abuse and Neglect Program
Children's Hospital of Philadelphia
34th St and Civic Center Blvd
Philadelphia, PA 19104
215/590-2058
215/590-2180 (Fax)
Director: Cindy W. Christian, MD

The Children's Hospital of Philadelphia identifies and treats more child abuse victims than any medical institution in Pennsylvania. It is the only children's hospital in the city that has an established program and fellowship in child abuse and neglect. Abused children are referred to Children's Hospital from physicians, hospitals, law enforcement, and social service agencies throughout the state of Pennsylvania and New Jersey. The hospital created the Children's Hospital Child Abuse Team in 1974. This multidisciplinary team consists of physicians, social workers, nurses, and other hospital personnel who have a long-standing interest and extensive experience in diagnosing and providing intervention for abused children. In addition to caring for physically abused and neglected children of all ages, the hospital has developed an expertise in caring for young children who are sexual abuse victims. In 1991, the hospital developed the CARE Clinic (Child Abuse Referral and Evaluation Clinic), which meets twice a week to evaluate and treat physically or sexually abused children. The CARE clinic is the only medical program in the Philadelphia area that specifically addresses the special medical needs of the youngest victims of sexual abuse. The Children's Hospital has a long-standing affiliation with SCAN, Inc, a unique social service agency that provides multidisciplinary services to Philadelphia families that are at risk for abuse and neglect. Members of the hospital's child abuse team serve as consultants to a number of Pennsylvania professionals who work with abused children, including the governor's office, Philadelphia medical examiner's office, the Philadelphia district attorney's office, the Philadelphia Department of Human Services, and other legal and social service communities, neighboring counties, and New Jersey.

Child Protection Team
The Milton S. Hershey Medical Center
Department of Pediatrics, H085
Penn State Geisinger Health System
PO Box 850
Hershey, PA 17033
717/531-6700
Director: Andrew S. Freiberg, MD
    215/531-6012

The Child Protection Team at The Milton S. Hershey Medical Center is a multidisciplinary team that serves several missions in the prevention, evaluation, and treatment of all forms of child abuse. Serving several counties in central Pennsylvania, the team regularly to discuss and collect data on all cases of child abuse referred to the hospital or associated clinics. It develops and implements protocols for the efficient evaluation of cases and oversees these strategies in the medical center. The team developed a lecture series for pediatric and med/peds residents on the recognition and evaluation of child abuse. As a regional trauma center, Hershey Medical Center cares for a large number of serious physical abuse cases in Central Pennsylvania.

CVMH Child Protection Team
1086 Franklin St
Johnstown, PA 15905
814/533-9000
814/539-6601 (Fax)
Director: Lawrence Rosenberg, MD
    814/536-8956

In this 10-year-old hospital/county-based child protective team, Dr Rosenberg has 150 child abuse referrals from four county areas. Student seminars are also provided.

Children's Advocacy Center
1107 Wilmington Rd
New Castle, PA 16101
412/658-4688
412/658-8810 (Fax)
Director: Judy Veon

The Children's Advocacy Center was begun to alleviate the trauma to abused children of having to go from place to place (ie, hospital, police station, child welfare, etc) and repeat themselves over and over. The CAC is set in a homey environment, and the resources come to the child. Therapy is also available at the home through the local mental health system. Abuse education and coordination of services are also part of the program.

Children's Seashore House

3405 Civic Center Blvd
Philadelphia, PA 19104-4388
215/895-3155
215/895-3587 (Fax)
Medical Director: Angelo P. Giardino, MD
Program Manager: Karen M. Hudson, MSW, LSW

Children's Seashore House is an abuse referral clinic for children with disabilities. Through a team approach including medicine, nursing, social work, psychology, and speech therapy, evaluations are completed to assess the risk of maltreatment. Referrals and recommendation are also offered.

Pediatric Medical Associates

2705 DeKalb Pike, Suite 205
Norristown, PA 19401
610/277-6400

1077 Rydal Rd, Suite 300
Rydal, PA 19046
215/572-0425
Contact: Steven A. Shapiro, DO

This private general pediatric practice with offices located in Norristown and Abington, Pennsylvania, has provided primary medical evaluations, and ongoing care to children under the age of 12 years who are victims of child abuse. A close affiliation over 14 years with the Montgomery County Office of Children and Youth Services provides the basis for referrals, which can be arranged within 24 hours on an as needed basis. Additionally, the group provides training and education on a regular basis for all members of the Montgomery County SCAN team.

Pediatric Practices of Northeastern Pennsylvania

1837 Fair Ave
Honesdale, PA 18431
717/253-5838
717/253-6678
Contact Physician: Paul H. Diamond, MD

Medical evaluations are provided in this group private general pediatric practice.

Sunbury Community Hospital Center for Child Protection

Sunbury Community Hospital
Sunbury, PA 17801
717/286-3333
717/286-3452 (Fax)
Director: P. J. Bruno, MD
717/286-7754

With the help of benevolent community conscious citizens and our legislators, the Center for Child Protection at Sunbury Community Hospital was started 2 to 3 years ago. The main thrust of the center is to evaluate children via a videotaped psychosocial interview, physical examination, as well as a colposcopic exam.

Rhode Island

ChildSafe — The Child Protection Program at Hasbro Children's Hospital

593 Eddy St
Co-Op 140
Providence, RI 02903
401/444-3996
Director: Carole Jenny, MD
Service Coordinator: Elizabeth Hrycko, MSSA

This program provides medical services for children when abuse or neglect is suspected or confirmed. The program operates an outpatient evaluation clinic where children can receive forensic interviews, comprehensive health assessments, and photo/video colposcopy. Expert consultation to inpatient and emergency services at Hasbro Children's Hospital is provided 24 hours per day. The service evaluates and manages cases of sexual abuse, physical abuse, neglect, medical neglect, failure to thrive, and factitious illness (Munchausen Syndrome by Proxy). Physicians provide expert witness testimony and medical/legal case evaluations. An active fellowship training program for pediatricians is part of the program's mission.

South Carolina

Abuse Recovery Center
5 Richland Medical Park Acc I, Area C
Columbia, SC 29203
803/765-7211

Directors: Allison DeFelice, MD
Anne Abel, MD

This program for medical evaluation of child abuse, both physical and sexual, is staffed by a physician, social worker, nurse, child life specialist, and volunteer part-time counselor. Although child abuse cases have been seen in the training program for several years, the clinic was just organized in September 1990.

Children's Advocacy Center of Spartanburg
100 Washington Pl
Spartanburg, SC 29302
864/515-9922

Medical Director: Nancy A. Henderson, MD
Executive Director: Dateria Johnson

This center opened in April 1996. Medical exams are performed at the center for suspected victims of child sexual abuse. Weekly staffings, an important part of the agency, involve the physician, DSS, law enforcement, GAL, mental health, and the solicitor's office. Therapy and extended assessments are also available at the center. Abuse education and coordination of services are a major part of this program.

Greenville Hospital System
701 Grove Rd
Greenville, SC 29605
864/455-7097

Director: Nancy Henderson, MD

The child sexual abuse clinic provides expert medical exams for all non-acute sexually abused children. The exams are performed with the help of child-life cases primarily referred from DSS and law enforcement. A separate facility for the evaluation of suspected victims may be provided within the next 6 months.

Medical University of South Carolina
Department of Pediatrics
MUSC Children's Hospital
Charleston, SC 29425
803/953-8459
803/792-2123 (Night or Weekend)
803/953-8459 (Fax)

Director: Sara E. Schuh, MD, MPH

The Medical University of South Carolina Department of Pediatrics has a full program for evaluation of children and adolescents for allegations of abuse and neglect. It includes both emergent and non-emergent cases, inpatient and outpatient. Intensive Care Unit admissions are available when indicated. Physician, nursing, and social work services and a patient advocate are available. Psychiatric support is also available when indicated.

Tennessee

Child Abuse Referral and Evaluation (CARE) Program
Vanderbilt University Medical Center
T-3320 Medical Center North
Nashville, TN 37232-2575
615/343-5747
615/343-5751 (Fax)

Medical Director: Suzanne P. Starling, MD

The CARE team provides forensic medical evaluations of hospitalized patients with suspected physical abuse or neglect. CARE provides multidisciplinary case review for all patients evaluated and expert medical testimony for child abuse cases. A weekly outpatient clinic provides comprehensive evaluations and forensic consultative services on cases of physical abuse, neglect and non-organic failure to thrive.

Childhelp, USA
2505 Kingston Pike
Knoxville, TN 37919
423/637-1753
423/544-7150 (Fax)

Director: Richard D. Willey

Children's Advocacy Center of Knox County offers a single child-friendly location in which victims of child sexual abuse can be interviewed by one member of a professional multidisciplinary child protective team, psychologically evaluated, and medically examined within 7 days of disclosure. The center houses offices for the Department of Children's Services, law enforcement, the district attorney, a psychologist, and a pediatric gynecologist.

Children's Advocacy Center of Hamilton County

909 Vine St
Chattanooga, TN 37403
423/266-6918
423/265-0620 (Fax)
Director: Nancy Ridge

The Children's Advocacy Center of Hamilton County is a child-friendly environment which provides coordination of services for child abuse victims. Children can receive sexual assault medical examinations, extended psychosocial assessments, and crisis counseling. The center maintains an expansive resource library related to child abuse and provides professional and community education focused on prevention.

Children's Advocacy Center of Sullivan County

PO Box 867
Bloutville, TN 37617
423/279-1222
423/323-0972 (Fax)
Executive Director: Karen Guidi

The Children's Advocacy Center of Sullivan County provides services to children who may have been victims of child physical and sexual abuse. In addition to medical exams, the program offers crisis intervention and counseling. The center provides court training for children and families and community education programs for the Tri-Cities area.

LeBonheur Center for Children in Crisis

2400 Poplar Ave, Suite 318
Memphis, TN 38112
901/327-4766
901/327-6135 (Fax)
Director: Gary Cook

As a department of LeBonheur Children's Medical Center exclusively focusing on child abuse issues, medical consultations are provided to LeBonheur inpatients to rule in/out child abuse; family evalua-

tions are conducted by a multidisciplinary team at the request of TN-Children's Services protective service workers; and outpatient treatment services are provided to victims of abuse/neglect and their parents. The center provides home visitation services to new teen mothers to prevent child abuse.

Memphis Sexual Assault Resource Center

1331 Union Ave
Suite 1150
Memphis, TN 38104
901/327-0233
901/274-2769 (Fax)
Manager: Brenda Cassinello

The Memphis Sexual Assault Resource Center is a multidisciplinary agency that provides forensic medicolegal evaluations of alleged victims of sexual assault/abuse for the investigating agencies. Other services of the agency include crisis intervention/counseling in the office and 24 hour hotline; legal assistance that includes pretrial conferences, court escort, victim's compensation, and night court for children; medicolegal/forensic evaluations that include medical screening, physical and material evidence collection; expert witness services to the courts including forensic evaluators and forensic serologists; community education that includes pathology of the crime and prevention instruction; and professional training to medical professionals, attorneys and legal professionals, and social professionals.

Our Kids, Inc

1900 Hayes St
Nashville, TN 37203
615/862-4211 (Clinic)
615/862-4127 (Administrative Office)
Medical Director: Suzanne Starling, MD, FAAP

The Our Kids Center provides medical and psychological evaluations and support for children who may have been sexually abused. Between 850 to 1000 children are seen each year from Davidson and surrounding counties. The center also provides training opportunities for professionals in the medical and psychosocial fields.

Patient Advocacy Committee

East Tennessee Children's Hospital
2018 Clinch Ave
Knoxville, TN 37901
423/541-8484

Chair: Mary Palmer Campbell, MD

This multidisciplinary group reviews all inpatients referred to the Department of Human Services. Inpatient and emergency medicine physicians, intensive care and hospital nursing services, chaplain, child life, social services, and home health care are all represented. The purpose is to ensure adequate investigating, reporting, and follow-up services to victims of child maltreatment.

Special Attention Clinic

East Tennessee Children's Hospital
2018 Clinch Ave
Knoxville, TN 37901
423/541-8710
423/541-8497

Director: Mary Palmer Campbell, MD

The Special Attention Clinic is for the medical evaluation of children believed to be sexually abused. Children are referred by DHS and local physicians after initial investigation and interviews. The evaluation includes a general physical exam, as well as genital and rectal exams using a colposcope with camera attachment. Findings are conveyed to the Department of Human Services and to local law enforcement, when indicated.

Texas

The ABC Center (for the Medical Evaluation of Child Victims of Abuse and Neglect)

Division of General Pediatrics
University of Texas Medical Branch
400 Harborside Dr
Galveston, TX 77555-1119
409/747-9298

Director: James L. Lukefahr, MD
409/772-1444

The ABC Center meets four days a week to evaluate children for alleged sexual or physical abuse. The center is staffed by a physician,

physician's assistant, and social worker. Most referrals are from regional child protection and law enforcement agencies. Evaluation consists of a brief interview followed by complete physical examination and colposcopy with photography. Videotaped forensic interviews are performed at the nearby Advocacy Center for Children of Galveston County, which also provides short-term counseling. ABC Center professionals participate in regional multidisciplinary case reviews and child death review teams. The center is the primary facility for child abuse training at the University of Texas Medical Branch, providing teaching experiences for pediatric residents as well as medical and allied health students. The center is linked to other Texas child abuse centers through the Texas Telemedicine Peer Review Network.

Alamo Children's Advocacy Center

7130 New Highway 90 West
San Antonio, TX 78227
210/358-3971

Medical Director: Nancy D. Kellogg, MD
Executive Director: Marlyn Gibbs

Agencies/disciplines currently housed at ACAC include a director, counselors, two physicians, a nurse practitioner, an advanced practice nurse, an RN, an assistant district attorney, detectives from Sex Crimes, and the sexual abuse unit from Child Protective Services. Services offered include counseling, medical evaluations, CPS assessments, child interviews, multidisciplinary reviews and staffings, court school for children, training for health professionals, community presentations, and testimony. The physicians and nurses are faculty at University of Texas Health Science Center at San Antonio; medical evaluations are scheduled 5 days per week. ACAC is linked to other Texas child abuse centers through the Texas Telemedicine Peer Review Network.

Child Advocacy, Research and Education (CARE) Center
Department of Pediatrics
Texas Tech University Health Sciences Center
3601 4th St
Lubbock, TX 79430
806/743-2121
Director: Barbara Camp Law, PA, CHA
Consultants: Richard M. Lampe, MD
      Mark Hall, MD
      806/743-2121

The CARE Center provides forensic evaluations, preventive education, multidisciplinary reviews, coordination of the Child Fatality Review Team, failure to thrive evaluations, and expert medical testimony for children who may have been abused or neglected. Education and training is provided to residents, medical students, partner agencies, and the community. A patient database, research, linkage with other centers, and consultation for area professionals is provided.

Child Advocacy Resource and Evaluation
Cook Children's Medical Center
800 Seventh Ave
Fort Worth, TX 76104
817/885-3953
817/870-7445 (Fax)
Director: Leah J. Lamb, DO
      drlamb@cookchildren.org (E-mail)

The CARE Team conducts medical interviews, medical and forensic evaluations, psychosocial assessments, and preventative education. It participates in multidisciplinary reviews for victims of sexual abuse, physical abuse, and neglect. The CARE Team serves as a resource for parents, primary care physicians, law enforcement, and the Texas Department of Protective and Regulatory Services. The CARE Team and other Cook Children's Medical Center health professionals work together to assess the family's needs and provide treatment and follow-up care. Social workers specializing in child protection issues are available to facilitate consultation, reporting, and crisis intervention. The CARE Team also make referrals to other community agencies for counseling needs.

Child Assessment Program
Children's Advocacy Center
1110 E. 32nd St
Austin, TX 78722
512/472-7279
Director: Beth Nauert, MD
      512/443-4800

This program meets 1/2 day weekly to evaluate children for alleged sexual abuse. Evaluation includes an interview of child (brief not video-taped) and a physical examination with colposcope and photos. A report is prepared for the referring physician or agency.

**Child Protection Program Team (CPPT)
of Driscol Children's Hospital**
3455 South Alameda Dr
Corpus Christi, TX 78466-6530
512/694-5100
512/851-6867 (Fax)
Director: William J. (Jerry) Reed, MD
      512/694-6426
Coordinator: Sonia Eddleman, RN

The team provides complete medical evaluations, including forensic/colposcopic and photographic evaluations, of children suspected of being abused or neglected. Staff includes social services, psychological services, and multidisciplinary team which meets twice weekly and collaborates with an advocacy center and peer review CARE and fatality review team.

Medical and Dental Clinic
Harris County Children's Protective Service
5100 Southwest Freeway
Houston, TX 77056
713/599-5595
Director: Kim K. Cheung, MD, PhD
      713/599-5588

Harris County CPS medical clinic provides comprehensive general pediatric care for children, with CPS involvement. Services include initial assessments for physical abuse and neglect, medical examinations for placement, well child care, and acute sick visits. Pediatric residents and medical students from University of Texas-Houston medical school receive some of their ambulatory training at the clinic, as well as education on recognition and prevention of child maltreatment. Other functions of the clinic include consultation for case workers and coordination of medical care for children in foster care. A dental clinic is also on site.

REACH Clinic
Children's Medical Center of Dallas
1935 Motor St
Dallas, TX 75235
214/640-6134

Directors: Janet Squires, MD
                Donna Persaud, MD

The core team is composed of two physicians, pediatric nurse practitioner, registered nurse, social worker and administrative coordinator. The medical staff is from the Department of Pediatrics of the University of Texas Southwestern Medical Center. The clinic provides medical consultation on child abuse cases primarily for Child Protective Services in Dallas county. The services include direct patient assessment in the inpatient and outpatient setting, and review of medical data and legal testimony. The team meets weekly for peer review and operates in collaboration with the Dallas Children's Advocacy Center. Several team members regularly give lectures and workshops on child abuse and related themes such as domestic violence.

Virginia

Abused Children's Center
Fairfax Hospital
3300 Gallows Rd
Falls Church, VA 22046
703/698-3505
703/698-2893 (Fax)

Medical Director: Michael Altieri, MD
SANE Coordinator: Sue Brown, RN, BSN,
                        CEN, SANE

The examination and treatment of children who may have been sexually assaulted requires special services, including a facility that is comforting for a child and has a caring approach on the part of the staff. The Abused Children's Center at Inova Fairfax Hospital is a cooperative effort by Inova Fairfax Hospital and law enforcement agencies. The center assists police and child protective agencies with the collection of evidence in

pediatric sexual abuse cases. The center is not a walk-in or self-referral center. Children are referred only by police and child protective services. In an area that is set apart from the rest of the emergency department, the police officer or the child protective services representative interviews the victim about the events. After the interview, the SANE nurse examines the victim for injuries and collects any evidence. The SANE nurse is trained to perform a detailed forensic exam, use a physical evidence recovery kit (PERK) and colposcopy imaging, perform certain medical/laboratory tests, and make any necessary referrals for follow-up care and counseling.

Child Advocacy Committee
Children's Hospital of The King's Daughters
800 W Olney Rd
Norfolk, VA 23508
804/628-7179

Director: John M. de Triquet, MD

The Child Advocacy Committee is charged with the review of all inpatients and outpatients evaluated for physical or sexual abuse. All children admitted to the Orthopedic or Burn Services are reviewed by a medical representative of the committee. The committee chairman serves as the primary medical consultant for the five regional Child Protective Services in southeastern Virginia.

Child Protection Team
Children's Medical Center
Virginia Commonwealth University
PO Box 980514
Richmond, VA 23298
804/828-7400

Medical Director: Miriam Bar-on, MD
Coordinator: Ruth Hall

The Child Protection Team (CPT) provides evaluative and consultative services to the medical community at large for children suspected of being abused or neglected. It serves as a referral source for CPS, law enforcement, and mental health workers to provide medical evaluations as needed. All children admitted with suspicious injuries are evaluated by team members. In addition, a major aspect of the team's activities is to provide training in the area of child abuse and neglect for medical professionals and others who work with children.

Washington

Brigid Collins House
PO Box 2633
Bellingham, WA 98227
360/734-4616

Executive Director: Byron Manering

Brigid Collins House is a child abuse treatment and prevention agency. The mission of the agency is to break the cycle of child abuse in Whatcom County. The goals are to promote the healthy development of all families, to prevent the onset of abuse through community outreach and education, and to provide immediate and comprehensive services to victims of child abuse. Programs include Healthy Families Whatcom County, for families beginning prenatally and ending when the child turns seven; Parents Helping Parents weekly drop in support groups; Family Support Team parent mentor program; the Nurturing Program for parents and children ages 4 to 12; school-based case management; child sexual abuse case management; and group therapy for children who have been sexually abused and their non-offending parents.

Children's Protection Team
Children's Hospital & Medical Center
4800 Sand Point Way NE
PO Box 5371, CH-76
Seattle, WA 98105-0371

Manager: Carol Mason, MEd
    206/526-2194

Clinical Director: Jill Cole, DSW
    206/526-2167

The multidisciplinary Children's Hospital Protection Program provides diagnostic and treatment services for children and adolescents with difficulties related to child abuse and neglect. The program also provides education and training for hospital staff, medical residents, nurses, and social workers in training. The multidisciplinary team of the Children's Protection Team consists of pediatricians, educators, nurses, social workers, psychiatrist, hospital counsel, security, and pastoral care. The team provides expert consultation to hospital staff and, on occasion, to the community in lieu of city child protection teams. Consultation is also available for medical diagnosis and treatment at

Children's Hospital and other hospital sites including area clinics. The program sponsors a clinic that does specialized child sexual abuse exams for children known to the medical center, supports advocacy efforts in the community, and provides staff for community participation in city child abuse review teams and expert witness testimony. Team members provide community education and present at national conferences on child abuse and neglect.

Clark County Child Abuse Intervention Center
700 NE 87th Ave
Vancouver, WA 98664
206/253-1230

Medical Director: John Stirling, MD

Medical evaluation of suspected victims of child sexual and/or physical abuse is provided in the Vancouver Clinic, a multispecialty group clinic serving SW Washington. Close liaison is provided with law enforcement and the county prosecutor's office, as well as with Children's Protective Services and community support services. The office provides clinical training for, and coordinates with, a hospital-based Sexual Assault Response Team to evaluate acute cases. Consultation is also provided to community Child Protection Teams and an Infant-Child Death Review Committee.

Harborview Sexual Assault Center
325 9th Ave, MX 359947
Seattle, WA 98104
206/521-1800

Medical Director: Naomi Sugar, MD

Harborview Sexual Assault Center provides emergency and non-emergency medical evaluations for children and adolescents referred primarily from King County (other Washington areas as needed). The program offers psychosocial evaluations, ongoing therapy, medical consultation, expert legal testimony, educational opportunities for practicing clinicians and residents, and local and statewide referral services for medical and mental health therapy. The center provides medical networking and educational resources for clinicians throughout the state. It is affiliated with University of Washington School of Medicine, Department of Pediatrics, and the School of Social Work.

Regional Center for Child Abuse and Neglect
Deaconess Medical Center
PO Box 248
Spokane, WA 99210-0248
509/623-7501
509/625-5132 (Fax)
Director: Alan Hendrickson, MD
Manager: Mary Ann Murphy

A collaborative effort among hospital, CPS, law enforcement, prosecutor, attorney general, and treatment provides for child abuse assessments. The program provides:

1. Comprehensive medical examinations, including colposcopy, for child victims of physical and sexual abuse and neglect;
2. Evidentiary interviews videotaped;
3. Multidisciplinary case planning (average of 8 professionals involved with each family) for decisions on: (a) legal action (civil and criminal); (b) placement and visitation; (c) social and health treatment plan for all family members.

The staff includes: a pediatrician, pediatric nurse practitioner, RN, manager, two social workers, secretary, three CPS social workers, and one detective.

Sexual Assault Clinic and Child Abuse Program
Mary Bridge Children's Hospital & Health Center
311 So L St
Tacoma, WA 98405
253/552-1478
253/552-1540 (Fax)
Medical Director: Yolanda Duralde, MD
Manager: Carolyn McDougal, MD

The Mary Bridge Sexual Assault Clinic Intervention Program is an outpatient non-acute forensic medical evaluation and psychosocial support program that serves birth to 18-year-old individuals who may have been sexually assaulted. The average age is 6, and percentage of female to male is 75% to 25%. An emergency department evaluation occurs immediately in rape and acute situations. Medical evaluation, medical treatment, and psychosocial services for physical assault occur through the Child Abuse Intervention Department. In development is the Child Abuse Prevention Program and an in-house child advocacy team. Professional staff includes physicians, social

workers, and nurses. Close interaction with law enforcement and Child Protective Service occurs. Psychosocial services include crisis intervention, case management, and support to child and family.

Sexual Assault Clinic
Providence St Peter Hospital
413 Lilly Road NE
Olympia, WA 98506
360/493-7469
Medical Director: Deborah K. Hall, MD

This clinic serves residents of Thurston, Lewis, Mason, Grays Harbor, Pacific, and Wahkiakum Counties. Children and adolescents are referred for concerns of possible sexual abuse. Social workers gather background history and behavior concerns pre-visit; physicians provide medical evaluation/ recommendations. Counseling is available, at little or no cost, for parents or guardians of children who have been abused. Forensic interviews of young children or adolescents are available to law enforcement or Child Protective Services. Sexual assault nurse examiners provide 24-hour call coverage in the Emergency Department for child and adult rape exams, collection of forensic evidence, and prevention of unintended pregnancy and/or STD infections.

Wisconsin

Child Abuse/Neglect Evaluation
Marshfield Children's
1000 N Oak St
Marshfield, WI 54449
715/387-5251
Director: Karen B. Mielke, MD

Children are examined and, when appropriate, interviewed by Dr Mielke. Appropriate cultures are taken. Photography is performed by a graphic arts specialist. Colposcopy with photography is used for the evaluation of sexual abuse. A social worker assists in scheduling and communication. Inpatient evaluations and interventions by a multidiscplinary team are provided when necessary. Psychological treatment services are available. Dr Mielke will testify by phone or in person in court. This is a specialty clinic of the 450 physician multispecialty Marshfield Clinic.

West Virginia

West Virginia University - Charleston Division and Women and Children's Hospital Sexual Abuse Team
800 Pennsylvania Ave
Charleston, WV 25302
304/348-2390
304/342-8288 (Fax)

Co-Directors: Joan M. Phillips, MD
                  Kathleen V. Previll, MD
                  304/342-8272

The West Virginia University Charleston Division Department of Pediatrics, in conjunction with Women and Children's Hospital, conducts a twice-weekly sexual abuse clinic staffed by a social worker, pediatric resident, and teaching pediatrician. Reports from this team are sent to the referring DHS worker, law enforcement, doctor, or referring attorney. Follow-up counseling, court action, or medical follow-up is arranged.

National Committee to Prevent Child Abuse (NCPCA)

Chapter Contacts

Sources of information and liaison to local parental support groups and child abuse prevention efforts in specific communities are provided in this section.

Alabama

Lynne Thrasher
205/355-7252
Staff Contact
North Alabama Chapter, NCPCA
PO Box 1247
613 Lafayette NE
Decatur, AL 35601

Glenda Trotter
205/271-5105
Executive Director
Greater Alabama Chapter, NCPCA
PO Box 230904,
2101 Eastern Blvd, Ste 26
Montgomery, AL 36123-0904

Alaska

Elizabeth Forrer
907/276-4994
Executive Director
South Central Alaska Chapter, NCPCA
3745 Community Park Loop, #102
Anchorage, AK 99508-3466

Arizona

Carole Brazsky
520/969-2308
Executive Director
Arizona Chapter, NCPCA
PO Box 63921
Phoenix, AZ 85082-3921

California

Julie Christine
916/498-8481
Executive Director
California Chapter, NCPCA
CA Consortium to PCA
926 J St, Ste 717
Sacramento, CA 95814-2707

Connecticut

Jane Bourns
203/747-6801
Director
Connecticut Chapter, NCPCA
Director Children's Services,
Wheeler Clinic
91 Northwest Dr
Plainville CT, 06062

Delaware

Karen de Rasmo/JoAnne Kasses
302/654-1102
Interim Co-Directors
Delaware Chapter, NCPCA
Delawareans United to PCA
Tower Office Park
240 N James St, Ste 103
Newport, DE 19804

District of Columbia

Barbara Lautman
202/223-0020
Executive Director
DC Chapter, NCPCA
PO Box 57194
Washington, DC 20037

Florida

Stephanie Meincke
904/448-5437
Executive Director
Florida Chapter, NCPCA
2728 Pablo St, Ste B
Tallahassee, FL 32308

Georgia

Sandra Wood
404/870-6565
Executive Director
Georgia Chapter, NCPCA
1375 Peachtree St, NE, Suite 200
Atlanta, GA 30309

Hawaii
Charles Braden
808/951-0200
Executive Director
Hawaii Chapter, NCPCA
1575 So Beretania St
Ste 201-202
Honolulu, HI 96826

Illinois
Don Schlosser
217/522-1129
Executive Director
Illinois Chapter, NCPCA
528 S 5th St, Ste 211
Springfield, IL 62701

Cynthia Savage
312/663-3520
Executive Director
Greater Chicago Council, NCPCA
332 S Michigan Ave, #1600
Chicago, IL 60604-4357

Roy Harley
309/764-7017
Executive Director
Quad Cities Affiliate, NCPCA
525 16th St
Moline, IL 61265

Indiana
Andie Marshall
317/634-9282
Executive Director
Indiana Chapter, NCPCA
One Virginia Ave, Ste 401
Indianapolis, IN 46204

Iowa
Steve Scott
515/252-0270
Executive Director
Iowa Chapter, NCPCA
3829 71st St, Ste A
Urbandale, IA 50322

Kansas
Robert L. Hartman
316/942-4261
Executive Director
Kansas Chapter, NCPCA
1365 N Custer, Box 517
Wichita, KS 67201

Kentucky
Jill Seyfred
606/275-1299
Executive Director
Kentucky Chapter, NCPCA
2401 Regency Rd, Ste 104
Lexington, KY 40503

Louisiana
Marketa Garner
504/346-0222
Executive Director
Louisiana Chapter, NCPCA
2351 Energy Dr, Ste 1010
Baton Rouge, LA 70808

Maine
Liz Kuhlman
207/778-6960
Executive Director
Franklin County Maine Chapter, NCPCA
69 North Main St
Farmington, ME 04938

Lucky Hollander
207/874-1120
Executive Director
Maine Association of Can Councils
Greater Maine Chapter, NCPCA
PO Box 912
Portland, ME 04104

Marilyn Staples
207/284-1337
Executive Director
York County Chapter, NCPCA
0 Dental Ave, PO Box 568
Biddeford, ME 04072

Maryland
Gloria Goldfaden
410/841-6599
Executive Director
Maryland Chapter, NCPCA
2530 Riva Road, Ste 3
Annapolis, MD 21401

Massachusetts
Jetta Bernier
617/742-8555
Executive Director
Massachusetts Chapter, NCPCA
14 Beacon St, #706
Boston, MA 02108

Michigan
Jean Smith
810/469-5180
Executive Director
Michigan Chapter, NCPCA
PO Box 12096
Lansing, MI 48901

Minnesota
Roy Garza
612/641-1568
Executive Director
Minnesota Chapter, NCPCA
450 N Syndicate St, Ste 290
St Paul, MN 55104

Mississippi
Donna McLaurin
601/366-0025
Executive Director
Mississippi Chapter, NCPCA
2906 N State, Ste 200
Jackson, MS 39216

Missouri
Lucia Erickson-Kincheloe
314/634-5223
Executive Director
Missouri Chapter, NCPCA
308 East High St
Jefferson City, MO 65101

Montana
Sarah Lipscomb
406/728-9449
Program Director
Montana Chapter, NCPCA
PO Box 7533
Missoula, MT 59807

Nevada
Paula Ford, PhD
702/368-1533
Executive Director
Nevada Chapter, NCPCA
5440 W Sahara, Ste 202
Las Vegas, NV 89102

New Hampshire
Monique Devine
603/225-5441
Acting Director
New Hampshire Chapter, NCPCA
PO Box 607
44 Warren St
Concord, NH 03302

New Jersey
Sharon Copeland
201/643-3710
Executive Director
New Jersey Chapter, NCPCA
35 Halsey, Ste 300
Newark, NJ 01702-3031

New Mexico
Trish Steindler
505/471-6909
NM Contact
RR 9, Box 10
Santa Fe, NM 87505

New York
James Cameron
518/445-1273
Executive Director
New York Chapter, NCPCA
134 S Swan St
Albany, NY 12210

North Carolina
Jennifer Tolle
919/829-8009
Executive Director
North Carolina Chapter, NCPCA
3344 Hillsborough St, Ste 100D
Raleigh, NC 26707

North Dakota
Kathy Mayer
701/223-9052
Executive Director
North Dakota Contact, NCPCA
418 E Rosser, Ste 303
Bismark, ND 58502-1213

Ohio
Debbie Sendek
614/722-6800
Executive Director
Ohio Chapter, NCPCA
700 Children's Drive
Columbus, OH 43205

Oklahoma
Debbie Richardson
405/525-0688
Executive Director
Oklahoma Chapter, NCPCA
2200 Classen Blvd, Ste 340
Oklahoma City, OK 73106

Pennsylvania
Terry Ferrier
717/393-4511
Executive Director
Central Pennsylvania Chapter
PO Box 7664
1917B Olde Homestead Lane
Lancaster, PA 17604

Rhode Island
Ted Whiteside
401/728-7920
Executive Director
Rhode Island Chapter, NCPCA
500 Prospect St
Pawtucket, RI 02860

South Carolina
Janice Bolin
803/747-1339
Executive Director
Low Country SC Chapter, NCPCA
5055 Lackawanna Blvd
North Charleston, SC 29406-4522

Beebe James
803/733-5430
Executive Director
Midlands Chapter, NCPCA
1800 Main St, #3A
Columbia, SC 29201

Russell Smith
803/467-7680
Executive Director
Piedmont Chapter, NCPCA
111 Mills Ave
Greenville, SC 29601-3671

Tennessee
Lynne Luther
615/227-2273
Executive Director
Tennessee NCPCA Contact
3010 Ambrose Ave
Nashville, TN 37207

Texas
Wendell Teltow
Executive Director
513/250-8483
Texas Chapter, NCPCA
12701 Research, Ste 303
Austin, TX 78759

Utah
Edward Witker
Staff Contact
801/532-3404
Utah Chapter, NCPCA
40 E South Temple, Ste 350-12
Salt Lake City, UT 84111-1003

Vermont
Linda Johnson
Executive Director
802/229-5724
Vermont Chapter, NCPCA
PO Box 829
141 Main St
Montpelier, VT 05601

Virginia
Barbara Rawn
Executive Director
804/775-1777
Virginia Chapter, NCPCA
224 E Broad St, Ste 302
Richmond, VA 23241

Washington
Bruce Garner
President
360/658-2164
Washington Chapter, NCPCA
1801 Grove St, Unit D
Marysville, WA 98270

West Virginia
Laurie McKeown
Coordinator
304/523-9587
West Virginia Contact
PO Box 1653
Huntington, WV 25717

Wisconsin
Sally Casper
Executive Director
608/256-3378
Wisconsin Chapter, NCPCA
214 N Hamilton
Madison, WI 53703

Wyoming
Rose Kor
Executive Director
307/637-8622
Wyoming Chapter, NCPCA
1120 Logan Ave
Cheyenne, WY 82001

AAP Chapters
Committees on Child Abuse and Neglect:

Chairperson Roster

Alabama
John F. Shriner, MD
Chairperson
334/432-1101
Child Advocacy Center
1351 Spring Hill Ave
Mobile, AL 36604-3210

Arkansas
Jerry G. Jones, MD
Chairperson
501/320-1013
Arkansas Children's Hospital
800 Marshall St
Little Rock, AR 72202-3510

Arizona
Kathryn A. Bowen, MD
Chairperson
520/881-4635
2731 E Simmons St
Tucson, AZ 85716-1045

California 1
David L. Kerns, MD
Chairperson
408/885-5405
Santa Clara Valley Medical Center
751 S Bascom Ave
San Jose, CA 95128

California 2
Jess Diamond, MD
Chairperson
805/326-2263
Department of Pediatrics
Kern Medical Center
1830 Flower St
Bakersfield, CA 93305-4144

California 3
David L. Chadwick, MD
Chairperson
619/576-5814
Children's Hospital & Health Center
Center for Child Protection, 5016
3020 Children's Way
San Diego, CA 92123-4223

California 4
Deborah Claire Stewart, MD
Chairperson
714/634-5106
Department of Pediatrics
U of CA Irvine Medical Center
101 The City Drive
Irvine, CA 92668

Colorado
Andrew Paul Sirotnak, MD
Chairperson
303/572-4609
1937 Eudora St
Denver, CO 80220-1252

Connecticut
Jeanne Marie Marconi, MD
Chairperson
203/838-8414
61 East Ave
Norwalk, CT 06851-4906

Florida
J. M. Whitworth, MD
Chairperson
904/549-4670
Children's Crisis Center, Inc
PO Box 40279
Jacksonville, FL 32203-0279

Georgia
Lynn Anne Platt, MD
Chairperson
912/350-8016
The Children's Hospital
Memorial Medical Center, Inc
PO Box 23089
Savannah, GA 31404-6283

Iowa
Randell Curtis Alexander, MD
Chairperson
319/353-6136
University of Iowa
Department of Pediatrics
209 Hospital School
Iowa City, IA 52242-1011

Illinois
Emalee G. Flaherty, MD
Chairperson
773/880-3763
2300 Children's Plaza # 16
Chicago, IL 60614

Indiana
Roberta Ann Hibbard, MD
Chairperson
317/630-2617
Department of Community & General Pediatrics
Myers Bldg D-530
1001 W 10th St
Indianapolis, IN 46202-2859

Maine
Lawrence Ronald Ricci, MD
Chairperson
207/879-6160
The Child Abuse Program @ Spurwink Clinic
17 Bishop St
Portland, ME 04103-1070

Denise Marie Miller, MD
Co-Chairperson
207/985-2467
51 High St
Kennebunk, ME 04043-2613

Massachusetts
Robert Peter Nelken, MD
Chairperson
508/475-4522
140 Haverhill St
Andover, MA 01810-1504

Jan E. Paradise, MD
Co-Chairperson
617/534-7902
2 Alexander Rd
Newton, MA 02161

Mississippi
Julia Ann Sherwood, MD
Chairperson
601/366-3649
876-A Lakeland Dr
Jackson, MS 39216-4644

Missouri
James Corbet Kelly, MD
Chairperson
816/234-3463
Department of Emergency Medicine
Children's Mercy Hospital
24th @ Gillham Road
Kansas City, MO 64108

Nebraska
Karen Higgins, MD
Chairperson
308/382-1100
PO Box 550
2444 W Faidley
Grand Island, NE 68803-4327

New Hampshire
Steven William Kairys, MD
Chairperson
603/650-4620
Department of Pediatrics/DMS
1 Medical Center Dr, HB7450
Lebanon, NH 03756

New York 1
Celeste Marie Madden, MD
Chairperson
315/471-0733
322 Farmer St
Syracuse, NY 13203-1306

New York 2
Roy Horowitz, MD
Chairperson
183 Mineola Blvd
Mineola, NY 11501-2524

New York 3
Linda Theil Cahill, MD
Chairperson
212/879-9829
530 E 72nd St
New York, NY 10021-4855

North Dakota
Jean Fahey, MD
Chairperson
701/235-0365
3114 26 Avenue SW
Fargo, ND 58103-5067

Ohio
Bernard J. Cullen, MD
Chairperson
419/893-2591
1350 Old Trail Road
Maumee, OH 43537-1943

Oklahoma
Marian Pilar Escobar, MD
Chairperson
405/222-9500
Southern Plains Medical Center
PO Box 1069
Chickasha, OK 73023-1069

Gwendolyn L. Gibson, MD
Chairperson
918/838-8188
University of Oklahoma
College of Medicine-Tulsa
2815 S Sheridan
Tulsa, OK 74129-1000

Oregon
Judith Ann (Jan) Bays, MD
Chairperson
503/331-2400
Emanuel Children's Hospital
2800 N Vancouver Ave
Portland, OR 97227-1630

Pennsylvania
Glen S. Bartlett, MD
Chairperson
717/533-7850
Hershey Pediatric Center
441 E Chocolate Ave
Hershey, PA 17033-1324

Pat J. Bruno, MD
Co-Chairperson
717/286-7754
369 N 11th St
Sunbury, PA 17801-1610

Tennessee
Robert V. Walling, MD
Chairperson
UT Medical Group
66 N Pauline
Memphis, TN 38105-5105

Texas
Nancy Denny Kellogg, MD
Chairperson
512/270-3971
Department of Pediatrics
7703 Floyd Curl Dr
San Antonio, TX 78284-7808

Utah
Helen L. Britton, MD
Chairperson
801/588-3650
Primary Children's Medical Center
100 N Medical Dr
Salt Lake City, UT 84113-1100

Vermont
George W. Brown, MD
Chairperson
206/253-1230
PO Box 4488
South Burlington, VT 05406-4488

Virginia
Viviana Skansi, MD
Chairperson
804/461-4111
18 The Koger Center
Suite 115
Norfolk, VA 23502

Washington
John Stirling, Jr, MD
Chairperson
715/387-5251
700 NE 87th Ave
Vancouver, WA 98664-1913

Wisconsin
Gerald E. Porter, MD
Chairperson
715/387-5251
803 S Adams Ave
Marshfield, WI 54449

Wyoming
Valerie Jean Bell, MD
Chairperson
307/635-7961
433 E 19th Ave
Cheyenne, WY 82001-4652

Federal Agency Contacts for Multi-Agency
Child Death Review Activities

Federal Agency	Primary Contact	Secondary Contact	Secondary Contact

Centers for Disease Control and Prevention (CDC)	Phil McClain, MS
	CDC
	National Center for
	  Injury Prevention
	  and Control
	1600 Clifton Road, NE
	Mailstop F41
	Atlanta, GA 30333
	770/488-4143
	770/488-4338 (Fax)
		Randy Hanzlick, MD
		CDC
		Mailstop F35
		4770 Buford Ave, NE
		Atlanta, GA 30341
		770/488-7087
		770/488-7044 (Fax)
			Shorunda Buchanan, PhD
			CDC
			Mailstop F35
			4770 Buford Ave, NE
			Atlanta, GA 30341
			770/488-7088
			770/448-7044 (Fax)

Centers for Disease Control and Prevention	Family and Intimate Violence Prevention Team CDC Mailstop K60 Buford Ave, NE Atlanta, GA 30341-3724 770/488-4410 770/488-4349	**Gib Parrish, MD** CDC Mailstop F35 4770 Buford Ave, NE Atlanta, GA 30341 770/488-7088 770/488-7044 (Fax)	

Congressional Research Service	**Ms Dale Robinson**
	Congressional Research
	  Service
	Education and Public
	  Welfare Division
	Library of Congress
	101 Independence Ave, SE
	Washington, DC 20540-7440
	202/707-2322
	202/707-7338 (Fax)		

Department of Defense	Department of Defense
	Bureau of Naval
	Personnel
	PERS-661 Delta
	Washington, DC 20370-6610
	703/697-0601
	703/697-6617 (Fax)
	  202/576-0373 (Fax)
		Paul Vasallo, MD
		Armed Forces Institute
		  of Pathology
		Office of the Medical
		  Examiner
		Washington, DC 20306-6000
		202/576-3232	

Department of Interior	**Marcella Giles** Attorney Advisor Department of Interior Office of Indian Affairs 1849 C St NW Mailstop 6456 Washington, DC 20240 202/208-6967 202/219-1791 (Fax)		

Federal Agency	Primary Contact	Secondary Contact	Secondary Contact
Department of Justice	**Mary Incontro** Deputy Chief Violent Crime Section US Department of Justice PO Box 7179 Washington, DC 20044- 7179 202/514-0849 202/514-8714 (Fax)	**Bernard Auchter** Program Manager National Institute of Justice Domestic Violence Program 633 Indiana Ave, NW, #867 Washington, DC 20531 202/307-0154 202/307-6394	**Winston C. Norman** Major Case Specialist, ViCAP Behavioral Science Unit Federal Bureau of Investigations Quantico, VA 22135 703/640-1207 703/640-1354 (Fax)
Indian Health Services	**Richard Kotomori, MD** Chief, Special Initiatives Section Indian Health Services 5600 Fishers Lane, Room 5A-41 Rockville, MD 20857 301/443-4646 301/443-7623 (Fax)	**Tom Welty, MD, MPH** Office of Epidemiology PHS Indian Hospital 3200 Canyon Lake Drive Rapid City, SD 57702 605/348-1900	
National Center for Health Statistics	**Lois Fingerhut** Special Assistant Injury Epidemiology National Center for Health Statistics 6525 Belcrest Road, Room 750 Hyattville, MD 20782 301/436-7026 301/436-8459 (Fax)	**Kenneth Kochanek, MA** Mortality Statistics Branch, NCHS Division of Vital Statistics 6525 Belcrest Road, Room 840 Hyattville, MD 20782 301/436-8884 301/436-7066 (Fax)	
National Institutes of Health - NICHD	**Marian Willinger, PhD** Center for Research for Mothers and Children, NICHD National Institutes of Health 6100 Executive Bl Room 4B03 Rockville, MD 20852 301/496-5575 301/402-2085 (Fax)		
NCCAN	**Emily Cooke** National Center on Child Abuse and Neglect PO Box 1182 Washington, DC 20013 202/205-8709 202/205-9721 (Fax)	**David Lloyd, Director** National Center on Child Abuse and Neglect PO Box 1182 Washington, DC 20013 202/205-8646	**Sally Flanzer** National Center on Child Abuse and Neglect PO Box 1182 Washington, DC 20013 202/205-8708 202/205-9721 (Fax)

Federal Agency	Primary Contact	Secondary Contact	Secondary Contact
NCCAN Clearinghouse	**Lenna Reid** National Clearinghouse on Child Abuse and Neglect Information PO Box 1182 Washington, DC 20013- 1182 800/394-3366 703/385-7565 (Fax)	**Sandi McLeod** National Clearinghouse on Child Abuse and Neglect Information PO Box 1182 Washington, DC 20013- 1182 800/394-3366 703/385-7565 (Fax)	
Office of Disease Prevention & Health Promotion	**Jim Harrell** Department Director Department of Health & Human Services Office of Disease Prevention & Health Promotion 200 Independence Ave, SW Washington, DC 20201 202/401-6295 202/205-9478 (Fax)		
Office of the Surgeon General	**Winnie Mitchell** Policy Analyst Office of the Surgeon General Room 736E, Humphrey Building Washington, DC 20201 202/690-6467 202/690-6498 (Fax)		
Public Health Service	**Juanita C. Evans, MSW** US Public Health Service Health Resources & Services Administration Maternal & Child Health Bureau 5600 Fishers Lane, Room 18A39 Rockville, MD 20857 301/443-4169 301/443-1296 (Fax)	**Jean Hathey, PhD** Director, Injury Prevention and EMSC Program US Public Health Service 5600 Fishers Lane, Room 18A39 Rockville, MD 20857 301/443-4026 301/443-1296 (Fax)	
US Advisory Board on Child Abuse and Neglect	**Deanne Tilton-Durfee** Chair, Fatalities Workgroup c/o Inter-Agency Council on Child Abuse and Neglect (ICAN) 4024 N Durfee Ave El Monte, CA 91732 818/455-4585 818/444-4851 (Fax)	**Preston Bruce** Executive Director United States Advisory Board on Child Abuse and Neglect Humphrey Building, Room 303-D Washington, DC 20201 202/690-7059 202/260-6309	

Federal Agency	Primary Contact	Secondary Contact	Secondary Contact
US Attorney's Office	**Kathryn Turmon** US Attorney's Office 555 4th Street NW Room 1810 Washington, DC 20001 202/514-7364		

National Association Contacts for Multi-Agency Child Death Review Activities

Association	Primary Contact	Secondary Contact	Secondary Contact
American Academy of Forensic Sciences	Mary E.S. Case, MD Saint Louis University 1402 S Grand St Louis, MO 63104 314/577-8298	John D. McDowell, DDS University of Colorado School of Dentistry Campus Box Office C284 4200 E 9th Ave Denver, CO 80262 313/270-6355	
American Academy of Pediatrics	Carole Jenny, MD American Academy of Pediatrics Child Abuse Section Children's Hospital 1056 E 19th St, Box B-138 Denver, CO 80218 303/861-6919 303/837-2791 (Fax)	Brahm Goldstein, MD Section on Critical Care, AAP Oregon Health Services Univ Department of Pediatrics 3181 SW Sam Jackson Park Rd Portland, OR 97201 503/494-8194	Tammy Piazza American Academy of Pediatrics Child Abuse Section 141 Northwest Point Blvd PO Box 927 Elk Grove Village, IL 60009 847/981-7880 847/228-5097 (Fax)
American Association for Child and Adolescent Psychiatry	August Cervini American Association for Child and Adolescent Psychiatry 3615 Wisconsin, NW Washington, DC 20016 202/966-7300 202/966-2891 (Fax)		
American Bar Association	Sarah Kaplan American Bar Association, Center on Children and the Law 740 15th St, NW Washington, DC 20005- 1009 202/662-1720 or 1009 202/662-1755 (Fax)	Susan Wells American Bar Association, Center on Children and the Law 740 15th St, NW Washington, DC 20005- 1009 202/942-4189 or 1009	
American Burn Association	G. Patrick Kealey, MD Chair, Prevention Committee Burn Treatment Center University of Iowa Hospital & Clinic 200 Hawkins Dr, 1504 JCP Iowa City, IA 52242 319/356-7892 or 1086 319/356-1304 or 8378 (Fax)		

Association	Primary Contact	Secondary Contact	Secondary Contact
American Hospital Association	**Bonnie Conners Jellen** Section for Maternal and Child Health, American Hospital Association 840 N Lake Shore Dr, 5E Chicago, IL 60611 312/280-4198		
American Humane Association	**Robyn Alsop** Coordinator of Information Services American Humane Association 63 Inverness Dr East Englewood, CO 80112-5117 303/792-9900 or 5117 303/792-5333 (Fax)		
American Medical Association	**Roger Brown, PhD** Director Department of Mental Health American Medical Association 515 N State St Chicago, IL 60610 312/464-5067 312/464-5841 (Fax)		
American Nurses Association	**Sarah R. Stanley, MS, RN** Interim Director, Dept of Practice, Policy & Economics American Nurses Association 600 Maryland Ave, SW, #100 West Washington, DC 20024-2571 202/651-7066 202/651-7001 (Fax)		
American Probation and Parole Association	**Mickey Neel** American Probation and Parole Association PO Box 11910 Lexington, KY 40578-1910 606/231-1939 606/231-1943 (Fax)	Ann Crowe American Probation and Parole Association PO Box 11910 Lexington, KY 40578-1910 606/231-1939 606/231-1949 (Fax)	

Association	Primary Contact	Secondary Contact	Secondary Contact
American Professional Society for Abused Children	Sheila Crow Co-Chair, Child Fatality Task Force American Professional Society for Abused Children (APSAC) PO Box 26901 4B4402CHO Oklahoma City, OK 73190 405/271-8858 405/271-2931 (Fax) E-mail: scrow@etowah.uokhse.edu	Dolores Brooks Executive Director American Professional Society for Abused Children (APSAC) 407 S Dearborn Ste 1300 Chicago, IL 60605 312/554-0166 312/939-8962 (Fax)	Randy Alexander, MD University of Iowa Hospital and School University of Iowa Iowa City, IA 52242 319/353-6136, ext 1011 319/356-8284
American Public Health Association	Michael Durfee, MD American Public Health Assoc Maternal Child Health Section Family Violence Committee 210 Starlight Crest La Canada, CA 91011 818/952-2053 818/952-2976 (Fax)	Ken Jarrost, PhD American Public Health Assoc Social Work Section c/o University of Pittsburgh 223 Parran Hall Pittsburgh, PA 15261 412/624-3102 412/624-5510 (Fax)	Pat West APHA Injury Control Section 2134 Spring St Philadelphia, PA 19103 215/568-7811 c/o Tom Vernon 212/575-4939
American Public Health Association	Mila Aroskar, PHN APHA Public Health Nursing Section c/o University of Minnesota School of Public Health 420 Delaware St, SE Minneapolis, MN 55455-0734 612/625-0615 612/624-3972 (Fax)	Ann Kith, RN, DRPH APHA Maternal Child Health c/o University of Southern Maine School of Nursing 96 Salmouth St Portland, ME 04103 207/780-4138 207/780-4997 (Fax)	
American Public Welfare Association	Betsy Thielman National Association of Public Child Welfare Administrators, American Public Welfare Assoc 810 First St, NE, Ste 500 Washington, DC 20002 202/682-0100 202/289-6555 (Fax)		
American Samoa	Fuala'au Hanipale American Samoa Govt Department of Human Resources Social Services Division Pago Pago, AS 96799 684/633-1222, ext 159		

Association	Primary Contact	Secondary Contact	Secondary Contact
Association for Death Education & Counseling	**Ben Wolfe, President** Association for Death & Education Counseling (ADEC) 638 Prospect Ave Hartford, CT 06105 203/586-7503 203/586-7550 (Fax)		
Association of Maternal Child Health Programs	**Tom Vitagione, Chief** Children and Youth Section, Department of Environment, Health and Natural Resources PO Box 27687 Raleigh, NC 27611-7687 919/733-7437 919/733-0488 (Fax)	Barbara Aliza Association of Maternal Child Health Programs 1350 Connecticut Ave, NW Washington, DC 202/775-0436 202/775-0061 (Fax)	
Association of SIDS Program Professionals	**Mary McClain, President** Association of SIDS Program Professionals Massachusetts Center for SIDS 818 Harrison Ave Boston, MA 02218 617/534-7437 617/534-5555 (Fax)	Shelia Marquez, RN, BSN Executive Director Colorado SIDS Program 6825 E Tennessee, #300 Denver, CO 80224 303/320-7771 303/322-8775 (Fax)	Deborah Frazier, Executive Director SIDS Program Arkansas Department of Health Division of Child & Adolescent Health 4815 Markham, Slot 41 Little Rock, AR 72205 501/661-2321
Association of State & Territorial Health Officers	**Mary McCall** Project Director Maternal Child Health Association of State & Territorial Health Officers 415 2nd St, NE Suite 200 Washington, DC 20002 202/546-5400 202/544-9349 (Fax)		
C. Henry Kempe Center	**Donald Bross, JD** C. Henry Kempe Center for the Prevention and Treatment of Child Abuse and Neglect 1825 Marion St Denver, CO 80218 (303) 321-3963 (303) 329-3523 (Fax)		

Association	Primary Contact	Secondary Contact	Secondary Contact
Children's Defense Fund	Mary Lee Allen Director Child Welfare and Mental Health Division Children's Defense Fund 25 E St, NW Washington, DC 20001 202/628-8787 202/662-3550		
Children's Safety Network National Injury & Violence Prevention	Anara Guard, MLS Research Associate Education & Development Center, Inc 55 Chapel St Newton, MA 02158-1060 617/969-7100 617/244-3436 (Fax)		

Council of State Governments	Mickey Neel
	Council of State
	  Governments
	PO Box 11910
	Lexington, KY 40578-1910
	606/231-1939
	606/231-1943 (Fax)
		Ann Crowe
		Council of State
		  Governments
		PO Box 11910
		Lexington, KY 40578-1910
		606/231-1939
		606/231-1943 (Fax)	

Harvard Injury Control Center	Ilana Lescohier, PhD
	Harvard Injury Control
	  Center
	Domestic Violence Division
	718 Huntington Ave
	Boston, MA 02115
	617/432-3770
	617/432-0190 (Fax)
	LESCHONIE@HSPH.
	  Harvard.Edu (E-mail)		

Humane Society of the United States	Randy Lockwood, PhD Humane Society of the United States 2100 L St, NW Washington, DC 20037 301/258-3030 301/258-3034 (Fax)		
International Association of Chiefs of Police	Chief Tom O'Laughlin Wellsley Police Department International Association of Chiefs of Police 485 Washington St Wellsley, MA 02181 617/235-0062 617/235-3830 (Fax)		

Association	Primary Contact	Secondary Contact	Secondary Contact
International Homicide Investigators Association	**Terry Green** President International Homicide Investigators Association PO Box 670 Quantico, VA 22134-0670 800/742-1007 703/670-0407 (Fax)		

National Association of Children's Hospitals & Related Institutions	**Shirley Girouard**
	 National Association of
	   Children's Hospitals &
	   Related Institutions
	   (NACHRI)
	 401 Wythe St
	 Alexandria, VA 22314
	 703/684-1355
	 703/684-1589 (Fax)		

National Association of Attorneys General	**Susan C. Munsat**
	 State Initiatives Counsel,
	   National Association of
	   Attorneys General
	 444 N Capitol St, NW
	 #339
	 Washington, DC 20001
	 202/434-8023
	 202/434-8008 (Fax)		

National Association of Counties	**Sandra Markwood** National Association of Counties 440 First St, NW 8th Floor Washington, DC 20001 202/942-4235 202/737-8480 (Fax)		

National Center for the Prosecution of Child Abuse	**Fatality Project**
	 National Center for the
	   Prosecution of Child
	   Abuse
	 99 Canal St Center Plaza
	 Ste 510
	 Alexandria, VA 22314
	 703/739-0321
	 703/836-3195 (Fax)		

National Committee for the Prevention of Child Abuse	**Karen McCurdy**
	 National Committee for
	   the Prevention of Child
	   Abuse
	 332 S Michigan Ave
	 Chicago, IL 60604
	 312/663-3520
	 312/939-8962 (Fax)		

Association	Primary Contact	Secondary Contact	Secondary Contact
National Court Appointed Special Advocate (CASA) Association	Michael S. Pirairio, CEO National Court Appointed Special Advocate (CASA) Association 2722 Eastlake Ave E Ste 220 Seattle, WA 98102 206/328-8588 206/323-8137 (Fax)		
National Fetal Infant Mortality Review Program	Kathy Buckley National Fetal Infant Mortality Review Program 409 12th St, SW Washington, DC 20024-2188 202/863-1630 202/484-5107 (Fax)		
National Governors' Association	Nolan Jones Director, Justice and Public Safety National Governors' Association 444 Capitol St, NW, #267 Washington, DC 20001 202/624-5360 202/624-5313 (Fax)		
National Organization of Victim Assistance	Cheryl Tyiska National Organization of Victim Assistance 1757 Park Rd, NW Washington, DC 20010 202/232-6682		
National Coalition Against Domestic Violence	Rita Smith National Coalition Against Domestic Violence PO Box 18749 Denver, CO 80218 303/839-1852 303/839-9251 (Fax)		
Society for Pediatric Pathology	Harry Wilson, MD Department of Pathology Providence Memorial Hospital 439 Eudora El Paso, TX 79902 915/545-7323 915/545-7073 (Fax)		

Association	Primary Contact	Secondary Contact	Secondary Contact

Society of Critical Care Medicine	Brahm Goldstein, MD
	Oregon Health Services
	  University
	Department of Pediatrics
	3181 SW Sam Jackson
	  Park Rd
	Portland, OR 97201
		Society of Critical Care Medicine
		8101 E Kaiser Blvd
		Anaheim, CA 92808-2214
		714/282-6000	

Zero to Three	Joan Miller
	  Project Coordinator
	Zero to Three
	National Center for Infants,
	  Toddlers and Families
	734 15th St, NW
	10th Floor
	Washington, DC 20005
	202/638-1133
	202/638-0851 (Fax)		

State and Regional Contacts for Multi-Agency Child Death Review Activities

State or Region	Primary Contact	Secondary Contact	Secondary Contact

Alabama	Thomas Miller, MD
	Director, Bureau of Family
	  Health Services
	State Public Health Services
	434 Monroe St
	Montgomery, AL 36130
	334/242-5661
	
	Debbie Wallace
	Corporate Foundation
	  for Children
	PO Box 1021
	Montgomery, AL 36102
	334/262-5993
	334/262-5990 (Fax)
		James R. Lauridson, MD
		State Medical Examiner
		Alabama
		Department of Forensic
		  Sciences
		PO Box 240591
		Montgomery, AL 38124
		334/242-3093
		334/260-8734 (Fax)
			Steve Aldridge
			District Attorney
			Madison County
			  Courthouse
			100 Northside Square
			Huntsville, AL
			205/532-3460

Alaska	Nina Kinney
	Department of Health
	  and Social Services
	Division of Family and
	  Youth Services
	PO Box 110630
	Juneau, AK 99811-0630
	907/465-3170
	907/465-3397 (Fax)
	
	Russ Webb
	Deputy Commissioner
	Department of Health
	  & Social Services
	PO Box 110601
	Juneau, AK 99811
	907/465-3030
	907/465-3068 (Fax)
		Anita Powell, NP
		Section of Maternal Child
		  and Family Health
		Alaska Public Health
		1231 Gambell St
		Anchorage, AK 99501
		907/279-4711
		907/274-1384 (Fax)	

Arizona	Robert Schackner, MA
	Manager, Child Fatality
	  Review Program
	Arizona Department
	  of Health Services
	  Commission
	Family Health Services
	1740 W Adams Street
	Phoenix, AZ 85007
	602/542-1875
	602/542-1265 (Fax)
		Bev Ogden
		Governor's Office
		  of Children
		Chair, State Child
		  Fatality Review Team
		1700 W Washington,
		  #404
		Phoenix, AZ 85007
		602/542-3191
		602/542-4644 (Fax)	

State or Region	Primary Contact	Secondary Contact	Secondary Contact

Arkansas	Debbie Roark
	Department of Human
	    Services
	Division of Children and
	    Family Services
	PO Box 1437-830
	Little Rock, AR 72203-1437
	501/682-2274
	501/682-2335 (Fax)
	
	Max Snowden
	Executive Director
	Commission on Child
	    Abuse, Rape and
	    Domestic Violence
	4301 W Markham,
	    Slot 606
	Little Rock, AR 72205
	501/661-7975
	501/661-7967 (Fax)
	rednison@comfmc.
	    uams.edu (E-mail)
		Jerry G. Jones, MD
		Director
		Program for Children
		    at Risk
		Arkansas Children's
		    Hospital
		800 Marshall St
		Little Rock, AR 72202-
		    3591
		501/320-1013
		501/320-3939 (Fax)
		JGJONES@exchange.nams
		    EDU (E-mail)
			Tony Davis, SIDS
			    Coordinator
			Arkansas Department
			    of Health
			4815 Markham, #17
			Little Rock, AR 72205
			501/661-2727
			501/661-2055 (Fax)

California	Michael Durfee, MD
	Regional Coordinator
	Los Angeles County
	    Department of Health
	    Services
	241 N Figueroa,
	    Room 306
	Los Angeles, CA 90012
	213/240-8146
	213/893-0919
	
	Anna Yee
	Los Angeles County
	    Inter-Agency Council
	    on Child Abuse and
	    Neglect (ICAN)
	4024 N Durfee Ave
	El Monte, CA 91732
	818/455-4585
	818/444-4851 (Fax)
		Patty O'Ran
		California Office of the
		    Attorney General
		Crime and Violence
		    Prevention Center
		1300 "I" St
		Sacramento, CA 95814
		916/324-7863
		916/327-2384 (Fax)
		
		Kay Ryan
		California Office of
		    Child Abuse Prevention
		744 P St, MS 9-100
		Sacramento, CA 95814
		916/657-3787
			Alex Kelter, MD
			State Department of
			    Health Services
			Injury and Violence
			    Prevention
			PO Box 942732
			Sacramento, CA 94234-
			    7320
			916/323-3480
			916/323-3682 (Fax)

Colorado	Jane Beveridge
	Colorado Department of
	    Social Services
	Division of Child Welfare
	1575 Sherman St
	Denver, CO 80203-1714
	303/866-5951
	303/866-4214 (Fax)
		Joe Carney
		Director, Vital Statistics
		Colorado Department
		    of Health
		4300 Cherry Creek Dr
		    South
		Denver, CO 80222-1530
		303/692-2249
		303/782-0095 (Fax)
			Deborah Haack
			Injury Prevention
			Colorado Department
			    of Health
			4300 Cherry Creek Dr
			    South
			Denver, CO 80222-1530
			303/692-2587
			303/782-0095 (Fax)

State or Region	Primary Contact	Secondary Contact	Secondary Contact
Connecticut	James Carr, Director Department of Children & Family Services 505 Hudson St Hartford, CT 06106 860/550-6420 860/566-8022 (Fax) Stacey Gerber Department of Children & Family Services 505 Hudson St Hartford, CT 06106 860/550-6465 860/566-8022 (Fax)	Betty Spivack, MD Department of Pediatrics Hartford Hospital 80 Seymour St Hartford, CT 06102 860/545-5000 860/545-4188 (Fax)	Dr Vincent Sullivan Department of Children and Family Services 505 Hudson St Hartford, CT 06106 860/550-6461 860/566-8022 (Fax)
Delaware	Richard Callery, MD Chief Medical Examiner 200 S Adams St Wilmington, DE 19801 302/577-3420 302/577-3416 (Fax)	Lori Sitler, Director Victim Witness Assistance Program Department of Justice Carvel State Office Building 820 N French Wilmington, DE 19801 302/577-2055 302/577-2479 (Fax)	
District of Columbia	Annie Goodson Acting Commissioner of Social Services Co-Chair, District of Columbia Child Fatality Review Committee (CFRC) 609 H St, NE 5th Floor Washington, DC 20002 202/727-5930 202/727-5971 (Fax)	Sharon D. James CFRC Coordinator Commission on Social Services 609 H St, NE 5th Floor Washington, DC 20002 202/727-5930 202/727-5971 (Fax)	Ryan Rainey United States Attorney's Office Co-Chair Regional Child Fatality Counsel 555 4th St, NW, 11-445 Washington, DC 20001 202/514-7192 202/514-8784 (Fax)
Florida	Patricia B. Hicks, QA Director Department of Children & Families Family Safety & Preservation 2729 Fort Knox Blvd Ste 160 Tallahassee, FL 32308 904/487-2006 904/921-2038 (Fax)		

State or Region	Primary Contact	Secondary Contact	Secondary Contact
Georgia	Eva Y. Pattilo Director Office of Child Fatality Review Children's Trust Fund Two Northside 75, Ste 125 Atlanta, GA 30318 404/352-6471 404/352-6051 (Fax) J. Tom Morgan DeKalb County District Attorney 700 DeKalb County Courthouse 556 N McDonough St Decatur, GA 30030 404/371-4728 404/371-2670 (Fax)	Denise Brooks Regional Coordinator Institute for Infant and Child Survival Office of the Medical Examiner 150 N Marietta Pkwy Marietta, GA 30060 404/590-0966 404/528-2207 (Fax)	Joseph L. Burton Chief Medical Examiner Metro Atlanta 150 N Marietta Pkwy Marietta, GA 30060 404/528-2200 404/528-2207 (Fax)
Guam	Mary Lou Taijeron Department of Public Health and Social Services PO Box 2816 Agana, Guam 96910 671/477-8966		
Hawaii	Loretta J. Fuddy, MSW, MPH Branch Chief, Maternal and Child Health Branch 741-A Sunset Ave Honolulu, HI 96861 808/733-9033 808/733-9032 (Fax)	Lisa Nakao Planner, Maternal & Child Health Branch 741-A Sunset Ave Honolulu, HI 96816 808/733-9022 808/733-9032 (Fax) Gwendolyn Costello USCINCPAC - Surgeons Office (J073) Box Medical Camp H.M. Smith Honolulu, HI 96861-5025 808/477-6956 808/477-3050 (Fax)	Therese Argoud Injury Prevention and Control Program State Department of Health 1250 Punchbowl St, #214 Honolulu, HI 96813 808/586-5940 808/586-5945 (Fax)
Idaho	Mardell Nelson Department of Health and Welfare 450 W State St Boise, ID 83720-5450 208/334-5700 208/334-6699 (Fax)	Ken Robbins Deputy Prosecuting Attorney Elmore County PO Box 607 Mountain, ID 83647 208/587-2144	

State or Region	Primary Contact	Secondary Contact	Secondary Contact

Illinois	Sharon O'Conner
	Cook County Office of the
	  Medical Examiner
	2121 W Harrison Street
	Chicago, IL 60612
	312/997-4509
	312/997-4400 (Fax)
		Neil Hochstadt, PhD
		State Task Force
		  Chairperson
		LaRabida Hospital
		E 65th and Lake
		  Michigan
		Chicago, IL 60649
		773/363-6700	

Indiana	Paula Ferguson
	Indiana Family and
	  Social Services
	  Administration
	Division of Family
	  and Children
	402 W Washington,
	  # W364
	Indianapolis, IN 46204
	317/232-4429
	317/232-4436 (Fax)
		Jim Stewart
		Marion County Office
		  of Family and Children
		145 S Meridian
		Indianapolis, IN 46225
		317/232-1773
			Suzanne O'Malley
			Marion County
			  Prosecutors Office
			Family Advocacy Center
			233 McCrea St, #1100
			Indianapolis, IN 46225
			317/327-6948

Iowa	Wayne McCracken
	Iowa Department of
	  Human Services
	Bureau of Individual
	  and Family
	Hoover State Office
	  Building, 5th Floor
	Des Moines, IA 50319
	515/281-8978
	515/281-4597 (Fax)
		Randy Alexander, MD
		University of Iowa
		  Hospital and Schools
		University of Iowa
		Iowa City, IA 52242-1011
		319/353-6136
		319/356-8284 (Fax)
			Sue Tesdohl, MSW
			St Luke's Child
			  Protection Center
			St Lukes Hospital
			Cedar Rapids, IA

Kansas	Betty M. Glover, LMSW
	Executive Director
	State Child Death Review
	  Board
	Office of the Attorney
	  General
	2nd Floor, Kansas Judicial
	  Center
	Topeka, KS 66612-1597
	913/296-7970
	913/296-0652 (Fax)
		Katherine J. Melhorn, MD
		Department of Pediatrics
		University of Kansas
		  School of Medicine-
		  Wichita
		3243 E Murdock, Level A
		Wichita, KS 67214
		316/688-3110
		316/688-3227 (Fax)
			Nancy Lindberg
			Assistant to the
			  Attorney General
			Office of the Attorney
			  General
			2nd Floor
			Judicial Center
			Topeka, KS 66612-1597
			913/296-2215
			913/296-6296 (Fax)

Kentucky	Sarah Wilding, RN
	Department for Social
	  Services
	Division of Maternal
	  & Child Health
	275 East Main St
	Frankfort, KY 40621
	502/564-2136
	502/564-3254 (Fax)
		Susan Pollack, MD
		Kentucky Injury Prevention
		  & Research Center
		1141 Red Mile Rd, Ste 2
		Lexington, KY 40536
		606/257-4954
		602/257-3909 (Fax)	

State or Region	Primary Contact	Secondary Contact	Secondary Contact

Louisiana	Cindy Phillips
	Department of Social
	  Services
	Office of Community
	  Services
	PO Box 3318
	Baton Rouge, LA 70821
	504/342-9928
	504/342-9087 (Fax)
		Larry Hebert, MD
		Medical Director
		Department of Health
		  and Hospitals
		PO Box 629
		Baton Rouge, LA 70821-
		  0629
		304/342-4770	

Maine	Larry Ricci, MD The Child Abuse Program The Spurwink Clinic 17 Bishop St Portland, ME 04103 207/879-6160 207/879-6161 (Fax)	Phyllis Merriam, LMSW Department of Human Services Child Protective Services 221 State St Augusta, ME 04333 207/287-5060 207/287-5062 (Fax)	

Maryland	Dan Timmel, LCSW
	MEDCHI
	1211 Cathedral St
	Baltimore, MD 21201
	410/539-0872
	410/547-0915 (Fax)
		Carolyn Fowler, PhD,
		  MPH
		Johns Hopkins University
		Center for Injury Research/
		  Policy
		543 Hampton House
		624 N Broadway
		Baltimore, MD 21205
		410/955-0442
		410/614-2797 (Fax)
			Anne Dixon, MD
			Deputy Chief Medical
			  Examiner
			State of Maryland
			Office of the Chief
			  Medical Examiner
			111 Penn St
			Baltimore, MD 21201
			410/333-3250
			410/333-3063 (Fax)

Massachusetts	Cindy Rodgers
	Massachusetts Department
	  of Public Health, Division
	  of Prevention
	250 Washington St
	4th Floor
	Boston, MA 02108-4619
	617/624-5424
	617/624-5075 (Fax)		

Michigan	Teri Covington
	Michigan Child Death
	  Program Coordinator
	Michigan Public Health
	  Institute
	2364 Woodlake Dr
	Okemos, MI 48864
	517/347-3145
	517/347-1962 (Fax)
		Doug Patterson
		Michigan Department
		  of Public Health
		PO Box 30195
		Lansing, MI 48906
		517/335-8922
		517/335-9222 (Fax)
			Cassandra Joubert
			Jackson
			Program Director
			Michigan Public Health
			  Institute
			One Ford Place, Ste 2D
			Detroit, MI 48202
			313/871-9275
			313/871-9298 (Fax)

State or Region	Primary Contact	Secondary Contact	Secondary Contact
Michigan	Joseph Kwiatkowski Cheboygan County Prosecuting Attorney 870 South Main St Cheboygan, MI 49721 616/627-8800 616/627-8405 (Fax)	Marilyn Poland, PhD Mutzel Hospital 4707 St Antoinne Detroit, MI 48201 313/577-1147	

Minnesota	Rebecca Santos
	Department of Human
	  Services
	Children's Services Division
	444 Lafayette Rd
	St Paul, MN 55155-3830
	612/215-9445
	612/296-6244 (Fax)
		Erin Sullivan Sutton
		Department of Human
		  Services
		Children's Services Division
		444 Lafayette Rd
		St Paul, MN 55155-3830
		612/296-2487
		612/296-6244 (Fax)	

Mississippi	Glenda Funchess
	University of Southern
	  Mississippi
	PO Box 5127
	Hattiesburg, MS 39406
	601/266-4516
	601/266-4391 (Fax)
		Dot Roberts
		Mississippi Department
		  of Human Services
		PO Box 352
		Jackson, MS 39205
		601/359-4482
		601/354-6660 (Fax)
			Larry LaFleur, PhD
			Associate Professor
			Department of Criminal
			  Justice
			University of Southern
			  Mississippi
			PO Box 9302
			Hattiesburg, MS 39406
			601/266-4509

Missouri	Richard Easter
	Chief Investigator
	State Technical Assistance
	  Team
	PO Box 88
	Jefferson City, MO 65103-
	  0088
	573/751-1479
		Maurine Hill
		Technical Investigator
		State Technical Assistance
		  Team
		PO Box 88
		Jefferson City, MO 65103-
		  0088
		573/751-1479	

Montana	Charles McCarthy
	Department of Family
	  Services
	PO Box 8005
	Helena, MT 59604-8005
	404/444-5900
	406/444-5956 (Fax)
		Nora Gerrity, MD
		Great Falls Clinic
		PO Box 5012
		Great Falls, MT 59403
		406/454-2171
		406/454-0455
			Christina Litchfield
			City-County Health
			  Department
			501 W Alder
			Missoula, MT 59802
			406/523-4750

Montana	Pamela Mayer
	Department of Family
	  Services
	PO Box 8005
	Helena, MT 59604
	406/444-5900
	406/444-5956 (Fax)
		Yvonne Bradford
		City-County Health
		  Department
		501 W Alder
		Missoula, MT 59802
		406/523-4750	

State or Region	Primary Contact	Secondary Contact	Secondary Contact
Nebraska	David Schor, MD Director, Maternal Child Health Nebraska Department of Health Services 301 Centennial Mall South Lincoln, NE 68509 402/471-2907 02/471-0383 (Fax)	Mary Jo Pankoke Department of Social Services PO Box 95026 Lincoln, NE 68509-5026 402/471-9320 402/471-9455 (Fax)	
Nevada	Maryellen White Nevada Department of Human Resources Division of Child and Family 711 E Fifth St Carson City, NV 89710 702/687-3023 702/687-1074 (Fax) Michael Capello Washoe County Department of Social Services PO Box 11130 Reno, NV 89520 702/328-2300 702/328-3788 (Fax)	Judy New Supervisor Clark County Department of Family and Youth Services 3401 E Bonanza Rd Las Vegas, NV 89101 702/455-5361 702/455-5592 (Fax)	Carol Stillian Clark County Department of Family and Youth Services 3401 E Bonanza Rd Las Vegas, NV 89101 702/455-5430 702/455-5479 (Fax)
New Hampshire	Sandra Matheson New Hampshire Department of Justice 33 Capitol St Concord, NH 03301 603/271-3671 603/271-2110 (Fax)	Sylvia Gale New Hampshire Division for Children and Youth 6 Hazen Dr Concord, NH 03301 603/271-4691 603/271-4729 (Fax)	
New Jersey	Donna Pincavage Governor's Task Force on Child Abuse and Neglect CN 700 Trenton, NJ 08625-0717 609/292-0888 609/292-6838 (Fax)	Robert Goode, MD New Jersey State Medical Examiner 325 Norfolk St Newark, NJ 07103 201/648-7259	
New Mexico	Dr Susan Nader New Mexico Department of Health 1190 St Francis Dr Santa Fe, NM 87501 505/827-2457 505/827-2329 (Fax)	Patricia McFeeley, MD Assistant Chief Medical Investigator University of New Mexico School of Medicine Albuquerque, NM 87131- 5091 505/272-0710 505/272-0727 (Fax)	

State or Region	Primary Contact	Secondary Contact	Secondary Contact
New York	**Tom Hess** Division of Family and Children's Services 40 North Pearl St Albany, NY 12243 518/474-9589 518/474-1842 (Fax) **Michael Baden, MD** Co-Director, Forensic Services New York State Police Building 22, State Campus Albany, NY 12226 518/457-8678 518/459-4220 (Fax)	**Jonathon Arden, MD** Office of Chief Medical Examiner King County Hospital Pathology Building, Room 141 451 Clarkson Ave Brooklyn, NY 11203 718/462-7177 718/756-7505 (Fax)	**June Bradley** Senior Investigator New York State Police Child Abuse Unit Building 22, State Campus Albany, NY 12226 518/458-8503 518/459-4220 (Fax)
North Carolina	**Marcia Herman-Giddens** Office of the Chief Medical Examiner Chapel Hill, NC 27599- 7580 919/966-2253 919/962-6263 (Fax) mherman-giddens@unc.edu (E-mail)	**Michael Sanderson, MPH** Local Child Fatality Prevention Teams Division of Maternal and Child Health PO Box 29597 Raleigh, NC 27626-0597 919/715-3296 919/715-3049 mherman-giddens@unc.edu (E-mail)	
North Dakota	**Gladys Cairns** North Dakota Department of Human Services/CFS 600 East Boulevard Ave Bismarck, ND 58505-0250 701/328-4806 701/328-2359 (Fax)	**Jon Rice, MD** Health Officer North Dakota Department of Health 600 East Boulevard Ave Bismarck, ND 58505-0200 701/328-2372 701/328-4727 (Fax)	**Jon Byers** North Dakota Attorney General's Office PO Box 1054 Bismarck, ND 58502-1054 701/328-5500 701/328-5510 (Fax)
Northern Mariana Islands	**Margaret Olopai-Taitano** Division of Youth Services Department of Community and Cultural Affairs PO Box 1000 Saipan, MP 96950 670/234-8950 670/322-2220 (Fax)	**Ebert-Santos, MD** Chief of Medical Staff Department of Public Health and Environ- mental Services PO Box 409 Saipan, MP 96950 670/234-8950 670/234-8930 (Fax)	**Chief of Criminal Division** Office of the Attorney General Administration Building, 2nd Floor Capitol Hill, MP 96950 670/322-4311 670/322-4320 (Fax)

State or Region	Primary Contact	Secondary Contact	Secondary Contact

Ohio	**Jean Schafer, Chief**
	Children's Services
	Ohio Department of
	   Human Services
	65 East State St
	5th Floor
	Columbus, OH 43215
	614/466-9824
	614/466-0164 (Fax)
	
	Patricia Eber
	Family & Children's
	   First Council
	830 Main St
	Ste 609
	Cincinnati, OH 45202
	513/632-7232
	513/632-6527 (Fax)
		Pam Schirner
		Franklin County
		   Children's Services
		1951 Gantz Rd
		Grove City, OH 43123
		614/275-2509
		614/275-2755 (Fax)
		
		Richard Schneider
		Prosecuting Attorney
		222 E Central Pkwy
		Cincinnati, OH 45202
		513/946-2305
		513/946-2291 (Fax)	

Oklahoma	**Sheila Thigpen**
	Administrator
	Center on Child Abuse
	   and Neglect
	Oklahoma Child Death
	   Review Board
	PO Box 26901
	CHO 4B, Room 4402
	Oklahoma City, OK 73190
	405/271-8858
	405/271-2931 (Fax)
		Kathryn Simms
		Child Abuse and
		   Neglect Section
		Department of Human
		   Services
		PO Box 25352
		Oklahoma City, OK 73125
		405/521-2283
		405/521-6684 (Fax)	

Oregon	**Chris Wheeler, MPH** State Technical Assistance Team Oregon Health Division 800 NE Oregon St, #21 Portland, OR 97232 503/731-8597 503/731-4157 (Fax)	**Grant Higgins, MD, MPH** Co-Chair CFR Team 800 NE Oregon St, #21 Portland, OR 97232 503/731-4829 503/731-4078 (Fax)	

Palau	**Dr A. H. Polloi**
	Director of Public Health
	Ministry of Health
	Republic of Palau
	PO Box 6027
	Koror, PW 96940
	680/488-2552
	680/488-1211 or 1725
	   (Fax)
		Administrator
		Behavioral Health Division
		PO Box 6027
		Koror, PW 96940
		680/488-1907
		680/488-1211 or 1725
		   (Fax)	

State or Region	Primary Contact	Secondary Contact	Secondary Contact
Pennsylvania	**Pat West** 2134 Spring St Philadelphia, PA 19103 215/568-7811 215/520-9177 (Fax)	**Chukwudi Onwuachi-Saunders, MD** City of Philadelphia Department of Health 1600 Arch St, 17th Floor Philadelphia, PA 19103 215/686-5047 215/568-2787 (Fax)	**Suzanne Yunghans** Administrator Pennsylvania Chapter American Academy of Pediatrics Dayton Building 610 Old Lancaster Rd Bryn Mawr, PA 19010-3809 215/520-9123 215/520-9177 (Fax)
Puerto Rico	**Maria L. Carrillo** Department of Social Services Families with Children Program PO Box 11398, Miramar Santurce, PR 00910 809/723-2127 809/723-1223		
Rhode Island	**Kenneth Fandetti** Department for Children and Their Families 610 Mt Pleasant Ave Building 1 Providence, RI 02908 401/457-4950 401/521-4570 (Fax) **Elizabeth Laposata, MD** Chief Medical Examiner 48 Orms St Providence, RI 02904 401/274-1333	**Laureen D'Ambra** Office of Child Advocate 260 W Exchange St Ste 2 Providence, RI 02903 401/277-6650 401/277-6652 (Fax)	**William Hollinshead, MD** Rhode Island Department of Health Division of Family Health 3 Capitol Hill Providence, RI 02908 401/277-2312 401/277-1442 (Fax)
South Carolina	**Lt Patsy Habben** Child Fatality Investigation Department South Carolina Law Enforcement Division PO Box 21398 Columbia, SC 29221 803/737-9000 803/896-7041 (Fax)	**H. Gratin Smith, MD** Pediatrician 150 Academy Ave Greenwood, SC 29646 864/227-4111 864/227-4883 (Fax)	
South Dakota	**Merlin Weyer** South Dakota Department of Social Services/CPS Kneip Building 700 Governor Dr Pierre, SC 57501 605/773-3227 605/773-4855 (Fax)	**Nancy Hoyme** Department of Health MCH Coordinator Anderson Building 445 E Capitol Pierre, SD 57501-3185 605/773-4476 605/773-5509 (Fax)	

State or Region	Primary Contact	Secondary Contact	Secondary Contact
Tennessee	Louis Martinez Department of Children's 　Services CPS 8th Floor 436 6th Ave, North Nashville, TN 37243 615/532-4624 615/532-6495 (Fax)	Debbie Johnson Director, Child/Adolescent 　Health Services Department of Health Tennessee Tower, 5H 436 6th Ave, North Nashville, TN 37243 615/532-5624 615/532-6495 (Fax)	
Texas	Anne Ramsey Project Coordinator Child Fatality Review Team 　Project Children's Justice Act Department of Protective 　& Regulatory Services PO Box 149030, MC E611 Austin, TX 78714 512/706-5029 512/450-3022 (Fax)	Lt Bill Walsh Dallas Police Department 106 Harwood, Room 225 Dallas, TX 75201 214/670-5936 214/670-5759 (Fax)	
Utah	Pat Rothermich CFS Specialist DFS/DSS PO Box 45500 Salt Lake City, UT 84145 801/538-4043 801/538-4016 (Fax)	Patricia Keller Director Violence & Injury 　Prevention Program Department of Health Division of Family Health 　Services PO Box 144240 Salt Lake City, UT 84114- 　4240 801/538-8161 801/538-6510 (Fax)	Mary Thompson Violence & Injury 　Prevention Program Department of Health Division of Family 　Health Services PO Box 144240 Salt Lake City, UT 84114- 　4240 801/538-6348 801/538-6510 (Fax)
Vermont	George W. Brown, MD Vermont Child Fatality 　Review Committee Child Protection Network 76 Glenn Rd Burlington, VT 05401-4131 802/863-9626	George Karson Department of Social 　and Rehabilitation 　Services 103 South Main St Waterbury, VT 05671- 　2401 802/241-2131 802/244-2980 (Fax)	
Virgin Islands	Angela R. Krigger Department of Human 　Services Knud Hansen Complex Building A 1303 Hospital Ground St Thomas, VI 00802 809/774-4393 809/774-0082 (Fax)	Catherine Scopino Human Services Knud Hansen Complex Building A 1303 Hospital Ground St Thomas, VI 00802 809/774-4393 809/774-0082 (Fax)	Carol Battuello Human Services 6179 Annas Hope St Croix, VI 00820 809/773-5303 809/773-1882 (Fax)

State or Region	Primary Contact	Secondary Contact	Secondary Contact
Virginia	Suzanne J. Keller Coordinator State Child Fatality Review Team 9 North 14th St Richmond, VA 23219 804/786-3174 804/371-8595 (Fax)	Marcella Fierro, MD Office of the Chief Medical Examiner 9 North 14th St Richmond, VA 23219 804/786-1033 804/371-8595 (Fax)	Meridith McEver Fairfax County Department of Human Development 12011 Government Center Pkwy Fairfax, VA 22035 703/324-7575
Washington	Lorrie Grevstad, RN, MN Nursing Consultant Community & Family Health PO Box 47880 Olympia, WA 95804-7880 360/753-6060 360/586-7868 (Fax)	Maxine Hayes, MD Assistant Secretary for Parent Child Health PO Box 47880 Olympia, WA 95804-7880 360/753-7021 360/586-7868 (Fax)	Donna White PO Box 47880 Olympia, WA 95804- 7880 360/753-5853 360/586-7868 (Fax)
West Virginia	Janice Binder State of West Virginia Juvenile Justice Committee 214 Dickenson St Charleston, WV 25301 304/558-3649 304/558-0831 (Fax)	Maureen Runyon Women and Children's Hospital 800 Pennsylvania Charleston, WV 25301 304/348-2391	Kathie King Office of Social Services Department of Health and Human Resources Room 850, Building 6 Charleston, WV 25305 304/558-7980 304/558-2059 (Fax)
Wisconsin	Mary Dibble Bureau for Children, Youth and Families Department of Health and Social Services 1 West Wilson St, Room 465 Madison, WI 53707 608/267-2245 Gregory A. Schmunk, MD Brown County Medical Examiner 305 E Walnut St, Room 602 PO Box 23600 Green Bay, WI 54305-3600 414/488-4185 414/448-4186 (Fax) gschmunk@pipeline.com (E-mail)	Jeffrey Jentzen, MD Milwaukee County Medical Examiner 933 W Highland Ave Milwaukee, WI 53233 414/223-1200	Sandra Nowack Wisconsin State Department of Justice 123 W Washington Ave PO Box 7857 Madison, WI 53707- 7857 608/266-7477 608/267-2223 (Fax)
Wyoming	Bill Rankin Department of Family Services Hathaway Building Cheyenne, WY 82002 307/777-3570 307/777-3693 (Fax)	LeeAnn Stephenson Department of Family Services Hathaway Building Cheyenne, WY 82002 307/777-3569 307/777-3693 (Fax)	Rick Robb Department of Family Services Hathaway Building Cheyenne, WY 307/777-7150 307/777-3693 (Fax)

American Professional Society on the Abuse of Children (APSAC)

Chapter Contacts

Alabama
Shirley Robinson, PhD
1818 Kensington Rd
Homewood, AL 35209
205/879-8460

Arkansas
Jan Church, PhD
Arkansas Children's Hospital
1120 Marshall St, Ste 401
Little Rock, AR 72202
501/320-3814

Arizona
Linda Gray
1115 W McDowell Rd
Phoenix, AZ 85007
602/257-8452

California
Michael Hertica, MFCC, Intern
Torrance Police Department
3300 Civic Center Dr
Torrance, CA 90503
310/375-0613

Colorado
Dan Jarboe, MA
Jefferson County Children's Advocacy Center
12100 W Alameda Pkwy
Lakewood, CO 80228
303/987-4888

Connecticut
Audrey Courtney, MSN
St Francis Hospital
Children's Center
114 Woodland St
Hartford, CT 06106
860/714-5912

District of Columbia
Ned Hitchcock II, MS
Division of Child Protection
Children's Hospital
111 Michigan Ave, NW
Washington, DC 20010-2970
202/884-6709

Florida
Donna Watson-Lawson, BSW
PO Box 140009
Gainesville, FL 32614-0009
352/374-5643

Georgia
Beatrice Yorker, JD, MS, RN
Georgia State School of Nursing
PO Box 4019
Atlanta, GA 30302
404/651-3046

Hawaii
Nalani Archibeque, PhD
Children's Advocacy Center
2200 Main St, Ste 660
Wailuku, Maui, HI 06763
808/244-4199

Idaho
Anna Sever
Department of Health and Welfare
450 W State St, 5th Floor
PO Box 83720
Boise, ID 83720-0036

Illinois
Thomas Ryan, MS
Childhood Trauma Treatment Program
342 Manor Court
Bolingbrook, IL 60140
630/739-0491

Indiana
Melissa Steinmetz, ACSW
66090 Oak Rd
Lakeville, IN 46536
219/656-4950

Kansas
Patricia Phillips, MN
UKS Medical Center, Pediatrics Dept.
39th and Rainbow Blvd
HCM 2013
Kansas City, KS 66103
913/588-7339

Kentucky
Barbara Norris, MA
2345 Cincinnati Pike
Georgetown, KY 40124
606/246-2310

Massachusetts
Debra Whitcomb, PhD
Education Development Center
55 Chapel St
Newton, MA 02158
617/969-7101

Maryland
Diane DePanfilis, PhD, MSW
UMD Baltimore School of Social Work
525 W Redwood St
Baltimore, MD 21201
410/706-3609

Maine
See NNEPSAC

Michigan
David L. Harrison, JD
270 Wimberly
Rochester Hills, MI 48306
810/651-8668

Minnesota
Vicki Nauschultz
Midwest Children's Resource Center
360 Sherman St #200
St Paul, MN 55102
612/220-6750

North Carolina
Nancy B. Lamb, JD
202 E Colonial Ave
Elizabeth City, NC 27909
919/331-4743

Nebraska
Mary Paine, MA
Lincoln Behavioral Health Clinic
3201 Pioneers Blvd
Ste 202
Lincoln, NE 66502
402/489-9959

New Hampshire
See NNEPSAC

New Jersey
Marsha Heiman, PhD
296 Amboy Ave
Metuchen, NJ 08840
908/548-8516

New Mexico
Sara Simon, MA
2600 Marble NE
Albuquerque, NM 87131
505/843-2190

New York
Ann Botash, MD
SUNY Health Sciences Center
Department of Pediatrics
90 Presidential Plaza
Syracuse, NY 13202
315/464-5831

NNEPSAC (Northern New England—ME, NH, VT)
Susan Bolduc, MSW
Moore Center Services
132 Titus Ave
Manchester, NH 03103
603/626-0824

Ohio
Kelly Castle
Columbus Police Department
120 Maroni Blvd
Columbus, OH 43215
614/645-4551

Oklahoma
Tricia Williams, JD
Center on Child Abuse and Neglect
PO Box 26901
CHO-48138
Oklahoma City, OK 73190
405/271-8858

Oregon
Bruce Spilde, LCSW
1707 Kauffman
Vancouver, WA 98661
503/331-2400

Pennsylvania
Darlene Pessein, MSW
Joseph J. Peters Institute
260 S Broad St, Ste 220
Philadelphia, PA 19102
235/693-0600

Rhode Island
Paul Graf
US Naval Investigative Service
144 Meverkunl Ave, 3rd Floor
Newport, RI 02841-1607
401/821-2241

South Carolina
Jerome Stewart, RN, LPC
Carolina Psychotherapy
2204 Divine St
Columbia, SC 29205
801/771-0243

Tennessee
Bonnie Beneke, MSW
5819 Old Harding Rd
Suite 204
Nashville, TN 37205
615/352-4439

Texas
Deborah Butler
Child Abuse Intervention Training Project
4801 Marine Creek Pkwy
Fort Worth, TX 76179
817/232-7703

Utah
Suzanne Mitchell, MSW
Children's Justice Center
257 Eleventh Ave
Salt Lake City, UT 84103
801/355-0781

Vermont
See NNEPSAC

Virginia
Cathy Krinick, JD
Law Offices
555 Denbeigh Blvd
Newport News, VA 23608
757/896-0111

Washington
Barbara Stone
Division of Child & Family Services
PO Box 45710
Olympia, WA 98504-5710
360/902-7822

Wisconsin
Thomas Fallon, JD
Department of Justice
123 W Washington St, Room 439
Madison, WI 53707-7857
608/264-9685

Application for Section Membership

Join one or more of the Academy's 43 surgical, medical subspecialty, or multidisciplinary Sections to get added value from your AAP membership.

Over 18,500 AAP members (35% of our membership) belong to at least one Section, including 9000 pediatric residents who automatically belong to the AAP Resident Section when they join as a Resident Fellow.

The primary purpose of AAP Sections is education. Programs developed by Sections constitute more than half of the educational programming at AAP Annual and Spring meetings. Sections are also involved in policy development, public education, and advocacy.

As a Section member you will have the opportunity to share ideas with and learn from colleagues who share your specific interests and/or subspecialty background.

Application Information

You may apply for up to 5 Sections with one application. All applicants for Section membership must be AAP members in good standing. Resident Fellows are not eligible to join Sections other than the Resident Section, which is automatically granted when AAP membership is approved.

All Section applications must be accompanied by an application processing fee of $35. Most Sections require that a current curriculum vitae be submitted with the application. Some Sections require additional sub-board certification beyond the initial certification in pediatrics granted by the American Board of Pediatrics (see criteria page for individual section requirements).

Applicants will be notified in writing when the application is complete and has been submitted to the appropriate Section Executive Committee for review and approval. All notifications of approval of Section membership will also be sent in writing. Most sections have established annual dues ($15-$65) to assist them in providing quality educational programs and information to section members. *Annual dues are not assessed until after the approval process is complete.*

For more information on Section membership criteria, the approval process, or individual Section activities, contact:

Section Membership Assistant
AAP Division of Member Services
141 Northwest Point Blvd
Elk Grove Village, IL 60007

800/433-9016, ext 7143
847/228-5005, ext 7143
847/228-5245 (FAX)

The American Academy of Pediatrics is committed to the attainment of optimal physical, mental, and social health for all infants, children, adolescents, and young adults.

Requirement Criteria

Section	Requirements	Section	Requirements
Adolescent Health	Fellow	Nephrology	Fellow 1 letter of recommen-dation from a Section member
Administration and Practice Management	Fellow	Neurology	Fellow or Specialty Fellow* At least one year training in neurosciences
Allergy & Immunology	Fellow Certified by the Sub-Board of Allergy & Immunology	Ophthalmology	Fellow or Specialty Fellow* Certified by the American Board of Ophthalmology and 50% of prac-tice devoted to care of children
Anesthesiology	Fellow or Specialty Fellow* Certified by the American Board of Anesthesiology		
Bioethics	Fellow	Orthopaedics	Fellow or Specialty Fellow* Certified by the American Board of Orthopaedic Surgery and 50% of practice devoted to the care of children
Cardiology	Fellow Certified by the Sub-Board of Pediatric Cardiology		
Child Abuse & Neglect	Fellow	Otolaryngology & Bronchoesophagology	Fellow or Specialty Fellow* Certi-fied by the American Board of Otolaryngology and 50% of prac-tice devoted to care of children
Children With Disabilities	Fellow		
Clinical Pharmacology & Therapeutics	Fellow	Pediatric Pulmonology	Fellow
Community Pediatrics	Fellow	Perinatal Pediatrics	Fellow
Computers & Other Technologies	Fellow	Plastic Surgery	Fellow or Specialty Fellow* Certified by the American Board of Plastic & Reconstructive Surgery and 50% of practice devoted to care of children
Critical Care	Fellow		
Dermatology	Fellow or Specialty Fellow*	Radiology	Fellow or Specialty Fellow* Certified by the American Board of Radiology or American Board of Nuclear Medicine and 50% of practice devoted to care of children
Developmental & Behavioral Pediatrics	Fellow		
Emergency Medicine	Fellow or Specialty Fellow*	Resident	Resident Fellow (automatic sec-tion membership) Post Residency Training Fellowship (by request)
Endocrinology	Fellow		
Epidemiology	Fellow		
Gastroenterology & Nutrition	Fellow	Rheumatology	Fellow 50% of practice devoted to rheumatologic care of children
Genetics & Birth Defects	Fellow or Specialty Fellow* Copy of C.V., statement of interest	School Health	Fellow
		Seniors	Fellow 55 years of age or older
Hematology-Oncology	Fellow 1 letter of recommenda-tion from a Section member, and a copy of C.V.	Sports Medicine & Fitness	Fellow
		Surgery	Fellow or Specialty Fellow* Certified by the American Board of Surgery and 50% of practice devoted to care of children
Home Health	Fellow		
Infectious Diseases	Fellow	Transport Medicine	Fellow
Injury & Poison Prevention	Fellow	Uniformed Services	Fellow Member of the Uniformed Services
International Child Health	Fellow	Urology	Fellow or Specialty Fellow* Certified by the American Board of Urology and 50% of practice devoted to care of children
Med/Peds**	Fellow		

* Specialty fellowships are available to physicians certified by a recognized specialty board other than pediatrics who devote at least 50% of their professional time to the care of pediatric-aged patients. Call 1-800/433-9016 ext 4720 to request an application.

** Provisional Section

American Academy of Pediatrics

☐ MD
☐ DO

Name

AAP ID #   Social Security Number   ☐ Home
                                                  ☐ Office

Address

City/State/Zip   Country   ☐ Home
                                                   ☐ Office

Phone   Fax   E-Mail

Date of Birth (Month/Day/Year)
If currently in the Armed Forces: Branch _____ Rank_____
Are you currently in the Public Health Service? ☐ yes ☐ no   Are you in the reserves? ☐ yes ☐ no

tegory of AAP Membership:

☐ Fellow   ☐ Emeritus Fellow
☐ Candidate Fellow   ☐ Post Residency Training Fellow

Certification: (Name of Board and Sub-Board if applicable)

_____
                                    Certification Date: _____

_____
                                    Certification Date: _____

Current Hospital Affiliation:

_____

_____

Application for Section(s) on: *Check no more than five (5)*

☐ Administration & Practice Management
☐ Adolescent Health
☐ Allergy & Immunology
☐ Anesthesiology
☐ Bioethics
☐ Cardiology
☐ Child Abuse & Neglect
☐ Children w/Disabilities
☐ Clinical Pharmacology and Therapeutics
☐ Community Pediatrics
☐ Computers & Other Technologies
☐ Critical Care
☐ Dermatology
☐ Developmental & Behavioral Pediatrics

☐ Emergency Medicine
☐ Endocrinology
☐ Epidemiology
☐ Gastroenterology & Nutrition
☐ Genetics and Birth Defects
☐ Hematology-Oncology
☐ Home Health
☐ Infectious Diseases
☐ Injury & Poison Prevention
☐ International Child Health
☐ Nephrology
☐ Neurology
☐ Ophthalmology
☐ Orthopaedics
☐ Otolaryngology & Bronchoesophagology

☐ Pediatric Pulmonology
☐ Perinatal Pediatrics
☐ Plastic Surgery
☐ Radiology
☐ Rheumatology
☐ School Health
☐ Senior Members
☐ Sports Medicine & Fitness
☐ Surgery
☐ Transport Medicine
☐ Uniformed Services
☐ Urology
Provisional Section
☐ Med/Peds
☐ _____

10. Current Medical School Appointment:

_____

_____

11. Current Professional Activities (private practice, industry or government position, university, etc.):

Type of Activity   Location   Date Started

_____

_____

12. Indicate areas of special interest pertaining to the Section(s) you are applying to:

_____

_____

13. What activities would you be interested in assisting the Section with (newsletter, educational program)?

_____

14. Graduate Medical Education:

Type   Institution   Dates

_____

_____

15. Honors:

_____

16. Society Memberships:

_____

_____

17. Publications: (Use additional sheets if necessary)

_____

_____

18. Signature of Applicant:

_____

All section applications must be accompanied by a $35 check for initiation fees.

Mail the completed forms and fee to:

Section Membership Assistant   **800/433-9016**, ext 7143
AAP Division of Member Services   **847/228-5005**, ext 7143
141 Northwest Point Blvd   **847/228-5245** (FAX)
Elk Grove Village, IL 60007   **E-mail:** membership@aap.org

WWW

Helpful Addresses and Telephone Numbers

American Academy of Pediatrics
141 Northwest Point Blvd
PO Box 927
Elk Grove Village, IL 60009-0927
800/433-9016

American Humane Association
63 Inverness Drive East
Englewood, CO 80112-5117
303/792-9900

American Medical Association
Division of Health Science
515 N State St
Chicago, IL 60610
312/464-5000

**American Professional Society
on the Abuse of Children**
407 S Dearborn St
Ste 1300
Chicago, IL 60605
312/554-0166

American Prosecutors Research Institute
99 Canal Center Plaza
Ste 510
Alexandria, VA 22314
703/739-0321

**Bureau of Justice Statistics
Clearinghouse (BJS)**
National Criminal Justice
Reference Service (NCJRS)
PO Box 6000
Rockville, MD 20850
800/732-3277

Center on Children and the Law
American Bar Association
750 N Lake Shore Dr
Chicago, IL 60611
312/988-5000

Child Welfare League of America
440 First St, NW, Third Floor
Washington, DC 20001-2085
202/638-2952

**National Center for the Prosecution of
Child Abuse**
99 Canal Center Plaza
Ste 510
Alexandria, VA 22314
703/739-0321

National Center on Child Abuse and Neglect
PO Box 1182
Washington, DC 20013-1182
202/205-8586

**National Clearinghouse on Child Abuse
and Neglect Information**
PO Box 1182
Washington, DC 20013-1182
800/394-3366

National Committee to Prevent Child Abuse
332 S Michigan Ave
Ste 1600
Chicago, IL 60604
312/663-3520

**National Criminal Justice Reference Service
(NCJRS)**
US Department of Justice
National Institute of Justice
PO Box 6000
Rockville, MD 20850
800/851-3420

**National Network of Children's
Advocacy Centers**
1319 F St, NW, Ste 1001
Washington, DC 20004-1106
202/639-0597

National Organization for Victim Assistance
1757 Park Road, NW
Washington, DC 20010 800/TRY-NOVA

National Resource Center on Child Sexual Abuse
107 Lincoln St
Huntsville, AL 35801
205/534-6868
Information Service:
800/KIDS-006

Index

Professionals
  knowledge of, 97–98
  psychological needs of, 8–9
Psychological abuse, 57, 122
Psychological impact of child maltreatment, 122–27
Psychological maltreatment rating scales, 58–59
Psychological needs of professionals, 8–9
Public disclosure of private information about victims of abuse, 99
  AAP policy statement on, 104
Punishment, corporal, 12–17

R

Radiologic skeletal survey, 68
Reabuse, 128–30
  parental substance abuse in, 183
Reasonable medical certainty, 21, 22
Religious objections to medical care, 99
  AAP policy statement on, 105–7
Retinal hemorrhage, 130–33
Rib fractures, 190–91
Rib injuries, 3

S

Schools, corporal punishment in, 16–17
Seat belts, injuries from, 5
Secondary brain injuries, 78
Severe emotional disturbances, 58
Sexual abuse, 52, 122–23, 125–26, 134–43
  AAP policy statement on guidelines for evaluation of, 144–50
  anatomic findings with, 137–38
  behavioral issues in, 138–39
  and contested divorce, 10
  and developmental disabilities, 42
  diagnosis of, 134–35
  expert testimony in, 22
  medical examination in diagnosing, 95–96
  prevention of, 121
  sibling studies on, 180
  use of dolls in interviewing child on, 95
Sexual assault of the adolescent, AAP policy statement on, 151–55
Sexually transmitted diseases, 156–62
  AAP policy statement on, 163–67
  AAP policy statement on gonorrhea in prepubertal children, 168–69
  ˈen impact/shaken baby syndrome, 7, 170–73
  ˈAP policy statement on, 174–77

Siblings, implications of shaken baby syndrome for, 173
Sibling studies, 178–81
Skull fractures, 68
  in shaken baby syndrome, 171
Sodium poisoning, 118
Spanking. *See* Corporal punishment
Spousal abuse, 46
Stairway falls, 64
Stairway-related injuries, 64–65
State and Regional Contacts for Multi-Agency Child Death Review Activities, 266–78
Statistics of child abuse, 181–82
Substance abuse disorders, 183–85
Sudden infant death syndrome (SIDS), 83, 85–86
  AAP policy statement on distinguishing from child abuse fatalities, 92–94
  criteria for distinguishing, from fatal child abuse, 87
Survivors of child abuse, substance use in, 185
Syphilis, 161–62

T

Testimony, court, 21–23
Thoracic trauma, 189–91
Tibial spiral fractures, 68
Timeout, 13, 15
Tin ear syndrome, 52
Transverse fractures, 68
Traumatization, vicarious, 7, 8

U

Upper gastrointestinal series (UGI), 4

V

Vicarious traumatization, 7, 8
Violence, domestic, 46–48
Vulvovaginitis, 162